Captain Rod and Basil

COASTAL LORAN COORDINATES

Volume 2
Great Lakes and Gulf of St. Lawrence

International Marine Publishing Company
Camden, Maine

Published by International Marine Publishing Company

10 9 8 7 6 5 4 3 2 1

Copyright © 1990 Rodney J. and Kyong S. Stebbins

Reproduction or publication of the content in any manner, without express permission of the publisher, is prohibited. No liability is assumed with respect to the use of the information herein. International Marine books are published by International Marine Publishing Company, a division of TAB BOOKS Inc. The name "International Marine" and the International Marine logo are trademarks of TAB BOOKS Inc. Printed in the United States of America.

Publications produced by WEAK INDUSTRIES, Inc. and TAB BOOKS, Inc. are not able to, nor intended to, supplant individual training, responsibility, any other navigational aids, charts, or judgment of the user, nor will the publisher, copyright owners, retailers, dealers, or distributors assume any responsibility whatsoever for damages arising from the use of this publication by anyone. The purchaser and users of this publication agree that, with the implementation of this publication, they will hold harmless WEAK INDUSTRIES, Inc., and TAB BOOKS, Inc., their owners, agents, publishers, distributors/dealers, retailers, and subsidiary corporations from damages arising from the use of information contained herein.

International Marine Publishing Company offers software for sale. For information and a catalog, please contact TAB Software Department, Blue Ridge Summit, PA 17294-0850.

Printed by Arcata Graphics, Kingsport, TN
Contributing authors: Will Cerney and Pierce Hoover

To add loran coordinates for reefs, wrecks, havens, ports, and passes to this book, write:

Rod and Susie Stebbins
WEAK INDUSTRIES, Inc.
9132 Blairmoor Road
Tampa, FL 33635-1322

Additional copies and information about this publication can be obtained from:

INTERNATIONAL MARINE PUBLISHING COMPANY
Division of TAB BOOKS, Inc.
Blue Ridge Summit, PA 17294-0850
(800)822-8158

WEAK INDUSTRIES, Inc.
9132 Blairmoor Road
Tampa, FL 33635-1322

Library of Congress Cataloging-in-Publication Data

Stebbins, Rodney J.
  [Coastal loran coordinates]
  Captain Rod and Susie Stebbins' coastal loran coordinates.
    p.   cm.
    Contents: -- v. 2. Great lakes and Gulf of Saint Lawrence.
  ISBN 0-87742-276-1 (v. 2)
    1. Loran -- United States -- Tables. 2. Boats and boating -- United States.
I. Stebbins, Susie S. II. Title. III. Title: Coastal loran coordinates.
VK561.U5S74 1990
623.89'32'0973 -- dc20

ABOUT THE AUTHORS

The Captain of the intrepid vessel Sancho and the husband of wonderful First Mate Susie is a retired civil engineer who specialized in concrete construction and consulting for fun and profit.

During his professional career as a consulting engineer, he traveled the wide world, working for many agencies whose concrete structures were in need of repair. He sat on five American Concrete Institute Committees and two Transportation Research Board Committees (researching epoxies, fibers, testing methods, polymers, and shotcrete) for a bit more than 12 years.

In the winter of 1981, the Stebbinses left Chicago, Illinois, with all of their belongings trailing behind them in trucks.

When they arrived in Tampa, Rod and Susie asked for directions to the salty Gulf of Mexico. Without hesitation, they drove to the beach, changed into their swimsuits, and, as one might predict of any tourist who arrives in the winter, they soaked themselves and got salty.

The next day, Rod and Susie went out looking not for a house, but for a boat. Their furniture and boat, dubbed Sancho, arrived almost simultaneously a few days later. While Susie put the house together, Rod got Sancho ready. In the process, Rod was transformed from a mild-mannered engineer into the man Susie lovingly calls her "Captain Bligh." In an unceremonious manner, Sancho was launched and christened with diet Coke and a trip to the Florida Keys.

The loran coordinates that were collected on their very first trip, right on through those recorded during their voyages in the year 1989, are contained in this book. In addition, many were donated by friends who believe that a loran without a destination is just about as sorry as "a Sancho without his Don Quixote."

The First Mate in this operation is the talented and pretty wife of Captain Rod. Only five feet tall, Susie is a giant on the boat. She stands her watch (day or night), navigates, drives, washes and polishes the boat, is usually the first in the water, outfishes most everyone else, and prepares the finest meals anywhere from almost anything she gathers from the sea. What's more, she takes time out for romance, sunrises, and sunsets.

When the Stebbinses first moved to Florida, Susie couldn't swim at all and believed that water deeper than two or three feet was strictly for the fish. By 1982, Susie was taking lessons in scuba diving, and in the spring of 1983, Susie, armed with her wetsuit and scuba equipment, joined her husband in exploring the deep. Together they form a highly complementary diving team.

During the next several years, they logged over 800 dives while identifying reefs and wrecks. As one might guess, Susie is the delight of this team.

Now in his fourth incarnation, the first Sancho was a 22-foot Glastron. The next four were Sea Rays that grew gradually from 24 to 27 to 30 feet in length, finally becoming the present-day Sancho, a 36-foot flybridge model.

Throughout his various reincarnations, Sancho has carried his charges all along the eastern seaboard. He has spent a four-month vacation in the Bahamas, a three-and-a-half-month vacation in the Florida Keys, and two weeks in the Dry Tortugas. Each year Sancho makes several trips from Tampa, Florida, to various points on the Florida coast.

An integral part of the team, Sancho has his vices too. He has a serious drinking problem that seems to be without end. In eight years, Sancho has consumed over 120,000 gallons of gasoline, and has logged an average of between 950 to 1,125 engine hours each year for seven years.

Sancho is Rod and Susie's "incomparable friend," perpetual in purpose and gracefully classic in line. He is a willing participant in the quest for the "impossible dream." With Sancho at the ready, Rod and Susie know their voyage will never end.

Also known as the Damned Cat, Garfeldasteinski is the only unwilling participant in the quest for coordinates, sunsets, sunrises, sunnin', funnin', divin', fishin', campin', and boatin'.

Captain Rod says, "The only reason the Damned Cat goes with us is because the First Mate loves to have her pet with her. If you were to ask the Damned Cat what she thinks about the whole idea, she would quickly hiss, spit twice, turn tail, and get seasick."

Looking at the Stebbins family, an outsider might think the crew just about the most unlikely combination of humanity imaginable.

Susie is a pretty Oriental lady, petite in stature, nicely groomed, conservative in dress, and swift to smile. Rod, on the other hand, is a born captain type: tall and portly, he is most often attired in boating shoes, shorts, and sport shirts, wears a short silver beard, and plays his "Captain Bligh" character with gusto. In the quiet of the evening, Susie reminds Captain Rod that he can continue to play captain just as long as he has her permission.

Captain Hal Carter of the Grouper Trouper of Seffner, Florida, has this to say about traveling with the Stebbinses: "It's similar to traveling with a Captain Bligh who has a purpose and a mission. Captain Rod was destined to be a captain; he barks orders with great conviction at the First Mate, yells at the Damned Cat, and demands that everything be in its place.

"Susie is the finest boat cook and First Mate any Captain Bligh could ever hope for. What the captain lacks, she more than makes up for in charm, willingness, and ability.

"While both insist on careful attention to details, each has a certain faraway manner that calms seas and assures those who meet them that there are good and colorful things left to dream about. Their dream is to traverse the plentiful waters of the eastern seaboard and to view the gorgeous colors of the crystal-clear waters of Florida.

"The Florida waters are better for the likes of the Stebbinses voyaging upon them. The world still has room for dreamers."

CONTENTS

CHAPTER 1:	Introduction	1
CHAPTER 2:	Finding A Waypoint	3
CHAPTER 3:	Loran Navigation	7
CHAPTER 4:	Boating Buddies	31
CHAPTER 5:	The Lowdown On Diving	38
CHAPTER 6:	Making Passes	39
	Georgian Bay	42
	Newfoundland	46
	Lake Erie	54
	Lake Huron	63
	Lake Michigan	67
	Lake Ontario	74
	Lake St. Clair	76
	Lake Superior	77
	Cape Breton Island	82
	Magdalen Islands	85
	New Brunswick	86
	Nova Scotia	89
	Prince Edward Island	99
	Quebec	101
	St. Lawrence Seaway	118
CHAPTER 7:	Heavenly Havens	125
CHAPTER 8:	Plentiful Ports	128
CHAPTER 9:	Reaching Rocks	144
CHAPTER 10:	Lovely Ledges	148
CHAPTER 11:	Reefs	151
CHAPTER 12:	Wrecks	154
CHAPTER 13:	Fine Fish'n	156
CHAPTER 14:	Sea Bounty	164
CHAPTER 15:	Daffynitions	169
CHAPTER 16:	Waypoint Log	172

CHAPTER 1

INTRODUCTION

This very handy publication was intended, from its inception, to be not much more than a book of destinations. This simply means that there are no predetermined routes given and the book won't tell you how to get to a rock, ledge, wreck, reef, or sea buoy. Instead, it lets you know that these things exist and provides the coordinates for them in the simplest method that exists today.

Water depths are listed for reference only and should not be considered absolutely accurate, as we have not yet been able to authenticate all water-depth listings. The contents of the book are broken down into subject categories, as found in the table of contents. All the coordinates were accumulated with the ASF (Automatic Secondary Factor) in the off position. To ensure maximum loran accuracy, turn the ASF off when searching for the waypoints listed herein.

The chapter on passes lists the principal buoys and other aids to navigation that can be found from the western end of Lake Superior eastward through the Great Lakes system (U.S. and Canadian shores), the St. Lawrence Seaway, the lower St. Lawrence River, the Gulf of St. Lawrence, and the shores of Nova Scotia and New Brunswick to the State of Maine border (where our *Coastal Loran Coordinates: Texas to Maine* edition takes over). All the other chapters, including those on havens, ports, rocks, ledges, reefs, wrecks, and fishing, are self-explanatory with regard to what is contained in each. Each chapter is the most complete available to the boater to date.

CREWS WHO CRUISE

To assist us in our search for coordinates, we have chartered five boats manned with retired husband-and-wife teams much like us. Each boat has the ability to take its passengers to dive spots to verify findings, and each of the members of these teams — known as our "WEAK" crews — love to fish, cruise, and camp along the way. All of them work very hard and have made significant contributions to the sport of recreational boating — to say nothing of their invaluable ability to search out and verify coordinates for this publication. Without our WEAK crews, the three regional editions of *Coastal Loran Coordinates* could not exist.

A very special thanks must go out to Captain Joe Potts, his lovely wife Sandy, and their 34-foot Sea Ray Brandy for their presence and encouragement; to Captain Hal Carter and his Grouper Trouper for his editing and constant scouring; to Captain Eddy Garcia, his wife Joanie, and their 43-foot Morgan Lady Joan for their great efforts and the one year they spent at sea assisting us.

We'd also like to thank the Fisherman Doctor David Deam for his contributions and encouragement, and Captain Terry Farner, his fishing family, and their vessel Special K for their fishing coordinates and constant vigilance. Last, but far from least, our thanks go to Captain Jim "London" Zonlick, his team, and their 36-foot Sea Ray Hunky Dory, for their diving and photographic expeditions during the 1988 season, and to Captain Ed Suarez, Jr. of Columbia, Maryland, for his help and expertise in locating and documenting wrecks. Their help is invaluable to us.

The combined efforts of our WEAK crews have helped us produce the finest loran coordinate reference books available. The growth of our Texas to Maine edition over the past couple of years is readily apparent. Our first edition was printed in April of 1986 and included 650 coordinates. Within 60 days we released an additional 200 coordinates, adding those we'd collected for the Florida Keys and the Bahamas. Our May 1987 edition contained more than 1,600 coordinates, and our May 1988 edition contained nearly 4,000 neat places to go. In 1989 our publication grew to more than 8,000 destination coordinates, and the 1990 edition contains more than 14,000, making it the largest publication of its kind available on the market at this time. (If you visit Florida, the Florida Keys, or the Bahamas, be sure to search for the silver dollars and the cases of wine we've placed around wrecks and reefs. Clues to their locations can be found in the Texas to Maine edition.)

We hope for similar growth in this Great Lakes/Gulf of St. Lawrence edition in the years to come. The guide has been great fun to create, and we hope it will provide as much fun for you in your days on the water.

ONWARD AND UPWARD

All in all, everyone is looking forward to 1990, when we can get underway again. We are still at the helm seeking sunsets and romantic havens to hole up in. So if you see our 36-foot Sea Ray Sancho, please rap on the door and join us for a cool one. If you see any of our hard-working WEAK crews plying about, please treat them to a cool one, as they provided many of the coordinates for our most enjoyable spots.

Good luck to you in your search, and may all you discover bring you great happiness.

CHAPTER 2

FINDING A WAYPOINT

When we think of finding a location on a map or chart, we usually think of the intersection of two visible bearings, like the meeting of two highways. Finding our way with a loran isn't too different, except that the destination is out in the middle of the puddle and there probably isn't anything to see except water, waves, and more water. That tends to make most of us wonder if we really have arrived!

Large objects such as wrecks, ledges, holes, domes, spikes, and mounds can readily be seen on a chart paper recorder or a video depth monitor, and your depth finder will tell you when you have arrived. But sometimes small items such as subtle bottom structure changes and gradual depth changes can't be seen on a sounder, and, as a result, it's easy to overlook a good fishing location.

With practice, you can learn to identify the type of bottom that is below the boat. Steel hulls may look like a malfunction, sandy bottoms will look different than rocky bottoms, and so on. Learn to operate your machinery, because this publication is not designed to teach you all about individual types of equipment; instead, it simply provides the destination coordinates.

COMMON MISTAKES

Before we discuss the techniques for arriving at a location, it is important that we help you understand that movement, however small, can make finding things quite frustrating. When it appears that you are dead in the water and that you are going nowhere fast, you are actually moving away from the very target you just came to find!

It is important to learn the limitations and functions of your chosen loran, to learn a reasonable method of determining when you're about to arrive at your chosen destination, and when, in fact, you're at ground zero.

Probably the most common mistake made in using the loran is failing to understand what the mission is. Ground zero is *not* the exact spot where you must drop anchor all of the time. If you're looking to fish or dive near a ledge, for example, it's only important that the divers be able to get to the ledge easily from the boat.

We like to place a marker on the ledge and then anchor the boat "downstream" from it. When the divers go down the anchor line, they can check their compasses and swim in the same direction to the ledge, which is upstream, while they are at their strongest.

When we are going to fish a ledge, we most always troll a zigzag course along the ledge, hoping to tease a fish into striking one of the $4.75 phony foods laced with sharpened barbed hooks. (It often seems to us that these hooks are placed strategically to warn the fish to stay away!)

Probably the next biggest mistake you can make with your loran is to operate the unit with the Automatic Secondary Factor (ASF) enabled (on) instead of disabled (off). Hard on the heels of this mistake is entering the coordinates incorrectly, like putting time delays (TDs) into the latitude/longitude (LAT/LON) mode and vice versa, making errors in interpolation, making errors in reading coordinates taken from the charts, forgetting to "seed" the loran, selecting the improper transmitting stations, and assuming that the loran is always right.

We have accepted invitations to assist our readers in understanding their lorans and the system. Without exception, within two hours they have all been able to take up "loraning" by themselves.

It seems that most people are intimidated by the way their loran's instructions are presented. It also seems that the people who write the instructions either know nothing about boating and what the loran is to be used for, or wrote the manual in a foreign language and then gave it to a fourth grader to translate.

OUR METHOD

Now that we have bitten the hand that feeds us, let's discuss finding our spots. The need for accuracy varies from chapter to chapter. If you are looking for a sea buoy in the fog, as might be described in the chapter on passes, or if you are looking for wrecks or reefs, it goes without saying that the "targets" (destinations) are smaller by comparison to the areas found in the chapters on rocks and fishing, which may include rocky or fishing areas that are acres across.

Once you've learned the basics of the loran, it is possible for you to find the large fields of rocky and fishing areas listed in this book, and, with a little practice, small objects are a piece of cake, too.

We do a lot of evening and night boating, now that we have made friends with our electronics. We are not as intimidated about finding our way home at night now that we have come to understand a few simple facts and techniques.

Our first night trip was a voyage for the books. Wow, were we concerned! To say that we were uptight would be a gross understatement. We had visions of falling into trenches, of night serpents snapping at our wake, of running out of gas, of having mechanical failures, and of just about everything else we could dream up — all of this after we had made exactly the same trip during daylight hours several times to make certain we would not fall off the edge of the world.

Now that we have made many such trips, we have made up "trip cards" that list each coordinate necessary to make a safe voyage. These trip cards remain on the boat, ready to be used should the visibility deteriorate due to haze, smog, fog, or rain. The confidence we have gained by using these cards, coupled with the use of our loran, has allowed us to use the boat much as we might use the car.

One of the first lessons we learned about traveling by loran with limited visibility is that it is best to slow to a speed that allows us to avoid hitting something or someone should we come upon them suddenly. We cruise at a speed of about six knots, which allows us to hear horns and whistles over the noise of our engines.

One evening, as we plowed through the fog, we almost rammed into a small boat that had set anchor due to the limited visibility. The fact that he had a small flashlight (which was getting weaker by the moment) was the only thing that prevented us from causing great damage. As it turned out, we were able to assist the boaters by towing them to a safe anchorage well out of harm's way, where we both stayed until the next morning.

GROUND ZERO

Hitting ground zero means to reach zero-zero on the nautical miles to the destination displayed on the screen of the loran. Probably the only time it is necessary to be that accurate is when finding a marker, a sea buoy in very limited visibility, or when it is necessary to find an unmarked reef or wreck. Suffice it to say that markers and sea buoys are already marked, so we will discuss finding the reefs, wrecks, and other small objects where accuracy is required.

The first step is to slow down. When we are within 0.20 nautical miles of our destination, we slow Sancho to idle speed while holding the compass heading to the destination. We change the screen of the loran so that we can see the notation "Distance to Destination," and watch it count down to 0.00, being very careful to hold the heading. There we deploy a marker, which is nothing more than an empty plastic milk bottle tied to a stout cord with a five-pound chunk of lead tied to the other end.

Once it is anchored, we make a wide swing to the right so that we can approach the marker with the bow into the wind. Once again, we're looking for 0.00 while monitoring the white line recorder for indications of the wreck or reef. When we have made a positive identification with the white line, disregarding 0.00, Susie sets the second marker in place after the Captain yells, "Now, honey!" Sancho then continues into the wind far enough to set the bow anchor, yet close enough to allow his stern to lie close the second marker.

If we are going to fish, we set markers to tell us if we are drifting right or left of the spot. If we are going to dive the site, we are positioned in a way that's best to protect the divers during their descent and ascent.

Incidentally, don't forget to have the dive flags up when the divers are in the water and to take them down again when the divers are out of the water, just in case someone else wants to approach the site.

Share the site by communicating about your activities with other boats in the area. Most important, leave the site clean, undisturbed, and unmarked. It takes the sea a long time to heal from an indiscretion.

When we leave, we lift our markers, secure the lines, and stow them for the next time. On the way home, we usually take a moment or two to have a cold drink and to apologize to each other for all of the screaming and hollering we did during the anchoring exercises.

WIT & WISDOM

Hull speed for a displacement hull can be calculated by multiplying the square root of the length of the water line (feet) by approximately 1.4, with the average range for the multiplier actually being 1.3 to 1.5.

I don't think we have ever made a good anchorage without one of us yelling out an unnecessary command or the other replying with an equally unnecessary something-or-other. Must be a part of boating, because it seems everyone does it.

When searching for good fishing or diving sites, look for the things that don't seem to fit the scenery, like a pile of rocks in the middle of a sand bar. That pile of rocks might be the first clue to a find of wealth; then again, it might just be a pile of rocks. This is the excitement that comes with exploring and researching destinations.

We will stay at the helm for a few more years and we will keep updating this guide. We trust all of our efforts will bring lots of exciting adventures for both the novice boater and the seasoned salt.

It's all done by researching and digging; then slow down and try to piece together the clues that are everywhere.

CHAPTER 3

LORAN NAVIGATION

By Will Cerney and Pierce Hoover

A special thanks to Sport Fishing Magazine for permission to reprint this text, which was compiled from articles in the magazine.

In the old days, sea captains subdued sextants, calibrated chronometers, and labored over log tables just to get an estimation of where in the world they were. Many an old salt would have been grateful for a machine that could simply tell him what part of the ocean he was in with any degree of accuracy.

With the advent of Satnav, loran, and, soon, GPS, oceangoing skippers now take it for granted that they can punch a few buttons and get their vessel's position almost anywhere in the world, all without doing any complicated mathematics or perching on the deck to take a sun sight.

In US coastal waters, it is the loran system that provides the quickest, least expensive, and most reliable electronic means of positioning a vessel. In the days of loran A and the early days of loran C, the machines could do nothing more that get a fix — it was up to the skipper to mark his charts, make his calculations, and navigate his vessel accordingly.

But with the miniaturization of computer technology has come a new breed of machines. The modern loran can do a lot more than just give loran numbers to be plotted on a grid. Skippers now rely on their lorans to steer them to and from their fishing grounds and harbors, to keep track of distances and speeds, and to store information on favorite fishing locations.

Such electronic assistance is a great boon to sailors, cruising skippers, and fishermen, who can now spend more time searching for secluded anchorages or fishing, and less time fiddling with charts.

The only problem is, some folks think a loran can take over and do all the navigating for them. True, you can punch a few numbers into a loran and it will take you there and back without any understanding on your part.

But at the very least, skippers who run offshore should have some idea of how their machines figure distances and headings, and they should be familiar with basic navigational techniques such as plotting and dead reckoning. A captain shouldn't rely on any one device, even a loran, to guide his boat, and he should be able to make his way home safely if the loran fails.

To operate safely offshore using a loran system as a primary tool of piloting, a skipper needs to have a clear understanding of what those numbers he punches into his machine mean, and of how the loran processes those numbers to help him steer to and from his destination.

THE LORAN SYSTEM

The word loran is an acronym for LOng RAnge Navigation. It is an electronic radio navigation system first developed during World War II as loran A. The system we now use is loran C, which was developed in the 1960s and put into service in the 1970s.

While the name says long range, loran C is really considered a medium-range system. For very precise, close-in navigational fixes, the offshore oil industry often uses such costly systems as portable microwave positioning, while ships at sea rely on the somewhat less precise fixes given by Omega and satellite navigation receivers. Loran C falls between the extreme accuracy of short-range microwave and the lesser accuracy of present-day worldwide systems.

With loran C, you can get a position up to 1,200 miles from the transmitting facility. When things are working right, loran can establish your position to within 100 to 1,000 yards of your actual location (this is known as accuracy), but if you know where you are, it can bring you back to within 50 to 75 feet of the same spot the next time (this is known as repeatability). Loran's excellent repeatability is ideally suited to fishermen searching for that choice piece of bottom they ran across last trip, and its accuracy is good enough to plot a course to distant harbors with confidence.

Loran coverage is not worldwide, but it is in operation along both coasts of the United States and Canada as well as the Great Lakes, in Hawaii, Europe, the Far East, and various other areas of the northern hemisphere. This coverage comes from several groups of loran transmitters known as chains. Each chain is made up of a master transmitter and several slaves that work together to provide position information. While all loran transmitter chains broadcast at the same frequency (100 KHz), they each have a unique signal pulse rate (known as a Group Repetition Interval, or GRI) that tells your machine which transmitter group it is listening to. But before we get into TDs, GRIs, and all the other terms, let's find out how a loran knows where you are.

LORAN THEORY

Loran is a time delay location system. In other words, it works on the assumption that radio signals travel at constant speeds and the longer it takes a signal to reach you, the farther you are from the source. By using three separate signal sources in a given loran chain, your unit can determine your position with a good deal of accuracy.

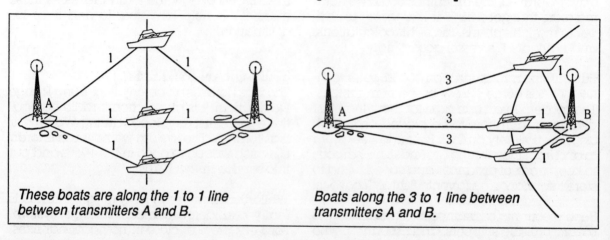

These boats are along the 1 to 1 line between transmitters A and B.

Boats along the 3 to 1 line between transmitters A and B.

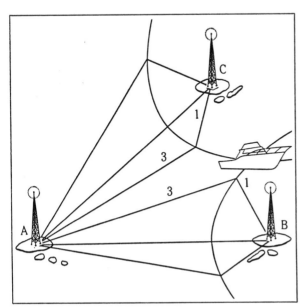
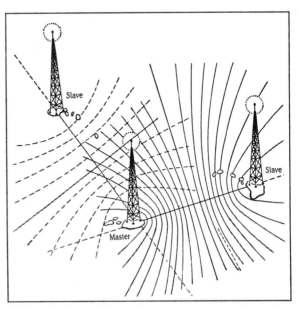

This boat is at the intersection of the AB 3 to 1 line and the AC 3 to 1 line.

A simple loran chain, with a master and two slave transmitters.

To understand the process, let's imagine two loran transmitters are set on islands several hundred miles apart. A direct line between these transmitters is known as the base line. Now, let's imagine that we are on a boat at the mid-point of that base line, halfway between the two islands. If both loran transmitters fired simultaneous signals (which they really don't), we would receive the signals at the same time.

The same would hold true if we moved at an angle 90 degrees to the base line, since the two stations would still be the same distance from our boat, no matter where we were along that line. We can call that line of all points equidistant from the two transmitters the one-to-one line, since it is established by measuring the time delay from transmission to reception. Technicians would call our one-to-one line a time delay line, or TD.

It makes sense that if we move our imaginary boat along the base line until we are closer to one transmitter than the other, we will get that signal sooner. If we are three times as far from one transmitter as from the other, the signal from the closer transmitter will get there three times as quickly. Plotting a line of all points that are three times as far from one transmitter as the other produces a curve, which we'll call the three-to-one time delay (TD) line, since it measures the amount of time it takes the signal to get from the transmitter to our position.

But even though the receiver knows we are somewhere along that three-to-one TD curve, it can't tell what part of the curve it is on. Finding the exact location along that curve requires a third transmitter.

What we need, then, is a third island transmitter that can work with one of our two existing transmitters to establish a position along a second time delay line.

Then, by finding the intersection of the two TD lines, we know where we are. So if the receiver says you are on a three-to-one TD line from transmitters A and B, and on the three-to-one line from transmitter A and C, you know you are at the exact spot where those two TD lines cross.

A real loran chain doesn't work exactly as our simplified one does, but the principles are the same. In reality, each chain has one master transmitter and several slave transmitters. TD lines are always based on readings between the master and one of the slaves, and the transmitters don't fire at the same time. Instead, the master fires and each slave follows at a predetermined interval. Each slave has a distinct delay interval and every loran chain in the world has a different group repetition interval (GRI); in other words, the interval at which the master and each of the slaves transmit their signals.

The northeastern United States, for example, works on a GRI of 9960, while the southeastern US uses a GRI of 7980 and the California coast operates on 9940. What these numbers represent is the time interval in which the master fires, is answered by each of the slaves, and fires again. These numbers are expressed in microseconds; a microsecond is one-millionth of a second!

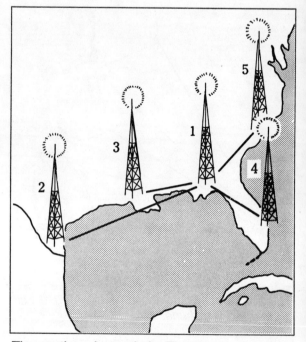

The southern loran chain. The master station (1) is in Malone, FL, with slave stations in (2) Raymondville, TX, (3) Grangeville, LA, (4) Jupiter, FL, and (5) Carolina Beach, NC.

To delve a bit farther into GRI, let's look at the southeastern US chain. The master, which is in Malone, Florida, fires once every 79,800 microseconds, and each of the four slaves — known as W, X, Y, and Z — follows after a predetermined delay. The W slave in Grangeville, Louisiana, fires 11,000 microseconds after the master; the X in Raymondville, Texas, follows after 23,000 microseconds; the Y in Jupiter, Florida, at 43,000 microseconds; and the Z in Carolina Beach comes last, at 59,000 microseconds.

So when a fisherman comes over the radio

and tells you he is in the 13,500 line at the 46,600, he is using the W and Y slaves in conjunction with the master to establish his position along the TD lines formed by W and the master and by Y and the master.

We should point out that there is no direct relationship between TD numbers and distance, because the lines curve and cross at different angles throughout the coverage area.

A modern loran can interpret signals down to hundredths of a microsecond, which can represent a distance as small as two or three boat lengths. For greatest accuracy, the TD lines used should intersect at as near a 90-degree angle as possible. Some modern lorans have a feature known as ATS (Automatic Transmitter Selection) or ASS (Automatic Slave Selection), which automatically selects the best TD line crossover angle for the particular location.

OPERATING SEQUENCE

The loran should be turned on and should be working before you start your day on the water. Unless your boat has a separate battery system for electronics, you should start your engines before turning on the loran. Otherwise, the sudden voltage drop created by the starter motor can blank out the loran and you will have to run through the cycling process again.

After you turn the loran on, it may take several minutes to lock onto the transmitters, depending on signal strength and local noise. If your machine has automatic transmitter selection, it will automatically select the two slave transmitters in the chain it considers to have the best crossing angle for your particular location. If you want to use a different slave, you will need to put the machine on manual select to make the change.

If you have a couple of minutes, you might run the loran through a signal-to-noise ratio (SNR) check. The SNR button checks each transmitter and tells you how strong the signal is in relation to interference and electrical noise. A low SNR reading means the transmitter signal is weak or you have a lot of interference. In either case, you might be in for trouble. Different manufactures have different values for SNR, and you should know the optimum and minimum values for your loran.

Once the loran is cycled out or locked on, you should make sure it is giving you a good reading by checking its output against a couple of known positions. A logical first checkpoint would be the dock, and you should know your dockside position and check it against what the machine says to make sure it knows you are in the same place as usual.

A good second checkpoint would be a marker or buoy outside the harbor or at the mouth of the channel. Before you get underway, enter that second checkpoint as waypoint one and you can run a check on your navigational functions, such as range and bearing. You might also want to leave that position in the memory to use as a destination on the trip home.

NAVIGATION FEATURES

Early lorans did nothing more than establish a position and display it in TD coordinates, which then had to be plotted on a loran C overprinted chart. Since then, a number of memory and navigation features have been built into loran units. Navigational units now convert TD coordinates to latitude and longitude and display the position as "lat" and "lon" readings.

It is possible to operate a loran in the latitude/longitude mode exclusively, and some users successfully plot courses and find fishing holes without ever knowing what a TD is. But it is important to remember that lat and lon are calculated from the loran's TDs, and are only as accurate as the TD coordinates themselves. We'll talk more about that later; for now, just remember that all loran machines measure position in TDs, even if they display it as latitude and longitude.

Most modern lorans have a built-in memory that stores TD or lat/lon information. This is quite useful for fishermen, who want to record their exact position when they find a fishing spot they like. If the fisherman saves that location in the loran's memory, it can consistently bring him back to within 50 or 75 feet of the same location in most coastal areas.

TD or lat/lon coordinates for a known location, such as an island, can also be entered into the loran and used to steer a course. But as with any method of navigation, a loran should never be relied on as an absolute or solitary source of piloting information. The two most common problems arising from using loran memory in navigation are wrong numbers and lack of navigational understanding.

If a wrong number is accidentally keyed into

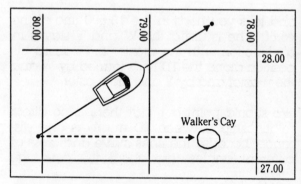

This skipper punched a wrong number into his loran without checking it and is not going to Walker's Cay.

the memory, the loran will take you to a place you don't want to visit. This problem becomes especially severe if the operator doesn't understand charts and lacks basic navigational skills.

Let's suppose, for example, that a boat owner without any navigational know-how plans a trip from Florida over to Walker's Cay in the Bahamas. A buddy gives him the numbers for Walker's Cay — latitude 27-14.38, longitude 78-24.08 — and tells our friend that there's nothing more to it than entering the numbers and going where the loran tells him to go.

But if our boat owner hits an eight instead of a seven when he is punching his latitude coordinates without double-checking (thus getting 28-14.38), the machine will tell him to go to a point 60 nautical miles north of the island (each degree of latitude equals 60 nautical miles). Add to that the possibility of a loran failure halfway through the trip and you can see that our friend has some problems.

A basic understanding of charts and dead reckoning is essential to piloting with a loran, and every skipper should make the effort to understand the relationship of the coordinates he feeds into his loran and the actual locations these numbers represent.

RANGE AND BEARING

When driving a boat, the direction from one spot to another is always expressed in terms of a compass heading between zero and 360 degrees, known as the bearing, while the actual distance between the two points is expressed in nautical miles, known as the range. For example, a boat at the mouth of Miami's Government Cut has range and bearing to the island of Bimini of 40 miles at 80 degrees.

Simple enough. Just steer a compass course of 80 degrees and 40 miles later you're in Bimini, right? Well, sort of. As you would expect, nothing is as simple as it seems. For starters, the bearing isn't necessarily the course you will need to steer by your compass to reach your destination.

Cross currents, polar magnetic variation, and compass irregularities work together to create differences between the numerical heading expressed on a chart and the compass heading you will actually need to steer to reach your destination. Before we get on with loran use, we'll have to take a short side trip to see how these various factors come into play.

TRUE AND MAGNETIC NORTH

Navigators speak of "magnetic north" and "true north," and it should be realized that the two aren't always the same thing. When you look at a chart plotted with latitude/longitude lines, north is always "up," in a direction parallel to the lines of longitude.

If you look at a globe, you will see that longitude lines aren't actually parallel; instead, they converge at the north pole. For the sake of mapmaking, we think of longitude lines as running parallel, a process known as a Mercator projection. This type of projection creates some irregularities when using navigation charts over long distances, but it has to do with other things besides true and magnetic north (to explain that, we'd have to get into spherical trigonometry).

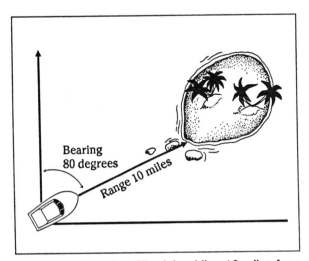

Range and Bearing: The island lies 10 miles from the boat; this distance is known as the range. The direction is 80 degrees from true north, which is known as the bearing.

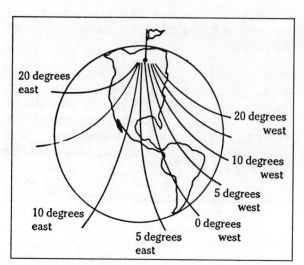

Magnetic variation occurs because the magnetic and true north poles are not identically located, and variation increases from 0 degrees along the west coast of Florida to as much as 20 degrees on other coastlines.

Whether you are using a globe or a Mercator projection chart, true north always refers to the direction to the top of the earth — the north pole. Readings taken from a chart are therefore automatically expressed in true north bearings.

It just so happens that one of the earth's centers of magnetic attraction lies near the north pole. Magnetic pieces of metal (like compasses) point to this magnetic north pole, which actually lies several hundred miles to the south of the real north pole. In some areas of the world, true and magnetic north are almost the same, while they differ by as much as 20 degrees in other locales.

In any one area, the angle of difference between true and magnetic north can be calculated, and it is known as the local magnetic variation. Navigators have long been aware of this fact, and add or subtract the magnetic variation difference when calculating what compass course to steer.

To make things even more complicated, scientists have discovered that this magnetic north pole moves a little bit every year. This means the magnetic variation in any particular area is increasing or decreasing by slight amounts each year.

To get range and bearing information from your loran, you must enter a destination (waypoint). The machine, which already knows where you are, calculates the distance and direction to your destination. The direction (bearing) is calculated in true north, but because lorans are now such smart little machines, many of them automatically convert the bearing to magnetic north. On some older machines, the magnetic variation for your area had to be entered annually, and it would have to be changed when visiting an area with a greater or lesser variation. New machines calculate magnetic variation for your particular spot automatically, and adjust that variation as you move across the earth's surface.

By the way, the automatic correction from true to magnetic north built into the loran can be turned on or off, and in some areas where there are substantial local anomalies in the magnetic field, it might be a good idea to turn the correction off and do the calculations for yourself.

COURSE ADJUSTMENTS

And now we come to the important point of all this explanation, the point that gets a lot of beginning navigators in trouble. Skippers, take heed: your loran is a smart little machine, but it can't tell you what number on your particular compass you should steer by to reach your destination. Sure, it can give you the bearing, either in true or magnetic north, but that bearing may be substantially different from the actual course you need to steer by the compass.

Cross currents, wind, and tides all need to be taken into consideration when figuring what course to run, but in addition to these variables, these is often an error in the compass itself, caused by objects on the boat.

Compasses are affected by objects in the local environment. Place a large metal object right next to the compass and you can see this for yourself. Radios with external speakers, video screens, metal equipment housings, tools, steel (but not aluminum) drink cans left on the console, and a host of other objects can affect a magnetic compass. (Wires forming a circuit that surrounds the compass create a magnetic field. To solve the problem, wires are run together in "twisted pairs." This way, the fields from the two wires will cancel each other out.)

The fluctuations of a magnetic compass are known as deviation, and wise old salts and sailors sometimes take the time to calculate precise compass deviations for their boats. Since deviation often will change with the boat's heading, the only way to figure deviation is to run between several points where you know the actual heading (say, from buoy one to buoy two, which you know is 170 degrees), then note the difference between what you know and what your compass reads for each heading. (Also, bear in mind that compass deviation will change when you reposition any of the objects that are affecting it.)

Thus, in the old days navigators calculated the course to steer by figuring the true north bearing and then by adding or subtracting both magnetic variation and compass deviation for the desired course heading. Next, they took into account tides, current, and the ship's leeway, finally arriving at a heading that was essentially an educated and precisely calculated guess. Sounds like a lot of work, doesn't it?

Trying to figure compass deviation and drift for all headings quickly takes all the fun out of boating. But since we're now using a loran to help with our navigation, we can do something that would make traditionalists who rely entirely on their magnetic compass and their esoteric navigational skills throw up their hands in horror.

As far as we're concerned, the compass is mostly an aid to steering. Sure, we should try to keep deviation to a minimum by mounting the compass away from interfering magnetic objects, and we should note any large deviations the compass may show, but with the loran on board, we don't have to rely on painfully exact course calculations and precise compass courses to get us to our destination.

Instead, we will give the loran the coordinates of our desired destination, let it do the figur-

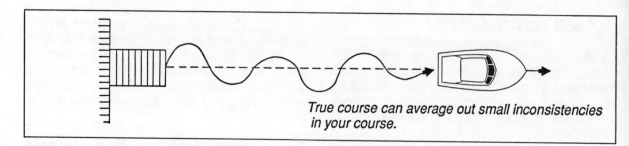

True course can average out small inconsistencies in your course.

ing, and then take off on an approximate compass heading. Once underway, we will use the compass mostly as a guide to steer by, keeping the bow in line with a number on the compass card. (If you are on a steady course, heading in the right direction, it really doesn't matter what that number is.) To keep on track, we will use the navigation software built into the loran — features like true course, ground speed, estimated time of arrival, and cross track error. Most loran users already know something about these functions, but we'll go over them just to make sure.

TRUE COURSE

You're heading out to the ledge, running at 24 knots. A buddy calls up on the VHF and asks what course you're running. You glance at the compass and tell him you're heading due east.

Well, maybe you are and maybe you aren't. The only thing you know for sure is that the needle on your compass lines up with the big E when you look at it. What about magnetic variation, and what about that windshield wiper motor that sits right next to the compass? Isn't the tide turning north at four knots, and didn't you make a few swings in the last few minutes to dodge floating junk?

The only way to know the real direction you have been traveling in is to use your loran. The setting known as true course (TC) can tell you what track you have been making across the ocean bottom.

To do this, the loran records your present position (waypoint zero), waits a little while, takes another position (waypoint one), then calculates the actual bearing between the two points. The machine keeps doing this at predetermined intervals, and when it has enough samples, it averages these waypoints to calculate your true bearing over the past few minutes, taking into account all the little jogs you took to avoid floating logs and any other helm changes you might have made. If you hold a steady course on the compass, the loran will give you an exact heading. If your course wavers slightly, the machine will give you an average course for the predetermined time interval it samples.

One very important, and often overlooked, element of this process is the length of the sampling interval the loran uses to calculate true course. On slow vessels, such as sailboats, the sampling interval must be fairly long to get a good average heading. But if the same long sampling period is used on a sportfisherman running at 30 knots, the TC function will

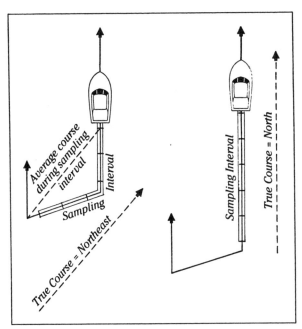

The true course setting has a built-in lag factor, which may cause the machine to appear inaccurate at times. In figure one, the skipper has turned the boat and is heading due north, but his loran still shows his true course as northeast. This is because of the lag of sampling intervals, which follows the boat's course like a string of railroad cars. In figure two, the sampling interval has "turned the corner." In other words, the lag of the true course samples has now adjusted to the new course.

lag far behind any helm changes and will not accurately represent your present course.

As a rule of thumb, the faster the boat is traveling, the shorter the sampling interval (known as the time filter) should be. If you consistently overrun your fishing hole (we'll explain why you do that in a minute), it might be an indication that your time filter is set for too long an interval, and you should make necessary adjustments, or discuss it with a knowledgeable electronics dealer.

GROUND SPEED

When your loran takes sample readings, it not only calculates bearing, it also keeps track of the distance you have traveled. When you set the loran in ground speed (GS) mode, it divides distance by time to figure boat speed. Once again, it is using a predetermined sampling interval, and displays average speed during that interval.

The loran's ground speed calculations are based on a straightline course, and, like the true course calculation, it is most accurate when you are maintaining a constant course. Zigzags and course changes will affect the average speed, just as they affect TC readings. In addition, the sampling interval your loran is set for will create a lag between present speed and average speed for the duration of the sampling period.

That may sound complicated, but it's easy to see it for yourself. Next time you are out on your boat, put your loran in GS mode, get up to speed for awhile, and then chop the throttle. You will notice that the loran takes a while to slow down, because it is averaging your present slow speed and your former fast speed. The longer it takes the loran's GS indicator to drop down to your present speed, the longer your sampling period (time filter). If you think that your loran's sampling period is too long, you might want to shorten it.

Now that you know how a loran figures course

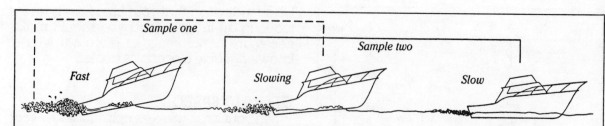

Ground speed is measured by tracking the boat's speed for a certain interval of time and averaging it. In sample one, the ground speed reading will be high, even though the skipper has come off a plane just as he got his ground speed reading. This is because he has been running fast through most of the sampling period. In sample two, the boat has been moving slowly through most of the sampling period, so the ground speed reading will be very close to the boat's actual speed.

and speed, you will see why so many fishermen overrun their waypoints. When you punch a destination in and tell the machine to give you direction to get there, it stays busy throughout the trip figuring true course, average speed across the bottom, and a whole lot of other things. As we've seen, all these calculations take time, and that lag time can cause you to overshoot your mark.

Let's say, for example, that your machine is set up to sample waypoints for 30 seconds to figure out headings and speed and cross track error and all those other things. That means that in range and bearing mode, it won't recognize you are at your destination until 30 seconds after you get there. If you are blasting along at 30 knots, that 30-second delay means you have overshot your point by a quarter of a mile. That's why smart skippers slow down a half mile or so before they get to their destination — this gives the loran time to catch up.

Of course, if you switch the machine back to latitude/longitude or TD display, you will get instantaneous position readouts — provided you can interpret them. But an easier way to cut down on unwanted lag might be to shorten up those sampling intervals for high-speed operation. (Keep in mind that a very short sampling interval will decrease your accuracy at trolling speeds.)

ETA AND VMG

By using range, bearing, and speed calculations, your loran can perform a couple of additional tricks that you may find useful at some point. Estimated time of arrival (ETA) is exactly what it sounds like. The loran looks at your speed and course to the desired destination, then calculates how long it will take you to get there if you maintain your present speed.

Velocity made good (VMG) is a function fishermen may or may not find useful. Sailboat captains, especially racers, find it almost invaluable. The VMG function remembers your

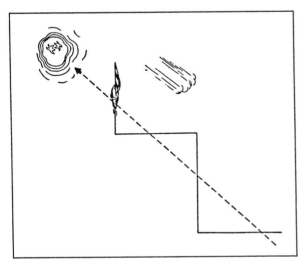
A sailboat uses the Velocity Made Good setting to keep track of its progress to its destination.

starting point and your destination, and updates you as to how far you have traveled in the direction of your destination.

If you were to punch in a destination waypoint 10 miles due east of the harbor, then motor only one mile east and spend the rest of the day trolling north and south, your VMG function wouldn't concern itself with your north/south wanderings, and would keep track of how far you still have to go to get to your original waypoint. Sailboat skippers who have to zig-zag at right angles to work their way into the wind often use VMG to keep track of their progress toward their upwind goal.

ASF

Earlier, we mentioned that loran works on the principle that radio waves travel at a constant speed. The truth is that the signals' speed over water and the speed over land are slightly different, which can have an effect on the accuracy of a loran fix. Several years ago, the Coast Guard began calculating the variances in loran signals created by various land masses. These corrections are known as Automatic Secondary Factors (ASF), and they represent the calculated differences between theoretical and actual TD positions when the distortion caused by land is added in.

Most new machines have ASF corrections built into the memory, while older units don't. A lot of boaters will never be aware of these corrections and couldn't care less. The most common problem resulting from ASF corrections comes from the fisherman who trades his old loran in for a new one. He may suddenly find that his fancy new machine can't find a lot of his favorite fishing spots.

Attacking the machine with profanity or a hammer is not the solution. In many such cases, the problem is that the old loran didn't have ASF corrections built in, and the fisherman's numbers were based on uncorrected machine readings. Since the new loran will automatically add in those corrections, it will take the boater to a slightly different location using the same coordinates.

If you have such a problem, the solution is to turn off the new loran's ASF correction program and take yourself to the fishing spot using your old numbers. Once you have found your place, switch the ASF back on and make a note of the new coordinates based on the machine's correction.

Remember, too, that all the coordinates printed in this publication were found with the ASF in the OFF position.

CROSS TRACK ERROR

The cross track error function (XTE, CTE, or CT) is a helpful feature for holding a course. The range and bearing mode tells you where to go and how far away you are, but it is the cross track that will help you steer a straight course to your destination. It does this by telling you if you are holding to that course line or if you are steering off to one side or another, which is your cross track error.

To understand the importance of knowing your cross track, let's look at a skipper who doesn't use it. Our captain has a very slow boat that he likes to run to a secluded island. Every trip, he punches the location of the island into his loran, and his range and bearing tell him to steer due east for 40 miles. Since his boat only does 10 knots, he figures it's okay to check the course every hour or so. He sets the autopilot and relaxes.

After making the same trip several times, our man begins to wonder why the loran always begins by telling him to steer 90 degrees, then 85 degrees the second hour, 40 degrees the third hour, and due north the fourth hour. He always ends up coming to the island from the south instead of from the west.

From an overhead vantage point, we can see what the skipper doesn't. The water between his home port and the island has a six-knot current flowing due south. As our captain steers in the direction of the island, he is pushed south by the current and has to make bigger and bigger corrections as he approaches his destination. The obvious solution, we would say, would be to "crab" into the current by steering a bit north of the island.

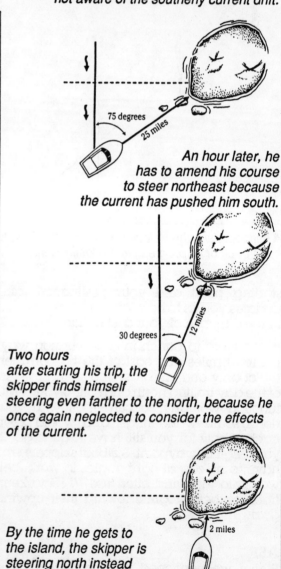

Starting from the marina, the skipper checks range and bearing on his loran and steers due east to the island, not aware of the southerly current drift.

An hour later, he has to amend his course to steer northeast because the current has pushed him south.

Two hours after starting his trip, the skipper finds himself steering even farther to the north, because he once again neglected to consider the effects of the current.

By the time he gets to the island, the skipper is steering north instead of east.

20

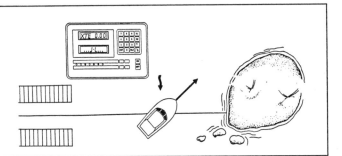

By setting his machine on the Cross Track Error setting, our skipper can run a straight course to the island. To him, it may seem as though he's heading northeast, but he is really only crabbing into the current to produce an easterly course.

Simple enough from a crow's vantage point, right? But not so obvious when you are on the water. That's when the loran's cross track error indicator becomes useful. If our friend had set his machine in the CTE mode and paid attention, it would have warned him when he first began to drift off to the south.

Most lorans do this by displaying the distance the boat has moved to one side or the other of the desired course. Current and wind drift can be compensated for by simply adjusting the boat's heading to keep it centered on the loran's display. Remember that a loran doesn't have any idea which way the nose of the boat is pointed; it only knows the direction to the destination and the true course you are running across the ocean bottom.

Thus, to those not aware of drift and the necessary correction angle, it may seem strange that the boat has to steer 80 degrees to reach a destination due east (90 degrees). But by following the loran's XTE display, a skipper will maintain the straightest course possible.

Note that the error away from the course line is usually displayed in hundredths of a nautical mile. A hundredth of a nautical mile is only 60 feet, a couple of boat lengths. If you have a cross track error of .02, that's only 120 feet. What that means is that you should not make large helm corrections to get back on course.

A distance of 120 feet isn't much error in the ocean and a small, gradual helm movement will get you back on course, while a large correction will probably send you too far on the other side of your desired heading. If you get way off your original course line you might want to reset the cross track error from your new position instead of steering way off course to get back to the old line.

CAUSE FOR ALARM

The additional features built into most new lorans include several useful alarm functions, including an anchor watch alarm, destination alarm, and cross track error alarm. The anchor watch does what the name implies. The machine keeps track of your anchored position and sounds an alarm if the boat drifts outside the limits you have set (a quarter mile, a half mile, or whatever). Setting a limit for the alarm allows you to swing at anchor without disturbance but alerts you in the event of a major position shift that signals a dragging anchor.

A destination alarm simply lets you know where you are within a certain distance (which you can specify) of your destination. A cross track error alarm monitors your course, and sounds a warning when you steer too far to one side or the other. You can set the limits of the cross track alarm so the machine tolerates the minor helm swings and only warns you when there is a major change in heading.

ROOM FOR ERROR

Once a skipper masters the basics of loran navigation, there is a temptation to let the machine do all the work. For example, let's follow a skipper as he leaves the Port Everglades channel in Fort Lauderdale, Florida, and heads north to Saint Mary's, Georgia. He punches in latitude and longitude for the sea buoy eight miles out of Saint Mary's (30.42.70, 81.19.00), hits his GOTO, and lets the machine guide him there, using range and bearing, cross track error, and all the other functions we've talked about.

First off, let's hope he checked a chart to make sure there are no islands or sandbars in his path. Second, let's hope he double-checked his coordinates before he entered them. If he hit an 80 instead of an 81 for his longitude, he'll be hunting for the sea buoy somewhere way to the east of the continental shelf.

But he's in luck this time. He entered the numbers correctly, and he looked a chart over to familiarize himself with the course he will be running. In other words, he is practicing good basic seamanship, using the loran as an aid to navigation instead of relying on it as his sole source of information.

After a long run up the coast, he finds himself at what his loran says is his destination, and there is no sea buoy there! After a few minutes of searching, his mate gives a yell and points to a shape on the horizon. The sea buoy is almost a mile away.

Loran is supposed to be accurate; what happened? It could have been one of a number of things (which we'll describe in more detail in the "Sources of Error" section). Maybe the ASF correction wasn't 100 percent. Maybe the sea buoy was moved. Buoys and channel markers are sometimes changed, and to stay updated on these changes, skippers should read the Coast Guard's *Notice to Mariners* and note such changes on their charts and logs.

Perhaps the TD lines our friend used gave a poor crossing angle, in which case he should switch to the stations with TD lines crossing as near 90 degrees as possible. Base line extension and poor crossover angles aren't a problem in Georgia, but in some areas on the fringes of loran coverage (like the Bahamas), poor crossover angles can reduce loran accuracy to a mile or more.

The point is, loran accuracy and repeatability is quite good, but you shouldn't trust your machine as the absolute authority on your position. Loran navigation should be backed up by a solid understanding of plotting and charting techniques and by good solid seamanship.

By the way, it might be a good thing that our

friend's loran didn't send him straight to the buoy. Improbable as it may seem, there are cases on record of skippers who entered the coordinates of a marker on their machine and ran, literally, right up on top of it. Such embarrassing and potentially dangerous collisions are rare, but you should still make a habit of slowing down the last half mile or so before reaching waypoint destinations set close to shore, shoals, or other hard objects.

A MATTER OF RECORD

Before we leave our friend to tie up at the Saint Mary's dock, there is one more piece of business that needs to be taken care of. After checking his *Notice to Mariners* to make sure the sea buoy wasn't moved by the Coast Guard, our skipper should enter the corrected loran coordinates for the buoy in his loran log book. That way, he will have the right numbers for his particular loran to refer to the next time he comes north.

All loran users should keep permanent written records of such corrections, as well as numbers for favorite fishing spots, harbor entrances, navigation hazards, and all waypoints that might by reused. Many lorans will store up to several hundred waypoints in the memory, but it would be unwise to trust the machine to remember everything without a backup. More than one skipper has had a lightning bolt, voltage jump, or simple machine failure wipe out years of valuable coordinates because he didn't back the machine's memory up with a written record.

FINDING A DIFFICULT WAYPOINT

Here's a little problem that you may have run into: you were out fishing one day and found a fantastic piece of bottom. You saved it in

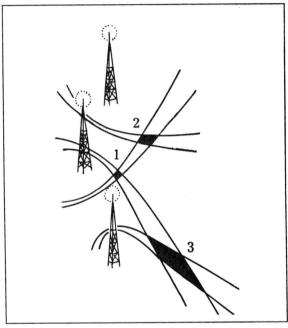

The double lines indicate the .1 TD margin of accuracy which loran can give us. Notice that in some areas where TDs intersect at nearly right angles (point 1), the area of uncertainty is relatively small, while the area increases as the angles become more acute (points 2 and 3).

the loran's memory as a waypoint, but when you tried to run back to the same spot on another trip, you couldn't find the bottom.

In a case like this, it might be the loran system itself that is causing you trouble, and an understanding of the system might help you find that bottom. If you know the TD coordinates for that spot, look on the chart and check the angle the lines cross at and the width between the TD lines. In areas along the curve where lines are spread and intersect at wide angles, there will be more surface area inside the TD grid.

The grid is the minimum time delay difference your machine can recognize. Newer machines can work in hundredths of TD units (although they may still display it in tenths), while older machines work in tenths. All points inside that grid will have the same TD coordinates.

If your machine is operating in latitude/longitude, the best it can do is to put you somewhere in that grid. By switching the machine to a TD readout, you can use a little trick to gain more accuracy. Begin by looking at a loran chart and figure which of your two slave stations has TD lines bunched closer together. Next, steer to a point along that narrower line and run down the line until you intersect the second TD. By doing this, you put yourself on a track that might be only 100 feet wide, while the track following the other TD line might be as wide as 500 or 600 feet.

ANCHORING ON A REEF

Finding a likely piece of structure isn't always enough. For bottom or drift fishing, you might want to anchor and leave yourself right above a particular spot. Instead of estimating wind and current drift and setting the anchor by guessing, you can use your loran to calculate exactly where to drop the hook so you can drift back to your spot.

To do this, put the boat right over the desired piece of bottom and enter this spot as a destination on your loran. Now, switch the machine to range and bearing mode and let the boat drift with the current for a few minutes.

For the sake of example, let's suppose you are in 100 feet of water and you plan to put out about 500 feet of anchor line. If you remember that each .01 of a nautical mile is 60 feet, you can figure that 500 feet is .08 nautical miles.

With this in mind, let the boat drift for awhile and then steer back on the bearing your loran tells you to. Continue past the destination on the same heading for about .08 nautical miles, plus a little extra to give the anchor time to sink. Then drop the hook. This will automatically put you upwind and upcurrent of your destination, and when your 500 feet of line is out, you will have drifted back.

By the way, if there is much current, your fishing lines won't go straight down, but will drift back behind the boat. If the current is much stronger than one knot, you should anchor even farther upcurrent so your lines will be over the structure when they drift back.

WARNING

Loran C is one of many aids to navigation. The prudent mariner should never depend on any single source of navigation information to the exclusion of others. You should also regularly plot and log loran C fixes during open-water navigation.

While your loran C set can tell you the direct course to steer to any given waypoint, it cannot tell you whether this is a safe course to follow. It doesn't tell you whether there is land or a dangerous reef in the way. You should always plot courses on a nautical chart before following the loran's recommended course.

SOURCES OF ERROR

This section is not intended to be a basic course in loran installation and operation, but is a troubleshooting guide for boaters who are already familiar with the operation of their particular machines. So we'll assume that you had your loran installed by a qualified dealer, who mounted it properly and adjusted everything correctly, and that you paid attention while he thoroughly explained the machine (as any reputable dealer should take the time to do).

We can call the first group of errors built-in errors, since they are inherent to the way loran works. There is really nothing you can do about system errors except understand them and try to minimize their effects.

The first, cross angle error, isn't really something that will show up on the screen as a bad number, but not understanding it could keep you from finding a waypoint. To explain cross angle errors, we need to remember how a loran receiver finds a position as the intersection of two TD lines, with the width of those lines being the minimum time delay distance your receiver can calculate. Again, these crossover lines are most accurate when they are nearest the base line, and when they intersect at close to a 90-degree angle. You begin to run into trouble when you use lines that are way out on a TD curve, or when two TD curves overlap at a large angle.

TD lines are measurable to within a tenth, and system accuracy is within plus or minus one-tenth. If you choose your time delay so that crossover angles are good, you'll have a repeatability of within 50 to 100 feet. If that seems like a big area to you, keep in mind that it is really only three or four boat lengths, and you couldn't stop that quickly if you were running at speed.

But you don't always have the best possible crossover angle, and you may find yourself above a rock pile with a TD intersection that is 100 feet in one direction, but 600 feet the other way. In such a case, you can use a little trick to increase your repeatability when you come back. Run up the narrower TD line, and cut your throttles as the wider number comes onto your screen.

Signal strength is a system variable that can shut your machine down. The most common cause of a weak signal is distance; the transmitter is just too far away. The best way to deal with weak signals is to avoid them by switching to a closer transmitter. For example, anyone looking at loran charts in Ft. Myers, Florida, might pick the Raymondville, Texas, and Jupiter, Florida, transmitters because the crossing angles look best. But the Texas transmitter is so far away that weak signals will disrupt operation from time to time. You would be better off using the stronger and closer transmitter in Grangeville, Louisiana, even though the crossover angles aren't as good.

Also, loran signals lag as they cross over land, so be aware of this if you are navigating in an area with a large landmass between you and the transmitter. For example, the Florida mainland lies between the Keys and all the transmitters in the southern chain. This can cause discrepancies of up to one mile on a loran fix. But this isn't really that bad, as this lag is fairly consistent and affects accuracy, but not repeatability in most cases.

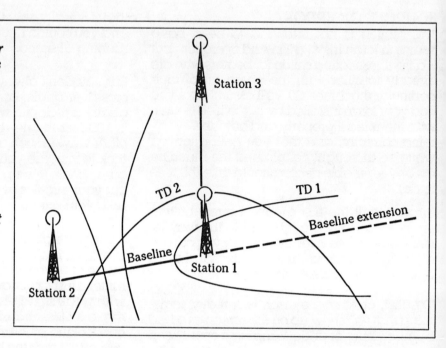

Base line extension error can occur when TD lines are very close to the transmitter. The steep curve made by transmitters 1 and 2 (TD 1) begins close to transmitter 1 and curves sharply behind it, where it is intersected by the transmitter 1 and 3 TD line (TD 2) in two distinct places. A loran receiver cannot tell the difference, and will give the same TD position for both places.

This means locals who already know where they are going have no problem. But transient boaters who are using the loran to steer a course by the charts might be in for a surprise.

Chart accuracy is something we too often take for granted. Just because a chart says a buoy is in a certain place doesn't mean it is always there. Check your *Notice to Mariners* for corrections, and generally be aware of discrepancies in the chart. For places you run to frequently, you might want to keep a corrections log that shows the difference in your reading and the chart numbers. In the end, if repeatability is our goal, we shouldn't worry about where a thing is as much as we should about how to get back there again. When accuracy is required, however, the skipper must leave a margin for error.

Base line extension is the final system fluke we will mention. A base line extension is an imaginary line that runs on beyond the two transmitters in a series. The closer you get to the base line extension, the less accurate your readings get. With TD lines very close to the extension, there is a possibility of duplicate readings (there are two places with the same loran number). Keep this in mind when you are traveling through these affected areas, and don't trust your navigation or autopilot when the numbers are close to the base line extension.

EQUIPMENT RELIABILITY

One of the biggest physical problems facing loran receivers is moisture. Unless your unit specifically says it is waterproof, don't assume that it is. Mount your loran in an enclosed area where spray and sea air can't get at it.

The next most common problem that affects receivers is poor power supply. If the loran is hooked into the same line as the starter battery, starting an engine or otherwise drawing a large surge of power can lock up the loran. The solution is to incorporate a second power supply just for the electronics.

Transmitter malfunctions are another source of potential error. Most transmitters have a back-up system, but lightning, power outages, or maintenance can take a station off the air for a while. To make sure your stations are working, check the SNR (signal-to-noise ratio) and look at each station to make sure they all read. If a station is off the air, switch to another. If the master is down, you may just have to wait.

ENVIRONMENTAL ERRORS
The third group of errors we can look at are environmental errors, which include things both inside and outside of the boat.

Weather can affect loran reception. If there is a cold front moving between you and a transmitter, you will lose half to three-quarters of your signal strength. There's really nothing you can do about a cold front, other than to be aware of it, and maybe try to find an unaffected transmitter. Local systems such as squalls can also affect reception.

The lightning that comes with a squall line doesn't affect the receiver (unless you get a direct hit), but the static buildup in the air will. If you start to notice a buzzing or humming sound, lay the antenna down and shut the loran off to protect the machine.

Antenna location can have a lot to do with loran reception. If your loran antenna is in the shadow of a larger VHF whip, you will lose reception. Try to set your antennas as far apart as possible, and use an extension on the loran antenna to get it up to the same height as the VHF.

Electronic noise is a problem for lorans. Alternators are a common culprit, but each vessel is different. To locate the source of any disruptive noise, turn on the SNR function, then start turning on different ship's systems until you locate the problem. Noise must be dealt with at the source, and you will have to depend on your electronics dealer to install the right filters to eliminate noise.

One common loran failure occurs in bad weather when windshield wipers are turned on. Not many people think to try the windshield wipers when they are checking the system back at the dock in good weather. The moral is, try to think of all possible sources of noise, as it could save you trouble later.

Noise in the local environment can disrupt a loran. If you have ruled out other possible sources of malfunction, pay attention to the area where the loran is located. Excessive heat build-up can make your electronics malfunction. To prevent this, make sure your receiver is adequately ventilated. Sometimes sunlight coming through a windshield can have a "greenhouse effect," so make sure your loran is not in direct sunlight.

Humidity is another cause of malfunction that may disappear once the machine dries out.

More than one irate loran owner has disconnected his inoperative system and carted it down to the dealer . . . where it worked perfectly. (It probably dried out on the way to the shop.) The best thing for you to do when a malfunction occurs is to be observant.

OPERATOR ERRORS

Lack of navigational skills has gotten more than one loran user in trouble. It's not enough simply to punch in numbers and go. You need to have an idea of how those numbers came about and where they are in relation to the rest of the ocean.

Carelessness is another source of problems. If you put the wrong numbers into the machine, it will send you to the wrong place. Take a little extra time to check your numbers before saving them.

Lack of system understanding is something you can't blame on the machine or anyone else. If you bought a used loran, or didn't get adequate instructions from your dealer, make the effort to learn your machine thoroughly. Read the manual, get a friend with a similar system to go over it with you, or take it to a dealer who has the time to explain things properly. Your loran can do a lot for you, but only if you know how to use it.

MORE ABOUT LORAN
by Rod and Susie Stebbins

Much has been written about the loran system, and for whose who would like to delve a bit more into the technical details, good books are available. Two of the best, because they are easy to understand, are *The Loran-C User's Guide* by Bonnie Dahl (Richardson's Marine Publishing, Inc., 1986), and *The Complete Loran-C Handbook* by Luke Melton (International Marine Publishing Company, 1986). The goals in the paragraphs that follow are to set straight one or two common misconceptions and to offer some commonsense advice on using the coordinates in this book to best advantage.

We have had the pleasure of having aboard our Sancho several brands of loran receivers to use for verification of coordinates, and we have yet to see much difference among them when reading TDs. Currently, we have four loran units aboard, and except for the time it takes each of them to settle down after a change in speed or direction has been initiated, they all agree consistently in the TD mode. Thus, we suggest in this book that reefs, wrecks, rocks, ledges, and the like ought to be located using TDs with the loran's ASF (Automated Secondary Factor) disabled. At least this way all of us will be using the same measurements in our searches. Please note, however, that when your destination is a charted aid to navigation, you should input the Lat/Lon rather than the TD coordinates as a waypoint in your loran, but only after "squaring" the loran receiver with the real world as described below. This applies to all the coordinates listed in Chapter 6 on "passes," and you'll find an explanation in the introduction to that chapter.

Why must the loran be reconciled to local geography? Because, while all lorans are consistent when displaying TDs at a given location, the same machines at the same location when asked to display latitudes and longitudes will not agree at all. This is true whether or not the ASFs provided by the factory are in operation; the root cause is in the software and the arithmetic conversions from TDs to Lat/Lons.

To help you understand loran's local limitations, we suggest you conduct the following exercises on one of those wonderful weekends when the weather is peaches and cream, and that you duplicate the test when the weather is less than nice. Also, verify a position or a range and bearing frequently — say, on the same day of each month — and save all your findings for the year. Not only will you know the local limitations, you will also know in subsequent years when the object of your affection is becoming a candidate for the shop or the scrap pile.

1. Initializing (seeding) your loran:

- *At a wet slip.* Determine the latitude and longitude of your slip as accurately as you possibly can and initialize (seed) your loran. This procedure is necessary with all lorans; using this "seed" your loran will subsequently pick the best loran transmitting chain and the two strongest slave or secondary stations within that chain. Based on local knowledge, change your secondary selection using manual override when advisable. Turn the loran on, seed it, and once it has settled down and is providing your present-position information, write down your position in TDs and Lat/Lon. We call this position "home," and we store the Lat/Lon into memory position 98 (loran capacity of 100) or 198 (loran capacity of 200). If you are able to determine a very accurate Lat/Lon position of "home" from the chart or an actual survey benchmark, note the difference your loran offers and save that information.
- *On a trailer.* Do the same as above, choosing for the site at which you enter your "seed" the place where you launch your boat regularly. Save that Lat/Lon coordinate.

2. Selecting test coordinates:

   Select five or six permanent navigational markers that are not likely to move or be moved and/or some geographical objects from a NOAA chart that are easy to get right next to in a boat. We use a coastal chart (scale of 1:40,000). Make sure you have the most recent edition of the chart. Scale as accurately as you can the Lat/Lons of each buoy or landmark, and list these coordinates on a piece of paper.

3. Verifying your loran's ability:

- Get underway to the first selected location. Position your boat just as close to the marker or object as you can get with bow and stern anchors.
- Once the loran has settled down for, say, 10 or 20 minutes, read the TDs and the Lat/Lons and record each of them as loran readings. Enter the TDs into the loran's waypoint memory so that you will have them available throughout the year. Note the difference between the loran's Lat/Lon and the Lat/Lon taken from the NOAA chart.
- You now know how far your loran's Lat/Lon deviates from the real world and the chart. In Sancho, we have tied ourselves

to a marker so that our loran antenna was just a few feet from it, only to be informed by our loran that we were as much as 0.08 nautical mile away. Eight one-hundredths of a nautical mile is only about 438 feet: close enough to see the marker, but no cigar.

- Still at the first location, check whether your loran will accept additional corrections; depending on the unit, this may be done by modifying the ASF, inserting "Additional Correction Factors," or inserting a "Current Position." If your loran has this capability, then your choice of a receiver was a wise one. If it does not, commit to memory how far "off position" you are and what you have to do to correct the error. (We are not aware of lorans on the market today that lack all ability to accept corrections.)
- With the correction factors in place, you should have a loran that is reconciled to the real world. All that is left is to verify that fact. Weigh your anchors and visit the next of the locations you have chosen. Be sure to set yourself up as you did at location #1. Allowing 10 to 20 minutes to settle down, record the TDs and Lat/Lons as before; you should find that the Lat/Lons are very close or identical to the coordinates you have measured from the chart.
- If you discover any difference, doublecheck your chart measurement for accuracy. We ought to be nearly splitting hairs, and you will probably find that you are as close as you are able to measure and interpolate to the coordinates you have taken from the chart.
- Verify each test location in turn and enter the proper coordinates into your loran. Note what has happened to your TDs as well.

4. Establishing your own benchmark:

- As soon as you have completed correcting your loran, return to port and secure your boat at a location that is easily accessed and will not likely be subject to change. This might be a gas dock, your wet slip (provided your wet slip is not covered or jammed in among buildings, masts, hills, etc.), a piling, or a floating dock that might be well out of the way.
- Note the exact location and record its TDs and Lat/Lon.
- Check this reference location often. Keep records of your findings, as you are likely to see slight variations each time. There is no reason for alarm; the loran system is simply "floating" about naturally. "Loran system float" is due to a multitude of factors, which include electronic interference "noises" on your boat or in the atmosphere, degree of humidity, condition of foliage and vegetation, etc. But these variations should be minor. As long as we remain in the TD mode and ignore the Lat/Lon, the loran will take us back to the same spot over and over again with uncanny accuracy.

The only time we seem to get confused or in trouble is when we try to make the loran geographically correct and agree with the local charting. The loran can accomplish this feat only by calculating the Lat/Lons from the TDs it sees. This is why we went through the exercises above, and why we entered in those additional corrections for the loran to use in its calculations.

CHAPTER 4

BOATING BUDDIES

Welcome to the world of loran owners, sailors, and boaters! Whether you are a seasoned salt or a novice, we are sure you will appreciate loran more as you discover the joys of boating and cruising it unlocks.

When we first started boating, we thought that a 10- to 20- mile trip was exciting, and when enroute, we were never quite sure we'd be able to survive the trip, since we didn't know what we were doing. We used to dream about taking vacations on a small boat. We would try to imagine just how we would make a three-week vacation on a 22-foot Glastron boat with a "cuddly" cuddy cabin work.

It seemed that we almost never had enough room, and over the years we kept buying bigger boats, with the same end result. No matter how large the boat, we never seemed to have quite enough room to take all the things we just knew we would be lost without!

It also seemed that the size of our boats increased with the scope of our abilities. Our first 22-foot boat was great for running around in small circles fast. There always seemed to be enough room for swimming suits, towels, lunch, and a small cooler. Then we started fishing, and when we added tackle for two, we needed a bigger boat. And so we bought a 24-foot Sea Ray with an aft stateroom (bedroom) for Christmas.

By the time the next fall arrived, we were armed with scuba certificates, and what with our diving gear, there was no continuing without an even larger boat soon. We justified it because we had just taken a couple of long trips. The first consisted of 350 miles and the second was a 980-miler over a three-week vacation. We soon found that traveling by small boat is very practical and quite easily done, even with the most modest of means.

But a friend of ours had that bigger boat, and every time we looked at it, we just knew it was the perfect boat for us. It was a twin-engine 27-foot Sea Ray, fully loaded with almost all the toys, including air conditioning and a custom-made livewell, which he used to keep live lobster in until dinner time.

Our friend's boat went up on the block, and within a couple of weeks, Sancho number three was ours. We settled down for awhile, knowing that we had arrived at the perfect size and that we were adequately equipped to do whatever we wanted to.

Then came the two-week trips, the six-week trips, the three months in the Bahamas, and the four and a half months in the Florida Keys.

One night on the way home to Tampa, we were cruising about 35 miles offshore when

---

> **HELPFUL HINT**
>
> Use your VHF radio for essential calls and remember that VHF Channel 16 is for emergencies only, not for radio checks, finding out how the fishing is, and general chatting. Once you have made contact with your party, go to another channel approved for general use. Your consideration will be greatly appreciated by all, including the Feds!

the skies clouded over and the rain came. The seas built, our windows were covered with salt spray, and we couldn't see anything but black outside. Though not in any real danger that night, we suddenly found ourselves in what seemed to be an unusually small boat.

That next Christmas we took delivery of our fourth Sancho and marveled at how big this 30-foot Sea Ray was, with its full 11-foot-wide beam. At last, a roller skating rink that floats! This was it — a generator and all the toys, including a radar. Happiness at last, right? Wrong.

Within the first year, Susie was already wishing for the boat of her dreams, a 36-foot Sea Ray with inboard engines and a football field for a cockpit. As of this printing, we have just taken delivery and will soon be out on the water. We are positive that this boat will have enough room . . . for now.

OUR FAVORITE THINGS

For us to define boating would require a lot of paper, because boating is as diverse as life itself. There are so many different aspects and facets of boating that it simply isn't possible to write about them all in one small volume.

Boat owners range from those who are casual about their pastime to the ardent "aficionados" who spend much of their lives reading, living, and breathing boating at every salty opportunity. We sincerely hope that by reading some of our text, you'll find for yourself some of the things that have become dear to our hearts. We will try to ring that certain bell or spark up the proverbial idea light that just might start a new hobby.

Just run your fingers down the list of destinations in this book, imagine the wrecks and the reefs, the many havens and endless ports that are not even listed, then close your eyes and drift off into that magic land called imagination to dream of trips that you will be taking... one of these days.

SNORKELING

The sport of snorkeling is something that can be done at one's own speed. When left to myself, I can actually fall asleep while floating and looking! Snorkeling is a very personal sport that is filled with colors and curiously shaped things that often defy the imagination.

Snorkeling can be done in water that is as shallow as six inches to a foot deep, depending on how fat you are. Susie can snorkel right up to the beach, but I have to snorkel out where the water is at least knee-deep, or else I'll wear part of my stomach off.

It isn't hard to learn how to snorkel. Just learn how to breathe through a tube without inhaling salt water. If you are hunting shells or treasure, it's a lot easier to float and kick with a mask and snorkel than it is to walk down the beach and bend over to pick up the same object.

Equipment needed: Snorkel, net-type bag, mask, and fins.

SCUBA DIVING

Scuba diving and boating are natural partners. We keep a couple of air tanks and our scuba gear on the boat at all times. We use this equipment to identify reefs, ledges, and wrecks, and find it useful for cleaning the bottom of the boat and inspecting the zinc anodes, trim tabs, and engine shafts. We use the equipment for hunting for something to eat, something to photograph, something to watch, and something to collect.

There are classes in scuba diving just about everywhere you turn. Equipment can be purchased new from dealers or used from the classified ads in the newspapers. Scuba diving used to be very expensive, but now just about anyone can afford the sport in varying degrees.

Scuba is a very natural addition to the boater's learned skills. If you don't wish to participate in the sport, you can be assured of missing out on about 80 percent of what the seas have to offer. Scuba diving is open to persons of almost any age. The young and bold dive deep and long, but even older folks can enjoy much of the underwater world if skill is tempered with good judgment.

We seldom dive deeper than about 45 to 50 feet. Most of the colors of the spectrum disappear below about 30 feet, and since we dive to see the colors, we are usually in shallow water.

But we also like the excitement of new adventure, such as exploring a new wreck or something of that sort, too, and, properly tempted, we have made some rather exciting and (we later felt) risky dives as well.

Equipment needed: Certification and about 300 pounds of diving equipment per diver.

CAMPING

Camping on the beaches is full of romance and fun. The campfires at the water's edge and the sing-alongs make for great fun. We used to camp with a tent and the works until we got our "bigger boat." Now we have the best of both worlds. We sleep in beds with sheets on them and slap the bugs with everyone else at the campfire.

We always keep a case or two of beer available for these events and never pass up the opportunity to share a case by the fire. We have met some of the nicest people camping,

---

DAFFYNITION

First Mate: (1) Wife and usually 50-percent owner of the vessel and accompanying debt. (2) The hardest-working member of the crew. (3) The only member of the crew that knows where anything is, as evidenced by the "get me" commands. (4) The person on the vessel who gets yelled at most of the time. (5) A multipurpose person capable of cooking, washing windows, polishing, looking for "things," getting "things," and knowing what the Captain is trying to say, all the while pretending that boating is great fun. (6) Kid tender. (7) Guest tender. (8) The only responsible person on the vessel, yet seldom allowed to drive. (9) Honey dearest. (10) Girlfriend or fiance. (11) Any person not at the helm. (12) The only person who can get even with the Captain and get away with it and always wins all of the arguments (one way or the other).

usually young and in love and full of life, adventure, and hopes for the future.

The feelings are contagious and we love to be near people going places, sharing sea stories and information of wonderful things gone by.

Beaches have a certain charm that invites people everywhere to remember their childhoods. Where else can you find all sorts of people prodding the sand, building sand castles, digging moats, basking, swimming, running, tossing and riding toys, and — oh my — wearing all of those tiny swimming suits? Susie has as much fun as I looking at all of the shapes of humanity, all clad in their least and some strutting their most.

There is nothing quite like a beach full of boaters with their boats anchored to and fro, parked side by side, each having its own story to tell.

Beaches are grand places for dreamers, but we have found that some are not the best for overnighting. Some beaches are quite tame, but some can be quite bumpy with a bit of wind.

This brings up learning from experience. We now lay out lots of anchor line when we are anticipating spending the night. We make sure that the stern anchor is going to stay put. By the way, our stern anchor is the same size as our bow anchor, thereby serving as a spare anchor as well.

We very often raft with other boats. We have discovered that one anchor will hold several boats quite well provided the current isn't too strong during the change of tides.

Once, while rafted up, we thought we would be safer with two anchors down. By morning the two anchor lines were fairly well braided, so we don't do that much anymore without well-placed stern anchors to keep the rafted boats from turning about themselves. We have not had the problem with one anchor that we have had with several. The number of anchors a rafting party should consider using is a judgment call.

When we are in doubt, we don't raft up; instead, we set our own anchor. Rafting boats together where there is the possibility of waves should be done with great care. Sailboats probably should never raft side by side lest their rigging get caught by some uncaring power yacht throwing a three-foot wake in passing. We have seen this happen, and the noise of masts colliding is heart-breaking.

When rafting power boats, large fenders at least 12 inches in diameter should be used, and the boats must be lashed together as tightly as possible. When boats are improperly lashed together with the wrong fenders, you can just about bank on damages.

Equipment needed: Friends and a case of beer.

BOATING

Boating to us encompasses many categories: cruising, fishing, water skiing, camping, cooking, social events, boating clubs, dining out along the waterways, powerboat races, watching or participating in sailing regattas, entertaining friends and business associates, using the boat as a summer cottage, and last, but in no way least, just plain putt-putting. It's great to travel fast or slowly and go nowhere as quickly or as slowly as one can.

Owning a boat is a unique kind of experience. We have not been able to figure out why we think that something that simply floats is so neat.

Susie and I were discussing this phenomenon. When I said, "I just don't know why we love it so much; you figure it out," she countered with, "It is easy to understand. If I can love you and not understand why, then you can love the boat and not understand it, too!" I guess she has it straight in her mind, so it must be okay.

Better than 50 percent of the pleasure of owning a boat is having your mate enjoy it as much or more than you do. We have just such a circumstance and enjoy all of the activities we've mentioned here during the course of the year. Our favorites are fishing, cruising, scuba diving, camping at our favorite gunkhole while rafted with dear friends, and looking forward to the next time we are going out — which is just about every week.

We first thought that cruising was a bit risky and truly an adventure. Now that we have taken many several-hundred-mile trips, we have come to the conclusion that cruising long distances is little more than a whole lot of little trips put together into one big journey.

Sometimes we make major crossings of large bodies of water when we can't see land for hours. But even then, we are rarely more than 35 miles from land and we are always well prepared. Sancho will have plenty of fuel, we will have plenty of supplies for meals, and we'll stock lots of water, soft drinks, and bait for fishing. Sancho has never let us down to date, but we are always prepared.

Preventive maintenance is the real answer to keeping the boat going. We change the oil and oil filters every 25 hours of running, we change the fuel/water separator filters every 50 hours, and we have a major tune-up every change of the season or no less than four times a year. The major tune-up includes checking ignition wiring, plugs, coils, condensers, rotors, and rotor caps. Now that we have an electronic ignition, we carry an extra unit on board.

Other spare parts that we keep on board include: a full set of fuses, a set of hand tools, a handful of wire connectors, a few feet of extra electrical wire (various sizes), two sets of fan belts, extra props, and extra prop nuts (we have lost the nuts while changing the props and a prop without nuts is embarrassing and impossible). A wrench to remove the prop nut is also a handy thing to have available. We carry containers with the proper hydraulic oil and engine oil. We always have enough engine oil to change the oil in one engine, at least. A couple of extra oil and separator filters make up the rest of the spares we have found necessary.

Cruising with loran and all the other little toys made for boats is neat and not at all confusing. Many of the electronic devices have multiple purposes, offering a certain redundancy that provides us with extra security. For example, the white line doubles as a depth finder, the radar doubles as a limited range finder, the loran doubles as a knot meter and a compass, the VHF doubles as a weather station/advisory, and the depth indicator doubles as a "passifier."

We think of our compass as the main instrument, and we like to imagine that the dial is similar to the doggie statue in the back window of a "Mexican taxi," with his head lazily moving about left to right, fore and aft. We're sure he's quietly thinking, "Ole, ole, ole."

We enjoy cruising about the coast at night while watching the shore lights. We have romantic moons, good wine, and soft music, without the threat of a midnight wrestling session with a crab trap line and float that are fouled in the props. We are either very lucky or the crabbers take their traps in at night. In the daytime, it's a different story.

We love to take long walks along the beaches while combing for meaningless treasure, and we have been tempted to buy an electronic metal detector so that we could have something else to carry in the boat. We will get that when we get our bigger boat . . . after our next bigger boat.

At anchor, we can usually be found swimming about, basking in the sun, or cleaning the water line and inspecting Sancho's bottom. There are plenty of things to do to the boat when cruising, such as checking the engine's various types of juices, including battery water levels and hydraulic reservoirs, soaping down bilges, wiping the engines down, cleaning those mysterious white spots from the Bimini top, scrubbing windows, polishing brightwork, oiling the teak, greasing the zerks of the steering and the outdrives, greasing the underwater zerks on the outdrives, polishing the boat, flushing the sand from the rope locker, washing down the fishing poles and diving gear, spraying the metal parts with silicone lubricant . . . And then there is the constant challenge of getting Susie to do all this while I do something "very important" that can't be interrupted even for a minute.

Susie always wants to know why it is that just when she finishes washing and polishing the windshields and gets her supplies put away, the largest bird in the county suddenly deposits its signature for everyone to see. I guess the only response to her dilemma is that she ought to be grateful that cows can't fly.

On any quiet evening at anchor, there is no serenity quite like that found while holding that special person and watching a sunset that brings on songs of eternal love and commitment. It seems Susie and I have more of these moments on the boat than at home. I guess this is why Sancho figures into our plans so often.

You don't have to have an expensive boat to discover all those special feelings and experiences. It doesn't matter if you're aboard a motoryacht, a sailboat, or a rowboat. With a little imagination and planning, the sunset will do the rest.

WIT & WISDOM
A displacement hull can best be described as a sea plow.

People who say that a boat is a hole in the water probably don't have a mate who shares the experiences of boating with them.

The sea has fed us emotionally as well as figuratively and when we have least expected it, it has provided splendid food for the table.

Now, let us try to summarize BOAT. It is a platform and vehicle for romance, beauty, togetherness, travel, excitement, and nourishment, and we doubt that many hobbies can offer quite that much. I often wonder what else there is worth having that Sancho is not already a part of providing.

Equipment needed. A boat and a bucket of money.

CHAPTER 5

THE LOWDOWN ON DIVING

Diving in the oceans and gulfs of the world requires proper training, including instruction in open-water diving skills. Deep dives are always hazardous and should be attempted only by those who are experienced and physically ready. Dives deeper than 25 feet in open waters should be planned carefully and attempted only with someone who has already made that particular dive.

Smart divers keep a knife handy and consider it a tool rather than a weapon. There is no telling when a diver may encounter the remains of some type of rope, net, or very stout monofilament fishing line that is impossible to cut or break by hand and often too stout to bite. If you become entangled, stay calm and use your knife to free yourself.

When tides change, so does the flow of water. Remember to check on whether the present water flow will remain the same throughout the duration of your dive or whether it will shift, leaving you with a long swim upcurrent. Swimming against currents and tides when you are tired after a dive can be very risky, if not impossible, especially if the current takes the boat and diver out of each other's sight.

Those new to open-water diving are advised to contact a dive shop in the area they plan to dive to learn the area's potential hazards and make sure they have the necessary skills. We urge everyone to know all there is to know about a dive before venturing into the water.

Always keep someone who can navigate, drive, and anchor the boat aboard when divers are in the water. If there is no one left topside to deal with unforeseen circumstances, the boat might not be there when you surface. The newspapers sometimes report a boat found drifting with nobody aboard.

The "boat keeper" should know the exact coordinates the divers entered the water, and he or she should monitor the boat's location with the loran to make sure it hasn't slipped anchor and departed the scene. The tender should also know when the divers are scheduled to surface and the maximum amount of time each diver can spend underwater.

When currents make it difficult for divers to stay near the boat, and often when there is no current, we run a line from the stern on a float, and drop a second anchor at the stern so that it almost reaches the bottom (it's usually within a foot or two). We call this our story pole. We attach a 40-foot line to our wrists and tie the other end to the story pole line with a large stainless steel snap. We have found this method best when diving in limited visibility and currents that are too strong to swim against easily.

On Sancho, we have a freshwater faucet in the cockpit, with a 25-foot hose attached for washing ourselves and our diving gear when we are done for the day. Of course, if we were diving in the sweet-water seas of the Great Lakes, this wouldn't be necessary! We also keep a spray can of silicone lubricant around to spray all of the metal pieces of our regulator and other diving equipment.

Last, when we are underway and the boat is bouncing about, we tie all of the tanks together with a line and lay them down. This keeps them from rolling about the cockpit and endangering life, limb, and the all-important pursuit of happiness.

CHAPTER 6

MAKING PASSES

This chapter works differently from those that follow, so a few words of explanation are in order. Beginning with Chapter 7, our chief business is life, liberty, and the pursuit of happiness — specifically, we'll be looking for fine anchorages and great spots for fishing and diving. Here in Chapter 6, however, we're pursuing aids to navigation — sea buoys, channel buoys, midchannel buoys, and primary and secondary lights — and this is serious business indeed. The Coast Guard fixes and records the locations of navaids not by TDs but by latitude and longitude, and so must we. If you should ever have to make an emergency call to the Coast Guard they will want to know your position, not in TDs but in degrees of latitude and longitude, and if you want help promptly you'd best know the answer.

Thus the controlling coordinates in this chapter are latitude and longitude, and from these the associated TDs have been calculated for your convenience using standard algorithms to which *no* ASF corrections have been applied. We have taken great care to ensure the accuracy of each latitude and longitude, but we cannot guarantee the same degree of accuracy for the TDs due to two mitigating factors: (1) The algorithms used to convert TDs to Lat/Lons or vice versa are not uniformly precise; and (2) the TDs overprinted on government charts are calculated not with the use of algorithms, but rather using theoretical rates of propagation of radio waves from loran transmitter locations. We do well always to remember that loran was conceived as an *approximate* position-fixing aid — as a means of finding the haystack in the field, not the needle in the haystack. With smarter, more sensitive machines and a growing database to work with, loran's users can now coax a level of performance from the system far beyond anything its originators conceived of. But we must be mindful, in doing so, of the limitations we sidestep but cannot eliminate. Loran supplements but does not replace chartwork, dead reckoning, and a navigator's care and skill.

For this chapter, proceed as follows: Initialize your loran receiver and "align" it with local geography as described near the end of Chapter 3. Then, when using the waypoints listed in this chapter, input latitudes and longitudes, *not* TDs. You may or may not want the ASF function enabled, depending on the model and its method of receiving additional local corrections from you, the user (as outlined in Chapter 3). Consult the manufacturer's instructions, and you should have no problem. When chartering or operating your own boat in unfamiliar waters, you may use the TDs as waypoints (again, with the ASF function disabled), but do so cautiously.

This chapter eliminates the need to search for charts, to measure, and then to interpolate coordinates. If your favorite pass and its markers are not found in this chapter, please understand that we did not omit it intentionally; we probably just haven't made it there yet! If you have an immediate need to see your coordinates printed in this book, turn your loran on, your ASF off, take the readings, and send them to us. We will make the entries and include the changes in the next printing.

No effort will be made by us to issue errata for pass buoys or markers that have been moved for whatever reason. We sincerely hope that each boater remains responsible enough to search throughout the volumes that contain "Notice to Mariners" when planning trips. Probably the only time that the cheese really gets binding is when we are approaching a new pass or a pass we have not been to for some time and it is dark, foggy, and the radar decides to take a vacation.

That is when Susie will always ask, "Honey, did you check to see if the buoy has been moved?" Like any good husband who doesn't want to alarm his mate or get into trouble with her (whichever the case may be), I respond, "Yes, dearest darling," while I maintain a 100 percent pucker.

HOW TO USE THIS CHAPTER

A word about the organization of this chapter: The coordinates are listed by province in the lower St. Lawrence, Gulf of St. Lawrence, and around the Atlantic shores of Nova Scotia and New Brunswick, with separate listings for Cape Breton Island and the Magdalen Islands. For the interior of the continent, listings are given by body of water, for each of the Great Lakes (with a separate listing for Georgian Bay), Lake St. Clair, and the St. Lawrence Seaway. Within each province or body of water the listings are given in order of descending longitude, west to east, skipping back and forth between United States and Canadian shores of the Great Lakes and between north and south shores of Prince Edward Island, Nova Scotia, etc.

DIVING IN

Hey, divers! Remember, it might be a good idea to look below at the manmade tripod structures and markers found near and in passes. Sometimes large meals can be found at the markers. Sometimes other types of treasures, such as fishing poles, tackle, and anchors, can be found nearby. Watch out for boaters, and be advised that a red flag in the channel might invite a "matador" instead of informing the oncoming boater that there is a precious person underwater.

Believe it or not, there are boaters out there who do not know the rules of the road and there are many who really don't care either. They'll just plow right on through where you are, so floating a diving flag is no insurance against propeller damage and/or serious injury.

We have learned to tie a floating flag to a line that is surrounded by an innertube painted bright red. Then, when we surface, we surface at the tube. We never dive, swim, or water ski in tight channels that boaters use for navigation.

Even with all of these precautions, beware of passes and areas that have markers, for you can be sure that there will be a boater coming along soon enough.

Remember that seldom are boaters allowed to tie boats and equipment directly to a buoy or buoy structure. Anchoring to the buoy may invite a not-so-welcome visit from the state police and/or Coast Guard.

We also have learned to have a boat watch aboard when everyone else is in the water. The boat watch will assure us we will not have to walk home.

TIDAL TIPS

Here's another important thing we discovered the hard way about traversing passes when the tides are running strong: Where there is a narrow pass or inlet, it is possible to run into water conditions that would chill the heart of Neptune himself. Fast running tides through a pass or inlet, coupled with a strong seasonal wind in the right direction, can make for impossible conditions.

We went sideways (broached) once and thought for a minute we were going to go swimming. Check local conditions before taking on a pass during strong tidal conditions. Be prepared to go somewhere else instead of following the desire to get through. It's always better to be safe than sorry.

UNCOMMON COURTESY

Arriving at passes is always something of an event on our boat. It seems we arrive at just about the same time as all the "redneck boaters" do. A "redneck boater" is a boater who has not read the book (and probably can't read), has no idea what consideration is, and is intent upon arriving at the dock in time to make life just a bit nervy. We are sure there are only a few of these peculiar breeds around. They could easily be spotted if given an IQ test because they'd flunk spectacularly.

Please remember that courtesy is probably the only thing boaters ought to have in common. We try to be courteous to all boaters, but it sure is hard to be nice in a gaggle of "redneck boaters." As a matter of fact, it is hard not to act just like them when faced with a lack of consideration.

PASSES

BODY OF WATER	PROV/STATE	NAME	LAT	LON	TD#1	TD#2	CHART
	LORAN C	5930 GRI ZULU	52-22.59	55-42.47			
	LORAN C	5930 GRI YANKEE	46-46.54	53-10.47			
GEORGIAN BAY	ONTARIO	GREEN POINT LIGHT Q34	46-17.55	84-07.03	30950.15	47958.77	2250
GEORGIAN BAY	ONTARIO	COYLE POINT N LIGHT Q30	46-16.75	84-06.95	30951.70	47965.39	2250
GEORGIAN BAY	ONTARIO	COYLE POINT LIGHT Q28	46-16.30	84-06.92	30952.66	47969.08	2250
GEORGIAN BAY	ONTARIO	CAMBRIA BANK LIGHT K33	46-19.48	84-06.20	30941.06	47945.24	2250
GEORGIAN BAY	ONTARIO	SAILORS ENCAMPMENT Q22	46-15.62	84-06.04	30949.70	47976.62	2250
GEORGIAN BAY	ONTARIO	SHOAL ISLAND	46-18.80	84-04.55	30934.06	47954.58	2250
GEORGIAN BAY	ONTARIO	RICHARDS LANDING	46-17.72	84-02.20	30924.30	47968.72	2250
GEORGIAN BAY	ONTARIO	WEST SISTER ROCK	46-18.22	83-54.93	30884.67	47981.51	2250
GEORGIAN BAY	ONTARIO	PLUMMER BANK K8	46-17.80	83-54.63	30884.07	47985.54	2250
GEORGIAN BAY	ONTARIO	PIRATE ISLAND LIGHT KE14	46-03.77	83-54.17	30915.22	48099.08	2251
GEORGIAN BAY	ONTARIO	HILTON BEACH	46-15.55	83-53.32	30882.36	48006.43	2250
GEORGIAN BAY	ONTARIO	ARCHIBALD ISLAND	46-04.48	83-53.10	30907.64	48095.69	2251
GEORGIAN BAY	ONTARIO	MACOMB ISLAND LIGHT KE9	46-04.88	83-52.47	30903.23	48093.84	2251
GEORGIAN BAY	ONTARIO	BURNT ISLAND REEF KE7	46-06.83	83-49.97	30884.91	48083.62	2251
GEORGIAN BAY	ONTARIO	KOSHAWONG POINT	46-07.75	83-48.77	30876.20	48078.86	2251
GEORGIAN BAY	ONTARIO	BRUCE MINES WHARF	46-17.83	83-47.39	30845.49	48001.66	2250
GEORGIAN BAY	ONTARIO	McKAY ISLAND	46-16.93	83-46.84	30844.58	48010.00	2250
GEORGIAN BAY	ONTARIO	NORTH SEINE ISLAND KE3	46-07.75	83-46.50	30863.85	48083.79	2251
GEORGIAN BAY	ONTARIO	O'DONNELL BANK LIGHT KE4	46-07.97	83-46.30	30862.25	48082.46	2251
GEORGIAN BAY	ONTARIO	SULPHUR ISLAND	46-08.68	83-36.38	30806.47	48098.04	2251
GEORGIAN BAY	ONTARIO	THESSALON POINT	46-14.23	83-34.12	30782.06	48059.04	2251
GEORGIAN BAY	ONTARIO	THESSALON BRKWTR	46-15.05	83-33.13	30774.94	48054.71	2251
GEORGIAN BAY	ONTARIO	MONK POINT	45-59.15	83-24.60	30762.05	48197.58	2251
GEORGIAN BAY	ONTARIO	COCKBURN ISLAND	45-57.62	83-19.12	30734.42	48220.38	2251
GEORGIAN BAY	ONTARIO	COCKBURN ISLAND BRKWTR	45-57.58	83-18.97	30733.65	48220.99	2251
GEORGIAN BAY	ONTARIO	MELDRUM BAY	45-55.43	83-06.77	30668.59	48260.91	2251
GEORGIAN BAY	ONTARIO	BATTURE ISLAND	45-58.22	83-04.25	30648.68	48243.80	2251
GEORGIAN BAY	ONTARIO	MISSISSAGI ISLAND	46-06.45	83-00.45	30611.68	48187.20	2259
GEORGIAN BAY	ONTARIO	COMB POINT	46-10.38	82-58.03	30591.10	48161.61	2268
GEORGIAN BAY	ONTARIO	BLIND RIVER LIGHT UP9	46-10.85	82-57.48	30587.21	48159.06	2268
GEORGIAN BAY	ONTARIO	CAPE ROBERT	45-49.80	82-48.62	30574.27	48336.89	2259
GEORGIAN BAY	ONTARIO	MILLS ISLAND	46-07.82	82-41.80	30504.37	48211.04	2259
GEORGIAN BAY	ONTARIO	GORE BAY	45-56.77	82-28.82	30447.20	48316.84	2257
GEORGIAN BAY	ONTARIO	LITTLE DETROIT	46-08.95	82-22.53	30393.83	48236.19	2268
GEORGIAN BAY	ONTARIO	SPANISH RIVER LIGHT UV2	46-10.88	82-22.25	30389.70	48222.35	2268
GEORGIAN BAY	ONTARIO	INNES ISLAND LIGHT J74	46-02.12	82-21.18	30395.36	48289.29	2257
GEORGIAN BAY	ONTARIO	BOYD ISLAND	46-07.47	82-20.22	30382.70	48251.07	2268
GEORGIAN BAY	ONTARIO	MIDDLE BANK LIGHT JD14	45-59.70	82-19.05	30386.38	48310.82	2257
GEORGIAN BAY	ONTARIO	KAGAWONG	45-54.57	82-15.65	30373.58	48354.51	2257
GEORGIAN BAY	ONTARIO	BEVERLY ISLAND	45-59.99	82-14.99	30362.52	48315.18	2257
GEORGIAN BAY	ONTARIO	MEREDITH ROCK	45-58.95	82-14.42	30360.58	48323.82	2257
GEORGIAN BAY	ONTARIO	CLAPPERTON ISLAND	46-03.28	82-14.25	30354.02	48291.98	2257

PASSES

BODY OF WATER	PROV/STATE	NAME	LAT	LON	TD#1	TD#2	CHART
GEORGIAN BAY	ONTARIO	GOOSEBERRY ISLAND	45-57.07	82-13.98	30360.49	48338.50	2257
GEORGIAN BAY	ONTARIO	ROBERTSON ROCK LIGHT J72	46-03.45	82-13.47	30349.32	48291.98	2257
GEORGIAN BAY	ONTARIO	CARTWRIGHT POINT	46-03.02	82-12.43	30343.89	48296.83	2257
GEORGIAN BAY	ONTARIO	LOGAN REEF LIGHT J71	46-02.00	82-11.17	30337.91	48306.39	2252
GEORGIAN BAY	ONTARIO	JAMES FOOTE PATCH J66	45-58.92	82-05.00	30305.95	48338.79	2286
GEORGIAN BAY	ONTARIO	NARROW ISLAND	45-59.47	81-58.72	30268.87	48344.35	2294
GEORGIAN BAY	ONTARIO	PICNIC ISLAND	45-59.47	81-56.87	30258.13	48347.14	2294
GEORGIAN BAY	ONTARIO	PICNIC ISLAND LIGHT J56	45-59.55	81-56.73	30257.23	48346.78	2294
GEORGIAN BAY	ONTARIO	LITTLE CURRENT	45-58.87	81-55.58	30251.27	48353.47	2294
GEORGIAN BAY	ONTARIO	MAGAZINE POINT LIGHT J44	45-58.94	81-55.50	30250.73	48353.08	2294
GEORGIAN BAY	ONTARIO	LITTLE CURRENT SWING BRIDGE	45-58.82	81-54.85	30247.08	48354.93	2294
GEORGIAN BAY	ONTARIO	GIBBONS POINT TURNING J31	45-58.67	81-54.33	30244.21	48356.79	2294
GEORGIAN BAY	ONTARIO	LONG POINT LIGHT J24	45-58.21	81-53.58	30240.32	48361.26	2294
GEORGIAN BAY	ONTARIO	STRAWBERRY ISLAND	45-58.40	81-51.27	30226.68	48363.29	2294
GEORGIAN BAY	ONTARIO	CARON REEF LIGHT J19	45-57.87	81-50.27	30221.38	48368.61	2294
GEORGIAN BAY	ONTARIO	STRAWBERRY ISLAND LIGHT J17	45-56.70	81-49.20	30216.29	48378.68	2205
GEORGIAN BAY	ONTARIO	MANITOWANING	45-44.70	81-48.48	30224.34	48467.22	2286
GEORGIAN BAY	ONTARIO	HEYWOOD ISLAND	45-55.50	81-47.25	30206.05	48390.21	2205
GEORGIAN BAY	ONTARIO	WHITEFISH RIVER	46-06.40	81-44.17	30178.34	48315.97	2286
GEORGIAN BAY	ONTARIO	DUNCAN CITY ROCK EE5	46-00.23	81-43.45	30179.53	48361.45	2205
GEORGIAN BAY	ONTARIO	CAROLINE ROCKS EE6	46-00.15	81-43.23	30178.32	48362.35	2205
GEORGIAN BAY	ONTARIO	CREAK ISLAND SHOAL	45-56.58	81-41.73	30172.73	48390.25	2205
GEORGIAN BAY	ONTARIO	WALL ISLAND	45-33.62	81-41.12	30191.29	48557.87	2235
GEORGIAN BAY	ONTARIO	LIGHTHOUSE POINT	45-15.46	81-40.38	30207.24	48691.93	2274
GEORGIAN BAY	ONTARIO	NORTH POINT	45-15.76	81-39.92	30203.91	48690.23	2274
GEORGIAN BAY	ONTARIO	CENTRE ISLAND BANK J16	45-55.13	81-39.37	30160.17	48404.03	2205
GEORGIAN BAY	ONTARIO	McELHINNEY LIGHT TD	45-18.92	81-38.12	30188.65	48669.04	2235
GEORGIAN BAY	ONTARIO	FLOWERPOT ISLAND	45-18.42	81-36.83	30180.97	48674.14	2235
GEORGIAN BAY	ONTARIO	BURNT ISLAND BANK J13	45-54.28	81-35.35	30137.28	48415.70	2205
GEORGIAN BAY	ONTARIO	CAPE SMITH N CHANNEL	45-47.02	81-34.92	30140.78	48468.54	2245
GEORGIAN BAY	ONTARIO	BEARS RUMP SHOAL NO T3	45-18.24	81-34.70	30167.54	48677.82	2235
GEORGIAN BAY	ONTARIO	KILLARNEY QUARRIES ENTR EA2	45-57.97	81-33.90	30125.88	48391.24	2205
GEORGIAN BAY	ONTARIO	CAMPBELL ROCK J12	45-49.62	81-33.23	30128.53	48452.05	2245
GEORGIAN BAY	ONTARIO	ANN LONG BANK E11	45-58.47	81-32.50	30117.36	48389.61	2205
GEORGIAN BAY	ONTARIO	SANDY COVE LEDGE	45-57.05	81-32.15	30116.37	48400.24	2205
GEORGIAN BAY	ONTARIO	KILLARNEY NORTHWEST	45-59.02	81-31.95	30113.75	48386.44	2205
GEORGIAN BAY	ONTARIO	KILLARNEY WEST ENTR	45-58.33	81-31.33	30110.65	48392.23	2205
GEORGIAN BAY	ONTARIO	LOBSTER POINT	45-58.80	81-30.92	30107.93	48389.44	2205
GEORGIAN BAY	ONTARIO	JACKMAN ROCK NO E1	45-57.98	81-29.63	30101.01	48397.06	2204
GEORGIAN BAY	ONTARIO	KILLARNEY EAST	45-58.10	81-29.33	30099.18	48396.62	2204
GEORGIAN BAY	ONTARIO	LONELY ISLAND WEST	45-33.63	81-29.15	30117.38	48572.43	2235
GEORGIAN BAY	ONTARIO	LONELY ISLAND	45-34.40	81-28.10	30110.23	48568.13	2235
GEORGIAN BAY	ONTARIO	HALFMOON ISLAND	45-26.12	81-27.85	30116.08	48628.21	2235
GEORGIAN BAY	ONTARIO	FLAT ROCK	45-58.98	81-25.58	30076.78	48395.47	2204

PASSES

BODY OF WATER	PROV/STATE	NAME	LAT	LON	TD#1	TD#2	CHART
GEORGIAN BAY	ONTARIO	CABOT HEAD	45-14.71	81-17.53	30060.65	48721.49	2235
GEORGIAN BAY	ONTARIO	GULL ISLAND	45-51.30	81-16.50	30028.24	48461.79	2245
GEORGIAN BAY	ONTARIO	LION'S HEAD HARBOUR	44-59.40	81-14.87	30057.44	48833.98	2282
GEORGIAN BAY	ONTARIO	ROOSTER REEF NO D86	45-55.17	81-13.98	30011.37	48437.72	2244
GEORGIAN BAY	ONTARIO	WIARTON	44-44.67	81-08.06	30026.09	48944.97	2282
GEORGIAN BAY	ONTARIO	COLPOYS BAY	44-46.78	81-07.38	30019.21	48930.42	2282
GEORGIAN BAY	ONTARIO	SURPRISE SHOAL NO T5	45-03.47	81-01.67	29966.01	48816.39	2282
GEORGIAN BAY	ONTARIO	CAPE CROKER	44-57.43	80-57.60	29943.32	48862.42	2282
GEORGIAN BAY	ONTARIO	NORTH KEPPEL WHARF	44-47.67	80-56.80	29945.52	48931.83	2282
GEORGIAN BAY	ONTARIO	OWEN SOUND MARINA	44-35.22	80-56.53	29954.93	49019.73	2271
GEORGIAN BAY	ONTARIO	OWEN SOUND PIER	44-34.84	80-56.35	29954.03	49022.52	2282
GEORGIAN BAY	ONTARIO	OWEN SOUND HARB NO T12	44-35.32	80-56.15	29952.14	49019.27	2271
GEORGIAN BAY	ONTARIO	SQUAW POINT SHOAL NO T9	44-37.08	80-54.98	29942.19	49007.61	2271
GEORGIAN BAY	ONTARIO	GRIFFITH ISLAND	44-51.05	80-53.37	29919.38	48910.53	2282
GEORGIAN BAY	ONTARIO	PYETTE POINT	44-44.22	80-53.30	29924.20	48958.53	2282
GEORGIAN BAY	ONTARIO	VAIL POINT SHOAL NO T7	44-44.75	80-47.30	29882.25	48958.82	2282
GEORGIAN BAY	ONTARIO	BYNG INLET LIGHT H	45-43.97	80-44.69	29842.08	48550.30	2293
GEORGIAN BAY	ONTARIO	BURTON BANK S LIGHT H12	45-44.57	80-40.88	29819.36	48550.32	2293
GEORGIAN BAY	ONTARIO	BURTON BANK LIGHT H13	45-44.65	80-40.73	29818.47	48549.93	2293
GEORGIAN BAY	ONTARIO	GEREAUX ISLAND	45-44.68	80-39.55	29811.47	48550.99	2293
GEORGIAN BAY	ONTARIO	BRITT TURNING LIGHT H19	45-45.00	80-39.46	29810.92	48548.90	2293
GEORGIAN BAY	ONTARIO	KEYSTONE ROCK LIGHT H21	45-45.23	80-39.00	29808.18	48547.82	2293
GEORGIAN BAY	ONTARIO	MEAFORD HARBOUR	44-36.58	80-35.40	29804.59	49022.63	2271
GEORGIAN BAY	ONTARIO	MEAFORD BRKWTR	44-36.77	80-35.38	29804.33	49021.33	2271
GEORGIAN BAY	ONTARIO	RABBIT ISLAND WEST END	45-46.04	80-34.52	29781.71	48547.09	2293
GEORGIAN BAY	ONTARIO	RABBIT ISLAND EAST END	45-46.09	80-34.30	29780.42	48546.99	2293
GEORGIAN BAY	ONTARIO	TIZARD ROCK LIGHT AL	45-34.08	80-33.30	29774.41	48629.77	2203
GEORGIAN BAY	ONTARIO	SEGUIN BANK NO P1	45-18.70	80-31.50	29764.27	48736.41	2284
GEORGIAN BAY	ONTARIO	CASTOR ISLAND	45-33.74	80-28.98	29748.19	48636.27	2203
GEORGIAN BAY	ONTARIO	PAVIS ISLAND	45-33.79	80-28.30	29744.07	48636.58	2203
GEORGIAN BAY	ONTARIO	PUSWAWA ISLAND	45-34.17	80-28.02	29742.39	48634.27	2203
GEORGIAN BAY	ONTARIO	POPLAR ISLAND	45-34.35	80-27.02	29736.36	48634.01	2203
GEORGIAN BAY	ONTARIO	JERGENS ISLAND	45-32.88	80-25.97	29729.88	48644.96	2203
GEORGIAN BAY	ONTARIO	BRIGNALL NARROWS	45-34.67	80-25.47	29727.02	48633.32	2203
GEORGIAN BAY	ONTARIO	ROGERS ISLAND	45-33.67	80-25.27	29725.71	48640.27	2203
GEORGIAN BAY	ONTARIO	PARRY SOUND APPROACH NO P2	45-20.73	80-25.18	29724.44	48728.02	2225
GEORGIAN BAY	ONTARIO	RED ROCK	45-21.60	80-24.48	29720.08	48722.72	2225
GEORGIAN BAY	ONTARIO	TURNING ISLAND	45-31.75	80-24.35	29719.94	48654.12	2203
GEORGIAN BAY	ONTARIO	OPECHEE ISLAND	45-35.52	80-24.13	29719.04	48628.86	2203
GEORGIAN BAY	ONTARIO	FARR ROCK LIGHT NO P7	45-21.42	80-22.77	29709.39	48725.40	2225
GEORGIAN BAY	ONTARIO	POINTE AU BARIL STATION	45-35.70	80-22.73	29710.64	48628.97	2203
GEORGIAN BAY	ONTARIO	THREE STAR SHOAL NO P10	45-21.57	80-21.88	29703.85	48725.14	2225
GEORGIAN BAY	ONTARIO	WESTERN ISLANDS	45-02.07	80-21.53	29701.63	48857.41	2289
GEORGIAN BAY	ONTARIO	ARIEL ROCK LIGHT NO P12	45-21.28	80-20.75	29696.78	48728.06	2225

PASSES

BODY OF WATER	PROV/STATE	NAME	LAT	LON	TD#1	TD#2	CHART
GEORGIAN BAY	ONTARIO	ARTHUR ORR ROCK NO P13	45-21.10	80-20.33	29694.15	48729.63	2225
GEORGIAN BAY	ONTARIO	NEW BANK LIGHT TN2	44-36.80	80-20.10	29697.02	49029.30	2201
GEORGIAN BAY	ONTARIO	GALNA POINT	45-25.27	80-19.87	29691.76	48701.89	2203
GEORGIAN BAY	ONTARIO	HALL ROCK SHOAL NO P16	45-20.47	80-19.56	29689.28	48734.52	2225
GEORGIAN BAY	ONTARIO	MIDDLE GROUND LIGHT P19	45-20.43	80-19.48	29688.77	48734.86	2225
GEORGIAN BAY	ONTARIO	TELEGRAPH ROCK NO P22	45-20.10	80-18.88	29684.99	48737.58	2225
GEORGIAN BAY	ONTARIO	HOOPER ISLAND SHOAL P24	45-19.78	80-18.30	29681.33	48740.22	2225
GEORGIAN BAY	ONTARIO	BORER BANK LIGHT P26	45-19.67	80-16.92	29672.69	48742.09	2225
GEORGIAN BAY	ONTARIO	NOTTAWASAGA ISLAND	44-32.31	80-15.54	29666.37	49061.77	2271
GEORGIAN BAY	ONTARIO	SPRUCE ISLAND SHOAL P27	45-19.83	80-15.50	29663.85	48742.18	2225
GEORGIAN BAY	ONTARIO	McCLELLAND ROCK P28	45-19.78	80-15.48	29663.72	48742.53	2225
GEORGIAN BAY	ONTARIO	CARLING ROCK NO P30	45-20.08	80-14.17	29655.60	48741.58	2225
GEORGIAN BAY	ONTARIO	LOCKERBIE ROCK NO TN11	44-32.23	80-13.81	29654.15	49063.11	2271
GEORGIAN BAY	ONTARIO	COLLINGWOOD LIGHT NO TN12	44-31.64	80-13.68	29653.40	49067.12	2271
GEORGIAN BAY	ONTARIO	COLLINGWOOD HARBOUR NO TN21	44-30.73	80-13.51	29652.46	49073.29	2271
GEORGIAN BAY	ONTARIO	SISTER ISLAND	45-20.00	80-11.87	29641.27	48743.98	2202
GEORGIAN BAY	ONTARIO	LOTTIE WOLF ROCK NO M2	44-55.75	80-10.41	29628.35	48907.37	2239
GEORGIAN BAY	ONTARIO	KILLBEAR POINT	45-19.97	80-10.23	29631.06	48745.49	2202
GEORGIAN BAY	ONTARIO	TURNING ISLAND S CHANNEL	45-12.70	80-09.95	29627.63	48794.29	2202
GEORGIAN BAY	ONTARIO	HOPE ISLAND	44-54.93	80-09.92	29625.05	48913.16	2239
GEORGIAN BAY	ONTARIO	ALVES POINT	45-23.48	80-09.75	29629.04	48722.45	2202
GEORGIAN BAY	ONTARIO	BEAUTY ISLAND	45-13.67	80-09.67	29626.06	48788.02	2202
GEORGIAN BAY	ONTARIO	CHRISTIAN ISLAND	44-47.18	80-09.38	29621.28	48965.30	2239
GEORGIAN BAY	ONTARIO	BARREL POINT	45-10.22	80-07.97	29614.52	48812.31	2202
GEORGIAN BAY	ONTARIO	SEVEN MILE NARROWS	45-15.62	80-06.73	29608.04	48777.23	2202
GEORGIAN BAY	ONTARIO	FIVE MILE NARROWS	45-16.23	80-05.90	29603.02	48773.80	2202
GEORGIAN BAY	ONTARIO	THREE MILE POINT	45-20.77	80-05.35	29601.06	48744.04	2202
GEORGIAN BAY	ONTARIO	McLAREN ISLAND EAST	45-16.54	80-05.18	29598.62	48772.29	2202
GEORGIAN BAY	ONTARIO	BUSTY SHOAL LIGHT P35	45-20.82	80-03.75	29591.20	48744.97	2226
GEORGIAN BAY	ONTARIO	THREE MILE GAP	45-17.67	80-03.50	29588.52	48766.06	2202
GEORGIAN BAY	ONTARIO	McKERREL ROCK NO P37	45-20.59	80-03.17	29587.54	48746.95	2226
GEORGIAN BAY	ONTARIO	SALT POINT	45-20.33	80-02.68	29584.41	48749.05	2226
GEORGIAN BAY	ONTARIO	ROSE POINT SWING BRIDGE	45-18.93	80-02.63	29583.57	48758.37	2226
GEORGIAN BAY	ONTARIO	JENKINS POINT	45-19.32	80-02.50	29582.92	48755.88	2226
GEORGIAN BAY	ONTARIO	PARRY SOUND HARBOUR P46	45-20.10	80-02.10	29580.74	48751.02	2226
GEORGIAN BAY	ONTARIO	BENNET BANK NO M3	44-52.41	80-01.47	29568.55	48934.98	2239
GEORGIAN BAY	ONTARIO	NOTTAWASAGA RIVER ENTR	44-32.20	80-00.50	29560.32	49069.17	2201
GEORGIAN BAY	ONTARIO	GIANTS TOMB	44-52.78	80-00.47	29561.98	48933.11	2239
GEORGIAN BAY	ONTARIO	RED ROCK GO HOME BAY	44-58.21	79-57.66	29544.84	48898.88	2202
GEORGIAN BAY	ONTARIO	SAWLOG POINT NO M6	44-52.43	79-57.10	29539.52	48937.34	2239
GEORGIAN BAY	ONTARIO	PENETANG NORTH WHARF	44-46.45	79-56.40	29533.41	48977.13	2218
GEORGIAN BAY	ONTARIO	NEWTON ISLANDS	44-56.45	79-56.32	29535.53	48911.28	2202
GEORGIAN BAY	ONTARIO	ASYLUM POINT	44-48.56	79-55.97	29531.01	48963.46	2218
GEORGIAN BAY	ONTARIO	WHISKY ISLAND	44-48.97	79-55.31	29526.69	48961.11	2218

PASSES

BODY OF WATER	PROV/STATE	NAME	LAT	LON	TD#1	TD#2	CHART
GEORGIAN BAY	ONTARIO	BREBEUF-McNICOLL NO M8	44-52.50	79-55.10	29526.28	48938.00	2202
GEORGIAN BAY	ONTARIO	KINDERSLEY ISLAND	44-54.93	79-54.43	29522.63	48922.39	2202
GEORGIAN BAY	ONTARIO	PINERY POINT NO M12	44-50.37	79-53.65	29516.01	48952.80	2202
GEORGIAN BAY	ONTARIO	MIDLAND BAY SHOAL NO M20	44-45.95	79-52.73	29508.56	48982.29	2221
GEORGIAN BAY	ONTARIO	SUCKER CREEK POINT	44-48.51	79-52.54	29508.04	48965.60	2202
GEORGIAN BAY	ONTARIO	CANDLEMAS SHOAL NO M13	44-49.25	79-52.48	29507.87	48960.77	2202
GEORGIAN BAY	ONTARIO	ARDILUAN ISLAND	44-54.12	79-51.13	29500.63	48929.57	2202
GEORGIAN BAY	ONTARIO	TONCH POINT LIGHT MN5	44-51.73	79-50.97	29498.68	48945.32	2202
GEORGIAN BAY	ONTARIO	ROBERTS ISLAND LIGHT MK	44-50.38	79-50.85	29497.39	48954.23	2202
GEORGIAN BAY	ONTARIO	TURNING ROCK HONEY HARBOUR	44-50.93	79-49.53	29488.84	48951.33	2202
GEORGIAN BAY	ONTARIO	FLAT POINT LIGHT MM4	44-46.57	79-48.24	29478.61	48980.48	2202
GEORGIAN BAY	ONTARIO	PORT McNICOLL LIGHT MM8	44-45.72	79-47.50	29473.33	48986.39	2223
GEORGIAN BAY	ONTARIO	STURGEON POINT MC4	44-46.30	79-45.30	29458.82	48983.68	2202
GEORGIAN BAY	ONTARIO	TURNING ROCK WAUBAUSHENE	44-46.33	79-44.40	29452.82	48983.93	2202
GEORGIAN BAY	ONTARIO	MARY ROCKS	44-46.20	79-43.40	29446.08	48985.25	2202
	NEWFOUNDLAND	CAPE ANGUILLE	47-54.00	59-24.70	Suggest	GPS	
	NEWFOUNDLAND	CODROY ISLAND	47-52.20	59-24.10	Suggest	GPS	
	NEWFOUNDLAND	CAPE RAY	47-37.30	59-18.30	Suggest	GPS	
	NEWFOUNDLAND	RED ISLAND	48-33.90	59-13.80	Suggest	GPS	
	NEWFOUNDLAND	VARDYS ISLAND (RHODE)	47-34.60	59-08.20	Suggest	GPS	
	NEWFOUNDLAND	PIKES ISLAND BRKWTR	47-34.50	59-07.90	Suggest	GPS	
	NEWFOUNDLAND	GRAVEYARD POINT BRKWTR	47-34.40	59-07.80	Suggest	GPS	
	NEWFOUNDLAND	PORT AUX BASQUES	47-34.00	59-07.00	Suggest	GPS	
	NEWFOUNDLAND	CHANNEL HEAD WHISTLE	47-33.90	59-06.60	Suggest	GPS	
	NEWFOUNDLAND	MARGAREE POINT	47-34.00	59-04.00	Suggest	GPS	
	NEWFOUNDLAND	POTATO ISLAND	47-34.90	58-59.10	Suggest	GPS	
	NEWFOUNDLAND	PITMANS ISLAND	47-34.80	58-58.80	Suggest	GPS	
	NEWFOUNDLAND	ILE AUX MORTS WHISTLE	47-34.00	58-58.50	Suggest	GPS	
	NEWFOUNDLAND	BAD NEIGHBOR ROCK BELL	47-34.50	58-54.20	Suggest	GPS	
	NEWFOUNDLAND	COLUMBIER ISLANDS	47-35.50	58-53.90	Suggest	GPS	
	NEWFOUNDLAND	GREAT BURNT ISLAND	47-35.70	58-53.60	Suggest	GPS	
	NEWFOUNDLAND	BEACH POINT SOUTH	48-45.90	58-47.00	Suggest	GPS	
	NEWFOUNDLAND	BEACH POINT BRKWTR	48-46.00	58-46.90	Suggest	GPS	
	NEWFOUNDLAND	LONG POINT	48-46.90	58-46.10	Suggest	GPS	
	NEWFOUNDLAND	PORT AU PORT BAY BELL	48-49.90	58-44.50	Suggest	GPS	
	NEWFOUNDLAND	CAINS ISLAND	47-36.00	58-42.20	Suggest	GPS	
	NEWFOUNDLAND	ROSE BLANCHE SHOALS	47-35.50	58-41.90	Suggest	GPS	
	NEWFOUNDLAND	ROSE BLANCHE POINT	47-35.90	58-41.50	Suggest	GPS	
	NEWFOUNDLAND	FOX BROOK	48-42.30	58-40.10	Suggest	GPS	
	NEWFOUNDLAND	BROAD COVE POINT	48-45.80	58-38.00	Suggest	GPS	
	NEWFOUNDLAND	SHAG ISLAND	48-52.30	58-35.00	Suggest	GPS	
	NEWFOUNDLAND	PORT HARMON	48-30.50	58-32.50	Suggest	GPS	
	NEWFOUNDLAND	PORT HARMON CHANNEL, W	48-30.60	58-32.40	Suggest	GPS	
	NEWFOUNDLAND	PORT HARMON CHANNEL, E	48-30.90	58-32.10	Suggest	GPS	

PASSES

BODY OF WATER	PROV/STATE	NAME	LAT	LON	TD#1	TD#2	CHART
	NEWFOUNDLAND	NORTH ICEBREAK	48-26.20	58-30.00	Suggest	GPS	
	NEWFOUNDLAND	ST GEORGES ICEBREAK	48-26.10	58-29.60	Suggest	GPS	
	NEWFOUNDLAND	SANDY POINT	48-27.40	58-29.40	Suggest	GPS	
	NEWFOUNDLAND	LITTLE PORT HEAD	49-07.00	58-26.00	Suggest	GPS	
	NEWFOUNDLAND	CHRISTMAS HEAD	47-40.50	58-23.50	Suggest	GPS	
	NEWFOUNDLAND	IRELAND ISLAND	47-37.90	58-22.50	Suggest	GPS	
	NEWFOUNDLAND	SOUTH HEAD ENTR	49-09.80	58-22.20	Suggest	GPS	
	NEWFOUNDLAND	WHITE POINT	49-08.50	58-21.20	Suggest	GPS	
	NEWFOUNDLAND	TORTOISE POINT	49-06.30	58-20.60	Suggest	GPS	
	NEWFOUNDLAND	OFFER ISLAND	47-38.40	58-13.70	Suggest	GPS	
	NEWFOUNDLAND	WOOD ISLAND	49-05.80	58-13.40	Suggest	GPS	
	NEWFOUNDLAND	FRENCHMANS HEAD	49-03.40	58-09.50	Suggest	GPS	
	NEWFOUNDLAND	EAGLE ISLAND	49-09.80	58-08.90	Suggest	GPS	
	NEWFOUNDLAND	MIDDLE ARM POINT	49-07.90	58-08.80	Suggest	GPS	
	NEWFOUNDLAND	TROUT RIVER ENTR	49-28.90	58-07.60	Suggest	GPS	
	NEWFOUNDLAND	MEADOWS POINT	48-59.50	58-03.80	Suggest	GPS	
	NEWFOUNDLAND	LOBSTER COVE HEAD	49-36.20	57-57.40	Suggest	GPS	
	NEWFOUNDLAND	WOODY POINT	49-30.30	57-54.90	Suggest	GPS	
	NEWFOUNDLAND	NORRIS POINT	49-30.90	57-52.80	Suggest	GPS	
	NEWFOUNDLAND	GADDS POINT	49-30.60	57-52.70	Suggest	GPS	
	NEWFOUNDLAND	COW HEAD	49-55.10	57-48.90	Suggest	GPS	
	NEWFOUNDLAND	WEST FLAT ISLAND	47-34.90	57-42.40	Suggest	GPS	
	NEWFOUNDLAND	PARSONS POND	50-10.80	57-42.40	Suggest	GPS	
	NEWFOUNDLAND	FURBER POINT	47-36.30	57-36.50	Suggest	GPS	
	NEWFOUNDLAND	BOAR ISLAND	47-36.20	57-35.20	Suggest	GPS	
	NEWFOUNDLAND	DANIELS COVE	50-14.50	57-34.80	Suggest	GPS	
	NEWFOUNDLAND	NORTHWEST HEADS	47-31.00	57-25.00	Suggest	GPS	
	NEWFOUNDLAND	POINT RICHE	50-41.90	57-24.70	Suggest	GPS	
	NEWFOUNDLAND	RAMEA	47-31.50	57-22.70	Suggest	GPS	
	NEWFOUNDLAND	PORT AU CHOIX	50-42.20	57-21.60	Suggest	GPS	
	NEWFOUNDLAND	BARBACE POINT FOG SIGNAL	50-43.80	57-20.80	Suggest	GPS	
	NEWFOUNDLAND	QUERRE ISLAND	50-43.20	57-20.00	Suggest	GPS	
	NEWFOUNDLAND	KEPPEL ISLAND	50-37.90	57-19.40	Suggest	GPS	
	NEWFOUNDLAND	HAWKE HARBOUR	50-35.70	57-15.80	Suggest	GPS	
	NEWFOUNDLAND	GREY RIVER POINT	47-34.00	57-07.00	Suggest	GPS	
	NEWFOUNDLAND	FEROLLE POINT	51-01.30	57-06.10	Suggest	GPS	
	NEWFOUNDLAND	WHITE ISLAND	50-55.80	57-01.80	Suggest	GPS	
	NEWFOUNDLAND	PENGUIN ISLANDS	47-23.00	56-59.00	Suggest	GPS	
	NEWFOUNDLAND	BRIG BAY	51-04.20	56-53.80	Suggest	GPS	
	NEWFOUNDLAND	CAPE LA HUNE	47-32.00	56-52.00	Suggest	GPS	
	NEWFOUNDLAND	SOPS ARM	49-45.00	56-48.00	Suggest	GPS	
	NEWFOUNDLAND	ANCHOR POINT	51-13.90	56-47.90	Suggest	GPS	
	NEWFOUNDLAND	ST-BARBE POINT	51-12.30	56-47.00	Suggest	GPS	
	NEWFOUNDLAND	ST-BARBE RANGE MK	51-11.90	56-45.80	Suggest	GPS	

PASSES

BODY OF WATER	PROV/STATE	NAME	LAT	LON	TD#1	TD#2	CHART
	NEWFOUNDLAND	FRANCOIS BAY	47-34.00	56-45.00	Suggest	GPS	
	NEWFOUNDLAND	FLOWERS COVE	51-17.70	56-44.80	Suggest	GPS	
	NEWFOUNDLAND	JACKSONS ARM	49-51.70	56-44.50	Suggest	GPS	
	NEWFOUNDLAND	NAMELESS POINT	51-18.80	56-44.50	Suggest	GPS	
	NEWFOUNDLAND	NEW HARBOUR ISLAND	47-35.70	56-39.50	Suggest	GPS	
	NEWFOUNDLAND	WESTPORT COVE	49-47.00	56-37.00	Suggest	GPS	
	NEWFOUNDLAND	GREAT HARBOUR DEEP	50-22.90	56-24.80	Suggest	GPS	
	NEWFOUNDLAND	POINT PLATE	46-49.40	56-24.20	Suggest	GPS	
	NEWFOUNDLAND	CAP BLANC	47-06.30	56-23.90	Suggest	GPS	
	NEWFOUNDLAND	SEAL COVE	49-55.80	56-22.90	Suggest	GPS	
	NEWFOUNDLAND	CAP COUPE "SPM" WHISTLE	46-45.00	56-21.00	Suggest	GPS	
	NEWFOUNDLAND	BASSE DE SAVOYARD WHISTLE	46-54.40	56-15.30	Suggest	GPS	
	NEWFOUNDLAND	FOURCHE HARBOUR	50-31.00	56-15.00	Suggest	GPS	
	NEWFOUNDLAND	MARNE SHOAL WHISTLE	46-43.90	56-13.40	Suggest	GPS	
	NEWFOUNDLAND	MAQUELON ROCKS BUOY	47-04.00	56-13.00	Suggest	GPS	
	NEWFOUNDLAND	TAYLOR ISLAND	47-38.00	56-13.00	Suggest	GPS	
	NEWFOUNDLAND	DUCKBILL POINT	50-36.00	56-12.00	Suggest	GPS	
	NEWFOUNDLAND	PASS ISLAND FOG SIGNAL	49-29.00	56-12.00	Suggest	GPS	
	NEWFOUNDLAND	PASS ISLAND	47-30.00	56-12.00	Suggest	GPS	
	NEWFOUNDLAND	LES ROCHERS WHISTLE	47-03.40	56-11.70	Suggest	GPS	
	NEWFOUNDLAND	BAIE VERTE	49-56.20	56-11.50	Suggest	GPS	
	NEWFOUNDLAND	BAD ROCK	50-47.00	56-10.00	Suggest	GPS	
	NEWFOUNDLAND	TETE DE GALENTRY	46-46.00	56-09.00	Suggest	GPS	
	NEWFOUNDLAND	DAWSON POINT	47-39.00	56-09.00	Suggest	GPS	
	NEWFOUNDLAND	ROCHER PETIT ST PIERRE	46-47.90	56-08.80	Suggest	GPS	
	NEWFOUNDLAND	RADDICKTON POINT	50-52.00	56-08.00	Suggest	GPS	
	NEWFOUNDLAND	PARTRIDGE POINT	50-09.00	56-08.00	Suggest	GPS	
	NEWFOUNDLAND	GROLE POINT	47-31.00	56-08.00	Suggest	GPS	
	NEWFOUNDLAND	ILE ST PIERRE	46-48.30	56-07.70	Suggest	GPS	
	NEWFOUNDLAND	WHITE POINT HARBOUR	50-43.30	56-07.00	Suggest	GPS	
	NEWFOUNDLAND	ENGLEE LIGHT	50-44.00	56-07.00	Suggest	GPS	
	NEWFOUNDLAND	GRANDE BASSE WHISTLE	46-47.20	56-06.20	Suggest	GPS	
	NEWFOUNDLAND	COACHMANS HARBOUR	50-03.30	56-05.70	Suggest	GPS	
	NEWFOUNDLAND	GREEN ISLAND	46-53.00	56-05.00	Suggest	GPS	
	NEWFOUNDLAND	FLEUR-DE-LYS HARBOUR	50-07.40	56-04.80	Suggest	GPS	
	NEWFOUNDLAND	MIDDLE ARM	49-42.30	56-04.50	Suggest	GPS	
	NEWFOUNDLAND	SPRINGDALE WHARF	49-29.90	56-03.80	Suggest	GPS	
	NEWFOUNDLAND	TINKER ROCK	47-37.00	56-03.00	Suggest	GPS	
	NEWFOUNDLAND	MAIN BROOK WHARF	51-10.00	56-00.00	Suggest	GPS	
	NEWFOUNDLAND	CAILLOUX ISLET	51-12.00	56-00.00	Suggest	GPS	
	NEWFOUNDLAND	COCK BANK WHISTLE	46-50.40	55-59.20	Suggest	GPS	
	NEWFOUNDLAND	FOX ISLAND	47-33.90	55-58.40	Suggest	GPS	
	NEWFOUNDLAND	SMITH HARBOUR	49-44.40	55-57.70	Suggest	GPS	
	NEWFOUNDLAND	LITTLE BAY ARM FERRY	49-35.40	55-56.20	Suggest	GPS	

PASSES

BODY OF WATER	PROV/STATE	NAME	LAT	LON	TD#1	TD#2	CHART
	NEWFOUNDLAND	BRENT ISLAND	51-15.00	55-56.00	Suggest	GPS	
	NEWFOUNDLAND	CAPE NORMAN	51-38.00	55-55.00	Suggest	GPS	
	NEWFOUNDLAND	SILVER POINT	50-53.00	55-54.00	Suggest	GPS	
	NEWFOUNDLAND	GAULTOIS HARBOUR	47-36.00	55-54.00	Suggest	GPS	
	NEWFOUNDLAND	CAPE FOX	50-52.00	55-54.00	Suggest	GPS	
	NEWFOUNDLAND	BEACHSIDE WHARF	49-38.60	55-53.40	Suggest	GPS	
	NEWFOUNDLAND	BRUNETTE ISLAND	47-15.00	55-52.00	Suggest	GPS	
	NEWFOUNDLAND	FORTUNE BAY HEAD	47-04.00	55-52.00	Suggest	GPS	
	NEWFOUNDLAND	CAPE MARK	47-45.00	55-52.00	Suggest	GPS	
	NEWFOUNDLAND	PACQUET HARBOUR	49-59.00	55-51.00	Suggest	GPS	
	NEWFOUNDLAND	SCHOONER ISLAND	51-37.00	55-51.00	Suggest	GPS	
	NEWFOUNDLAND	BAY D'ESPOIR	47-47.00	55-51.00	Suggest	GPS	
	NEWFOUNDLAND	WESTERN BREAKWATER	47-05.00	55-50.00	Suggest	GPS	
	NEWFOUNDLAND	NIPPERS ISLANDS	49-47.00	55-50.00	Suggest	GPS	
	NEWFOUNDLAND	FORTUNE HARBOURBUOY	47-05.00	55-50.00	Suggest	GPS	
	NEWFOUNDLAND	ROCKY POINT, BRETON	47-29.00	55-48.00	Suggest	GPS	
	NEWFOUNDLAND	SULEY ANN COVE FERRY	49-38.00	55-48.00	Suggest	GPS	
	NEWFOUNDLAND	SAGONA ISLAND, NW	47-22.00	55-48.00	Suggest	GPS	
	NEWFOUNDLAND	ALANS ISLAND, BLUFF HD	46-51.00	55-48.00	Suggest	GPS	
	NEWFOUNDLAND	ROBERTS ARM	49-29.30	55-47.90	Suggest	GPS	
	NEWFOUNDLAND	SAGONA ISLAND FOG SIGNAL	47-22.00	55-47.80	Suggest	GPS	
	NEWFOUNDLAND	MACKS ISLAND NORTH	49-39.00	55-47.00	Suggest	GPS	
	NEWFOUNDLAND	LITTLE BAY ISLANDS	49-39.00	55-47.00	Suggest	GPS	
	NEWFOUNDLAND	LITTLE BAY ISLAND	49-38.00	55-46.00	Suggest	GPS	
	NEWFOUNDLAND	GRAND BANK BRKWTR	47-06.00	55-45.00	Suggest	GPS	
	NEWFOUNDLAND	PILLYS ISLAND FERRY WHARF	49-34.00	55-44.00	Suggest	GPS	
	NEWFOUNDLAND	ST-BARBE ISLANDS	50-12.00	55-43.00	Suggest	GPS	
	NEWFOUNDLAND	LUSHES BIGHT	49-36.00	55-43.00	Suggest	GPS	
	NEWFOUNDLAND	SOUTHERN POINT	49-35.40	55-42.90	Suggest	GPS	
	NEWFOUNDLAND	GULL ROCK	49-41.00	55-41.00	Suggest	GPS	
	NEWFOUNDLAND	MOUSE ISLAND	51-19.00	55-39.00	Suggest	GPS	
	NEWFOUNDLAND	GOOSE COVE	51-19.00	55-39.00	Suggest	GPS	
	NEWFOUNDLAND	MID ISLAND	50-42.00	55-38.00	Suggest	GPS	
	NEWFOUNDLAND	BULL POINT/COOMBS COVE	47-27.00	55-38.00	Suggest	GPS	
	NEWFOUNDLAND	LA SCIE, SLEEPY PT	49-58.00	55-37.00	Suggest	GPS	
	NEWFOUNDLAND	TRITON ISLAND	49-33.00	55-36.00	Suggest	GPS	
	NEWFOUNDLAND	BOXEY POINT	47-24.00	55-35.00	Suggest	GPS	
	NEWFOUNDLAND	HARBOUR ROCK	51-22.00	55-34.00	Suggest	GPS	
	NEWFOUNDLAND	BLACK HEAD	46-54.00	55-34.00	Suggest	GPS	
	NEWFOUNDLAND	LONG ISLAND	49-36.00	55-34.00	Suggest	GPS	
	NEWFOUNDLAND	ANTHONY HARBOUR ENTR	51-22.00	55-34.00	Suggest	GPS	
	NEWFOUNDLAND	FISHING POINT	51-21.00	55-33.00	Suggest	GPS	
	NEWFOUNDLAND	DRUNKARDS POINT BELL	46-54.00	55-31.00	Suggest	GPS	
	NEWFOUNDLAND	ENGLISH HARBOUR WEST	47-27.00	55-30.00	Suggest	GPS	

P A S S E S

BODY OF WATER	PROV/STATE	NAME	LAT	LON	TD#1	TD#2	CHART
	NEWFOUNDLAND	GRIQUET HARBOUR	51-33.00	55-27.00	Suggest	GPS	
	NEWFOUNDLAND	QUIRPON HARBOUR, NE	51-36.00	55-27.00	Suggest	GPS	
	NEWFOUNDLAND	CAPE BAULD	51-38.00	55-26.00	Suggest	GPS	
	NEWFOUNDLAND	PARTRIDGE POINT	51-35.00	55-25.00	Suggest	GPS	
	NEWFOUNDLAND	ST JACQUES ISLAND	47-28.00	55-25.00	Suggest	GPS	
	NEWFOUNDLAND	BELLARAM HARBOUR	47-31.00	55-25.00	Suggest	GPS	
	NEWFOUNDLAND	LEADING TICKLES	49-30.00	55-24.00	Suggest	GPS	
	NEWFOUNDLAND	LEAMINGTON PT WHARF	49-21.00	55-23.00	Suggest	GPS	
	NEWFOUNDLAND	GARNISH ENTRANCE	47-14.00	55-22.00	Suggest	GPS	
	NEWFOUNDLAND	GULL ISLAND	49-59.90	55-21.50	Suggest	GPS	
	NEWFOUNDLAND	MIDDLE HEAD	46-54.00	55-21.00	Suggest	GPS	
	NEWFOUNDLAND	MILL POINT EAST	49-09.00	55-20.00	Suggest	GPS	
	NEWFOUNDLAND	COTTRELLS COVE POINT	49-29.00	55-18.00	Suggest	GPS	
	NEWFOUNDLAND	COTTRELLS COVE WHARF	49-30.00	55-17.00	Suggest	GPS	
	NEWFOUNDLAND	LOWER SANDY POINT	49-13.00	55-17.00	Suggest	GPS	
	NEWFOUNDLAND	BELLENS POINT	49-32.00	55-14.00	Suggest	GPS	
	NEWFOUNDLAND	CORBIN HARBOUR LG PT	46-57.00	55-14.00	Suggest	GPS	
	NEWFOUNDLAND	GRASSY ISLANDS	49-15.80	55-13.70	Suggest	GPS	
	NEWFOUNDLAND	CABBAGE HARBOUR	49-20.00	55-13.00	Suggest	GPS	
	NEWFOUNDLAND	MAL BAL ISLAND	47-37.00	55-12.00	Suggest	GPS	
	NEWFOUNDLAND	LITTLE BURIN ISLAND	46-58.90	55-11.50	Suggest	GPS	
	NEWFOUNDLAND	STAG ROCK	47-02.00	55-11.00	Suggest	GPS	
	NEWFOUNDLAND	SHALLOWAY ISLAND	47-00.00	55-10.00	Suggest	GPS	
	NEWFOUNDLAND	DODDING HEAD	47-00.00	55-09.00	Suggest	GPS	
	NEWFOUNDLAND	UPPER BLACK ISLAND	49-25.00	55-08.00	Suggest	GPS	
	NEWFOUNDLAND	LONG HARBOUR POINT	47-35.00	55-08.00	Suggest	GPS	
	NEWFOUNDLAND	IRON ISLAND	47-02.40	55-07.30	Suggest	GPS	
	NEWFOUNDLAND	STURGEON COVE HEAD	49-31.00	55-07.00	Suggest	GPS	
	NEWFOUNDLAND	DUCK ROCK	47-09.00	55-05.00	Suggest	GPS	
	NEWFOUNDLAND	GO BY POINT	47-08.00	55-05.00	Suggest	GPS	
	NEWFOUNDLAND	TIDES COVE POINT	47-07.00	55-04.00	Suggest	GPS	
	NEWFOUNDLAND	ST MICHAELS ISLAND	49-17.50	54-59.30	Suggest	GPS	
	NEWFOUNDLAND	RED HARBOUR HEAD	47-17.00	54-59.00	Suggest	GPS	
	NEWFOUNDLAND	STANLEY ROCKS BELL	47-15.00	54-59.00	Suggest	GPS	
	NEWFOUNDLAND	ST BERNARDS BRKWTR	47-32.00	54-58.00	Suggest	GPS	
	NEWFOUNDLAND	COLLINS ISLAND	47-16.00	54-57.00	Suggest	GPS	
	NEWFOUNDLAND	KNIGHTS ISLAND, NE	49-25.00	54-55.00	Suggest	GPS	
	NEWFOUNDLAND	STEERING ROCK	47-21.00	54-54.00	Suggest	GPS	
	NEWFOUNDLAND	RAGGED POINT	47-33.00	54-53.00	Suggest	GPS	
	NEWFOUNDLAND	MORETONS HARBOUR	49-35.00	54-52.00	Suggest	GPS	
	NEWFOUNDLAND	MORETONS HARBOUR	49-35.00	54-51.00	Suggest	GPS	
	NEWFOUNDLAND	ODERIN HARBOUR ENTR	47-18.00	54-49.00	Suggest	GPS	
	NEWFOUNDLAND	S TWILLINGATE	49-41.00	54-48.00	Suggest	GPS	
	NEWFOUNDLAND	SUMMERFORD WHARF	49-30.00	54-47.00	Suggest	GPS	

P A S S E S

BODY OF WATER	PROV/STATE	NAME	LAT	LON	TD#1	TD#2	CHART
	NEWFOUNDLAND	TICKLE POINT SHOAL	49-39.00	54-46.00	Suggest	GPS	
	NEWFOUNDLAND	TWILLINGATE WHARF	49-40.00	54-46.00	Suggest	GPS	
	NEWFOUNDLAND	TERRENCEVILLE WHARF	47-40.00	54-44.00	Suggest	GPS	
	NEWFOUNDLAND	DUCK ISLAND	49-36.00	54-43.00	Suggest	GPS	
	NEWFOUNDLAND	LONG ISLAND POINT	47-18.00	54-42.00	Suggest	GPS	
	NEWFOUNDLAND	PETIT FORTE HARBOUR	47-23.00	54-40.00	Suggest	GPS	
	NEWFOUNDLAND	SHIP ISLAND	49-31.10	54-35.90	Suggest	GPS	
	NEWFOUNDLAND	MARTICOT ISLAND	47-20.00	54-35.00	Suggest	GPS	
	NEWFOUNDLAND	BACALHAO ISLAND W	49-41.00	54-33.00	Suggest	GPS	
	NEWFOUNDLAND	DRAM ISLAND	49-35.00	54-32.00	Suggest	GPS	
	NEWFOUNDLAND	FAREWELL HARBOUR F WHARF	49-33.00	54-29.00	Suggest	GPS	
	NEWFOUNDLAND	VICTORIA COVE	49-21.00	54-28.00	Suggest	GPS	
	NEWFOUNDLAND	STEERING ISLAND	49-31.00	54-27.00	Suggest	GPS	
	NEWFOUNDLAND	SMOKER ISLAND	49-37.00	54-27.00	Suggest	GPS	
	NEWFOUNDLAND	TICKLE POINT, N	49-40.00	54-25.00	Suggest	GPS	
	NEWFOUNDLAND	CHARGE ISLAND, S	49-34.00	54-24.00	Suggest	GPS	
	NEWFOUNDLAND	RUTH ISLAND, E	49-41.00	54-22.00	Suggest	GPS	
	NEWFOUNDLAND	GRASSY ISLANDS	49-28.00	54-19.00	Suggest	GPS	
	NEWFOUNDLAND	MAN OF WAR COVE	49-34.00	54-18.00	Suggest	GPS	
	NEWFOUNDLAND	STAG HARBOUR	49-33.00	54-18.00	Suggest	GPS	
	NEWFOUNDLAND	SEAL COVE	49-43.00	54-17.00	Suggest	GPS	
	NEWFOUNDLAND	CARMENVILLE WHARF	49-24.00	54-17.00	Suggest	GPS	
	NEWFOUNDLAND	FOGO ISLAND HARBOUR	49-44.00	54-16.00	Suggest	GPS	
	NEWFOUNDLAND	BLUNDON'S ISLAND	49-33.00	54-14.00	Suggest	GPS	
	NEWFOUNDLAND	ROCKY BAY	49-26.90	54-13.80	Suggest	GPS	
	NEWFOUNDLAND	ST MARY'S CAY WHISTLE	46-42.00	54-13.00	Suggest	GPS	
	NEWFOUNDLAND	CAPE ST MARY'S	46-49.00	54-12.00	Suggest	GPS	
	NEWFOUNDLAND	TINKER ROCK	49-35.00	54-11.00	Suggest	GPS	
	NEWFOUNDLAND	ST BRIDES FOG SIGNAL	46-55.00	54-11.00	Suggest	GPS	
	NEWFOUNDLAND	STOREHOUSE ISLAND	49-49.00	54-11.00	Suggest	GPS	
	NEWFOUNDLAND	CANN ISLAND, SELDOM HARB	49-35.00	54-11.00	Suggest	GPS	
	NEWFOUNDLAND	PUBLIC WHARF	49-44.00	54-10.00	Suggest	GPS	
	NEWFOUNDLAND	JOE BATTS ARM ROCKS	49-44.00	54-10.00	Suggest	GPS	
	NEWFOUNDLAND	JOE BATTS POINT	49-05.00	54-09.00	Suggest	GPS	
	NEWFOUNDLAND	JOE BATTS ARM	49-44.00	54-09.00	Suggest	GPS	
	NEWFOUNDLAND	BURNT PT, SELDOM COVE	49-36.00	54-09.00	Suggest	GPS	
	NEWFOUNDLAND	RED ISLAND HARBOUR	47-24.00	54-09.00	Suggest	GPS	
	NEWFOUNDLAND	NORTH HARBOUR POINT	47-49.00	54-06.00	Suggest	GPS	
	NEWFOUNDLAND	LITTLE FOGO ISLAND	49-49.00	54-05.00	Suggest	GPS	
	NEWFOUNDLAND	IRONSKULL ROCK	47-27.00	54-05.00	Suggest	GPS	
	NEWFOUNDLAND	LONG ISLAND POINT	47-41.70	54-04.90	Suggest	GPS	
	NEWFOUNDLAND	TILTON HARBOUR, W	49-42.00	54-04.00	Suggest	GPS	
	NEWFOUNDLAND	RED ISLAND SHOAL WHISTLE	47-24.00	54-03.00	Suggest	GPS	
	NEWFOUNDLAND	POINT LANCE WHISTLE	46-47.00	54-03.00	Suggest	GPS	

PASSES

BODY OF WATER	PROV/STATE	NAME	LAT	LON	TD#1	TD#2	CHART
	NEWFOUNDLAND	BUFFETT ISLAND	47-31.60	54-03.00	Suggest	GPS	
	NEWFOUNDLAND	ARGENTINA WHISTLE "A"	47-20.00	54-02.00	Suggest	GPS	
	NEWFOUNDLAND	BORDEAUX ISLAND	47-44.00	54-02.00	Suggest	GPS	
	NEWFOUNDLAND	SOUND ISLAND POINT	47-47.40	54-01.10	Suggest	GPS	
	NEWFOUNDLAND	COME BY CHANCE	47-49.00	54-01.00	Suggest	GPS	
	NEWFOUNDLAND	VERDE POINT	47-14.00	54-01.00	Suggest	GPS	
	NEWFOUNDLAND	ARGENTINA BELL "A2"	47-20.00	53-59.00	Suggest	GPS	
	NEWFOUNDLAND	HARE BAY	48-51.00	53-59.00	Suggest	GPS	
	NEWFOUNDLAND	ARGENTINA BUOY "A6"	47-19.00	53-58.00	Suggest	GPS	
	NEWFOUNDLAND	MUSGRAVE HARBOUR	49-28.00	53-58.00	Suggest	GPS	
	NEWFOUNDLAND	ARGENTINA BELL "A4"	47-20.00	53-58.00	Suggest	GPS	
	NEWFOUNDLAND	BRACH WEST BRKWTR	46-53.00	53-57.00	Suggest	GPS	
	NEWFOUNDLAND	MUDDY POINT	49-27.00	53-57.00	Suggest	GPS	
	NEWFOUNDLAND	MUDDY SHAG ISLAND	49-29.00	53-56.00	Suggest	GPS	
	NEWFOUNDLAND	SHAG ROCKS	47-25.00	53-55.00	Suggest	GPS	
	NEWFOUNDLAND	FOX HARBOUR	47-19.30	53-54.60	Suggest	GPS	
	NEWFOUNDLAND	FISHERMANS WHARF	49-01.10	53-52.70	Suggest	GPS	
	NEWFOUNDLAND	PICKFORD ISLAND	49-32.00	53-51.00	Suggest	GPS	
	NEWFOUNDLAND	N PENGUIN ISLAND, E	49-27.00	53-48.00	Suggest	GPS	
	NEWFOUNDLAND	HAPPY ADVENTURE BAY	48-38.00	53-46.00	Suggest	GPS	
	NEWFOUNDLAND	OFFER WADHAM ISLAND	49-36.00	53-46.00	Suggest	GPS	
	NEWFOUNDLAND	GRINDSTONE HEAD	48-59.00	53-43.00	Suggest	GPS	
	NEWFOUNDLAND	LITTLE HEARTS EASE	48-01.40	53-41.30	Suggest	GPS	
	NEWFOUNDLAND	PENNGS COVE	48-50.10	53-41.20	Suggest	GPS	
	NEWFOUNDLAND	GREAT COLINET ISLAND	47-01.00	53-41.00	Suggest	GPS	
	NEWFOUNDLAND	HARE CUT POINT	48-53.00	53-39.00	Suggest	GPS	
	NEWFOUNDLAND	SALVAGE HARBOUR	48-41.00	53-38.00	Suggest	GPS	
	NEWFOUNDLAND	PUFFIN FLAT ISLAND	48-47.00	53-37.00	Suggest	GPS	
	NEWFOUNDLAND	GOOSEBERRY HARBOUR	48-53.00	53-37.00	Suggest	GPS	
	NEWFOUNDLAND	LA HAYE POINT	46-54.30	53-36.90	Suggest	GPS	
	NEWFOUNDLAND	SHOE COVE POINT	49-02.00	53-36.00	Suggest	GPS	
	NEWFOUNDLAND	BENBURRY ROCK BUOY "JV4"	49-07.00	53-36.00	Suggest	GPS	
	NEWFOUNDLAND	CAPE PINE	46-37.00	53-36.00	Suggest	GPS	
	NEWFOUNDLAND	LUMSDEN	49-19.00	53-36.00	Suggest	GPS	
	NEWFOUNDLAND	CANDLE COVE ROCKS	49-06.00	53-36.00	Suggest	GPS	
	NEWFOUNDLAND	ST SHOTTS FOG SIGNAL	46-37.00	53-36.00	Suggest	GPS	
	NEWFOUNDLAND	LITTLE DENIER ISLAND	48-41.00	53-35.00	Suggest	GPS	
	NEWFOUNDLAND	SEINE ROCK	49-04.00	53-34.30	Suggest	GPS	
	NEWFOUNDLAND	WESLEYVILLE HARBOUR	49-08.00	53-34.00	Suggest	GPS	
	NEWFOUNDLAND	BENNETS HIGH ISLAND	49-08.00	53-34.00	Suggest	GPS	
	NEWFOUNDLAND	SCAMMELS LOOKOUT	49-04.00	53-34.00	Suggest	GPS	
	NEWFOUNDLAND	POUND ROCKS	49-04.00	53-34.00	Suggest	GPS	
	NEWFOUNDLAND	SOUTH POUND ISLAND	49-06.00	53-34.00	Suggest	GPS	
	NEWFOUNDLAND	HOPEALL HEAD	47-38.00	53-34.00	Suggest	GPS	

PASSES

BODY OF WATER	PROV/STATE	NAME	LAT	LON	TD#1	TD#2	CHART
	NEWFOUNDLAND	GREENSPOND HARBOUR	49-04.00	53-34.00	Suggest	GPS	
	NEWFOUNDLAND	PUFFIN ISLAND	49-04.00	53-33.00	Suggest	GPS	
	NEWFOUNDLAND	MOTION ISLAND	48-06.00	53-33.00	Suggest	GPS	
	NEWFOUNDLAND	POUND COVE	49-10.00	53-32.00	Suggest	GPS	
	NEWFOUNDLAND	BLACK ISLAND	49-08.00	53-32.00	Suggest	GPS	
	NEWFOUNDLAND	WHITEWAY	47-42.00	53-29.00	Suggest	GPS	
	NEWFOUNDLAND	KENNYS ROCKS	49-13.00	53-28.00	Suggest	GPS	
	NEWFOUNDLAND	WESTERN HEAD BELL	48-38.00	53-27.00	Suggest	GPS	
	NEWFOUNDLAND	RAGGED ISLANDS	48-14.00	53-27.00	Suggest	GPS	
	NEWFOUNDLAND	GULL ISLAND, CAPE FREELS	49-15.00	53-26.00	Suggest	GPS	
	NEWFOUNDLAND	STEVENSON'S ISLETS	49-10.00	53-25.00	Suggest	GPS	
	NEWFOUNDLAND	POWELLS HEAD	46-41.40	53-24.20	Suggest	GPS	
	NEWFOUNDLAND	HEARTS CONTENT HARBOUR	47-53.00	53-23.00	Suggest	GPS	
	NEWFOUNDLAND	CABOT ISLAND	49-10.00	53-22.00	Suggest	GPS	
	NEWFOUNDLAND	CHARGE ROCK WHISTLE "JX"	49-15.00	53-22.00	Suggest	GPS	
	NEWFOUNDLAND	JEANS HEAD, N	47-55.60	53-21.90	Suggest	GPS	
	NEWFOUNDLAND	BLOODY POINT	47-54.90	53-21.60	Suggest	GPS	
	NEWFOUNDLAND	FORT POINT, TRINITY HARB	48-22.00	53-21.00	Suggest	GPS	
	NEWFOUNDLAND	KINGS COVE	48-35.00	53-19.00	Suggest	GPS	
	NEWFOUNDLAND	BAIT ROCKS, COLEYS PT	47-35.00	53-15.00	Suggest	GPS	
	NEWFOUNDLAND	HANTS HARBOUR	48-01.00	53-15.00	Suggest	GPS	
	NEWFOUNDLAND	SHIP HEAD	47-41.00	53-14.00	Suggest	GPS	
	NEWFOUNDLAND	POINT OF BEACH	47-41.00	53-13.00	Suggest	GPS	
	NEWFOUNDLAND	CONCEPTION HARBOUR	47-26.40	53-12.60	Suggest	GPS	
	NEWFOUNDLAND	PORT DE GRAVE, N BRKWTR	47-35.30	53-12.60	Suggest	GPS	
	NEWFOUNDLAND	PORT DE GRAVE, S BRKWTR	47-35.20	53-12.60	Suggest	GPS	
	NEWFOUNDLAND	HORSE CHOPS	48-21.00	53-12.00	Suggest	GPS	
	NEWFOUNDLAND	CONCEPTION BAY BUOY	47-42.00	53-12.00	Suggest	GPS	
	NEWFOUNDLAND	BALLYHACK	47-27.00	53-12.00	Suggest	GPS	
	NEWFOUNDLAND	NEWMANS COVE	48-35.10	53-11.70	Suggest	GPS	
	NEWFOUNDLAND	NORTH HEAD	47-33.00	53-11.00	Suggest	GPS	
	NEWFOUNDLAND	GREEN PT/BAY ROBERTS	47-36.00	53-10.00	Suggest	GPS	
	NEWFOUNDLAND	CARBONEAR BAY WHISTLE	47-45.00	53-10.00	Suggest	GPS	
	NEWFOUNDLAND	CARBONEAR ISLAND	47-44.00	53-10.00	Suggest	GPS	
	NEWFOUNDLAND	HARBOUR GRACE ISLANDS	47-43.00	53-09.00	Suggest	GPS	
	NEWFOUNDLAND	SALMON COVE POINT	47-28.00	53-09.00	Suggest	GPS	
	NEWFOUNDLAND	BONAVISTA WHISTLE BUOY	48-39.00	53-09.00	Suggest	GPS	
	NEWFOUNDLAND	SQUARRY ISLAND	48-39.00	53-08.00	Suggest	GPS	
	NEWFOUNDLAND	BLOW ME DOWN BLUFF	47-25.70	53-07.70	Suggest	GPS	
	NEWFOUNDLAND	BONAVISTA BRKWTR	48-38.90	53-07.10	Suggest	GPS	
	NEWFOUNDLAND	HOLYROOD GEN PLANT	47-26.60	53-06.40	Suggest	GPS	
	NEWFOUNDLAND	CATALINA HARBOUR	48-31.00	53-05.00	Suggest	GPS	
	NEWFOUNDLAND	CAPE BONAVISTA	48-42.00	53-05.00	Suggest	GPS	
	NEWFOUNDLAND	CAPE RACE	46-39.50	53-04.50	Suggest	GPS	

PASSES

BODY OF WATER	PROV/STATE	NAME	LAT	LON	TD#1	TD#2	CHART
	NEWFOUNDLAND	MANUEL ISLAND	48-31.00	53-04.00	Suggest	GPS	
	NEWFOUNDLAND	GREEN ISLAND	48-30.00	53-03.00	Suggest	GPS	
	NEWFOUNDLAND	WESTERN BAY HEAD	47-53.00	53-03.00	Suggest	GPS	
	NEWFOUNDLAND	BURNT POINT	48-31.00	53-03.00	Suggest	GPS	
	NEWFOUNDLAND	BRANDIES SHOAL	48-30.00	53-02.00	Suggest	GPS	
	NEWFOUNDLAND	OLD PELICAN ISLAND	48-05.00	53-02.00	Suggest	GPS	
	NEWFOUNDLAND	OUTER BREAKWATER	48-05.20	53-00.70	Suggest	GPS	
	NEWFOUNDLAND	INNER BREAKWATER	48-05.20	53-00.50	Suggest	GPS	
	NEWFOUNDLAND	LONG POND	47-31.10	52-58.70	Suggest	GPS	
	NEWFOUNDLAND	RENEWS HEAD BUOY	46-54.00	52-55.00	Suggest	GPS	
	NEWFOUNDLAND	BELL ISLAND	47-39.00	52-55.00	Suggest	GPS	
	NEWFOUNDLAND	NORTHERN HEAD	46-58.00	52-54.00	Suggest	GPS	
	NEWFOUNDLAND	BEAR COVE POINT	46-56.40	52-53.60	Suggest	GPS	
	NEWFOUNDLAND	FERRYLAND HEAD	47-01.00	52-52.00	Suggest	GPS	
	NEWFOUNDLAND	PORTUGAL COVE	47-37.60	52-51.60	Suggest	GPS	
	NEWFOUNDLAND	SW PT, BACCALIEU IS	48-06.00	52-49.00	Suggest	GPS	
	NEWFOUNDLAND	BACCALIEU ISLAND	48-09.00	52-48.00	Suggest	GPS	
	NEWFOUNDLAND	CAPE ST FRANCIS	47-49.00	52-47.00	Suggest	GPS	
	NEWFOUNDLAND	BAY BULLS	47-19.00	52-45.00	Suggest	GPS	
	NEWFOUNDLAND	FORT AMHERST	47-34.00	52-41.00	Suggest	GPS	
	NEWFOUNDLAND	NORTH HEAD	47-34.00	52-41.00	Suggest	GPS	
	NEWFOUNDLAND	CHAIN ROCKS	47-34.00	52-41.00	Suggest	GPS	
	NEWFOUNDLAND	CAPE SPEAR	47-31.00	52-37.00	Suggest	GPS	
	NEWFOUNDLAND	VIRGIN ROCKS WHISTLE	46-29.00	50-46.00	Suggest	GPS	
	NEWFOUNDLAND	ST PIERRE HARB ENTR	46-46.70	46-10.10	Suggest	GPS	
	NEWFOUNDLAND	TREPASSEY HARBOUR	46-43.00	43-23.00	Suggest	GPS	
LAKE ERIE		WALBRIDGE PARK RANGE	41-36.90	83-34.80	43569.66	56536.05	14846
LAKE ERIE		MAUMEE RIVER BRKWTR "A"	41-37.60	83-32.70	43578.60	56557.18	14847
LAKE ERIE		OTTAWA RIVER SKI RAMP	41-42.70	83-29.60	43619.30	56606.90	14846
LAKE ERIE		MANHATTAN RANGE	41-41.60	83-28.20	43614.78	56613.79	14847
LAKE ERIE		BAY VIEW PARK BUOY 50	41-41.60	83-28.00	43615.19	56615.50	14847
LAKE ERIE		LUNA PIER MARINA NO 1	41-48.70	83-26.40	43666.03	56661.40	14846
LAKE ERIE		LUNA PIER MARINA NO 2	41-48.70	83-26.40	43666.03	56661.40	14846
LAKE ERIE		MAUMEE BAY NO 40	41-42.70	83-26.00	43626.75	56637.54	14847
LAKE ERIE		TOLEDO BEACH MARINA RANGE	41-49.70	83-24.80	43676.07	56679.50	14846
LAKE ERIE		OTTER CREEK RANGE	41-51.00	83-24.00	43686.38	56692.17	14846
LAKE ERIE		BOLLES HARB ENTR NO 15	41-52.30	83-22.80	43697.55	56708.20	14846
LAKE ERIE		BOLLES HARB ENTR NO 10A	41-52.10	83-22.60	43696.67	56708.99	14846
LAKE ERIE		MAUMEE BAY NO 30	41-44.40	83-22.40	43645.73	56675.89	14847
LAKE ERIE		STERLING STATE PARK "A"	41-54.20	83-20.00	43716.16	56740.44	14846
LAKE ERIE		SANDY CREEK RANGE	41-55.50	83-19.80	43725.15	56747.98	14846
LAKE ERIE		TOLEDO HARBOR LIGHT	41-45.70	83-19.70	43660.21	56704.75	14847
LAKE ERIE		SANDY CREEK ENTR NO 1	41-55.40	83-19.50	43725.15	56750.06	14846
LAKE ERIE		COOLEY CANAL W BRKWTR	41-40.60	83-17.00	43631.34	56704.98	14846

PASSES

BODY OF WATER	PROV/STATE	NAME	LAT	LON	TD#1	TD#2	CHART
LAKE ERIE		COOLEY CANAL E BRKWTR	41-40.60	83-17.00	43631.34	56704.98	14846
LAKE ERIE		TOLEDO WW INTAKE CRIB	41-42.00	83-16.00	43643.01	56719.79	14846
LAKE ERIE		MONROE HARBOR APPR NO 1	41-51.90	83-15.00	43711.89	56772.48	14846
LAKE ERIE		SWAN CREEK RANGE	41-58.60	83-14.70	43756.77	56804.89	14846
LAKE ERIE		ENRICO PERMI PWR INTAKES	41-58.60	83-14.70	43756.77	56804.89	14846
LAKE ERIE		TOLEDO HARBOR ENTR NO 2	41-49.40	83-11.90	43701.97	56787.73	14847
LAKE ERIE		METRO PARK MARINA RANGE	42-03.20	83-11.60	43793.73	56851.42	14848
LAKE ERIE		GIBRALTER N CHANNEL RANGE	42-05.90	83-11.20	43812.07	56866.70	14848
LAKE ERIE		MILLEVILLE BEACH LIGHT	42-02.60	83-11.20	43790.75	56852.13	14848
LAKE ERIE		POINT MOUILLEE ACCESS NO 1	42-00.20	83-11.20	43775.12	56841.53	14848
LAKE ERIE		MOBIL OIL BUOY NO 1	42-08.20	83-10.40	43828.66	56883.53	14848
LAKE ERIE		FORD YACHT CLUB NO 1	42-05.30	83-10.20	43810.51	56872.45	14848
LAKE ERIE		TOLEDO TRAFFIC BUOY	41-50.10	83-10.10	43710.64	56806.18	14847
LAKE ERIE		HURON VALLEY OUTFALL "W"	42-03.10	83-09.90	43796.97	56865.29	14848
LAKE ERIE		HURON VALLEY OUTFALL "E"	42-03.10	83-09.80	43797.20	56866.13	14848
LAKE ERIE		HURON VALLEY OUTFALL "C"	42-03.10	83-09.80	43797.20	56866.13	14848
LAKE ERIE		HICKORY ISLAND BUOY 1	42-04.40	83-09.70	43805.85	56872.69	14848
LAKE ERIE		GROSSE ILE YACHT CLUB	42-05.30	83-09.00	43813.27	56882.54	14848
LAKE ERIE		DETROIT LIME CO LIGHT	42-17.70	83-09.00	43891.87	56936.73	14848
LAKE ERIE		DETROIT RIVER LIGHT	42-00.10	83-08.50	43780.61	56863.89	14830
LAKE ERIE		GROSSE ILE S CHAN RANGE	42-11.10	83-08.50	43851.57	56912.14	14848
LAKE ERIE		WYANDOTTE CHANNEL NO 2	42-11.10	83-08.40	43851.80	56912.97	14848
LAKE ERIE		HACKETT'S REACH NO D31	42-01.77	83-08.33	16449.87	56872.67	2123
LAKE ERIE		LIVINGSTON CHANNEL "DL1"	42-02.50	83-08.20	43796.97	56876.97	14848
LAKE ERIE		MAMAJUDA SHOAL BUOY	42-10.90	83-08.20	43851.00	56913.77	14848
LAKE ERIE		HACKETT'S REACH NO D24	42-00.77	83-08.20	16451.79	56869.37	2123
LAKE ERIE		FIGHTING ISLAND S LIGHT	42-10.40	83-08.10	43848.05	56912.43	14848
LAKE ERIE		MAMAJUDA LIGHT	42-11.50	83-08.10	43855.05	56917.23	14848
LAKE ERIE		BAR POINT PIER "33D"	42-02.40	83-08.10	43796.55	56877.38	14848
LAKE ERIE		DETROIT RIVER PIER NO 30	42-01.50	83-08.10	43790.68	56873.43	14848
LAKE ERIE		DETROIT RIVER PIER NO D30	42-01.60	83-08.10	16450.30	56873.87	2123
LAKE ERIE		GRASSY ISLAND LIGHT	42-13.50	83-08.00	43867.93	56926.78	14848
LAKE ERIE		WYANDOTTE JUNCTION BUOY	42-14.40	83-08.00	43873.60	56930.70	14848
LAKE ERIE		HACKETT'S REACH NO D32	42-02.17	83-07.95	16449.31	56877.63	2123
LAKE ERIE		DETROIT RIVER NO 37D	42-03.10	83-07.80	43801.79	56882.98	14848
LAKE ERIE		TURTLE CREEK RANGE	41-36.90	83-07.70	43625.52	56768.52	14846
LAKE ERIE		ERIE PAVING BUOY "A"	41-41.50	83-07.60	43657.60	56789.62	14830
LAKE ERIE		LIVINGSTON CHANNEL NO 77D	42-08.50	83-07.50	43837.33	56909.15	14848
LAKE ERIE		AMHERSTBURG CHAN NO 46D	42-03.80	83-07.50	43807.03	56888.58	14848
LAKE ERIE		AMHERSTBURG CHAN NO 45D	42-03.80	83-07.50	43807.03	56888.58	14848
LAKE ERIE		BAR POINT RANGE "49D"	42-04.20	83-07.40	43809.86	56891.18	14848
LAKE ERIE		LIVINGSTON CHANNEL ENTR	42-08.20	83-07.30	43835.88	56909.52	14848
LAKE ERIE		DETROIT RIVER NO 14	41-57.80	83-07.30	43768.21	56863.93	14848
LAKE ERIE		AMHERSTBURG CHAN NO 51D	42-04.70	83-07.20	43813.56	56895.05	14848

PASSES

BODY OF WATER	PROV/STATE	NAME	LAT	LON	TD#1	TD#2	CHART
LAKE ERIE		BALLARDS REEF CHAN NO 71D	42-07.40	83-07.10	43831.21	56907.71	14848
LAKE ERIE		AMHERSTBURG REACH NO 65D	42-06.80	83-07.10	43827.35	56905.08	14848
LAKE ERIE		AMHERSTBURG CHAN NO 53D	42-05.20	83-07.10	43817.03	56898.09	14848
LAKE ERIE		LIMEKILN CROSSING NO 69D	42-07.30	83-07.00	43830.80	56908.11	14848
LAKE ERIE		AMHERSTBURG CHAN NO 61D	42-06.00	83-07.00	43822.43	56902.42	14848
LAKE ERIE		FIGHTING I NO 104D	42-15.00	83-07.00	43879.74	56941.64	14848
LAKE ERIE		GR LAKES STL SHOAL NO 1	42-15.70	83-06.90	43884.37	56945.51	14848
LAKE ERIE		LIMEKILN CROSSING RANGE	42-07.70	83-06.90	43833.60	56910.69	14848
LAKE ERIE		WEST SISTER LIGHT	41-44.65	83-06.82	43680.00	56810.40	
LAKE ERIE		HACKETT'S REACH RANGE	42-05.80	83-06.80	43821.60	56903.23	14848
LAKE ERIE		LONG BEACH RANGE	41-36.70	83-06.80	43626.05	56775.41	14846
LAKE ERIE		FIGHTING I ANCH NO 2	42-15.10	83-06.80	43880.84	56943.75	14848
LAKE ERIE		FORT MALDEN RANGE	42-06.90	83-06.70	43828.93	56908.88	14848
LAKE ERIE		WEST SISTER I LIGHT	41-44.20	83-06.60	43678.32	56810.08	14830
LAKE ERIE		DETROIT RIVER NO 1	41-54.80	83-06.40	43750.36	56858.38	14830
LAKE ERIE		DETROIT EDISON CELL NO 2	42-16.20	83-06.40	43888.69	56951.84	14848
LAKE ERIE		DETROIT EDISON CELL NO 1	42-16.30	83-06.40	43889.32	56952.27	14848
LAKE ERIE		FIGHTING I ANCH LIMIT	42-15.70	83-06.30	43885.80	56950.51	14848
LAKE ERIE		GREEN COVE MARINA NO 1	41-36.80	83-06.20	43628.03	56781.02	14846
LAKE ERIE		DETROIT RIVER NO D108	42-18.80	83-04.00	43910.67	56983.02	14848
LAKE ERIE		INTERNATIONAL BDRY "H"	41-52.00	83-04.00	43737.04	56866.55	14830
LAKE ERIE		DAVID BEASE PWR PLANT	41-36.40	83-03.80	43630.38	56799.98	14846
LAKE ERIE		RIVERFRONT S ENTR NO 2	42-19.40	83-03.30	43916.09	56991.42	14848
LAKE ERIE		RIVERFRONT S ENTR NO 1	42-19.30	83-03.30	43915.47	56990.99	14848
LAKE ERIE		RIVERFRONT N ENTR NO 1	42-19.40	83-03.20	43916.33	56992.25	14848
LAKE ERIE		RIVERFRONT N ENTR NO 2	42-19.40	83-03.10	43916.57	56993.09	14848
LAKE ERIE		CRIB REEF BUOY NO 7	41-38.80	82-60.00	43655.39	56843.25	14830
LAKE ERIE		MIDDLE SISTER I LIGHT	41-51.00	82-60.00	43739.34	56896.36	14830
LAKE ERIE		MIDDLE SISTER ISLAND	41-51.00	82-59.90	16473.29	56897.21	2123
LAKE ERIE		NUGENTS CANAL PT W ENTR	41-30.60	82-59.80	43597.94	56809.38	14846
LAKE ERIE		DETROIT BOAT CLUB LIGHT	42-20.50	82-59.10	43933.13	57031.06	14848
LAKE ERIE		MEMORIAL PARK MARINA	42-21.00	82-59.00	43936.48	57034.01	14848
LAKE ERIE		INTERNATIONAL BDRY "G"	41-49.30	82-58.90	43730.29	56898.38	14830
LAKE ERIE		LAKE FRONT MARINA RANGE	41-31.50	82-58.40	43607.33	56825.42	14846
LAKE ERIE		LAKE FRONT MARINA W LIGHT	41-31.50	82-58.30	43607.55	56826.30	14846
LAKE ERIE		WATERWORKS INTAKE CRIB	42-21.10	82-58.00	43939.55	57042.75	14848
LAKE ERIE		BELLE ISLE LIGHT	42-20.60	82-57.60	43937.42	57043.97	14848
LAKE ERIE		WM LIVINGSTONE MEM LIGHT	42-20.80	82-57.30	43939.40	57047.32	14848
LAKE ERIE		WATERWORKS INTAKE LAGOON	42-21.00	82-57.30	43940.64	57048.16	14848
LAKE ERIE		FLEMING CHANNEL NO D110	42-20.50	82-57.10	43938.03	57047.71	14848
LAKE ERIE		PORTAGE RIVER	41-31.68	82-56.52	43611.80	56842.70	
LAKE ERIE		PECHE ISLAND LIGHT	42-20.90	82-56.50	43941.99	57054.40	14848
LAKE ERIE		PORT CLINTON INTAKE CRIB	41-31.20	82-56.40	43609.47	56841.49	14846
LAKE ERIE		PORT CLINTON LIGHT 2	41-31.10	82-56.20	43609.19	56842.79	14846

PASSES

BODY OF WATER	PROV/STATE	NAME	LAT	LON	TD#1	TD#2	CHART
LAKE ERIE		COLCHESTER EAST	41-58.93	82-55.85	16461.33	56966.11	2123
LAKE ERIE		WINDMILL POINT LIGHT	42-21.50	82-55.80	43947.44	57062.77	14848
LAKE ERIE		PECHE ISLAND BUOY	42-20.50	82-55.30	43942.45	57062.72	14848
LAKE ERIE		INTERNATIONAL BDRY "F"	41-47.00	82-54.20	43725.21	56928.76	14830
LAKE ERIE		COLCHESTER REEF LIGHT	41-56.00	82-54.00	43786.89	56969.26	14830
LAKE ERIE		COLCHESTER REEF	41-55.95	82-53.52	16467.86	56973.15	2123
LAKE ERIE		WILLOW POINT BUOY NO 5	41-26.50	82-53.50	43581.83	56846.49	14842
LAKE ERIE		WILLOW POINT BUOY NO 3	41-26.70	82-53.40	43583.49	56848.21	14842
LAKE ERIE		WILLOW POINT BUOY NO 1	41-26.70	82-53.20	43583.92	56849.96	14842
LAKE ERIE		EAST SISTER ISLAND	41-49.45	82-52.23	43745.60	56956.40	
LAKE ERIE		NORTH HARBOR SHOAL	41-50.44	82-52.21	43752.40	56960.80	
LAKE ERIE		NORTH HARBOR ISLAND	41-50.18	82-52.14	43750.80	56960.30	
LAKE ERIE		CATAWBA I BUOY NO 1	41-34.60	82-52.10	43643.06	56893.46	14844
LAKE ERIE		GREEN ISLAND LIGHT	41-38.70	82-52.10	43672.11	56911.10	14844
LAKE ERIE		COLONY CLUB MARINA LIGHT	41-33.20	82-51.40	43634.60	56893.52	14844
LAKE ERIE		CATAWBA CLIFFS HARBOR	41-34.30	82-51.30	43642.68	56899.11	14844
LAKE ERIE		N HARBOUR IS REEF NO E13	41-51.00	82-51.20	16477.62	56971.75	2123
LAKE ERIE		NORTH HARBOR I REEF "E13"	41-51.00	82-51.00	43760.00	56973.46	14830
LAKE ERIE		SOUTH BASS ISLAND LIGHT	41-37.70	82-50.50	43668.61	56920.65	14844
LAKE ERIE		T EDISON BRIDGE BUOY "B"	41-29.10	82-50.00	43608.16	56888.12	14844
LAKE ERIE		T EDISON BRIDGE BUOY "A"	41-29.00	82-50.00	43607.43	56887.69	14844
LAKE ERIE		W SHORE SKI RAMP LIGHT	41-27.90	82-49.90	43599.68	56883.85	14844
LAKE ERIE		NORTH BASS ISLAND NO 4	41-41.10	82-49.60	43694.61	56943.04	14844
LAKE ERIE		W HARBOR JUNCTION LIGHT	41-33.50	82-49.50	43640.92	56911.31	14842
LAKE ERIE		BIG CHICK ISLAND	41-46.79	82-49.36	43733.90	56969.60	
LAKE ERIE		SANDUSKY PWR LINE "A"	41-29.00	82-49.00	43609.59	56896.39	14844
LAKE ERIE		NEW GEM BEACH	41-34.70	82-48.96	43649.80	56921.30	
LAKE ERIE		W HARBOR ACCESS CH NO 3	41-33.90	82-48.90	43645.10	56918.23	14842
LAKE ERIE		SANDUSKY BAY SKI JUMP LIGHT	41-28.50	82-48.80	43606.40	56896.00	14844
LAKE ERIE		NORTH BASS CAN	41-44.32	82-48.63	43718.40	56965.30	
LAKE ERIE		PERRY MEMORIAL MON LIGHT	41-39.20	82-48.60	43683.47	56943.55	14844
LAKE ERIE		E HARBOR W BRKWTR LIGHT	41-33.70	82-48.20	43645.21	56923.46	14842
LAKE ERIE		E HARBOR E BRKWTR LIGHT	41-33.70	82-48.20	43645.21	56923.46	14842
LAKE ERIE		MARINE CITY DOCK LIGHT	41-32.00	82-48.00	43633.44	56917.93	14842
LAKE ERIE		MIDDLE HARBOR SHOAL NO 1	41-34.20	82-47.70	43649.90	56929.94	14842
LAKE ERIE		BALLAST ISLAND CAN	41-40.91	82-47.25	43697.70	56962.70	
LAKE ERIE		CHANNEL GROVE MARINA	41-32.20	82-47.20	43636.64	56925.73	14842
LAKE ERIE		BALLAST ISLAND LIGHT	41-40.70	82-47.00	43697.67	56963.81	14844
LAKE ERIE		EAST HARBOR ENTR NO 2	41-32.60	82-47.00	43639.96	56929.18	14842
LAKE ERIE		CEDAR CREEK EAST	42-00.64	82-46.73	16462.79	57051.12	2123
LAKE ERIE		LAKEVIEW E ENTR LIGHT	41-32.40	82-46.40	43639.84	56933.54	14842
LAKE ERIE		SCHROCKS MARINA E BRKWTR	41-32.60	82-46.10	43641.95	56937.02	14842
LAKE ERIE		INTERNATIONAL BDRY "E"	41-42.90	82-45.60	43716.34	56985.32	14844
LAKE ERIE		DANBURY BRKWTR LIGHT	41-30.30	82-45.50	43626.64	56932.42	14844

PASSES

BODY OF WATER	PROV/STATE	NAME	LAT	LON	TD#1	TD#2	CHART
LAKE ERIE		KINGSVILLE	42-01.57	82-43.90	16462.50	57079.20	2181
LAKE ERIE		STANDARD SLAG DOCK	41-32.70	82-43.80	43647.77	56957.45	14842
LAKE ERIE		KELLEYS ISLAND POPEYE'S	41-36.14	82-43.10	43673.20	56978.30	
LAKE ERIE		BAY POINT MARINA LIGHT	41-30.20	82-43.00	43631.43	56953.78	14842
LAKE ERIE		TURINSKY BOAT BASIN	41-32.40	82-42.90	43647.60	56964.00	14842
LAKE ERIE		MARBLEHEAD LIGHT	41-33.02	82-42.85	43651.30	56967.20	
LAKE ERIE		MARBLEHEAD LIGHT	41-32.20	82-42.70	43646.60	56964.89	14842
LAKE ERIE		MOSELEY CHANNEL RANGE	41-29.20	82-42.20	43625.90	56956.50	14845
LAKE ERIE		PATTERY PK MARINA S ENTR	41-27.80	82-42.10	43615.89	56951.44	14845
LAKE ERIE		SANDUSKY BAY RANGE	41-28.50	82-42.10	43621.01	56954.41	14845
LAKE ERIE		PELEE ISLAND W WHARF	41-46.00	82-42.00	43746.39	57029.63	14830
LAKE ERIE		EAST COVE BUOY NO 1	41-27.60	82-41.90	43614.86	56952.33	14845
LAKE ERIE		SADLER SAILING BASIN NO 1	41-27.50	82-41.90	43614.13	56951.90	14845
LAKE ERIE		SANDUSKY STGHT CH RANGE	41-29.50	82-41.80	43628.97	56961.27	14845
LAKE ERIE		CEDAR POINT WATER INTAKE	41-29.00	82-41.60	43625.77	56960.89	14845
LAKE ERIE		PELEE ISLAND W WHARF	41-45.82	82-41.50	16491.03	57033.18	2123
LAKE ERIE		CAMP PATOS LIGHT	41-37.00	82-40.90	43685.22	57000.94	14844
LAKE ERIE		INTERNATIONAL BDRY "D"	41-40.60	82-40.80	43711.13	57017.09	14844
LAKE ERIE		SANDUSKY HARBOR PIER	41-30.00	82-40.50	43635.50	56974.72	14845
LAKE ERIE		SANDUSKY HARB DEV NO 1	41-27.70	82-40.20	43619.33	56967.59	14845
LAKE ERIE		SCUDDER BRKWTR LIGHT	41-49.00	82-40.00	43771.98	57059.60	14830
LAKE ERIE		SCUDDER WHARF LIGHT	41-49.00	82-40.00	43771.98	57059.60	14830
LAKE ERIE		SANDUSKY HARB DEV NO 4	41-27.60	82-39.90	43619.26	56969.78	14845
LAKE ERIE		SANDUSKY MUNICIPAL CRIB	41-27.20	82-39.80	43616.54	56968.97	14845
LAKE ERIE		SCUDDER WHARF	41-48.85	82-39.58	16487.04	57062.59	2181
LAKE ERIE		SCUDDER BRKWTR	41-48.95	82-39.52	16486.90	57063.53	2181
LAKE ERIE		LEAMINGTON HARBOUR	42-01.43	82-36.19	16466.69	57144.53	2181
LAKE ERIE		TURNING LIGHTED BUOY "E10"	41-52.60	82-36.10	43806.23	57108.39	14830
LAKE ERIE		LEAMINGTON BRKWTR WEST	42-01.18	82-36.10	16467.20	57144.27	2181
LAKE ERIE		LEAMINGTON BRKWTR	42-01.18	82-36.10	16467.20	57144.27	2181
LAKE ERIE		PELEE PASSAGE NO E10	41-52.58	82-36.10	16482.50	57108.30	2123
LAKE ERIE		LEAMINGTON HARBOUR ENTR	42-01.53	82-36.05	16466.57	57146.15	2181
LAKE ERIE		SAWMILL CREEK ENTR	41-25.00	82-36.00	43608.64	56992.88	14830
LAKE ERIE		SAWMILL CREEK ENTR	41-25.00	82-35.60	43609.52	56996.38	14830
LAKE ERIE		PELEE PASSAGE	41-51.24	82-34.92	16485.38	57112.86	2123
LAKE ERIE		INTERNATIONAL BDRY "C"	41-40.60	82-34.90	43724.79	57068.27	14830
LAKE ERIE		MIDDLE GROUND BUOY "E9"	41-51.40	82-34.80	43801.06	57114.56	14830
LAKE ERIE		PELEE PASS MID GROUND E9	41-51.37	82-34.80	16485.22	57114.43	2123
LAKE ERIE		STURGEON CREEK	42-00.53	82-34.58	16469.17	57154.58	2123
LAKE ERIE		TRAFFIC LIGHTED "EEE"	41-51.80	82-34.50	43804.56	57118.82	14830
LAKE ERIE		PELEE PASSAGE "EEE"	41-51.92	82-34.50	16484.44	57119.33	2123
LAKE ERIE		STURGEON CREEK ENTRANCE	42-00.53	82-34.50	16469.21	57155.27	2123
LAKE ERIE		GRUBB REEF LIGHT NO E8	41-51.92	82-33.65	16484.87	57126.66	2123
LAKE ERIE		GRUBB REEF BUOY "E8"	41-51.90	82-33.60	43807.43	57127.01	14830

PASSES

BODY OF WATER	PROV/STATE	NAME	LAT	LON	TD#1	TD#2	CHART
LAKE ERIE		HURON HARB INNER E LIGHT	41-23.90	82-32.90	43607.28	57015.36	14843
LAKE ERIE		HURON HARBOR LIGHT	41-24.30	82-32.60	43610.93	57019.67	14843
LAKE ERIE		HURON HARBOR ENTR NO 1	41-24.50	82-32.20	43613.31	57024.01	14843
LAKE ERIE		PELEE POINT BUOY "EP2"	41-52.10	82-30.50	43816.35	57154.59	14830
LAKE ERIE		POINT PELEE NO EP2	41-52.17	82-30.50	16486.04	57154.88	2123
LAKE ERIE		PELEE PASSAGE NO E6	41-49.20	82-28.20	16492.17	57162.39	2123
LAKE ERIE		SOUTHEAST SHOAL "EE"	41-48.70	82-27.85	16493.17	57163.35	2123
LAKE ERIE		SOUTHEAST SHOAL NO "EE"	41-48.70	82-27.80	43799.15	57163.78	14830
LAKE ERIE		SOUTHEAST SHOAL LIGHT	41-49.60	82-27.80	43805.48	57167.52	14830
LAKE ERIE		SOUTHEAST SHOAL	41-49.58	82-27.78	16491.75	57167.61	2123
LAKE ERIE		WHEATLEY	42-03.62	82-27.73	16466.93	57226.06	2181
LAKE ERIE		TWO CREEKS	42-04.50	82-26.77	16465.76	57237.91	2100
LAKE ERIE		NOAA WEATHER BUOY 45005	41-41.10	82-24.00	43754.15	57165.11	14830
LAKE ERIE		VERMILLION W PIER NO 4	41-25.70	82-21.90	43645.46	57119.19	14826
LAKE ERIE		INTERNATIONAL BDRY "A"	41-42.40	82-19.80	43773.67	57207.06	14826
LAKE ERIE		BEAVER CREEK E OUTER LIGHT	41-26.30	82-15.10	43665.64	57181.25	14826
LAKE ERIE		LORAIN REEF BUOY "A"	41-28.10	82-12.90	43684.41	57207.98	14841
LAKE ERIE		LAKEVIEW PARK E LIGHT	41-28.00	82-12.00	43685.77	57215.45	14841
LAKE ERIE		LAKEVIEW PARK W LIGHT	41-27.80	82-11.90	43684.48	57215.49	14841
LAKE ERIE		LORAIN HARBOR NO 2	41-28.60	82-11.40	43691.72	57223.19	14841
LAKE ERIE		KANSAS AVENUE BUOY	41-29.00	82-10.00	43698.07	57237.11	14826
LAKE ERIE		INTERNATIONAL BDRY "Y"	41-47.10	82-09.30	43833.60	57317.79	14826
LAKE ERIE		AVON INTAKE BRKWTR	41-30.00	82-03.00	43722.43	57302.55	14826
LAKE ERIE		AVON LAKE OBSTR BUOY	41-30.70	81-59.10	43737.26	57339.60	14826
LAKE ERIE		RONDEAU INNER HARBOR	42-15.67	81-54.43	16460.44	57559.73	2181
LAKE ERIE		CROWN INTAKE BUOY	41-31.00	81-53.00	43754.59	57394.28	14826
LAKE ERIE		BRAD STREET LANDING	41-29.00	81-52.00	43741.64	57394.82	14826
LAKE ERIE		POINTE AUX PINS	42-15.42	81-51.33	16462.63	57585.46	2100
LAKE ERIE		ROCKY RIVER LIGHT NO 1	41-29.50	81-50.30	43749.72	57411.78	14826
LAKE ERIE		MOSS POINT REEF "B"	41-30.20	81-47.60	43761.88	57438.32	14826
LAKE ERIE		MOSS POINT REEF "A"	41-30.20	81-47.10	43763.13	57442.70	14826
LAKE ERIE		CLEVELAND WW INTAKE CRIB	41-33.00	81-45.00	43790.09	57472.57	14826
LAKE ERIE		EDGEWATER PARK NO 1	41-29.80	81-43.70	43768.57	57470.86	14839
LAKE ERIE		CLEV HARB W BRKWTR NO 5	41-29.80	81-43.60	43768.82	57471.74	14839
LAKE ERIE		CLEVELAND HARB W PIER	41-30.50	81-43.10	43775.54	57478.99	14839
LAKE ERIE		LAKESIDE/FOREST CTY YC "A"	41-37.90	81-41.50	43836.72	57523.20	14826
LAKE ERIE		CUYAHOGA RIVER NO 1	41-29.10	81-40.60	43770.93	57495.17	14839
LAKE ERIE		POINTE AUX PINS LIGHT	42-14.88	81-39.93	16469.90	57681.75	2181
LAKE ERIE		EAST 55TH ST MARINA ENTR	41-31.90	81-39.20	43796.38	57518.90	14839
LAKE ERIE		CLEVELAND HARB E ENTR	41-32.60	81-39.10	43802.09	57522.64	14839
LAKE ERIE		GORDON PARK DISP LIGHT "B"	41-32.50	81-38.30	43803.37	57529.25	14839
LAKE ERIE		GORDON PARK DISP LIGHT "A"	41-32.60	81-38.00	43804.92	57532.29	14839
LAKE ERIE		LAKESIDE/FOREST CTY YC "C"	41-35.50	81-35.10	43834.99	57569.51	14826
LAKE ERIE		NE YACHT CLUB OUTER LIGHT	41-34.40	81-35.10	43826.45	57565.04	14826

PASSES

BODY OF WATER	PROV/STATE	NAME	LAT	LON	TD#1	TD#2	CHART
LAKE ERIE		EUCLID BEACH PIER	41-35.50	81-34.20	43837.35	57577.40	14826
LAKE ERIE		WILDWOOD E PIER	41-35.30	81-34.00	43836.32	57578.34	14826
LAKE ERIE		WILDWOOD PARK C BRKWTR	41-35.30	81-34.00	43836.32	57578.34	14826
LAKE ERIE		WILDWOOD PARK W BRKWTR	41-35.30	81-34.00	43836.32	57578.34	14826
LAKE ERIE		WILDWOOD PARK E BRKWTR	41-35.40	81-34.00	43837.10	57578.75	14826
LAKE ERIE		LAKESIDE/FOREST CTY YC "B"	41-39.20	81-33.60	43867.49	57597.66	14826
LAKE ERIE		EUCLID INTAKE BUOY	41-37.50	81-30.80	43861.84	57615.31	14826
LAKE ERIE		EASTLAKE INTAKE BRKWTR	41-40.50	81-26.50	43896.59	57665.10	14825
LAKE ERIE		CHAGRIN W PIER LIGHT	41-40.60	81-26.30	43897.90	57667.26	14825
LAKE ERIE		CHAGRIN E PIER LIGHT	41-40.60	81-26.20	43898.17	57668.13	14825
LAKE ERIE		MENTOR HARB YACHT CLUB	41-43.50	81-21.00	43934.77	57725.33	14825
LAKE ERIE		PAINESVILLE INTAKE NO 1	41-45.40	81-17.90	43958.00	57760.06	14825
LAKE ERIE		FAIRPORT HARB E PIER	41-45.70	81-16.80	43963.39	57770.89	14825
LAKE ERIE		FAIRPORT HARB W PIER	41-45.70	81-16.80	43963.39	57770.89	14825
LAKE ERIE		PORT AUTHORITY RAMP	41-45.60	81-16.70	43962.90	57771.37	14825
LAKE ERIE		FAIRPORT HARB BUOY "A"	41-46.00	81-16.00	43967.95	57779.09	14837
LAKE ERIE		ASHTABULA BRKWTR BUOY "B"	41-46.00	81-15.70	43968.79	57781.72	14825
LAKE ERIE		FAIRPORT HARB E BRKWTR	41-46.10	81-15.40	43970.41	57784.75	14837
LAKE ERIE		PORT STANLEY	42-39.53	81-12.82	16426.52	58001.28	2181
LAKE ERIE		PORT STANLEY E BRKWTR	42-39.47	81-10.37	16428.00	58022.08	2181
LAKE ERIE		PORT BRUCE	42-39.33	81-00.67	16433.66	58104.92	2100
LAKE ERIE		PORT BRUCE LIGHT	42-32.88	80-58.22	16451.80	58105.44	2100
LAKE ERIE		GENEVA-ON-THE-LAKE NO 1	41-51.50	80-53.10	44077.00	58001.43	14836
LAKE ERIE		PORT BURWELL W BRKWTR	42-37.93	80-48.57	16444.13	58204.84	2181
LAKE ERIE		PORT BURWELL APPROACH	42-38.18	80-48.47	16443.51	58206.48	2181
LAKE ERIE		ASHTABULA HARBOR LIGHT	41-55.10	80-47.80	44120.77	58061.87	14836
LAKE ERIE		ASHTABULA INNER BRKWTR	41-54.70	80-47.70	44118.02	58061.20	14836
LAKE ERIE		ASHTABULA E BRKWTR	41-54.80	80-46.50	44122.46	58072.11	14836
LAKE ERIE		CONNEAUT HARB W BRKWTR	41-58.80	80-33.50	44193.86	58201.43	14824
LAKE ERIE		PORT ROWAN	42-37.22	80-26.78	16458.49	58391.49	2110
LAKE ERIE		ST WILLIAMS	42-39.30	80-24.35	16454.24	58418.72	2110
LAKE ERIE		LONG POINT INNER BAY EC10	42-37.12	80-21.37	16461.92	58438.23	2110
LAKE ERIE		WALNUT CREEK BRKWTR LIGHT	42-04.60	80-14.30	44301.05	58391.69	14824
LAKE ERIE		PORT DOVER MARINA	42-46.84	80-11.69	16439.69	58549.42	2181
LAKE ERIE		PORT DOVER LIGHT EA10	42-45.68	80-10.98	16443.60	58552.51	2110
LAKE ERIE		BLUFF BAR LIGHT NO EA11	42-35.77	80-09.52	16472.59	58537.55	2110
LAKE ERIE		ERIE YACHT CLUB RANGE	42-07.00	80-08.00	44340.66	58455.84	14835
LAKE ERIE		LONG POINT BAY "N"	42-42.90	80-07.34	16453.95	58576.65	2110
LAKE ERIE		PRESQUE ISLE LIGHT	42-09.90	80-06.90	44366.34	58476.03	14824
LAKE ERIE		PRESQUE ISLE PARK RANGE	42-09.40	80-06.80	44362.92	58475.11	14835
LAKE ERIE		PRESQUE ISLE PARK NO 7	42-09.20	80-06.80	44361.42	58474.39	14835
LAKE ERIE		PRESQUE ISLE PARK NO 5	42-09.20	80-06.80	44361.42	58474.39	14835
LAKE ERIE		PRESQUE ISLE PARK NO 6	42-09.20	80-06.70	44361.76	58475.26	14835
LAKE ERIE		PRESQUE ISLE BAY NO 1	42-09.50	80-06.70	44364.02	58476.34	14835

PASSES

BODY OF WATER	PROV/STATE	NAME	LAT	LON	TD#1	TD#2	CHART
LAKE ERIE		NANTICOKE STN NO EN1	42-44.60	80-05.77	16449.85	58594.85	2110
LAKE ERIE		NANTICOKE STN NO EN2	42-44.38	80-05.43	16450.71	58597.22	2110
LAKE ERIE		ERIE HARB ENTR NO 10	42-08.90	80-05.30	44364.32	58486.48	14835
LAKE ERIE		ERIE HARB ENTR NO 12	42-08.80	80-05.30	44363.56	58486.12	14835
LAKE ERIE		NANTICOKE STN NO EN5	42-45.13	80-05.02	16448.70	58602.77	2110
LAKE ERIE		ERIE HARB ENTR RANGE	42-09.10	80-04.90	44367.21	58490.71	14835
LAKE ERIE		ERIE HARBOR NO 8	42-09.10	80-04.90	44367.21	58490.71	14835
LAKE ERIE		NANTICOKE STN NO EN6	42-44.95	80-04.75	16449.40	58604.64	2110
LAKE ERIE		STELCO APPROACH NO ET11	42-46.83	80-04.62	16443.78	58610.66	2110
LAKE ERIE		NANTICOKE STN NO EN7	42-45.47	80-04.58	16447.93	58607.48	2110
LAKE ERIE		STELCO WHARF	42-46.88	80-04.58	16443.64	58611.14	2110
LAKE ERIE		STELCO APPROACH NO ET14	42-47.07	80-04.55	16443.08	58611.89	2110
LAKE ERIE		JOHN E LAMPE MARINA NO 1	42-08.90	80-04.50	44367.08	58493.50	14835
LAKE ERIE		JOHN E LAMPE MARINA NO 2	42-08.90	80-04.40	44367.43	58494.38	14835
LAKE ERIE		STELCO APPROACH NO ET12	42-46.93	80-04.37	16443.61	58613.09	2110
LAKE ERIE		STELCO APPROACH NO ET1	42-46.25	80-04.32	16445.72	58611.77	2110
LAKE ERIE		ERIE HARBOR PIER LIGHT	42-09.40	80-04.30	44371.55	58497.07	14835
LAKE ERIE		STELCO APPROACH NO ET2	42-46.29	80-04.15	16445.70	58613.35	2110
LAKE ERIE		NANTICOKE STN NO EN8	42-45.50	80-04.08	16448.13	58611.90	2110
LAKE ERIE		NANTICOKE BRKWTR	42-47.79	80-04.00	16441.17	58618.50	2110
LAKE ERIE		STELCO WHARF LIGHT "NTB"	42-45.90	80-04.00	16446.97	58613.64	2110
LAKE ERIE		NANTICOKE SHOAL NO EA8	42-43.70	80-03.63	16453.78	58611.06	2110
LAKE ERIE		NANTICOKE STN NO EN9	42-46.20	80-03.58	16446.30	58618.06	2110
LAKE ERIE		HAMMERMILL OBSTR BUOY	42-08.80	80-03.50	44369.78	58501.93	14835
LAKE ERIE		NANTICOKE STN NO EN10	42-46.07	80-03.42	16446.79	58619.11	2110
LAKE ERIE		ERIE HARBOR ENTR NO 2	42-09.80	80-03.20	44378.37	58508.18	14835
LAKE ERIE		LONG POINT LIGHT	42-32.90	80-03.00	44542.46	58586.09	14820
LAKE ERIE		LONG POINT	42-32.92	80-02.95	16484.05	58586.59	2110
LAKE ERIE		NANTICOKE STN NO EN11	42-46.73	80-02.87	16445.09	58625.59	2110
LAKE ERIE		NANTICOKE STN NO EN12	42-46.63	80-02.73	16445.48	58626.55	2110
LAKE ERIE		NANTICOKE WHARF ENTR	42-47.75	80-02.63	16442.08	58630.28	2110
LAKE ERIE		NANTICOKE STN E ENTR	42-47.70	80-02.52	16442.30	58631.10	2110
LAKE ERIE		NANTICOKE STN NO EN15	42-47.28	80-02.49	16443.62	58630.29	2110
LAKE ERIE		NANTICOKE STN NO EN16	42-47.30	80-02.38	16443.62	58631.30	2110
LAKE ERIE		NANTICOKE STN NO EN14	42-47.03	80-02.27	16444.52	58631.56	2110
LAKE ERIE		WILLIS DISTR CO DOCK	42-10.50	80-00.60	44392.69	58533.53	14823
LAKE ERIE		TECUMSEH REEF EA6	42-47.65	79-43.47	16453.58	58796.52	2120
LAKE ERIE		BARCELONA HARB E BRKWTR	42-20.70	79-35.90	44557.52	58786.05	14823
LAKE ERIE		PORT MAITLAND E PIER	42-51.19	79-34.71	16447.15	58880.88	2140
LAKE ERIE		MOHAWK ISLAND NO EA4	42-48.82	79-31.03	16457.22	58907.64	2120
LAKE ERIE		DUNKIRK LIGHT	42-29.60	79-21.20	44676.87	58943.68	14823
LAKE ERIE		DUNKIRK BRKWTR W NO 4	42-29.30	79-20.50	44677.50	58948.96	14823
LAKE ERIE		DUNKIRK BRKWTR E NO 2	42-29.40	79-20.20	44679.37	58951.90	14823
LAKE ERIE		DUNKIRK BRKWTR W NO 1	42-23.00	79-20.20	44633.78	58931.92	14823

PASSES

BODY OF WATER	PROV/STATE	NAME	LAT	LON	TD#1	TD#2	CHART
LAKE ERIE		PORT COLBORNE BUOY "E"	42-49.40	79-17.00	44820.09	59031.36	14820
LAKE ERIE		PORT COLBORNE LIGHT "E"	42-49.38	79-16.97	16463.86	59031.58	2120
LAKE ERIE		PORT ALBINO LIGHT	42-52.20	79-16.20	44839.40	59044.10	14820
LAKE ERIE		PORT COLBORNE W BRKWTR	42-52.20	79-16.20	44839.40	59044.10	14820
LAKE ERIE		PORT COLBORNE E3	42-52.20	79-16.17	16454.59	59044.36	2042
LAKE ERIE		PORT COLBORNE W BRKWTR	42-52.20	79-16.17	16454.59	59044.36	2042
LAKE ERIE		PORT COLBORNE OUTER BRKWTR	42-51.77	79-15.30	16456.62	59051.09	2042
LAKE ERIE		PORT COLBORNE	42-52.05	79-15.18	16455.71	59052.69	2042
LAKE ERIE		PORT COLBORNE CHAN BUOY	42-52.18	79-15.02	16455.35	59054.34	2042
LAKE ERIE		PORT COLBORNE E BRKWTR	42-52.00	79-15.00	16455.99	59054.16	2042
LAKE ERIE		COLBORNE WHARF 19	42-52.38	79-14.97	16454.67	59055.18	2042
LAKE ERIE		COLBORNE CRIB 3 LIGHT	42-52.49	79-14.93	16454.30	59055.74	2042
LAKE ERIE		COLBORNE WHARF 17	42-52.70	79-14.92	16453.56	59056.25	2042
LAKE ERIE		PORT COLBORNE HARBOUR	42-52.03	79-14.90	16455.95	59055.09	2042
LAKE ERIE		CASSADAY POINT "EA2"	42-50.40	79-13.57	16462.44	59063.41	2120
LAKE ERIE		CATTARAUGUS CREEK NO 2	42-34.30	79-08.40	44759.49	59070.13	14823
LAKE ERIE		CATTARAUGUS CREEK NO 1	42-34.30	79-08.30	44759.89	59071.01	14823
LAKE ERIE		POINT ABINO	42-50.10	79-05.80	16468.24	59130.70	2120
LAKE ERIE		CHIPPAWA LIGHT	43-03.80	79-02.90	44953.90	59178.45	14832
LAKE ERIE		NIAGARA FALLS SAFETY "A"	43-04.40	79-01.70	44961.61	59189.51	14832
LAKE ERIE		BIG SIX MILE CREEK LIGHT	43-01.60	79-00.70	44951.68	59194.42	14832
LAKE ERIE		NIAGARA MOHAWK PWR LIGHT	43-04.20	78-60.00	44967.39	59203.84	14832
LAKE ERIE		BUCKHORN I INTAKE CRIB	43-04.00	78-60.00	44966.41	59203.59	14832
LAKE ERIE		HOOKER ELEC OUTFALL CRIB	43-03.90	78-59.60	44967.52	59206.90	14832
LAKE ERIE		LA SALLE YACHT CLUB	43-04.40	78-59.30	44971.15	59210.09	14832
LAKE ERIE		BEAVER I ST PARK E ENTR	42-57.50	78-57.30	44944.21	59217.86	14832
LAKE ERIE		GRAND ISLAND RANGE	42-58.70	78-56.80	44952.52	59224.00	14832
LAKE ERIE		LITTLE RIVER RANGE	43-04.50	78-56.20	44984.00	59236.79	14832
LAKE ERIE		WAVERLY SHOAL "EU"	42-51.70	78-56.20	44917.01	59217.70	14833
LAKE ERIE		EAST RIVER MARINA N ENTR	42-58.10	78-56.00	44952.63	59230.04	14832
LAKE ERIE		ERIE CTY WATER BUOY "ECWA"	42-57.90	78-55.90	44951.98	59230.61	14832
LAKE ERIE		ASHLAND REFINERY LIGHT	42-60.00	78-55.80	44963.26	59234.50	14832
LAKE ERIE		BUFFALO HARBOR BUOY	42-50.20	78-55.40	44911.75	59221.91	14833
LAKE ERIE		MIDDLE REEFS "EU4"	42-52.73	78-55.27	16465.22	59227.68	2120
LAKE ERIE		BUFFALO INTAKE CRIB LIGHT	42-52.80	78-54.70	44929.32	59232.78	14833
LAKE ERIE		STRAWBERRY I CUT NO 1	42-56.60	78-54.70	44950.00	59239.05	14832
LAKE ERIE		UPPER RANGE LIGHT	42-57.20	78-54.60	44953.59	59240.84	14832
LAKE ERIE		JAFCO MARINA N LIGHT	42-56.60	78-54.60	44950.41	59239.91	14832
LAKE ERIE		JAFCO MARINA S LIGHT	42-56.60	78-54.60	44950.41	59239.91	14832
LAKE ERIE		WANAKAH INTAKE CRIB NO 2	42-45.10	78-54.30	44886.14	59221.21	14822
LAKE ERIE		BUFFALO INTAKE CRIB LIGHT	42-54.50	78-54.30	44940.32	59239.17	14833
LAKE ERIE		BUFFALO HARB JUNCTION B	42-52.00	78-54.00	44927.71	59237.48	14833
LAKE ERIE		FISHERIES CONTROL SITE	42-51.20	78-54.00	44923.20	59236.03	14833
LAKE ERIE		OLD BRKWTR N END LIGHT	42-52.70	78-53.90	44932.04	59239.59	14833

PASSES

BODY OF WATER	PROV/STATE	NAME	LAT	LON	TD#1	TD#2	CHART
LAKE ERIE		N BRKWTR S END LIGHT	42-52.80	78-53.80	44933.01	59240.64	14833
LAKE ERIE		FISHERIES CONTROL SITE	42-50.70	78-53.50	44922.41	59239.49	14833
LAKE ERIE		BUFFALO USCG SLIP LIGHT	42-52.70	78-53.50	44933.68	59243.08	14833
LAKE ERIE		N TONAWANDA INTAKE CRIB	43-01.50	78-53.50	44980.13	59256.35	14832
LAKE ERIE		TONAWANDA ISLAND NO 1	43-01.40	78-53.20	44980.84	59258.80	14832
LAKE ERIE		SMITH BOYS MARINA N LIGHT	43-01.80	78-52.90	44984.04	59261.90	14832
LAKE ERIE		GENERAL MILLS DOCK NO 2	42-52.30	78-52.60	44935.14	59250.25	14833
LAKE ERIE		S BUFFALO DIKE NO 2	42-50.20	78-52.50	44923.67	59247.31	14833
LAKE ERIE		LACKAWANNA E PIER LIGHT	42-49.90	78-51.70	44925.25	59253.76	14833
LAKE ERIE		LACKAWANNA W PIER LIGHT	42-49.80	78-51.70	44924.68	59253.57	14833
LAKE ERIE		UNION CANAL LIGHT	42-50.90	78-51.60	44931.38	59256.49	14833
LAKE ERIE		WHITEFISH BAR "C"	42-39.20	70-17.67	13673.64	60287.68	2110
LAKE HURON		PICKEREL CHAN ENTR NO 2	45-24.90	84-47.70	31325.37	48307.62	14886
LAKE HURON		BURT LAKE OBSTR BUOY	45-24.90	84-47.70	31325.37	48307.62	14886
LAKE HURON		MACKINAC BRIDGE RACON	45-48.90	84-43.70	31224.89	48108.81	14881
LAKE HURON		MACKINAC BRIDGE NO 1	45-48.40	84-42.50	31220.02	48115.98	14881
LAKE HURON		GROS CAP REEFS LIGHT	46-30.70	84-36.90	31069.70	47778.28	14884
LAKE HURON		ROUND ISLAND LIGHT	45-50.60	84-36.90	31183.18	48110.63	14881
LAKE HURON		BIRCH POINT RANGE	46-26.00	84-31.40	31054.38	47830.57	14884
LAKE HURON		ROUND ISLAND NO 32	46-26.00	84-31.40	31054.38	47830.57	14884
LAKE HURON		POINTE AUX PINS LIGHT	46-27.80	84-28.40	31034.52	47823.72	14884
LAKE HURON		CHEBOYGAN RIVER RANGE	45-38.90	84-28.30	31172.05	48230.09	14881
LAKE HURON		POINTE AUX PINS RANGE	46-28.10	84-28.30	31033.24	47821.56	14884
LAKE HURON		POINTE AUX PINS BAY "P18"	46-28.40	84-27.90	31030.45	47820.17	14884
LAKE HURON		BRUSH POINT RANGE	46-27.70	84-27.80	31031.74	47826.06	14884
LAKE HURON		BRUSH POINT DAYBEACON	46-28.30	84-27.50	31028.68	47822.00	14884
LAKE HURON		CHEBOYGAN RIVER ENTR NO 2	45-39.90	84-27.40	31164.00	48223.58	14881
LAKE HURON		LES CHENEAUXS W ENTR NO 1	45-57.80	84-27.10	31109.32	48073.25	14885
LAKE HURON		FOURTEEN FOOT SHOAL LIGHT	45-40.80	84-26.10	31154.05	48218.84	14881
LAKE HURON		BOIS BLANC LIGHT	45-48.60	84-25.30	31126.31	48154.63	14881
LAKE HURON		VIDAL SHOALS N BUOY "QM14"	46-30.90	84-23.20	31000.36	47812.10	14884
LAKE HURON		CANADIAN CANAL U RANGE	46-30.90	84-22.30	30995.81	47814.38	14884
LAKE HURON		VIDAL SHOALS CHAN RANGE	46-30.30	84-21.80	30994.77	47820.45	14884
LAKE HURON		LES CHENEAUXS I NO 5	45-57.40	84-21.20	31078.74	48090.39	14885
LAKE HURON		CANADIAN CANAL ENTR "QM1"	46-30.50	84-20.50	30987.69	47822.13	14884
LAKE HURON		CANADIAN CANAL L RANGE	46-30.90	84-20.50	30986.70	47818.94	14884
LAKE HURON		LES CHENEAUXS I NO 1	45-56.90	84-20.00	31073.94	48098.16	14885
LAKE HURON		SAULT STE MARIE WHARF	46-30.20	84-19.70	30984.38	47826.54	14884
LAKE HURON		LITTLE RAPIDS CUT NO 101	46-29.40	84-18.30	30979.23	47836.44	14883
LAKE HURON		ISLE ISIDORE LIGHT	45-58.20	84-18.30	31060.85	48090.46	14885
LAKE HURON		PENNY ISLAND POINT NO 1	45-56.90	84-17.10	31057.96	48104.00	14885
LAKE HURON		BAYFIELD ROCK RANGE	46-29.30	84-17.00	30972.86	47840.48	14884
LAKE HURON		LAKE NICOLET JUNCTION	46-27.60	84-17.00	30977.04	47854.06	14883
LAKE HURON		FRECHETTE POINT RANGE	46-27.30	84-16.70	30976.25	47857.20	14883

PASSES

BODY OF WATER	PROV/STATE	NAME	LAT	LON	TD#1	TD#2	CHART
LAKE HURON		McKAY BAY RANGE	45-59.00	84-16.50	31048.92	48087.98	14885
LAKE HURON		LAKE NICOLET NO 88	46-26.80	84-16.10	30974.41	47862.69	14883
LAKE HURON		SIX MILE POINT RANGE	46-26.40	84-16.00	30974.89	47866.13	14883
LAKE HURON		DARK HOLE E RANGE	46-15.90	84-15.90	31000.83	47950.96	14883
LAKE HURON		UPPER NICOLET RANGE	46-27.30	84-15.90	30972.16	47859.18	14883
LAKE HURON		CROW ISLAND LEADING LIGHT	45-58.10	84-14.40	31040.02	48100.23	14885
LAKE HURON		SUGAR ISLAND LIGHT	46-24.70	84-14.00	30968.80	47884.66	14883
LAKE HURON		LAKE NICOLET NO 80	42-23.60	84-13.80	31882.74	49982.71	14883
LAKE HURON		WEST NEEBISH CHAN NO 54	46-22.80	84-13.60	30971.43	47900.87	14883
LAKE HURON		OAK RIDGE RANGE	46-17.10	84-12.90	30982.06	47948.45	14883
LAKE HURON		WEST NEEBISH CHAN NO 48	46-21.20	84-12.80	30971.26	47915.65	14883
LAKE HURON		WEST NEEBISH CHAN NO 29	46-16.90	84-12.50	30980.47	47951.02	14883
LAKE HURON		WEST NEEBISH CHAN RANGE	46-20.30	84-12.30	30970.90	47924.10	14883
LAKE HURON		MIDDLE NEEBISH RANGE	46-19.90	84-11.10	30965.64	47930.20	14883
LAKE HURON		MIDDLE NEEBISH LIGHT 62	46-20.10	84-11.00	30964.63	47928.83	14883
LAKE HURON		MIDDLE NEEBISH CHAN NO 61	46-20.00	84-11.00	30964.87	47929.63	14883
LAKE HURON		ROCK CUT LOW LEADING LIGHT	46-15.10	84-10.60	30975.04	47970.08	14883
LAKE HURON		LOWER NICOLET W RANGE	46-19.50	84-10.60	30964.03	47934.61	14883
LAKE HURON		LOWER NICOLET E RANGE	46-19.50	84-10.50	30963.51	47934.85	14883
LAKE HURON		HAMMOND BAY HARBOR LIGHT	45-35.60	84-09.70	31077.56	48298.32	14881
LAKE HURON		MIDDLE NEEBISH CHAN NO 54	46-19.60	84-09.60	30958.55	47936.20	14883
LAKE HURON		WEST NEEBISH CHAN NO 9	46-12.60	84-09.00	30972.91	47994.07	14883
LAKE HURON		MARTIN REEF LIGHT	45-54.80	84-08.90	31019.02	48139.88	14881
LAKE HURON		PUMPKIN POINT BUOY NO 2	46-23.50	84-08.40	30942.77	47907.84	14883
LAKE HURON		SPECTACLE REEF LIGHT	45-46.40	84-08.20	31038.25	48211.07	14881
LAKE HURON		BIRCH POINT BUOY 16	46-22.20	84-08.20	30944.88	47918.70	14883
LAKE HURON		HARWOOD POINT W RANGE	46-19.30	84-07.30	30947.26	47944.08	14883
LAKE HURON		MUNUSCONG CHANNEL NO 39	46-18.60	84-07.20	30948.46	47949.93	14883
LAKE HURON		POINT OF WOODS RANGE	46-16.30	84-07.20	30954.13	47968.42	14883
LAKE HURON		DARK HOLE W RANGE	46-15.90	84-07.00	30954.07	47972.11	14883
LAKE HURON		STRIBLING POINT RANGE	46-18.80	84-06.90	30946.40	47949.04	14883
LAKE HURON		JOHNSONS POINT NO 19	46-15.30	84-06.10	30950.80	47979.05	14883
LAKE HURON		SAILORS ENCAMPMENT RANGE	46-15.70	84-05.80	30948.23	47976.53	14883
LAKE HURON		WINTER POINT RANGE LIGHT	46-15.70	84-05.80	30948.23	47976.53	14883
LAKE HURON		RAINS WHARF RANGE LIGHT	46-15.30	84-05.70	30948.69	47979.99	14883
LAKE HURON		POINT AUX FRENES LIGHT	46-07.90	84-01.50	30944.69	48049.38	14882
LAKE HURON		POINT AUX FRENES NO 21	46-08.20	84-01.20	30942.33	48047.62	14882
LAKE HURON		ROUND ISLAND LIGHT	46-06.60	84-01.20	30946.33	48060.57	14882
LAKE HURON		COAL DOCK LIGHT	46-05.20	84-00.80	30947.69	48072.82	14882
LAKE HURON		HAY POINT RANGE LIGHT	46-07.70	83-60.00	30937.11	48054.37	14882
LAKE HURON		SWEETS POINT LIGHT	46-02.30	83-56.20	30929.96	48106.56	14882
LAKE HURON		FORTY MILE POINT LIGHT	45-29.20	83-54.80	31010.18	48382.06	14864
LAKE HURON		SAGINAW RIVER NO 26	43-33.20	83-54.40	31414.99	49383.11	14867
LAKE HURON		SQUAW ISLAND LIGHT	46-02.30	83-54.30	30919.56	48110.69	14882

PASSES

BODY OF WATER	PROV/STATE	NAME	LAT	LON	TD#1	TD#2	CHART
LAKE HURON		DE TOUR REEF LIGHT	45-56.90	83-54.20	30932.54	48154.73	14882
LAKE HURON		PIRATE ISLAND BUOY "KE14"	43-03.80	83-54.20	31541.44	49639.14	14882
LAKE HURON		DETOUR HARBOR ENTR NO 2	45-59.70	83-54.00	30924.39	48132.41	14882
LAKE HURON		PIPE ISLAND LIGHT	45-60.00	83-54.00	30923.64	48129.97	14882
LAKE HURON		DRUMMOND ISLAND SHOAL NO 8	45-59.30	83-53.80	30924.29	48136.09	14882
LAKE HURON		FRYING PAN ISLAND LIGHT	45-59.20	83-53.70	30923.99	48137.11	14882
LAKE HURON		TWINS LIGHT	46-01.60	83-53.50	30916.92	48118.09	14882
LAKE HURON		KAWKAWLIN RIVER RANGE	43-39.50	83-53.10	31379.52	49329.21	14867
LAKE HURON		MACOMB ISLAND BUOY "KE9"	46-04.90	83-52.50	30903.35	48093.61	14882
LAKE HURON		SAGINAW BAY NO 32	43-39.10	83-51.00	31366.20	49334.54	14867
LAKE HURON		SAGINAW BAY NO 34	43-38.70	83-51.00	31367.84	49338.02	14867
LAKE HURON		SAGINAW BAY LIGHT	43-39.00	83-51.00	31366.61	49335.41	14867
LAKE HURON		SAGINAW BAY NO 33	43-39.00	83-50.90	31365.90	49335.50	14867
LAKE HURON		SAGINAW BAY NO 31	43-39.10	83-50.80	31364.77	49334.71	14867
LAKE HURON		SAGINAW BAY NO 30	43-39.70	83-50.50	31360.18	49329.75	14867
LAKE HURON		SAGINAW BAY NO 29	43-50.40	83-50.40	31316.49	49236.77	14867
LAKE HURON		ESSEXVILLE RANGE LIGHT	43-37.40	83-50.30	31368.16	49349.93	14867
LAKE HURON		SAGINAW BAY NO 28	43-40.20	83-50.10	31355.29	49325.76	14867
LAKE HURON		SAGINAW BAY NO 27	43-40.20	83-50.00	31354.58	49325.84	14867
LAKE HURON		SAGINAW BAY OBSTR "A"	43-40.30	83-49.90	31353.46	49325.07	14867
LAKE HURON		ROGERS CITY HARBOR NO 2	45-25.50	83-48.40	30983.02	48425.15	14864
LAKE HURON		ROGERS CITY HARBOR NO 1	45-25.50	83-48.40	30983.02	48425.15	14864
LAKE HURON		CALCITE BRKWTR LIGHT	45-25.00	83-46.40	30972.57	48433.04	14864
LAKE HURON		SAGINAW BUOY NO 11	43-44.70	83-46.20	31309.44	49290.20	14867
LAKE HURON		SAGINAW BUOY NO 1	43-49.60	83-42.10	31261.15	49251.67	14867
LAKE HURON		NORTH PIER LIGHT NO 4	44-01.20	83-40.00	31202.50	49154.03	14863
LAKE HURON		POINT AU GRES BUOY	44-01.20	83-40.00	31202.50	49154.03	14863
LAKE HURON		NORTH POINT MARINA BRKWTR	44-02.80	83-39.20	31191.04	49141.15	14863
LAKE HURON		NORTH POINT MARINA NO 1	44-02.70	83-39.20	31191.40	49142.00	14863
LAKE HURON		NORTH POINT MARINA NO 2	44-02.80	83-39.10	31190.34	49141.26	14863
LAKE HURON		OAKHURST PARK MARINA	43-37.80	83-37.10	31271.40	49357.13	14863
LAKE HURON		NATL GYPSUM CO RANGE	44-14.30	83-32.40	31103.15	49050.50	14863
LAKE HURON		GRAVELLY SHOAL LIGHT	44-01.20	83-32.30	31148.72	49161.88	14863
LAKE HURON		ALABASTER TRAMWAY RANGE	44-11.30	83-31.90	31110.12	49076.52	14863
LAKE HURON		NATL GYPSUM CO NO 1	44-13.80	83-31.00	31095.27	49056.31	14863
LAKE HURON		CHARITY I SHOAL NO 5	44-06.50	83-29.80	31112.37	49119.45	14863
LAKE HURON		PRESQUE ISLE LIGHT	45-21.40	83-29.50	30881.08	48493.04	14864
LAKE HURON		EAST TAWAS INTAKE BUOY	44-16.40	83-29.40	31075.42	49036.11	14863
LAKE HURON		PRESQUE ISLE HARBOR RANGE	45-20.30	83-29.40	30883.37	48502.24	14864
LAKE HURON		SEBEWAING YACHT CLUB LIGHT	43-44.30	83-27.80	31178.94	49309.14	14863
LAKE HURON		PARTRIDGE POINT MARINA	45-01.10	83-27.20	30922.15	48664.31	14864
LAKE HURON		TAWAS LIGHT	44-15.20	83-26.90	31062.32	49049.04	14863
LAKE HURON		JERRYS MARINA RANGE	44-15.70	83-26.30	31056.51	49045.49	14863
LAKE HURON		ALPENA LIGHT	45-03.60	83-25.40	30903.81	48646.39	14864

PASSES

BODY OF WATER	PROV/STATE	NAME	LAT	LON	TD#1	TD#2	CHART
LAKE HURON		STONEPORT LIGHT	45-17.80	83-25.10	30863.73	48530.02	14864
LAKE HURON		THUNDER BAY QUARRIES RANGE	45-04.10	83-25.00	30899.91	48642.88	14864
LAKE HURON		SAND POINT MIDCHANNEL	43-55.90	83-24.80	31114.78	49213.82	14863
LAKE HURON		HURON PORTLAND CEM RANGE	45-04.10	83-24.50	30896.77	48643.66	14864
LAKE HURON		YACHT CLUB JUNCTION BUOY	45-02.90	83-24.10	30897.56	48654.18	14864
LAKE HURON		THUNDER BAY WRECK "WR2"	45-03.70	83-23.60	30892.20	48648.34	14864
LAKE HURON		ROCKPORT HARBOR LIGHT	45-12.30	83-22.90	30864.64	48578.70	14864
LAKE HURON		MIDDLER ISLAND LIGHT	45-11.60	83-19.30	30844.13	48590.18	14864
LAKE HURON		AU SABLE N PIERHEAD	44-24.40	83-19.00	30978.18	48980.84	14863
LAKE HURON		STONEYCROFT POINT LIGHT	45-06.40	83-18.50	30852.82	48633.98	14864
LAKE HURON		LAKESHORE TERMINAL RANGE	44-40.20	83-17.20	30917.81	48851.75	14864
LAKE HURON		HARRISVILLE W BRKWTR	44-39.60	83-17.00	30918.26	48856.97	14864
LAKE HURON		STURGEON POINT LIGHT	44-42.70	83-16.30	30904.54	48832.23	14864
LAKE HURON		THUNDER BAY TRAFFIC BUOY	44-58.60	83-15.00	30851.51	48703.13	14864
LAKE HURON		MISSISSAGI STRAIT	45-53.60	83-13.50	30710.90	48262.77	2267
LAKE HURON		THUNDER BAY ISLAND LIGHT	45-02.20	83-11.70	30820.85	48678.48	14864
LAKE HURON		NORDMEER WRECK "WR1"	45-08.10	83-09.30	30790.47	48634.05	14863
LAKE HURON		PORT AUSTIN BRKWTR NO 4	44-03.20	82-59.60	30909.67	49175.05	14863
LAKE HURON		PORT AUSTIN REEF LIGHT	44-04.90	82-58.90	30899.26	49161.77	14863
LAKE HURON		GREAT DUCK ISLAND	45-38.50	82-57.80	30650.44	48409.46	2266
LAKE HURON		GREAT DUCK ISLAND LIGHT	45-38.50	82-57.80	30650.44	48409.46	14862
LAKE HURON		NOAA WEATHER BUOY 45003	45-17.90	82-46.50	30624.27	48589.26	14864
LAKE HURON		POINT AUX BARQUES NO 1	44-02.60	82-45.40	30808.87	49191.17	14862
LAKE HURON		POINT AUX BARQUES LIGHT	44-01.40	82-42.60	30792.06	49202.85	14862
LAKE HURON		HARBOR BEACH NO 3	43-50.90	82-38.40	30792.90	49289.19	14862
LAKE HURON		HARBOR BEACH NO 4	43-51.00	82-38.40	30792.60	49288.40	14862
LAKE HURON		HARBOR BEACH NO 2	43-50.70	82-38.10	30791.27	49290.95	14862
LAKE HURON		HARBOR BEACH NO 1	43-50.60	82-38.10	30791.58	49291.75	14862
LAKE HURON		HARBOR BEACH LIGHT	43-50.70	82-37.90	30789.79	49291.07	14862
LAKE HURON		PORT SANILAC LIGHT	43-25.80	82-32.40	30827.44	49489.31	14862
LAKE HURON		PORT SANILAC BRKWTR NO 2	43-25.80	82-32.10	30825.09	49489.40	14862
LAKE HURON		LEXINGTON BRKWTR NO 2	43-16.00	82-31.40	30852.73	49565.63	14862
LAKE HURON		FORT GRATIOT LIGHT	43-00.40	82-25.30	30858.47	49685.71	14862
LAKE HURON		NOAA WEATHER BUOY 45008	44-17.10	82-25.20	30622.58	49092.10	14860
LAKE HURON		LAKE HURON CUT NO 7	43-03.60	82-25.10	30845.51	49661.45	14862
LAKE HURON		POINT EDWARD RANGE	43-00.20	82-25.00	30856.75	49687.23	14862
LAKE HURON		LAKE HURON CUT NO 2	43-00.55	82-24.90	30854.70	49684.59	2260
LAKE HURON		CASEVILLE HARBOR BRKWTR	43-56.90	82-17.10	30616.46	49254.71	14863
LAKE HURON		PROVIDENCE BAY	45-39.05	82-16.53	30401.04	48469.69	2266
LAKE HURON		PROVIDENCE BAY WHARF	45-39.50	82-16.10	30397.76	48466.92	2266
LAKE HURON		SOUTH BAYMOUTH LIGHT JS2	45-32.23	82-01.61	30319.53	48541.70	2273
LAKE HURON		INKSTER ROCK LIGHT JS5	45-33.12	82-01.10	30315.17	48535.74	2273
LAKE HURON		KETTLE POINT	43-13.03	82-00.93	30618.76	49592.11	2260
LAKE HURON		KETTLE POINT LIGHT	43-13.00	82-00.90	30618.62	49592.34	14862

PASSES

BODY OF WATER	PROV/STATE	NAME	LAT	LON	TD#1	TD#2	CHART
LAKE HURON		McGRAW POINT LIGHT JS8	45-33.33	82-00.85	30313.35	48534.51	2273
LAKE HURON		COVE ISLAND LIGHT "T"	45-19.90	81-50.93	30269.14	48647.00	2235
LAKE HURON		WEST SISTER SHOAL J2	45-22.08	81-47.87	30246.88	48634.48	2235
LAKE HURON		O'BRIEN PATCH "TC"	45-20.43	81-46.52	30240.39	48648.28	2235
LAKE HURON		LUCAS ISLAND NO J3	45-23.50	81-46.52	30236.57	48625.60	2235
LAKE HURON		GRAND BEND	43-18.80	81-46.00	30480.73	49550.88	2260
LAKE HURON		LUCAS ISLAND	45-23.60	81-45.98	30233.04	48625.51	2235
LAKE HURON		POINT CLARK LIGHT	44-04.40	81-45.50	30361.53	49215.03	14862
LAKE HURON		SOUTHWEST BANK NO TA1	45-14.03	81-45.44	30241.67	48696.85	2274
LAKE HURON		POINT CLARK	44-04.37	81-45.43	30361.07	49215.29	2261
LAKE HURON		GODERICH N BRKWTR	43-44.79	81-44.25	30397.42	49360.77	2291
LAKE HURON		GODERICH S BRKWTR	43-44.72	81-44.18	30397.05	49361.30	2291
LAKE HURON		COVE ISLAND	45-19.62	81-44.12	30226.12	48657.05	2235
LAKE HURON		COVE ISLAND LIGHT	45-19.60	81-44.10	30226.01	48657.22	14862
LAKE HURON		CAPE HURD	45-13.26	81-43.75	30231.75	48704.42	2274
LAKE HURON		GODERICH MAIN LIGHT	43-44.60	81-43.60	30392.84	49362.38	14862
LAKE HURON		GODERICH MAIN	43-44.53	81-43.48	30392.08	49362.93	2291
LAKE HURON		BAYFIELD WHARF	43-34.20	81-42.50	30410.50	49439.02	2260
LAKE HURON		STOKES BAY ENTR "VK"	44-56.75	81-28.10	30149.21	48841.39	2292
LAKE HURON		LOGIE ROCK LIGHT VC2	44-27.68	81-27.02	30182.23	49054.42	2291
LAKE HURON		LYAL ISLAND	44-57.05	81-25.12	30128.79	48841.89	2200
LAKE HURON		PORT ELGIN S BRKWTR	44-24.36	81-24.37	30168.35	49080.30	2291
LAKE HURON		PORT ELGIN N BRKWTR	44-26.71	81-24.35	30164.54	49063.22	2291
LAKE HURON		CHANTRY ISLAND	44-29.40	81-24.15	30159.00	49043.79	2292
LAKE HURON		SOUTHAMPTON LIGHT VJ2	44-30.55	81-23.68	30153.92	49035.75	2292
LAKE HURON		McNAB POINT	44-28.38	81-23.60	30156.60	49051.57	2292
LAKE HURON		SAUGEEN RIVER LIGHT VJ3	44-30.18	81-23.31	30151.82	49038.68	2292
LAKE HURON		KETTLE POINT REEF NO V4	43-14.38	72-03.07	28006.56	49413.33	2260
LAKE MICHIGAN		BRAYS POINT LIGHT	44-00.40	88-31.20	32792.34	48494.10	14916
LAKE MICHIGAN		STOCKBRIDGE HARB ENTR NO 2	44-04.00	88-20.10	32731.46	48496.01	14916
LAKE MICHIGAN		COLUMBIA PARK LIGHT	43-54.80	88-19.80	32781.88	48596.29	14916
LAKE MICHIGAN		COLUMBIA PARK RANGE	43-54.90	88-19.70	32780.94	48595.56	14916
LAKE MICHIGAN		CEDAR LOCK NO 36	44-16.80	88-19.50	32659.10	48361.11	14916
LAKE MICHIGAN		HIGH CLIFF STATE PARK	44-10.00	88-17.70	32689.31	48440.30	14916
LAKE MICHIGAN		CONCRETE STRUCTURE "A"	44-16.90	88-16.10	32645.67	48372.39	14916
LAKE MICHIGAN		RAPIDE CROCHE NO 24	44-19.00	88-11.00	32614.75	48368.40	14916
LAKE MICHIGAN		RAPIDE CROCHE NO 22	43-19.10	88-10.90	32957.57	49016.91	14916
LAKE MICHIGAN		SUAMICO RIVER ENTR NO 3	44-37.80	88-00.50	32474.46	48207.85	14910
LAKE MICHIGAN		SUAMICO RIVER OBSTR BUOY	44-37.80	88-00.40	32474.06	48208.20	14910
LAKE MICHIGAN		PROCTOR & GAMBLE CO LIGHT	44-30.90	88-00.30	32509.49	48280.76	14918
LAKE MICHIGAN		GREEN BAY HARB DISPOSAL	44-32.30	88-00.20	32501.78	48266.43	14918
LAKE MICHIGAN		SUAMICO BUOY NO 1	44-37.80	88-00.20	32473.27	48208.91	14910
LAKE MICHIGAN		GREEN BAY HARB ENTR NO 29	44-33.50	87-59.60	32493.13	48255.98	14918
LAKE MICHIGAN		GREEN BAY HARBOR RANGE	44-34.80	87-59.00	32483.98	48244.50	14918

PASSES

BODY OF WATER	PROV/STATE	NAME	LAT	LON	TD#1	TD#2	CHART
LAKE MICHIGAN		GREEN BAY HARBOR RANGE	44-35.40	87-57.50	32474.85	48243.52	14918
LAKE MICHIGAN		GREEN BAY HARB ENTR LIGHT	44-39.20	87-54.10	32441.54	48215.87	14918
LAKE MICHIGAN		PENSAUKEE HARBOR LIGHT	44-49.30	87-53.90	32389.57	48112.02	14910
LAKE MICHIGAN		MILWAUKEE METRO BUOY "C"	43-01.50	87-53.80	32999.16	49267.91	14924
LAKE MICHIGAN		MILWAUKEE MUNI PIER RANGE	43-02.20	87-53.70	32994.34	49260.49	14924
LAKE MICHIGAN		MILWAUKEE TANKER PIER	43-00.90	87-53.40	33001.33	49275.82	14924
LAKE MICHIGAN		MILWAUKEE S DISP NO 2	42-60.00	87-53.00	33005.39	49287.05	14924
LAKE MICHIGAN		MILWAUKEE BRKWTR LIGHT	43-01.60	87-52.90	32994.85	49269.68	14924
LAKE MICHIGAN		MILWAUKEE N ENTR NO 1	43-02.60	87-52.80	32988.13	49258.95	14924
LAKE MICHIGAN		MILWAUKEE N ENTR NO 2	43-02.70	87-52.80	32987.50	49257.84	14924
LAKE MICHIGAN		MILWAUKEE S ENTR NO 2	43-00.50	87-52.60	33000.58	49282.79	14924
LAKE MICHIGAN		MILWAUKEE S ENTR LIGHT	43-00.50	87-52.60	33000.58	49282.79	14924
LAKE MICHIGAN		MILWAUKEE N POINT LIGHT	43-03.90	87-52.30	32977.88	49246.20	14924
LAKE MICHIGAN		McKINLEY PARK OBSTR BUOY	43-03.50	87-51.90	32978.76	49251.88	14924
LAKE MICHIGAN		PORT WASHINGTON BRKWTR	43-23.20	87-51.80	32856.68	49035.74	14904
LAKE MICHIGAN		PORT WASHINGTON NO 2	43-23.20	87-51.80	32856.68	49035.74	14904
LAKE MICHIGAN		PORT WASHINGTON W BRKWTR	43-23.30	87-51.80	32856.07	49034.65	14904
LAKE MICHIGAN		GREAT LAKES HARB RANGE	42-18.60	87-49.90	33265.71	49758.31	14905
LAKE MICHIGAN		MILWAUKEE S POINT NO 1	42-59.40	87-49.80	32996.00	49303.82	14904
LAKE MICHIGAN		OAK CREEK RANGE LIGHT	42-50.90	87-49.40	33048.77	49399.21	14904
LAKE MICHIGAN		OCONTO HARBOR S PIER LIGHT	44-53.90	87-49.30	32348.01	48081.05	14910
LAKE MICHIGAN		WAUKEGAN S HARB MARINA NO 1	42-21.40	87-49.30	33244.14	49728.73	14904
LAKE MICHIGAN		WAUKEGAN S HARB MARINA NO 2	42-21.40	87-49.20	33243.73	49729.04	14904
LAKE MICHIGAN		SYDNEY McLOUTH WRECK "WR2"	44-49.80	87-48.80	32366.33	48124.88	14910
LAKE MICHIGAN		LAKE FOREST BRKWTR LIGHT	42-14.00	87-48.70	33292.46	49813.70	14905
LAKE MICHIGAN		LAKE FOREST JETTY LIGHT	42-14.00	87-48.70	33292.46	49813.70	14905
LAKE MICHIGAN		RUNAWAY BAY ENTR N LIGHT	42-29.60	87-48.50	33185.36	49639.33	14904
LAKE MICHIGAN		KENOSHA LIGHT	42-35.40	87-48.50	33146.60	49574.52	14904
LAKE MICHIGAN		WAUKEGAN SHOALS NO 1	42-21.40	87-47.70	33237.57	49733.64	14904
LAKE MICHIGAN		WAUKEGAN SHOALS NO 3	42-21.40	87-47.70	33237.57	49733.64	14904
LAKE MICHIGAN		KENOSHA HARBOR ENTR NO 1	42-35.30	87-47.70	33143.95	49578.09	14904
LAKE MICHIGAN		ZION INTAKE BUOY "A"	42-26.70	87-47.40	33200.36	49675.15	14904
LAKE MICHIGAN		HIGHLAND PARK BRKWTR LIGHT	42-11.40	87-47.20	33304.33	49847.54	14905
LAKE MICHIGAN		DREDGE 906 WRECK BUOY "WR"	42-58.20	87-47.00	32991.93	49325.83	14904
LAKE MICHIGAN		RACINE YACHT CLUB S BRKWTR	42-44.10	87-46.60	33081.29	49483.41	14925
LAKE MICHIGAN		RACINE LAUNCH BASIN ENTR	42-43.70	87-46.60	33083.91	49487.86	14925
LAKE MICHIGAN		RACINE E ENTR LIGHT	42-44.00	87-46.20	33080.27	49485.75	14925
LAKE MICHIGAN		RACINE REEF BUOY NO 1	42-43.50	87-46.00	33082.70	49491.92	14925
LAKE MICHIGAN		WIND POINT LIGHT	42-46.90	87-45.50	33058.39	49455.66	14904
LAKE MICHIGAN		RACINE REEF LIGHT	42-43.60	87-44.20	33074.45	49496.28	14925
LAKE MICHIGAN		WIND POINT N SHOAL NO 14	42-47.60	87-43.60	33045.78	49453.66	14904
LAKE MICHIGAN		SHEBOYGAN RADIO BEACON	43-45.00	87-42.20	32687.25	48829.87	14922
LAKE MICHIGAN		SHEBOYGAN GEN STATION	43-45.00	87-41.50	32684.25	48832.10	14903
LAKE MICHIGAN		SHEBOYGAN BRKWTR LIGHT	43-45.00	87-41.50	32684.25	48832.10	14922

PASSES

BODY OF WATER	PROV/STATE	NAME	LAT	LON	TD#1	TD#2	CHART
LAKE MICHIGAN		GROSSEPOINT LIGHT	42-04.00	87-41.00	33330.23	49949.30	14927
LAKE MICHIGAN		WILMETTE HARBOR PIER LIGHT	42-04.80	87-40.80	33323.75	49940.86	14905
LAKE MICHIGAN		EVANSTON LAUNCH FACILITY	42-02.70	87-40.30	33336.43	49965.98	14927
LAKE MICHIGAN		EVANSTON BRKWTR LIGHT	42-02.70	87-40.30	33336.43	49965.98	14927
LAKE MICHIGAN		HOLLYWOOD AVE BRKWTR LIGHT	41-59.20	87-40.00	33359.97	50006.35	14927
LAKE MICHIGAN		FARWELL AVE BRKWTR LIGHT	42-00.40	87-39.40	33348.89	49994.52	14927
LAKE MICHIGAN		MANITOWOC PIER LIGHT	44-05.50	87-39.10	32558.20	48620.63	14922
LAKE MICHIGAN		SILVER CREEK WEST LIGHT	44-04.80	87-39.00	32561.63	48628.39	14922
LAKE MICHIGAN		MANITOWOC HARB JUNCTION	44-05.60	87-39.00	32557.22	48619.89	14922
LAKE MICHIGAN		WILMETTE WRECK BUOY "WR2"	42-05.70	87-39.00	33309.72	49935.88	14905
LAKE MICHIGAN		SILVER CREEK LIGHT	44-03.30	87-39.00	32569.93	48644.32	14922
LAKE MICHIGAN		ICE BOOM EAST LIGHT	44-05.70	87-38.90	32556.24	48619.15	14922
LAKE MICHIGAN		SILVER CREEK EAST LIGHT	44-04.70	87-38.90	32561.76	48629.77	14922
LAKE MICHIGAN		MANITOWOC HARBOR NO 5	44-05.70	87-38.90	32556.24	48619.15	14922
LAKE MICHIGAN		ICE BOOM WEST LIGHT	44-05.60	87-38.90	32556.79	48620.21	14922
LAKE MICHIGAN		MANITOWOC HARBOR NO 4	44-06.70	87-38.90	32550.73	48608.55	14922
LAKE MICHIGAN		MANITOWOC HARBOR BUOY	44-05.60	87-38.80	32556.36	48620.54	14922
LAKE MICHIGAN		MANITOWOC HARBOR NO 2	44-05.60	87-38.80	32556.36	48620.54	14922
LAKE MICHIGAN		FOSTER AVE PIER LIGHT	41-58.80	87-38.80	33357.69	50014.30	14927
LAKE MICHIGAN		MANITOWOC BRKWTR LIGHT	44-05.60	87-38.60	32555.50	48621.19	14922
LAKE MICHIGAN		BELMONT HARBOR LIGHT	41-56.50	87-38.00	33370.66	50042.54	14927
LAKE MICHIGAN		MONTROSE BRKWTR LIGHT	41-57.80	87-37.90	33360.95	50028.13	14927
LAKE MICHIGAN		DIVERSEY HARB ENTR S BRKWTR	41-55.90	87-37.90	33374.52	50049.60	14928
LAKE MICHIGAN		DIVERSEY YACHT HARB RANGE	41-55.90	87-37.80	33374.09	50049.88	14928
LAKE MICHIGAN		DIVERSEY HARB ENTR N BRKWTR	41-55.90	87-37.80	33374.09	50049.88	14928
LAKE MICHIGAN		MARINETTE LITTLE RIVER	45-02.70	87-37.50	32256.35	48032.88	14909
LAKE MICHIGAN		CHICAGO N AVE JETTY LIGHT	41-54.90	87-37.20	33378.66	50062.87	14928
LAKE MICHIGAN		OAK STREET BRKWTR NO 3	41-54.00	87-37.00	33384.25	50073.60	14928
LAKE MICHIGAN		OAK STREET BRKWTR NO 2	41-54.00	87-37.00	33384.25	50073.60	14928
LAKE MICHIGAN		BURNHAM PARK HARBOR LIGHT	41-51.10	87-36.60	33403.40	50107.52	14928
LAKE MICHIGAN		CHICAGO HARB S BRKWTR NO 1	41-52.50	87-36.60	33393.30	50091.68	14928
LAKE MICHIGAN		OAK STREET BRKWTR LIGHT	41-54.20	87-36.40	33380.22	50073.00	14928
LAKE MICHIGAN		NORTHERLY ISLAND BUOY "ZA"	41-51.10	87-36.40	33402.54	50108.07	14928
LAKE MICHIGAN		31st STREET JETTY LIGHT	41-50.40	87-36.30	33407.15	50116.27	14928
LAKE MICHIGAN		MENOMINEE INNER BRKWTR	45-06.40	87-36.00	32232.37	48000.82	14917
LAKE MICHIGAN		WILSON AVENUE INTAKE CRIB	41-58.00	87-35.50	33349.09	50032.56	14927
LAKE MICHIGAN		GROSSEPOINT BUOY NO 4	42-08.30	87-35.40	33275.83	49916.75	14905
LAKE MICHIGAN		CHICAGO HARBOR LIGHT	41-53.30	87-35.40	33382.33	50085.94	14928
LAKE MICHIGAN		MENOMINEE PIER LIGHT	45-05.70	87-35.10	32231.93	48010.98	14917
LAKE MICHIGAN		PESHTIGO REEF LIGHT	44-57.40	87-34.80	32270.63	48095.85	14910
LAKE MICHIGAN		MENOMINEE ENTRANCE NO 2	45-06.00	87-34.70	32228.83	48009.36	14917
LAKE MICHIGAN		CHICAGO HARBOR NO 1	41-53.20	87-34.30	33378.21	50090.07	14928
LAKE MICHIGAN		WILLIAM E DEVER CRIB	41-55.00	87-34.30	33365.29	50069.73	14928
LAKE MICHIGAN		TWO RIVERS N PIER LIGHT	44-08.60	87-33.60	32517.37	48605.48	14903

P A S S E S

BODY OF WATER	PROV/STATE	NAME	LAT	LON	TD#1	TD#2	CHART
LAKE MICHIGAN		FOUR-MILE CRIB LIGHT	41-52.40	87-32.70	33376.90	50103.43	14927
LAKE MICHIGAN		CALUMET RIVER ENTR LIGHT	41-43.90	87-31.80	33434.61	50202.04	14929
LAKE MICHIGAN		NORTH SLIP SOUTH LIGHT	41-44.30	87-31.80	33431.68	50197.50	14929
LAKE MICHIGAN		NORTH SLIP RANGE	41-44.40	87-31.80	33430.95	50196.37	14929
LAKE MICHIGAN		TWO CREEKS INTAKE LIGHT	44-17.10	87-31.60	32462.66	48522.41	14903
LAKE MICHIGAN		CALUMET HARBOR DISP AREA	41-43.90	87-31.40	33432.82	50203.08	14929
LAKE MICHIGAN		INDIANA HARBOR NO 7	41-43.80	87-31.00	33431.76	50205.26	14929
LAKE MICHIGAN		INDIANA HARBOR LIGHT	41-44.30	87-30.50	33425.85	50200.89	14929
LAKE MICHIGAN		NIPSO OBSTR BUOY "B"	41-41.90	87-30.50	33443.43	50228.09	14929
LAKE MICHIGAN		RAWLEY POINT LIGHT	44-12.70	87-30.50	32481.51	48572.14	14903
LAKE MICHIGAN		NIPSO OBSTR BUOY "A"	41-42.00	87-30.40	33442.25	50227.21	14929
LAKE MICHIGAN		KEWAUNEE N PIER NO 4	44-37.60	87-29.80	32347.76	48315.10	14903
LAKE MICHIGAN		HAMMOND INTAKE CRIB	41-42.20	87-29.80	33438.07	50226.50	14929
LAKE MICHIGAN		INDIANA HARBOR NO 1	41-43.10	87-29.70	33431.02	50216.55	14929
LAKE MICHIGAN		KEWAUNEE PIER LIGHT	44-27.50	87-29.60	32398.96	48420.28	14903
LAKE MICHIGAN		INDIANA HARB BRKWTR	41-43.50	87-29.60	33427.63	50212.28	14929
LAKE MICHIGAN		GREEN ISLAND LIGHT	45-03.30	87-29.50	32219.69	48054.41	14909
LAKE MICHIGAN		WHIHALA BEACH BRKWTR	41-41.10	87-29.30	33443.88	50240.24	14929
LAKE MICHIGAN		AMERICAN OIL BUOY "A"	41-40.80	87-28.30	33441.53	50246.18	14929
LAKE MICHIGAN		EAST SHOAL NO 4	41-44.00	87-28.20	33417.60	50210.18	14929
LAKE MICHIGAN		NORTHEAST SHOAL NO 2	41-45.60	87-28.00	33404.99	50192.58	14929
LAKE MICHIGAN		KEWAUNEE SHOAL LIGHT	44-27.10	87-27.90	32393.60	48429.93	14903
LAKE MICHIGAN		INDIANA HARBOR NO 2	41-41.10	87-26.80	33432.42	50246.52	14929
LAKE MICHIGAN		INDIANA HARBOR NO 1	41-41.20	87-26.60	33430.76	50245.89	14929
LAKE MICHIGAN		INDIANA HARBOR E BRKWTR	41-40.90	87-26.50	33432.50	50249.54	14929
LAKE MICHIGAN		SHERWOOD POINT LIGHT	44-53.60	87-26.00	32251.50	48164.16	14910
LAKE MICHIGAN		ALGOMA PIER LIGHT	44-36.40	87-25.80	32336.43	48340.55	14910
LAKE MICHIGAN		INDIANA HARBOR S BULKHEAD	41-39.60	87-25.20	33436.02	50267.44	14929
LAKE MICHIGAN		BUFFINGTON HARBOR RANGE	41-38.50	87-25.10	33443.67	50280.14	14927
LAKE MICHIGAN		STURGEON BAY ENTR LIGHT	44-52.10	87-24.90	32254.06	48183.03	14919
LAKE MICHIGAN		BUFFINGTON BRKWTR LIGHT	41-38.80	87-24.60	33439.11	50277.95	14927
LAKE MICHIGAN		STURGEON BAY NO 27	44-51.60	87-24.30	32253.90	48190.10	14919
LAKE MICHIGAN		OUTER SHOAL WRECK BUOY	41-46.00	87-23.70	33382.07	50198.68	14929
LAKE MICHIGAN		STURGEON BAY NO 21	44-50.40	87-23.30	32255.42	48205.59	14919
LAKE MICHIGAN		STURGEON BAY LEAD LIGHT	44-49.90	87-23.00	32256.57	48211.65	14919
LAKE MICHIGAN		MONUMENT SHOAL NO 5	44-59.60	87-22.80	32208.57	48114.27	14910
LAKE MICHIGAN		CEDAR RIVER PIER LIGHT	45-24.40	87-21.10	32086.02	47873.93	14909
LAKE MICHIGAN		INDIANA SHOAL NO 2	41-43.40	87-20.90	33387.72	50234.68	14927
LAKE MICHIGAN		STURGEON BAY RANGE	44-48.70	87-20.10	32249.73	48233.35	14919
LAKE MICHIGAN		STURGEON BAY NO 7	44-48.30	87-19.80	32250.38	48238.39	14919
LAKE MICHIGAN		CHAMBERS ISLAND NO 3	45-14.40	87-19.80	32125.96	47976.75	14909
LAKE MICHIGAN		STURGEON BAY NO 12	44-48.80	87-19.80	32247.92	48233.32	14919
LAKE MICHIGAN		GARY E PIER LIGHT	47-37.50	87-19.40	31576.89	46704.63	14927
LAKE MICHIGAN		GARY BRKWTR LIGHT	41-37.80	87-19.20	33420.65	50301.80	14927

PASSES

BODY OF WATER	PROV/STATE	NAME	LAT	LON	TD#1	TD#2	CHART
LAKE MICHIGAN		STURGEON BAY NO 6	44-47.60	87-18.80	32249.41	48248.76	14919
LAKE MICHIGAN		STURGEON BAY LIGHT	44-47.70	87-18.80	32248.91	48247.74	14919
LAKE MICHIGAN		STURGEON BAY N PIER LIGHT	44-47.50	87-18.60	32249.02	48250.42	14919
LAKE MICHIGAN		CANAL SHOAL BUOY NO 1	44-45.30	87-18.30	32258.57	48273.76	14919
LAKE MICHIGAN		STURGEON BAY NO 2	44-46.70	87-17.40	32247.64	48262.43	14919
LAKE MICHIGAN		GARY BULKHEAD LIGHT	41-37.40	87-17.30	33414.27	50310.52	14927
LAKE MICHIGAN		LILLA HAMMAR LIGHT NO 1	45-04.10	87-16.80	32160.94	48089.15	14909
LAKE MICHIGAN		EAGLE BLUFF LIGHT	45-10.10	87-14.20	32121.44	48038.12	14909
LAKE MICHIGAN		HORSESHOE ISLAND LIGHT	45-10.60	87-12.70	32112.53	48038.16	14909
LAKE MICHIGAN		WHITEFISH POINT NO 10	44-51.90	87-11.40	32195.36	48229.14	14910
LAKE MICHIGAN		BURNS W JETTY NO 1	41-38.00	87-10.70	33376.54	50317.54	14905
LAKE MICHIGAN		WHALEBACK SHOAL NO 4	45-22.80	87-10.10	32045.62	47927.05	14909
LAKE MICHIGAN		JACKSONPORT SHOAL NO 2	44-57.90	87-09.20	32156.61	48175.96	14910
LAKE MICHIGAN		BAILYTOWN WATER INTAKE	41-38.90	87-07.40	33352.76	50313.88	14905
LAKE MICHIGAN		BAILEYS HARBOR DIR LIGHT	45-04.20	87-07.20	32117.86	48119.63	14909
LAKE MICHIGAN		SEVASTOPOL BRKWTR NO 1	45-04.20	87-07.20	32117.86	48119.63	14910
LAKE MICHIGAN		BAILEYS HARBOR NO 1	45-02.80	87-06.90	32123.08	48134.51	14909
LAKE MICHIGAN		NOAA WEATHER BUOY 45007	42-41.90	87-06.40	32910.70	49617.50	14901
LAKE MICHIGAN		FORD RIVER SHOAL NO 5	45-38.50	87-03.40	31947.81	47798.41	14908
LAKE MICHIGAN		CANA ISLAND LIGHT	45-05.30	87-02.80	32092.89	48122.91	14909
LAKE MICHIGAN		ESCANABA LIGHT	45-44.70	87-02.20	31916.44	47743.70	14915
LAKE MICHIGAN		ROWLEY BAY NO 3	45-11.60	87-01.60	32058.43	48064.67	14909
LAKE MICHIGAN		SQUAW POINT LIGHT	45-49.90	87-00.20	31886.20	47701.64	14915
LAKE MICHIGAN		SAUNDERS POINT LIGHT	45-50.90	87-00.10	31881.66	47692.63	14915
LAKE MICHIGAN		MINNEAPOLIS SHOAL LIGHT	45-34.90	86-59.90	31947.80	47844.54	14908
LAKE MICHIGAN		DRISCO SHOAL NO 2	45-33.30	86-57.80	31945.35	47866.84	14908
LAKE MICHIGAN		PLUM ISLAND RANGE	45-18.20	86-57.20	32008.75	48014.39	14909
LAKE MICHIGAN		PLUM ISLAND BUOY NO 1	45-19.30	86-56.80	32002.04	48005.01	14909
LAKE MICHIGAN		WAVERLY SHOAL NO 5	45-17.10	86-56.70	32011.41	48026.71	14909
LAKE MICHIGAN		DETROIT HARBOR NO 11	45-20.50	86-56.20	31993.99	47995.30	14909
LAKE MICHIGAN		BOYER BLUFF LIGHT	45-25.20	86-56.20	31973.29	47949.86	14909
LAKE MICHIGAN		DETROIT HARBOR ENTR LIGHT	45-19.90	86-56.20	31996.66	48001.12	14909
LAKE MICHIGAN		NINE-FOOT SHOAL NO 3	45-16.50	86-56.10	32011.37	48034.49	14909
LAKE MICHIGAN		PLUM I OUTER SHOAL NO 1	45-13.90	86-55.80	32021.70	48060.81	14909
LAKE MICHIGAN		SHIPYARD I MARINA NO 2	45-20.50	86-55.70	31991.73	47996.92	14909
LAKE MICHIGAN		PILOT ISLAND LIGHT	45-17.10	86-55.20	32004.60	48031.55	14909
LAKE MICHIGAN		MICHIGAN CITY E PIER LIGHT	41-43.70	86-54.70	33248.92	50282.87	14905
LAKE MICHIGAN		NORTH DOCK LIGHT	45-20.40	86-54.60	31987.19	48001.45	14909
LAKE MICHIGAN		PORT DES MORTS ENTR	45-13.80	86-53.90	32013.48	48067.85	14909
LAKE MICHIGAN		JACKSON HARBOR LIGHT	45-24.20	86-51.00	31954.13	47976.36	14909
LAKE MICHIGAN		JACKSON HARBOR NO 1	45-25.20	86-50.90	31949.32	47967.06	14909
LAKE MICHIGAN		POTTAWATOMIE LIGHT	45-25.70	86-49.70	31941.69	47966.13	14909
LAKE MICHIGAN		FISHERMAN SHOAL NO 6	45-21.60	86-46.20	31943.51	48016.71	14909
LAKE MICHIGAN		ST MARTIN ISLAND LIGHT	45-30.20	86-45.50	31903.17	47936.60	14909

PASSES

BODY OF WATER	PROV/STATE	NAME	LAT	LON	TD#1	TD#2	CHART
LAKE MICHIGAN		NEW BUFFALO HARBOR NO 1	41-48.10	86-45.00	33162.09	50249.41	14905
LAKE MICHIGAN		ROCK ISLAND BUOY "RI"	45-26.10	86-44.50	31916.16	47978.93	14909
LAKE MICHIGAN		LITTLE GULL ISLAND NO 2	45-29.50	86-42.90	31894.24	47951.58	14909
LAKE MICHIGAN		FAIRPORT FIVE-FOOT NO 2	45-37.80	86-40.60	31848.82	47880.40	14908
LAKE MICHIGAN		FAYETTE BUOY NO 2	45-43.30	86-40.30	31824.84	47829.80	14908
LAKE MICHIGAN		POVERTY ISLAND LIGHT	45-31.30	86-40.00	31873.26	47943.71	14909
LAKE MICHIGAN		SUMMER ISLAND LIGHT	45-34.30	86-37.70	31850.06	47922.63	14909
LAKE MICHIGAN		LITTLE SABLE LIGHT	43-39.00	86-32.40	32386.58	49087.08	14907
LAKE MICHIGAN		NOVADOC WRECK BUOY "WR1"	43-41.90	86-31.10	32363.43	49060.02	14907
LAKE MICHIGAN		BIG SABLE LIGHT	44-03.50	86-30.90	32245.09	48837.96	14907
LAKE MICHIGAN		ST JOSEPH N PIER LIGHT	42-07.00	86-29.70	32941.21	50066.76	14930
LAKE MICHIGAN		LUDINGTON N BRKWTR	43-57.20	86-28.20	32264.47	48909.19	14937
LAKE MICHIGAN		LUDINGTON INNER S BRKWTR	43-57.20	86-27.70	32261.83	48910.41	14937
LAKE MICHIGAN		LUDINGTON INNER N BRKWTR	43-57.30	86-27.70	32261.29	48909.39	14937
LAKE MICHIGAN		LUDINGTON SOUTH PIER	43-57.10	86-27.60	32261.83	48911.68	14937
LAKE MICHIGAN		PENTWATER S PIER NO 4	43-46.90	86-26.60	32311.76	49018.91	14907
LAKE MICHIGAN		WHITE LAKE NO 5	43-22.50	86-25.20	32441.69	49275.11	14935
LAKE MICHIGAN		WHITE LAKE NO 7	43-22.50	86-25.00	32440.58	49275.54	14935
LAKE MICHIGAN		WHITE LAKE NO 9	43-22.60	86-23.80	32433.35	49277.04	14935
LAKE MICHIGAN		WHITE LAKE NO 11	43-23.10	86-22.70	32424.35	49274.15	14935
LAKE MICHIGAN		WHITE LAKE PIER NO 1	43-23.50	86-22.00	32418.15	49271.46	14935
LAKE MICHIGAN		WHITE LAKE NO 12	43-23.50	86-22.00	32418.15	49271.46	14935
LAKE MICHIGAN		WHITE LAKE NO 15	43-23.20	86-21.30	32415.97	49276.04	14935
LAKE MICHIGAN		WHITE LAKE NO 14	43-24.10	86-21.30	32410.79	49266.69	14935
LAKE MICHIGAN		MUSKEGON S BRKWTR LIGHT	43-13.50	86-20.80	32469.60	49378.07	14934
LAKE MICHIGAN		MANISTEE HARB N PIER LIGHT	44-15.10	86-20.80	32132.19	48745.61	14938
LAKE MICHIGAN		MUSKEGON N PIER LIGHT	43-13.70	86-20.50	32466.72	49376.58	14934
LAKE MICHIGAN		MUSKEGON N PIER LIGHT	43-14.00	86-19.70	32460.43	49375.04	14934
LAKE MICHIGAN		HARBOUR TOWNE ENTR NO 2	43-13.70	86-19.50	32461.05	49378.56	14934
LAKE MICHIGAN		HARBOUR TOWNE ENTR NO 1	43-13.70	86-19.50	32461.05	49378.56	14934
LAKE MICHIGAN		YACHT CLUB DOCK LIGHT	43-13.20	86-19.30	32462.85	49384.16	14934
LAKE MICHIGAN		MANISTEE LAKE NO 1	44-15.20	86-18.60	32120.09	48750.10	14938
LAKE MICHIGAN		LAKE MUSKEGON RANGE	43-13.00	86-18.50	32459.48	49387.82	14934
LAKE MICHIGAN		MANISTEE LAKE NO 3	44-14.90	86-18.30	32120.03	48753.86	14938
LAKE MICHIGAN		MANISTEE LAKE NO 5	44-14.60	86-18.20	32121.02	48757.12	14938
LAKE MICHIGAN		MANISTEE LAKE NO 9	44-14.20	86-18.10	32122.51	48761.39	14938
LAKE MICHIGAN		BEAR LAKE ENTR W LIGHT	43-14.40	86-17.90	32447.86	49374.42	14934
LAKE MICHIGAN		SOUTH HAVEN S PIER LIGHT	42-24.10	86-17.30	32753.52	49902.50	14906
LAKE MICHIGAN		WIGGINS POINT SHOAL NO 4	45-50.50	86-16.90	31688.24	47837.64	14908
LAKE MICHIGAN		PORTAGE LAKE N PIER	44-21.60	86-16.10	32074.86	48692.22	14907
LAKE MICHIGAN		ARCADIA ENTR BUOY	44-29.00	86-15.40	32034.89	48620.33	14907
LAKE MICHIGAN		GRAND HAVEN S PIER ENTR	43-03.50	86-15.40	32497.84	49492.63	14933
LAKE MICHIGAN		POINT BETSIE LIGHT	44-41.50	86-15.30	31974.71	48497.19	14907
LAKE MICHIGAN		FRANKFORT N BRKWTR	44-37.80	86-15.00	31990.60	48534.37	14907

PASSES

BODY OF WATER	PROV/STATE	NAME	LAT	LON	TD#1	TD#2	CHART
LAKE MICHIGAN		CONSUMER POWER CO NO 1	43-15.10	86-14.90	32426.62	49372.99	14934
LAKE MICHIGAN		MANISTIQUE LIGHT	45-56.70	86-14.80	31654.77	47787.90	14908
LAKE MICHIGAN		LAKE BETSIE ANCH "A"	44-37.80	86-13.90	31984.90	48537.24	14907
LAKE MICHIGAN		SS CITY OF MILWAUKEE LIGHT	44-37.80	86-13.90	31984.90	48537.24	14907
LAKE MICHIGAN		LAKE BETSIE ANCH "E"	44-37.70	86-13.70	31984.34	48538.75	14907
LAKE MICHIGAN		PORT SHELDON BRKWTR S LIGHT	42-54.00	86-13.10	32541.45	49595.68	14906
LAKE MICHIGAN		SAUGATUCK HARB OLD NO 1	42-39.90	86-13.00	32627.44	49743.04	14906
LAKE MICHIGAN		SAUGATUCK S PIER LIGHT	42-40.60	86-12.90	32622.49	49735.87	14906
LAKE MICHIGAN		LAKE MACATAWA LIGHT NO 1	42-46.30	86-12.00	32581.86	49677.77	14932
LAKE MICHIGAN		LAKE MACATAWA SKI JUMP	42-46.60	86-11.90	32579.41	49674.79	14932
LAKE MICHIGAN		S MANITOU I SHOAL NO 8	44-57.50	86-10.10	31874.91	48355.44	14912
LAKE MICHIGAN		SLEEPING BEAR BUOY NO 7	44-54.10	86-10.00	31889.62	48388.54	14912
LAKE MICHIGAN		LAKE MACATAWA NO 5	42-46.70	86-09.90	32566.74	49676.90	14932
LAKE MICHIGAN		LAKE MACATAWA NO 9	42-46.70	86-09.70	32565.53	49677.21	14932
LAKE MICHIGAN		LAKE MACATAWA NO 11	42-46.70	86-09.00	32561.29	49678.30	14932
LAKE MICHIGAN		LAKE MACATAWA NO 13	42-46.90	86-08.40	32556.44	49677.15	14932
LAKE MICHIGAN		LAKE MACATAWA NO 15	42-47.20	86-07.70	32550.35	49675.11	14932
LAKE MICHIGAN		LAKE MACATAWA NO 17	42-47.40	86-07.30	32546.70	49673.66	14932
LAKE MICHIGAN		LAKE MACATAWA NO 19	42-47.60	86-07.20	32544.88	49671.73	14932
LAKE MICHIGAN		GRAND RIVER WARNING BEACON	43-01.00	86-01.20	32428.29	49542.85	14933
LAKE MICHIGAN		BOULDER REEF NO 1	45-35.20	85-59.00	31661.61	48031.37	14911
LAKE MICHIGAN		N MANITOU SHOAL LIGHT	45-01.20	85-57.40	31793.37	48354.00	14912
LAKE MICHIGAN		SEUL CHOIX POINT LIGHT	45-55.30	85-54.70	31564.65	47861.76	14911
LAKE MICHIGAN		PORT INLAND NO 2	45-54.30	85-52.70	31558.64	47876.62	14911
LAKE MICHIGAN		PORT INLAND LIGHT	45-57.80	85-52.60	31545.46	47845.71	14911
LAKE MICHIGAN		PORT INLAND INNER RANGE	45-58.20	85-52.20	31542.09	47843.34	14911
LAKE MICHIGAN		PORT INLAND OUTER RANGE	45-58.10	85-52.20	31542.45	47844.23	14911
LAKE MICHIGAN		GULL ISLAND LIGHT	45-42.70	85-50.60	31591.34	47987.07	14911
LAKE MICHIGAN		NOAA WEATHER BUOY 45002	45-01.40	85-45.80	31731.68	48382.16	14912
LAKE MICHIGAN		LELAND HARBOR NO 1	45-01.40	85-45.80	31731.68	48382.16	14912
LAKE MICHIGAN		TOTAL PETRO LIGHT	44-47.00	85-38.20	31752.49	48537.13	14913
LAKE MICHIGAN		ZEPHYR CO LIGHT	44-47.00	85-38.20	31752.49	48537.13	14913
LAKE MICHIGAN		TRAVERSE CITY BRKWTR	44-47.30	85-37.90	31749.54	48535.00	14913
LAKE MICHIGAN		TRAVERSE BEACH BUOY NO 8	44-47.60	85-37.40	31745.50	48533.34	14913
LAKE MICHIGAN		NORTHPORT NORTH LIGHT	45-07.80	85-36.70	31656.77	48345.21	14913
LAKE MICHIGAN		BOARDMAN RIVER W PIER	44-45.90	85-36.60	31748.48	48551.35	14913
LAKE MICHIGAN		LANSING SHOALS LIGHT	45-54.20	85-33.70	31465.68	47932.20	14911
LAKE MICHIGAN		GRAND TRAVERSE LIGHT	45-12.60	85-33.00	31617.72	48310.02	14913
LAKE MICHIGAN		ST JAMES LIGHT	45-44.60	85-30.50	31483.62	48026.16	14911
LAKE MICHIGAN		MISSION POINT LIGHT	45-01.10	85-30.40	31650.29	48423.16	14913
LAKE MICHIGAN		CUTTY SARK HARB N BRKWTR	44-46.10	85-30.40	31713.31	48563.86	14913
LAKE MICHIGAN		CUTTY SARK HARB S BRKWTR	44-46.00	85-30.40	31713.74	48564.80	14913
LAKE MICHIGAN		ST JAMES HARBOR NO 1	45-44.00	85-29.80	31482.21	48033.40	14911
LAKE MICHIGAN		GARDEN ISLAND SHOAL NO 1	45-52.10	85-28.50	31446.99	47965.19	14911

P A S S E S

BODY OF WATER	PROV/STATE	NAME	LAT	LON	TD#1	TD#2	CHART
LAKE MICHIGAN		NAUBINWAY ISLAND LIGHT	46-04.50	85-26.70	31395.75	47861.86	14911
LAKE MICHIGAN		GR TRAVERSE SHOAL NO 3	45-08.10	85-26.40	31600.25	48367.95	14913
LAKE MICHIGAN		ELK RAPIDS BRKWTR	44-54.20	85-25.00	31649.13	48500.30	14913
LAKE MICHIGAN		HOG ISLAND REEF "HI"	45-43.50	85-20.40	31435.83	48063.02	14911
LAKE MICHIGAN		CHARLEVOIX NORTH PIER	45-19.30	85-15.90	31500.09	48291.18	14942
LAKE MICHIGAN		CHARLEVOIX SOUTH PIER	45-19.00	85-15.90	31501.22	48293.89	14942
LAKE MICHIGAN		BELVEDERE CLUB DOCK "A"	45-18.90	85-15.00	31496.72	48296.99	14942
LAKE MICHIGAN		NW MARINE YACHT BASIN NO 3	45-18.40	85-14.70	31496.98	48302.24	14942
LAKE MICHIGAN		PINE RIVER NO 3	45-18.90	85-14.70	31495.10	48297.71	14942
LAKE MICHIGAN		SIMMONS REEF NO 2	45-54.20	85-12.90	31360.65	47989.04	14911
LAKE MICHIGAN		DAHLIA SHOAL NO 9	45-37.50	85-12.80	31417.32	48135.88	14911
LAKE MICHIGAN		ILE AUX GALETS NO 7	45-40.90	85-11.00	31395.99	48110.43	14911
LAKE MICHIGAN		HATERS DOCK NO 6	45-14.30	85-10.70	31490.63	48348.94	14942
LAKE MICHIGAN		ILE AUX GALETS LIGHT	45-40.60	85-10.30	31393.35	48114.85	14911
LAKE MICHIGAN		GRAYS REEF LIGHT	45-46.00	85-09.20	31369.09	48070.25	14911
LAKE MICHIGAN		GRAYS REEF NO 3	45-45.80	85-08.40	31365.60	48074.06	14911
LAKE MICHIGAN		ILE AUX GALETS NO 2	45-41.00	85-08.10	31380.39	48116.93	14911
LAKE MICHIGAN		WHITE SHOAL LIGHT	45-50.50	85-08.10	31348.25	48033.84	14911
LAKE MICHIGAN		NEW SHOAL NO 3	45-49.20	85-08.00	31352.07	48045.41	14911
LAKE MICHIGAN		NEW SHOAL NO 1	45-49.20	85-04.80	31335.41	48053.66	14911
LAKE MICHIGAN		HARBORAGE MARINA ENTR NO 2	45-12.60	85-01.40	31445.56	48385.87	14942
LAKE MICHIGAN		STATE STREET PIER	45-25.80	84-59.50	31387.25	48272.31	14913
LAKE MICHIGAN		HARBOR SPRINGS ANCH "B"	45-25.60	84-59.10	31385.77	48275.03	14913
LAKE MICHIGAN		FORD PARK CHANNEL NO 1	45-25.60	84-58.90	31384.68	48275.50	14913
LAKE MICHIGAN		LITTLE TRAVERS LIGHT	45-25.20	84-58.60	31384.45	48279.75	14913
LAKE MICHIGAN		HARBOR SPRINGS ANCH "A"	45-25.60	84-58.40	31381.95	48276.68	14913
LAKE MICHIGAN		ST HELENA LIGHT	45-51.30	84-51.80	31260.38	48068.39	14881
LAKE MICHIGAN		PORT INLAND RADIO BEACON	45-58.10	82-52.60	30582.26	48265.91	14911
LAKE MICHIGAN		HOLLAND HARBOR N BRKWTR	42-46.40	82-12.90	30806.92	49789.06	14932
LAKE ONTARIO		BURLINGTON BAY BEACON	43-18.10	79-47.40	16335.87	58819.66	14802
LAKE ONTARIO		GIBRALTAR PT BEACON	43-36.80	79-23.20	16251.73	59035.20	14802
LAKE ONTARIO		PORT WELLER OUTER LIGHT	43-14.70	79-13.10	16362.96	59103.05	14822
LAKE ONTARIO		PORT WELLER BUOY	43-14.70	79-13.10	16362.96	59103.05	14822
LAKE ONTARIO		PORT WELLER ENTR RANGE	43-13.40	79-13.00	16368.94	59102.57	14822
LAKE ONTARIO		PORT WELLER E BRKWTR	43-14.70	79-12.90	16363.03	59104.73	14822
LAKE ONTARIO		FORT MISSISSAUGA LIGHT	43-15.70	79-04.60	16361.13	59175.29	14816
LAKE ONTARIO		NIAGARA BAR NO 2	43-19.00	79-04.30	16345.23	59180.19	14816
LAKE ONTARIO		FORT NIAGARA LIGHT	43-15.70	79-03.60	16361.45	59183.67	14816
LAKE ONTARIO		LEWISTON SKI JUMP LIGHT	43-10.40	79-03.00	16386.41	59184.03	14816
LAKE ONTARIO		WILSON HARBOR NO 2	43-19.20	78-50.20	16347.61	59297.28	14806
LAKE ONTARIO		OLCOTT LIGHT	43-20.40	78-43.20	16342.56	59355.32	14806
LAKE ONTARIO		WAUTOMA SHOAL NO 1	43-21.10	77-48.20	16332.65	59793.44	14805
LAKE ONTARIO		BRADDOCK POINT LIGHT	43-20.00	77-46.00	16339.36	59811.98	14805
LAKE ONTARIO		PROCTOR POINT LIGHT	43-58.30	77-44.80	16039.20	59729.13	14802

PASSES

BODY OF WATER	PROV/STATE	NAME	LAT	LON	TD#1	TD#2	CHART
LAKE ONTARIO		BRADDOCK BAY ENTR LIGHT	43-18.70	77-42.60	16346.88	59839.95	14805
LAKE ONTARIO		MAIN DUCK ISLAND NO 7	43-50.00	77-40.50	16098.87	59778.42	14802
LAKE ONTARIO		RIGNEY BLUFF BUOY	43-16.50	77-38.10	16360.37	59877.93	14815
LAKE ONTARIO		ROCHESTER HARBOR LIGHT	43-15.80	77-36.00	16364.27	59895.04	14815
LAKE ONTARIO		SCOTCH BONNET I LIGHT	43-53.90	77-32.50	16050.60	59815.55	14802
LAKE ONTARIO		IRONDEQUOIT BAY NO 2	43-14.30	77-32.00	16372.91	59927.93	14804
LAKE ONTARIO		PULTNEYVILLE INNER RANGE	43-17.00	77-11.10	16324.57	60063.12	14804
LAKE ONTARIO		PULTNEYVILLE YACHT CLUB	43-17.10	77-11.10	16323.69	60062.77	14804
LAKE ONTARIO		PULTNEYVILLE RANGE	43-16.90	77-11.00	16325.26	60064.08	14804
LAKE ONTARIO		PULTNEYVILLE NO 1	43-17.10	77-10.90	16323.30	60064.00	14804
LAKE ONTARIO		POINT PETRE LIGHT	43-50.30	77-09.20	16021.87	59954.90	14802
LAKE ONTARIO		SODUS OUTER LIGHT	43-16.60	76-58.50	16297.56	60135.73	14814
LAKE ONTARIO		SODUS LIGHT NO 6	43-16.20	76-58.40	16301.00	60137.83	14814
LAKE ONTARIO		DAVENPORT MARINE DOCK	43-13.50	76-55.60	16317.78	60162.70	14814
LAKE ONTARIO		PRINCE EDWARD PT LIGHT	43-56.20	76-51.50	15907.66	60014.76	14802
LAKE ONTARIO		TRAVERSE SHOAL "K14"	43-54.20	76-50.80	15923.06	60025.12	14802
LAKE ONTARIO		PORT BAY ENTR NO 1	43-18.30	76-50.20	16253.62	60167.91	14804
LAKE ONTARIO		FALSE DUCKS BANK "K12"	43-56.00	76-49.00	15899.67	60025.82	14802
LAKE ONTARIO		FALSE DUCKS LIGHT	43-56.90	76-47.90	15887.12	60026.93	14802
LAKE ONTARIO		WILLIAM SHOAL "K11"	43-55.50	76-47.80	15899.39	60032.54	14802
LAKE ONTARIO		FAIR HAVEN BRKWTR NO 2	43-21.00	76-42.50	16196.50	60187.41	14803
LAKE ONTARIO		MAIN DUCK ISLAND LIGHT	43-55.90	76-38.30	15855.53	60067.26	14802
LAKE ONTARIO		THE DUCKS BUOY NO 10	43-51.60	76-35.70	15882.82	60092.53	14802
LAKE ONTARIO		NINE MILE POINT LIGHT	44-09.10	76-33.40	15714.92	60036.19	14802
LAKE ONTARIO		PIGEON ISLAND LIGHT	44-04.00	76-33.00	15758.58	60056.04	14802
LAKE ONTARIO		S CHARITY SHOAL NO 9	43-59.00	76-32.50	15801.12	60076.02	14802
LAKE ONTARIO		WEST CHANNEL NO 2	43-28.00	76-31.20	16077.21	60196.76	14813
LAKE ONTARIO		WEST PIER HEAD LIGHT	43-28.40	76-31.00	16072.52	60195.83	14813
LAKE ONTARIO		E CHARITY SHOAL LIGHT	44-02.20	76-28.80	15754.91	60076.59	14802
LAKE ONTARIO		GALLOO ISLAND SHOAL NO 3	43-53.60	76-28.30	15829.70	60109.64	14811
LAKE ONTARIO		E CHARITY SHOAL BUOY	44-01.30	76-27.70	15757.67	60083.41	14802
LAKE ONTARIO		ALLEN OTTY SHOAL NO 2	44-03.80	76-27.00	15731.96	60076.61	14802
LAKE ONTARIO		GALLOO ISLAND LIGHT	43-53.30	76-26.70	15824.54	60115.75	14811
LAKE ONTARIO		RESEARCH BUOY "B"	43-31.30	76-19.40	15983.44	60215.70	14803
LAKE ONTARIO		STONEY POINT LIGHT	43-50.30	76-17.90	15806.04	60152.06	14811
LAKE ONTARIO		MEXICO PT B LAUNCH NO 2	43-31.60	76-15.50	15958.23	60223.46	14803
LAKE ONTARIO		MEXICO PT B LAUNCH NO 1	43-31.50	76-15.40	15958.52	60224.02	14803
LAKE ONTARIO		MEXICO POINT LIGHT	43-31.40	76-15.30	15958.81	60224.58	14803
LAKE ONTARIO		PORT ONTARIO NO 2	43-34.60	76-12.30	15913.13	60220.19	14803
LAKE ONTARIO		HENDERSON HARB ANCH "A"	43-51.10	76-12.20	15767.86	60164.00	14811
LAKE ONTARIO		SACKETS HARBOR LIGHT	43-56.60	76-08.70	15700.16	60153.72	14811
LAKE ONTARIO		NAVY PT MARINE DOCK 4	43-57.00	76-07.30	15688.81	60155.77	14811
LAKE ONTARIO		CHERRY ISLAND LIGHT	43-59.20	76-04.70	15655.00	60154.54	14811
LAKE ONTARIO		BLACK RIVER ENTR NO 1	43-59.20	76-04.70	15655.00	60154.54	14811

PASSES

BODY OF WATER	PROV/STATE	NAME	LAT	LON	TD#1	TD#2	CHART
LAKE ONTARIO		BLACK RIVER ENTR NO 2	43-59.10	76-04.60	15655.30	60155.12	14811
LAKE ST CLAIR	MICH/ONT	PECHE ISLAND RANGE	42-21.60	82-54.40	31249.22	49984.79	14853
LAKE ST CLAIR	MICH/ONT	GROSSE POINT PIER	42-23.00	82-54.00	31240.02	49974.04	14853
LAKE ST CLAIR	MICH/ONT	CLUB DOCK LIGHT	42-23.00	82-53.80	31238.36	49973.97	14853
LAKE ST CLAIR	MICH/ONT	CRESCENT SAIL YACHT CLUB	42-24.10	82-53.10	31227.94	49965.40	14853
LAKE ST CLAIR	MICH/ONT	GROSSE POINT LIGHT 2	42-24.30	82-53.00	31226.28	49963.86	14853
LAKE ST CLAIR	MICH/ONT	MILLER MEMORIAL LIGHT	42-27.80	82-52.80	31210.08	49937.19	14853
LAKE ST CLAIR	MICH/ONT	MARTIN DRAIN LIGHTS	42-28.90	82-52.80	31205.54	49928.80	14853
LAKE ST CLAIR	MICH/ONT	MARATHON OIL CO LIGHT	42-28.30	82-52.80	31208.02	49933.38	14853
LAKE ST CLAIR	MICH/ONT	MILK RIVER DRAIN NO 1	42-27.60	82-52.30	31206.77	49938.57	14853
LAKE ST CLAIR	MICH/ONT	GAUKLER SHOAL JUNCTION	42-28.50	82-51.50	31196.43	49931.50	14853
LAKE ST CLAIR	MICH/ONT	SELFRIDGE FIELD RANGE	42-36.90	82-49.20	31143.17	49866.82	14853
LAKE ST CLAIR	MICH/ONT	SELFRIDGE FIELD NW BRKWTR	42-36.70	82-48.90	31141.51	49868.30	14853
LAKE ST CLAIR	MICH/ONT	SELFRIDGE FIELD C BRKWTR	42-36.70	82-48.80	31140.69	49868.28	14853
LAKE ST CLAIR	MICH/ONT	SELFRIDGE FIELD SE BRKWTR	42-36.60	82-48.80	31141.09	49869.04	14853
LAKE ST CLAIR	MICH/ONT	BLUE LAGOON RANGE	42-36.10	82-47.70	31134.05	49872.66	14853
LAKE ST CLAIR	MICH/ONT	SALT RIVER RANGE	42-39.30	82-47.10	31116.28	49848.08	14853
LAKE ST CLAIR	MICH/ONT	SALT RIVER ENTR W LIGHT	42-39.20	82-47.10	31116.67	49848.84	14853
LAKE ST CLAIR	MICH/ONT	SALT RIVER ENTR E LIGHT	42-39.20	82-47.10	31116.67	49848.84	14853
LAKE ST CLAIR	MICH/ONT	HURON POINTE YACHT CLUB	42-35.60	82-46.90	31129.48	49876.32	14853
LAKE ST CLAIR	MICH/ONT	LOTTIVUE ENTR NO 2	42-39.30	82-45.70	31104.78	49847.86	14853
LAKE ST CLAIR	MICH/ONT	LAKE ST CLAIR LIGHT	42-27.90	82-45.30	31147.40	49934.28	14853
LAKE ST CLAIR	MICH/ONT	POINT HURON BUOY NO 1	42-33.20	82-44.90	31122.62	49894.13	14853
LAKE ST CLAIR	MICH/ONT	CLINTON RIVER NO 3	42-35.60	82-44.70	31111.32	49875.87	14853
LAKE ST CLAIR	MICH/ONT	ST CLAIR FLATS OLD CHANN	42-32.30	82-41.60	31098.88	49900.12	14852
LAKE ST CLAIR	MICH/ONT	N CHANNEL ENTR NO 1	42-32.30	82-41.60	31098.88	49900.12	14852
LAKE ST CLAIR	MICH/ONT	ST CLAIR CUTOFF CHANN	42-31.00	82-41.40	31102.44	49909.84	14853
LAKE ST CLAIR	MICH/ONT	ST CLAIR FLATS NO 1	42-31.20	82-41.30	31100.80	49908.31	14852
LAKE ST CLAIR	MICH/ONT	ST CLAIR FLATS NO 2	42-31.10	82-41.20	31100.37	49909.04	14852
LAKE ST CLAIR	MICH/ONT	ST CLAIR PIER X32/1	42-30.90	82-41.10	31100.34	49910.52	14853
LAKE ST CLAIR	MICH/ONT	ST CLAIR FLATS NO 5	42-31.60	82-40.80	31095.04	49905.17	14852
LAKE ST CLAIR	MICH/ONT	OLD CLUB BRKWTR	42-32.40	82-40.00	31085.20	49898.95	14852
LAKE ST CLAIR	MICH/ONT	BELVEDERE BOAT CLUB	42-38.00	82-39.50	31058.86	49856.63	14852
LAKE ST CLAIR	MICH/ONT	ST CLAIR FLATS CANAL	42-33.00	82-39.10	31075.33	49894.21	14853
LAKE ST CLAIR	MICH/ONT	ST CLAIR PIER	42-31.80	82-39.00	31079.28	49903.19	14853
LAKE ST CLAIR	MICH/ONT	FAIR HAVEN ENTR NO 1	42-39.90	82-39.00	31047.28	49842.16	14853
LAKE ST CLAIR	MICH/ONT	N CHANNEL YACHT CLUB NO 2	42-37.70	82-38.90	31055.09	49858.77	14852
LAKE ST CLAIR	MICH/ONT	MAYBURY HIGHWAY NO 10	42-33.30	82-38.30	31067.50	49891.75	14852
LAKE ST CLAIR	MICH/ONT	ST CLAIR LIGHT X44	42-32.20	82-37.40	31064.39	49899.76	14853
LAKE ST CLAIR	MICH/ONT	ST CLAIR LIGHT X43	42-32.20	82-37.40	31064.39	49899.76	14853
LAKE ST CLAIR	MICH/ONT	ST CLAIR LIGHT X47	42-32.80	82-36.40	31053.69	49895.01	14853
LAKE ST CLAIR	MICH/ONT	ST CLAIR LIGHT X48	42-32.70	82-36.20	31052.42	49895.70	14853
LAKE ST CLAIR	MICH/ONT	ST CLAIR LIGHT X50	42-32.90	82-35.50	31045.80	49894.02	14853
LAKE ST CLAIR	MICH/ONT	ST CLAIR BUOY A14	42-33.10	82-35.20	31042.52	49892.45	14853

PASSES

BODY OF WATER	PROV/STATE	NAME	LAT	LON	TD#1	TD#2	CHART
LAKE ST CLAIR	MICH/ONT	SQUIRREL ISLAND RANGE	42-33.20	82-35.00	31040.46	49891.64	14853
LAKE ST CLAIR	MICH/ONT	S CHANNEL NO A20	42-33.80	82-34.80	31036.44	49887.11	14852
LAKE ST CLAIR	MICH/ONT	HARSENS ISLAND RANGE	42-34.30	82-34.60	31032.80	49883.33	14852
LAKE ST CLAIR	MICH/ONT	SQUIRREL ISLAND NO A26	42-35.50	82-32.70	31012.32	49873.89	14852
LAKE ST CLAIR	MICH/ONT	WALPOLE ISLAND NO A30	42-36.20	82-31.50	30999.62	49868.38	14852
LAKE ST CLAIR	MICH/ONT	RUSSELL ISLAND LIGHT	42-36.60	82-31.40	30997.24	49865.38	14852
LAKE ST CLAIR	MICH/ONT	WALPOLE ISLAND LIGHT	42-36.30	82-31.40	30998.41	49867.62	14852
LAKE ST CLAIR	MICH/ONT	RUSSELL ISLAND NO 33	42-36.80	82-31.30	30995.63	49863.87	14852
LAKE ST CLAIR	MICH/ONT	WALPOLE ISLAND NO A32	42-36.70	82-31.10	30994.36	49864.56	14852
LAKE ST CLAIR	MICH/ONT	WALPOLE I FERRY BRKWTR	42-36.90	82-30.90	30991.93	49863.03	14852
LAKE ST CLAIR	MICH/ONT	WALPOLE ISLAND NO A34	42-37.30	82-30.70	30988.72	49860.00	14852
LAKE ST CLAIR	MICH/ONT	WILLOW POINT LIGHT	42-38.60	82-30.70	30983.70	49850.30	14852
LAKE ST CLAIR	MICH/ONT	MARINE CITY BUOY "A"	42-42.10	82-30.00	30964.49	49823.99	14852
LAKE ST CLAIR	MICH/ONT	COURTRIGHT LIGHT	42-48.40	82-28.70	30930.02	49776.51	14852
LAKE ST CLAIR	MICH/ONT	STOKES POINT WHARF	42-44.10	82-28.70	30946.17	49808.79	14852
LAKE ST CLAIR	MICH/ONT	HARTS LANDING NO A46	42-47.30	82-28.30	30930.84	49784.73	14852
LAKE ST CLAIR	MICH/ONT	RECORS POINT DOCK	42-45.50	82-28.30	30937.59	49798.24	14852
LAKE ST CLAIR	MICH/ONT	MOORETOWN LIGHT	42-50.40	82-28.10	30917.65	49761.39	14852
LAKE ST CLAIR	MICH/ONT	STAG ISLAND SHOAL	42-51.90	82-28.00	30911.29	49750.07	14852
LAKE ST CLAIR	MICH/ONT	KESSEL POINT LIGHT	42-45.10	82-27.90	30935.80	49801.18	14852
LAKE ST CLAIR	MICH/ONT	BOWERS CREEK DIR LIGHT	42-46.20	82-27.80	30930.84	49792.92	14852
LAKE ST CLAIR	MICH/ONT	STAG ISLAND BUOY "AM3"	42-53.80	82-27.60	30901.04	49735.70	14852
LAKE ST CLAIR	MICH/ONT	DUPONT LIGHTED BUOY	42-54.00	82-27.50	30899.49	49734.18	14852
LAKE ST CLAIR	MICH/ONT	CORUNNA RANGE LIGHT	42-53.20	82-27.40	30901.61	49740.21	14852
LAKE ST CLAIR	MICH/ONT	ST CLAIR RIVER NO A60	42-55.20	82-27.30	30893.47	49725.10	14852
LAKE ST CLAIR	MICH/ONT	BLUE WATER BRIDGE NO A64	42-59.80	82-25.40	30861.43	49690.26	14852
LAKE ST CLAIR	MICH/ONT	POINT EDWARD NO A62	42-59.70	82-25.40	30861.79	49691.02	14852
LAKE ST CLAIR	MICH/ONT	PORT HURON CAR FERRY	42-57.90	82-25.40	30868.24	49704.64	14852
LAKE ST CLAIR	MICH/ONT	ST CLAIR/BLACK RIV LIGHT	42-58.40	82-25.20	30864.81	49700.85	14852
LAKE SUPERIOR		ALLQUES ORE DOCK NO 3	46-42.10	96-01.10	33003.57	45123.09	14975
LAKE SUPERIOR		WARROAD RANGE LIGHT	48-54.00	95-18.40	32515.48	44024.31	14999
LAKE SUPERIOR		BIRCH POINT LIGHT	49-09.90	95-14.00	32459.60	44003.49	14999
LAKE SUPERIOR		BUFFALO POINT LIGHT	48-60.00	95-13.90	32489.89	44010.38	14999
LAKE SUPERIOR		BUFFALO POINT MARINA ENTR	49-02.50	95-13.70	32481.86	44007.78	14999
LAKE SUPERIOR		GULL ROCK LIGHT	48-59.00	95-03.60	32476.71	44004.36	14999
LAKE SUPERIOR		PENASSE ISLAND LIGHT	49-22.30	94-57.50	32395.42	44009.71	14999
LAKE SUPERIOR		FLAG ISLAND BUOY NO 2	49-20.10	94-53.20	32395.05	44012.09	14999
LAKE SUPERIOR		OAK ISLAND LIGHT NO 1	49-18.20	94-53.10	32400.66	44010.94	14999
LAKE SUPERIOR		BOUCHA ISLAND LIGHT	49-17.70	94-49.20	32395.77	44014.54	14999
LAKE SUPERIOR		OAK POINT LIGHT	48-52.60	94-41.20	32460.27	44005.21	14999
LAKE SUPERIOR		WHEELER POINT NO 4	48-50.40	94-41.20	32467.21	44003.88	14999
LAKE SUPERIOR		BURTON ISLAND LIGHT	48-57.00	94-37.00	32439.46	44014.18	14999
LAKE SUPERIOR		ROCKY POINT LIGHT	48-57.50	94-32.30	32429.98	44023.87	14999
LAKE SUPERIOR		PORT FRANCES RANIER BRIDGE	48-36.80	93-22.00	32369.70	44442.05	14998

PASSES

BODY OF WATER	PROV/STATE	NAME	LAT	LON	TD#1	TD#2	CHART
LAKE SUPERIOR		ROBERTS ISLAND LIGHT NO 2	48-37.20	93-16.00	32356.83	44475.86	14998
LAKE SUPERIOR		CANOE CHANNEL NO 4	48-37.00	93-15.60	32356.71	44479.36	14998
LAKE SUPERIOR		FRANSEN ISLAND LIGHT NO 2	48-37.70	93-15.10	32353.45	44478.51	14998
LAKE SUPERIOR		CANOE CHANNEL NO 17	48-36.40	93-10.90	32349.52	44510.79	14998
LAKE SUPERIOR		BALD ROCK LIGHT NO 8	48-37.40	93-10.90	32346.24	44505.23	14998
LAKE SUPERIOR		BIG AMERICAN ISLAND NO 19	48-36.30	93-09.00	32346.12	44522.69	14998
LAKE SUPERIOR		CAPSTAN REEF LIGHT	48-38.10	93-03.00	32328.38	44548.36	14998
LAKE SUPERIOR		MACKENZIE ISLAND LIGHT	48-36.50	92-56.40	32320.42	44596.30	14998
LAKE SUPERIOR		BRULE ISLAND LIGHT	48-35.80	92-54.00	32317.88	44614.44	14998
LAKE SUPERIOR		CANOE CHANNEL NO 34	48-33.60	92-53.40	32323.90	44630.79	14998
LAKE SUPERIOR		HITCHCOCK ISLAND NO 36	48-32.60	92-53.20	32326.80	44637.94	14997
LAKE SUPERIOR		HITCHCOCK BAY BUOY NO 35	48-33.20	92-53.10	32324.61	44634.94	14998
LAKE SUPERIOR		GULL ROCKS LIGHT	48-33.80	92-46.60	32309.41	44669.60	14997
LAKE SUPERIOR		NAMAKAN ISLAND "N"	48-27.10	92-42.80	32323.79	44733.38	14993
LAKE SUPERIOR		GAGNON POINT NO 6	28-28.60	92-42.70	33764.13	50726.86	14994
LAKE SUPERIOR		SQUAW NARROWS NO 4	48-29.00	92-42.10	32316.04	44725.32	14994
LAKE SUPERIOR		FOX ISLAND NO 4	48-26.20	92-40.00	32321.01	44755.56	14993
LAKE SUPERIOR		SURVEYORS ISLAND NO 43	48-31.10	92-37.70	32299.95	44737.91	14997
LAKE SUPERIOR		ST LOUIS BAY S RANGE	46-44.10	92-08.70	32623.65	45830.89	14975
LAKE SUPERIOR		ST LOUIS BAY RANGE	46-44.20	92-08.70	32623.27	45829.88	14975
LAKE SUPERIOR		ST LOUIS BAY NO 14	46-44.10	92-08.70	32623.65	45830.89	14975
LAKE SUPERIOR		ST LOUIS RIVER RANGE	46-43.20	92-08.60	32626.95	45840.55	14975
LAKE SUPERIOR		HOWARDS BAY BUOY NO 2	46-44.70	92-06.10	32615.79	45837.10	14975
LAKE SUPERIOR		DULUTH HARBOR BASIN NO 5	46-46.10	92-05.80	32609.70	45824.31	14975
LAKE SUPERIOR		HARBOR COVE MARINA NO 1	46-46.30	92-05.60	32608.49	45823.23	14975
LAKE SUPERIOR		DULUTH HARB S BRKWTR	46-46.70	92-05.50	32606.72	45819.65	14975
LAKE SUPERIOR		DULUTH HARB S BRKWTR	46-46.80	92-05.30	32605.91	45819.60	14975
LAKE SUPERIOR		DULUTH HARB N PIER LIGHT	46-46.90	92-05.30	32605.52	45818.58	14975
LAKE SUPERIOR		BARKERS ISLAND MARINA NO 5	46-42.80	92-02.90	32616.35	45871.58	14975
LAKE SUPERIOR		SUPERIOR FRONT CHAN RANGE	46-42.40	92-02.10	32616.19	45879.45	14975
LAKE SUPERIOR		SUPERIOR HARB BASIN NO 1	46-42.30	92-01.00	32614.21	45885.68	14975
LAKE SUPERIOR		SUPERIOR INNER S PIER	46-42.40	92-00.80	32613.39	45885.61	14975
LAKE SUPERIOR		SUPERIOR INNER N PIER	46-42.50	92-00.80	32613.00	45884.59	14975
LAKE SUPERIOR		SUPERIOR N BRKWTR LIGHT	46-42.70	92-00.50	32611.56	45883.99	14975
LAKE SUPERIOR		SUPERIOR ENTRY S BRKWTR	46-42.60	92-00.40	32611.74	45885.48	14975
LAKE SUPERIOR		KNIFE RIVER HARB ENTR	46-56.60	91-46.70	32527.06	45812.10	14966
LAKE SUPERIOR		TWO HARBORS W BRKWTR	47-00.70	91-40.50	32497.19	45802.90	14975
LAKE SUPERIOR		TWO HARBORS E BRKWTR	47-00.60	91-40.30	32497.12	45804.86	14966
LAKE SUPERIOR		TWO HARBORS LIGHT	47-00.80	91-39.70	32494.97	45805.91	14966
LAKE SUPERIOR		TACONITE HARB E PIER NO 2	47-31.60	91-34.40	32367.18	45548.66	14967
LAKE SUPERIOR		PORT WING E PIER LIGHT	46-47.60	91-23.20	32507.78	46015.25	14966
LAKE SUPERIOR		PELLET ISLAND LIGHT	47-16.20	91-15.90	32380.13	45781.80	14967
LAKE SUPERIOR		SILVER BAY RADIO BEACON	47-16.90	91-15.90	32377.50	45775.46	14967
LAKE SUPERIOR		BEAVER ISLAND LEADING LIGHT	47-16.80	91-15.90	32377.88	45776.37	14967

PASSES

BODY OF WATER	PROV/STATE	NAME	LAT	LON	TD#1	TD#2	CHART
LAKE SUPERIOR		BEAVER ISLAND LIGHT	47-16.80	91-15.50	32376.90	45778.41	14967
LAKE SUPERIOR		SILVER BAY LIGHT	47-17.20	91-15.50	32375.40	45774.79	14967
LAKE SUPERIOR		CORNUCOPIA E PIER LIGHT	46-51.60	91-06.30	32451.11	46059.38	14966
LAKE SUPERIOR		SAND ISLAND LIGHT	47-00.20	90-56.20	32392.28	46028.05	14973
LAKE SUPERIOR		TACONITE HARBOR RADIO BEACON	47-31.30	90-55.40	32273.04	45754.41	14967
LAKE SUPERIOR		6th AVE BREAKWALL LIGHT	46-39.90	90-54.30	32467.50	46230.54	14974
LAKE SUPERIOR		WASHBURN HARB S BRKWTR	46-40.00	90-53.30	32464.56	46234.39	14974
LAKE SUPERIOR		ASHLAND HARB BRKWTR S LIGHT	46-36.00	90-53.20	32480.41	46273.79	14974
LAKE SUPERIOR		ASHLAND HARB B RAMP NO 2	46-36.00	90-53.20	32480.41	46273.79	14974
LAKE SUPERIOR		ASHLAND HARB B RAMP NO 1	46-36.00	90-53.20	32480.41	46273.79	14974
LAKE SUPERIOR		CENTRAL AVE DOCK LIGHT	46-40.10	90-53.00	32463.40	46234.86	14974
LAKE SUPERIOR		ASHLAND HARBOR BRKWTR	46-37.70	90-52.20	32471.01	46262.02	14974
LAKE SUPERIOR		BAYFIELD HARB N BRKWTR	46-48.60	90-48.70	32418.53	46174.11	14973
LAKE SUPERIOR		BAYFIELD HARB S BRKWTR	46-48.50	90-48.70	32418.93	46175.06	14973
LAKE SUPERIOR		CHEQUAMEGON POINT LIGHT	46-43.70	90-48.60	32437.74	46221.41	14973
LAKE SUPERIOR		RASPBERRY ISLAND LIGHT	46-58.30	90-48.30	32379.45	46084.82	14973
LAKE SUPERIOR		LA POINTE HARBOR W BRKWTR	46-46.70	90-47.40	32422.71	46198.52	14973
LAKE SUPERIOR		MADELINE ISLAND BRKWTR	46-46.70	90-47.40	32422.71	46198.52	14973
LAKE SUPERIOR		LA POINTE HARBOR E BRKWTR	46-46.70	90-47.30	32422.45	46199.02	14973
LAKE SUPERIOR		RED CLIFF BRKWTR LIGHT	46-51.20	90-47.30	32404.65	46156.30	14973
LAKE SUPERIOR		LA POINTE LIGHT	46-43.70	90-47.10	32433.88	46228.67	14973
LAKE SUPERIOR		DEVILS ISLAND LIGHT	47-04.80	90-43.70	32342.38	46047.67	14973
LAKE SUPERIOR		LITTLE MANITOU ISLAND LIGHT	46-57.70	90-41.10	32363.06	46125.85	14973
LAKE SUPERIOR		STOCKTON I HARB E ENTR	46-54.90	90-33.10	32352.84	46191.02	14973
LAKE SUPERIOR		MICHIGAN ISLAND LIGHT	46-52.30	90-29.80	32354.21	46231.27	14973
LAKE SUPERIOR		SAXON HARBOR W BRKWTR	46-33.80	90-26.30	32418.83	46423.59	14965
LAKE SUPERIOR		SAXON HARBOR E BRKWTR	46-33.80	90-26.30	32418.83	46423.59	14965
LAKE SUPERIOR		GULL ISLAND LIGHT	46-54.40	90-25.30	32333.80	46233.62	14973
LAKE SUPERIOR		OUTER ISLAND LIGHT	47-04.60	90-25.00	32293.38	46141.85	14973
LAKE SUPERIOR		GRAND MARINA NO 1	47-44.60	90-20.40	32132.95	45824.58	14967
LAKE SUPERIOR		GRAND MARINA LIGHT	47-44.70	90-20.30	32132.32	45824.29	14967
LAKE SUPERIOR		GRAND MARINA HARB NO 7	47-44.60	90-20.10	32132.13	45826.10	14967
LAKE SUPERIOR		BLACK RIVER EAST BRKWTR	46-40.10	90-02.90	32328.22	46474.22	14965
LAKE SUPERIOR		BLACK RIVER WEST BRKWTR	46-40.10	90-02.90	32328.22	46474.22	14965
LAKE SUPERIOR		NOAA WEATHER BUOY 45006	47-19.90	89-51.60	32141.77	46170.95	14967
LAKE SUPERIOR		GRAND PORTAGE PIER	47-57.60	89-40.90	31976.71	45921.77	14967
LAKE SUPERIOR		HAT POINT GONG NO 1	47-57.90	89-38.60	31969.00	45930.78	14967
LAKE SUPERIOR		GRAND PORTAGE BAY ENTR	47-57.20	89-38.30	31970.51	45937.46	14967
LAKE SUPERIOR		VICTORIA ISLAND	48-04.87	89-21.63	31895.60	45961.71	2311
LAKE SUPERIOR		ONOTONAGON BELL NO 1	46-53.00	89-20.00	32148.78	46555.32	14965
LAKE SUPERIOR		ONOTONAGON HARB W PIER	46-52.80	89-19.80	32148.93	46558.04	14965
LAKE SUPERIOR		ONOTONAGON HARB E PIER	46-52.70	89-19.70	32149.00	46559.39	14965
LAKE SUPERIOR		MINK POINT	48-08.37	89-18.15	31873.68	45953.20	2311
LAKE SUPERIOR		JARVIS ROCK LIGHT	48-06.20	89-17.60	31879.16	45971.38	14968

PASSES

BODY OF WATER	PROV/STATE	NAME	LAT	LON	TD#1	TD#2	CHART
LAKE SUPERIOR		JARVIS ROCK	48-06.17	89-17.58	31879.20	45971.69	2311
LAKE SUPERIOR		KAMINISTIQUIA RIVER	48-21.72	89-15.35	31822.29	45873.79	2314
LAKE SUPERIOR		MISSION RIVER ENTR A14	48-21.33	89-13.05	31816.68	45887.34	2314
LAKE SUPERIOR		MISSION RIVER ENTR BRKWTR	48-21.23	89-13.02	31816.90	45888.16	2314
LAKE SUPERIOR		KAMINISTIQUIA R ENTR S	48-23.53	89-12.83	31809.07	45873.55	2314
LAKE SUPERIOR		KAMINISTIQUIA R TERM ENTR D7	48-23.58	89-12.67	31808.43	45873.97	2314
LAKE SUPERIOR		THUNDER BAY LIGHT E8	48-26.02	89-12.65	31800.71	45857.78	2314
LAKE SUPERIOR		THUNDER BAY LIGHT E9	48-25.50	89-12.62	31802.25	45861.38	2314
LAKE SUPERIOR		THUNDER BAY S ENTR	48-24.73	89-12.35	31803.86	45867.79	2314
LAKE SUPERIOR		THUNDER BAY LIGHT E3	48-25.92	89-12.21	31799.71	45860.53	2314
LAKE SUPERIOR		MISSION CHANNEL ENTRANCE	48-21.00	89-12.07	31814.80	45894.21	2314
LAKE SUPERIOR		MISSION CHANNEL LIGHT A8	48-21.08	89-12.02	31814.39	45893.91	2314
LAKE SUPERIOR		KAMINISTIQUIA RIVER ENTR	48-23.88	89-12.00	31805.49	45875.13	2314
LAKE SUPERIOR		KAMINISTIQUIA RIVER ENTR D1	48-23.76	89-11.94	31805.69	45876.22	2314
LAKE SUPERIOR		THUNDER BAY CENTRAL ENTR	48-25.90	89-11.87	31798.76	45862.27	2314
LAKE SUPERIOR		THUNDER BAY MAIN	48-25.97	89-11.75	31798.19	45862.37	2314
LAKE SUPERIOR		OLD DUMPING GROUND SHOAL P2	48-23.13	89-10.69	31803.94	45886.36	2314
LAKE SUPERIOR		THUNDER BAY N ENTR	48-26.63	89-10.63	31792.78	45863.29	2314
LAKE SUPERIOR		MISSION CHANNEL APPR AA2	48-21.25	89-10.57	31809.52	45899.61	2314
LAKE SUPERIOR		PIE ISLAND	48-13.75	89-10.50	31833.23	45951.55	2311
LAKE SUPERIOR		WELCOME SHOAL LIGHT A6	48-20.57	89-08.55	31805.60	45913.77	2314
LAKE SUPERIOR		WELCOME ISLAND	48-22.17	89-07.23	31796.59	45909.14	2314
LAKE SUPERIOR		ANGUS ISLAND	48-14.15	89-00.43	31801.35	45996.06	2311
LAKE SUPERIOR		ANGUS ISLAND LIGHT	48-14.20	89-00.40	31801.10	45995.84	14968
LAKE SUPERIOR		HARE ISLAND REEF LIGHT A2	48-17.92	88-59.20	31785.63	45975.68	2311
LAKE SUPERIOR		THUNDER CAPE	48-18.12	88-56.32	31776.17	45987.70	2311
LAKE SUPERIOR		THUNDER CAPE LIGHT	48-18.10	88-56.30	31776.17	45987.93	14968
LAKE SUPERIOR		CHAMPLAIN POINT	49-46.00	88-53.50	31518.56	45500.86	NONE
LAKE SUPERIOR		SISKIWIT BAY BUOY "SB"	47-53.40	88-53.20	31846.51	46179.99	14976
LAKE SUPERIOR		ROCK OF AGES LIGHT	47-53.40	88-53.20	31846.51	46179.99	14976
LAKE SUPERIOR		TROWBRIDGE ISLAND	48-17.57	88-52.42	31765.88	46009.54	2311
LAKE SUPERIOR		TROWBRIDGE ISLAND LIGHT	48-17.60	88-52.40	31765.73	46009.41	14968
LAKE SUPERIOR		ISLE ROYALE LIGHT	47-56.90	88-45.70	31811.18	46188.28	14976
LAKE SUPERIOR		POINT PORPHYRY LIGHT	48-20.40	88-38.90	31714.93	46051.99	14968
LAKE SUPERIOR		POINT PORPHYRY	48-20.40	88-38.90	31714.93	46051.99	2301
LAKE SUPERIOR		KEWEENAW W BRKWTR LIGHT	47-14.00	88-37.90	31933.59	46562.99	14972
LAKE SUPERIOR		KEWEENAW UPPER ENTR LIGHT	47-14.10	88-37.80	31932.89	46562.60	14972
LAKE SUPERIOR		KEWEENAW W REVETMENT LIGHT	47-13.60	88-37.60	31934.03	46567.68	14972
LAKE SUPERIOR		KEWEENAW UPPER ENTR NO 72	47-13.60	88-37.50	31933.70	46568.12	14972
LAKE SUPERIOR		LILY POND LEADING LIGHT	47-12.00	88-37.10	31938.16	46583.34	14972
LAKE SUPERIOR		OSCEOLA POINT LIGHT	47-07.40	88-35.60	31949.90	46628.90	14972
LAKE SUPERIOR		ROCK HARBOR W ENTR	48-05.70	88-34.40	31746.62	46175.29	14976
LAKE SUPERIOR		PILGRIM POINT LIGHT	47-06.40	88-30.40	31935.93	46660.15	14972
LAKE SUPERIOR		SHAGANASH ISLAND	48-26.17	88-28.83	31665.57	46058.38	2302

PASSES

BODY OF WATER	PROV/STATE	NAME	LAT	LON	TD#1	TD#2	CHART
LAKE SUPERIOR		SAND POINT LIGHT	46-47.10	88-28.00	32000.02	46838.41	14964
LAKE SUPERIOR		KEWEENAW W ENTR LIGHT	46-58.10	88-25.90	31951.15	46750.92	14972
LAKE SUPERIOR		GROS CAP	49-39.50	88-25.50	31454.41	45650.83	NONE
LAKE SUPERIOR		BLAKE POINT LIGHT	48-11.50	88-25.40	31699.38	46174.32	14976
LAKE SUPERIOR		PASSAGE ISLAND LIGHT	48-13.40	88-22.00	31682.48	46176.09	14968
LAKE SUPERIOR		McKELLAR ISLAND	49-58.05	88-15.10	31379.19	45607.27	6050
LAKE SUPERIOR		OMBABIKA ISLAND	50-07.25	88-15.00	31357.57	45567.25	6050
LAKE SUPERIOR		LITTLE FLATLAND ISLAND	49-43.72	88-14.50	31411.64	45676.45	NONE
LAKE SUPERIOR		GRAND TRAVERS BAY HARB NO 2	47-11.40	88-14.20	31861.90	46687.82	14964
LAKE SUPERIOR		THE VIRGINS	49-29.03	88-13.22	31444.13	45755.11	6050
LAKE SUPERIOR		RUSSELL ISLAND	49-54.07	88-12.30	31380.40	45636.79	6050
LAKE SUPERIOR		RED WILLOW ISLAND	49-41.25	88-10.50	31405.78	45705.03	NONE
LAKE SUPERIOR		EAGLE HARBOR LIGHT	47-27.70	88-09.60	31788.98	46573.97	14964
LAKE SUPERIOR		EAGLE HARBOR SHOAL NO 1	47-27.90	88-09.50	31787.96	46572.80	14964
LAKE SUPERIOR		EAGLE HARBOR RANGE LIGHT	47-27.30	88-09.10	31788.62	46579.32	14964
LAKE SUPERIOR		LAMB ISLAND	48-36.23	88-08.57	31571.26	46081.55	2312
LAKE SUPERIOR		HOLDEN SHOAL LIGHT J8	48-56.65	88-08.42	31513.93	45955.57	2312
LAKE SUPERIOR		CRICHTON ISLAND	48-57.12	88-06.32	31506.04	45961.78	2312
LAKE SUPERIOR		VERT ISLAND	48-56.60	88-02.10	31494.08	45982.91	2312
LAKE SUPERIOR		HURON ISLAND LIGHT	46-57.80	87-59.80	31859.71	46863.57	14964
LAKE SUPERIOR		MACINNES POINT	48-55.73	87-55.70	31476.01	46015.28	2312
LAKE SUPERIOR		COPPER HARBOR RANGE	47-28.20	87-52.00	31725.42	46644.45	14964
LAKE SUPERIOR		COPPER HARB ENT "CH"	47-28.70	87-51.80	31723.04	46641.30	14964
LAKE SUPERIOR		COPPER HARBOR LIGHT	47-28.50	87-51.60	31722.99	46643.73	14964
LAKE SUPERIOR		NOAA WEATHER BUOY 45001	48-01.30	87-43.40	31589.77	46428.53	14960
LAKE SUPERIOR		SIMPSON ISLAND	48-50.45	87-41.43	31443.82	46107.19	2312
LAKE SUPERIOR		BIG BAY POINT NO 1	46-51.70	87-41.30	31813.49	46991.18	14963
LAKE SUPERIOR		BIG BAY POINT LIGHT	46-50.50	87-40.80	31815.97	47003.53	14963
LAKE SUPERIOR		GULL ROCK LIGHT	47-25.00	87-39.80	31692.11	46720.39	14964
LAKE SUPERIOR		BARWIS ROCK LIGHT JC	48-50.22	87-36.95	31429.70	46127.16	2312
LAKE SUPERIOR		MANITOU LIGHT	47-25.20	87-35.20	31674.63	46737.52	14964
LAKE SUPERIOR		BATTLE ISLAND LIGHT	48-45.10	87-33.40	31431.46	46173.66	14960
LAKE SUPERIOR		BATTLE ISLAND ISLAND	48-45.10	87-33.40	31431.46	46173.66	2312
LAKE SUPERIOR		ROSSPORT POINT	48-49.53	87-32.90	31418.13	46148.09	2312
LAKE SUPERIOR		ROSSPORT HARBOUR ENTR	48-49.53	87-31.37	31413.05	46154.37	2312
LAKE SUPERIOR		GRANITE ISLAND LIGHT	46-43.30	87-24.70	31780.32	47128.99	14963
LAKE SUPERIOR		MARQUETTE LIGHT	46-32.80	87-22.60	31810.88	47229.21	14970
LAKE SUPERIOR		PRESQUE ISLE HARB BRKWTR	46-34.40	87-22.40	31804.11	47215.81	14970
LAKE SUPERIOR		STANNARD ROCK LIGHT	47-11.00	87-13.50	31640.08	46938.38	14963
LAKE SUPERIOR		SLATE ISLAND	48-37.27	86-59.75	31336.94	46358.80	2303
LAKE SUPERIOR		SLATE ISLAND LIGHT	48-37.30	86-59.70	31336.69	46358.81	14960
LAKE SUPERIOR		JACKFISH BAY	48-47.37	86-58.90	31308.60	46297.77	2305
LAKE SUPERIOR		BAY FURNACE LIGHT	46-26.30	86-41.50	31664.96	47435.86	14963
LAKE SUPERIOR		GRAND ISLAND LIGHT	46-33.70	86-40.90	31635.98	47373.41	14963

PASSES

BODY OF WATER	PROV/STATE	NAME	LAT	LON	TD#1	TD#2	CHART
LAKE SUPERIOR		MUNISING RANGE	46-24.90	86-39.70	31662.27	47454.39	14963
LAKE SUPERIOR		TROUT POINT NO 2	46-27.10	86-35.80	31637.52	47448.55	14963
LAKE SUPERIOR		NOAA WEATHER BUOY 45004	47-33.00	86-30.40	31402.48	46926.25	14960
LAKE SUPERIOR		HAWKINS ISLAND	48-43.20	86-25.87	31202.33	46450.01	2306
LAKE SUPERIOR		SKIN ISLAND	48-43.68	86-23.65	31193.24	46455.18	2304
LAKE SUPERIOR		AU SABLE LIGHT	46-40.30	86-08.40	31472.55	47427.67	14963
LAKE SUPERIOR		OTTER ISLAND	48-06.72	86-04.03	31208.31	46773.85	2308
LAKE SUPERIOR		GRAND MARAIS OF REFUGE	46-41.30	85-58.50	31425.32	47451.68	14962
LAKE SUPERIOR		GR MARAIS OF REFUGE NO 1	46-40.80	85-58.20	31425.57	47456.84	14962
LAKE SUPERIOR		MICHIPICOTEN ISLAND W END	47-43.08	85-57.35	31241.84	46967.79	2308
LAKE SUPERIOR		CARIBOU ISLAND	47-20.38	85-49.53	31270.28	47166.38	2310
LAKE SUPERIOR		CARIBOU ISLAND LIGHT	47-20.40	85-49.50	31270.10	47166.33	14960
LAKE SUPERIOR		DAVIEAUX ISLAND	47-41.69	85-48.67	31209.99	47007.85	2315
LAKE SUPERIOR		MICHIPICOTEN ISLAND LIGHT	47-45.20	85-35.80	31148.13	47025.30	14960
LAKE SUPERIOR		MICHIPICOTEN ISLAND	47-45.25	85-35.75	31147.81	47025.11	2309
LAKE SUPERIOR		LITTLE LAKE HARBOR NO 2	46-43.10	85-21.80	31252.16	47551.24	14962
LAKE SUPERIOR		LITTLE LAKE HARBOR NO 3	46-43.00	85-21.80	31252.45	47552.06	14962
LAKE SUPERIOR		CRISP POINT LIGHT	46-45.10	85-15.50	31217.02	47553.75	14962
LAKE SUPERIOR		HURSLEY ISLAND	47-35.77	85-02.55	31029.68	47201.14	2307
LAKE SUPERIOR		GARGANTUA ISLAND	47-33.50	84-57.80	31014.18	47232.43	2315
LAKE SUPERIOR		WHITEFISH POINT LIGHT	46-46.30	84-57.40	31128.32	47596.68	14962
LAKE SUPERIOR		MICHIPICOTEN HARBOUR	47-56.55	84-54.45	30950.04	47076.77	2315
LAKE SUPERIOR		MICHIPICOTEN RIVER ENTR	47-55.99	84-51.12	30937.18	47090.99	2315
LAKE SUPERIOR		PANCAKE SHOAL BUOY	46-54.20	84-50.70	31076.03	47553.06	14960
LAKE SUPERIOR		PANCAKE SHOAL NO X2	46-54.50	84-50.30	31073.38	47551.84	2300
LAKE SUPERIOR		ROWE ISLAND	47-26.42	84-47.60	30985.07	47315.49	2307
LAKE SUPERIOR		COPPERMINE POINT	46-59.08	84-47.20	31047.37	47524.81	2307
LAKE SUPERIOR		MAMAINSE HARBOUR	47-02.25	84-47.19	31039.57	47500.20	2315
LAKE SUPERIOR		SINCLAIR ISLAND	47-22.50	84-42.56	30971.20	47359.50	2315
LAKE SUPERIOR		MONTREAL POINT	47-14.50	84-39.00	30972.92	47429.86	2307
LAKE SUPERIOR		CORBEIL POINT NO XA4	46-52.70	84-37.50	31016.99	47601.74	14962
LAKE SUPERIOR		MAPLE ISLAND	46-46.17	84-34.83	31020.10	47660.31	14962
LAKE SUPERIOR		GOULAIS BAY	46-41.77	84-31.38	31014.10	47704.33	2315
	CAPE BRETON I	HENRY ISLAND ENTRANCE	45-58.60	61-36.00	14333.90	42714.82	
	CAPE BRETON I	PORT HOOD ISLAND	46-01.00	61-33.40	14343.93	42688.75	
	CAPE BRETON I	MURPHY POND BRKWTR	46-01.50	61-32.70	14345.89	42682.31	
	CAPE BRETON I	PORT HOOD ISLAND PIER	46-01.00	61-32.50	14343.32	42683.09	
	CAPE BRETON I	LITTLE JUDIQUE WHARF	45-57.50	61-31.70	14325.68	42692.27	
	CAPE BRETON I	JUDIQUE WHARF	46-05.10	61-27.90	14359.98	42637.21	
	CAPE BRETON I	MABOU HARBOUR	46-05.10	61-27.90	14359.98	42637.21	
	CAPE BRETON I	INVERNESS HARBOUR BRKWTR	46-13.70	61-19.60	14394.48	42548.11	
	CAPE BRETON I	INVERNESS HARBOUR RANGE	46-13.60	61-19.20	14393.73	42546.03	
	CAPE BRETON I	MARGAREE ISLAND	46-21.50	61-16.00	14427.28	42490.55	
	CAPE BRETON I	MARGAREE HARBOUR RANGE	46-26.40	61-06.80	14441.85	42409.90	

PASSES

BODY OF WATER	PROV/STATE	NAME	LAT	LON	TD#1	TD#2	CHART
	CAPE BRETON I	MARGAREE HARBOUR	46-26.50	61-06.60	14442.13	42408.18	
	CAPE BRETON I	CERBERUS ROCK WHISTLE	45-27.60	61-06.30	14164.06	42651.27	
	CAPE BRETON I	CRICHTON HEAD	45-30.70	61-06.30	14179.59	42639.86	
	CAPE BRETON I	ARICHAT HEAD	45-30.40	61-06.10	14178.02	42639.77	
	CAPE BRETON I	NEW WHARF	45-30.90	61-05.10	14180.13	42631.92	
	CAPE BRETON I	WHYCOCOMAGH/LOVETT PT	45-57.70	61-04.70	14310.00	42523.82	
	CAPE BRETON I	BEACH POINT	45-30.20	61-03.40	14176.00	42624.32	
	CAPE BRETON I	LA POINTE WHARF	46-36.20	61-03.20	14481.04	42340.41	
	CAPE BRETON I	GRAND ETANG BRKWTR	46-33.10	61-02.80	14467.58	42352.89	
	CAPE BRETON I	GRAND ETANG HARBOUR	46-33.00	61-02.60	14466.99	42352.11	
	CAPE BRETON I	MARACHE POINT ENTRANCE	45-28.80	61-02.10	14168.54	42621.73	
	CAPE BRETON I	ENRAGEE POINT	46-39.00	61-01.60	14491.46	42316.58	
	CAPE BRETON I	GRANDIQUE POINT	45-35.60	61-01.40	14201.91	42591.99	
	CAPE BRETON I	CAPE HOGAN	45-28.00	61-00.70	14164.06	42616.33	
	CAPE BRETON I	EASTERN HARBOUR RANGE	46-38.00	61-00.70	14486.54	42315.81	
	CAPE BRETON I	CHETICAMP HARBOUR BUOY	46-38.80	61-00.60	14489.79	42311.25	
	CAPE BRETON I	CAVEAU POINT ENTR	46-39.00	61-00.10	14490.21	42307.10	
	CAPE BRETON I	HAWK ISLAND	45-35.70	60-59.70	14201.70	42581.39	
	CAPE BRETON I	LITTLE NARROWS ENTRANCE	45-60.00	60-59.00	14317.38	42479.11	
	CAPE BRETON I	PETIT DE GRAT BELL BUOY	45-29.00	60-58.50	14168.23	42599.50	
	CAPE BRETON I	PETITE DE GRAT INNER RANGE	45-29.80	60-58.40	14172.15	42595.91	
	CAPE BRETON I	PETIT DE GRAT WHISTLE	45-28.30	60-58.30	14164.69	42600.91	
	CAPE BRETON I	LITTLE NARROWS RANGE	45-60.00	60-58.20	14316.91	42474.20	
	CAPE BRETON I	COWLEY POINT BRKWTR	45-30.10	60-57.80	14173.42	42591.21	
	CAPE BRETON I	PETITE DE GRAT ISLET	45-29.70	60-57.80	14171.44	42592.71	
	CAPE BRETON I	QUETIQUE ISLAND	45-36.60	60-57.50	14205.18	42564.71	
	CAPE BRETON I	PETIT DE GRAT INLET	45-31.10	60-57.10	14178.08	42583.28	
	CAPE BRETON I	BOURGEOISE INLET	45-37.50	60-57.00	14209.34	42558.23	
	CAPE BRETON I	MORRISON COVE RANGE	46-00.70	60-56.30	14319.02	42459.56	
	CAPE BRETON I	PETITE ANSE RANGE	45-29.70	60-56.10	14170.82	42582.57	
	CAPE BRETON I	MCIVER POINT RANGE	46-02.10	60-55.50	14325.00	42448.66	
	CAPE BRETON I	GREEN ISLAND	45-28.70	60-54.00	14165.15	42573.82	
	CAPE BRETON I	CAP RONDE	45-34.60	60-53.40	14193.77	42547.85	
	CAPE BRETON I	ST PETERS BELL BUOY	45-37.10	60-53.40	14205.89	42538.19	
	CAPE BRETON I	JEROME POINT	45-39.00	60-52.40	14214.63	42524.77	
	CAPE BRETON I	HELEN ISLAND	45-40.00	60-51.40	14219.00	42514.84	
	CAPE BRETON I	ORPHEUS ROCK BELL	45-28.70	60-51.20	14164.17	42557.20	
	CAPE BRETON I	BEAVER ISLAND	45-40.50	60-50.10	14220.83	42505.07	
	CAPE BRETON I	CAPE GEORGE	45-44.10	60-48.70	14237.33	42482.29	
	CAPE BRETON I	PLEASANT BAY BELL VC1	46-50.50	60-48.30	14526.98	42174.55	
	CAPE BRETON I	IONA GOVT WHARF	45-57.80	60-48.20	14301.01	42422.48	
	CAPE BRETON I	DERBY POINT	45-56.40	60-48.10	14294.51	42427.82	
	CAPE BRETON I	GREGORY ISLAND	45-42.60	60-48.10	14229.95	42484.70	
	CAPE BRETON I	PLEASANT BAY	46-50.00	60-48.00	14524.75	42175.25	

PASSES

BODY OF WATER	PROV/STATE	NAME	LAT	LON	TD#1	TD#2	CHART
	CAPE BRETON I	GRAND NARROWS BRIDGE	45-57.50	60-47.90	14299.46	42421.94	
	CAPE BRETON I	PLEASANT BAY BRKWTR	46-50.00	60-47.90	14524.67	42174.62	
	CAPE BRETON I	GILLIS POINT	46-01.40	60-46.70	14316.61	42397.89	
	CAPE BRETON I	LOWER L'ARDOISE WHISTLE	45-34.80	60-46.00	14191.83	42502.96	
	CAPE BRETON I	KIDSTON ISLAND	46-05.60	60-45.10	14334.64	42369.79	
	CAPE BRETON I	BONE ISLAND BUOY	46-05.10	60-44.80	14332.22	42370.15	
	CAPE BRETON I	KIDSTON ISLAND ENTR	46-06.00	60-44.60	14336.14	42364.97	
	CAPE BRETON I	LITTLE HARBOUR WHARF	45-35.00	60-44.50	14192.21	42493.27	
	CAPE BRETON I	MACRAE POINT BUOY	46-06.00	60-40.50	14333.68	42339.98	
	CAPE BRETON I	MACKENZIE POINT	46-07.00	60-39.00	14337.23	42326.41	
	CAPE BRETON I	POINT CLEAR	46-05.50	60-36.00	14328.81	42314.88	
	CAPE BRETON I	CAPE ST LAWRENCE	47-02.50	60-36.00	14562.64	42033.68	
	CAPE BRETON I	L'ARCHEVEQUE COVE FOG SIGNAL	45-37.30	60-34.40	14199.19	42424.32	
	CAPE BRETON I	BEACH POINT	46-17.40	60-32.50	14378.53	42239.37	
	CAPE BRETON I	MAN OF WAR POINT	46-11.20	60-32.20	14351.58	42266.16	
	CAPE BRETON I	OTTER HARBOUR RANGE	46-13.10	60-31.80	14359.57	42255.02	
	CAPE BRETON I	ST ESPRIT ISLAND	45-37.30	60-29.30	14197.22	42394.23	
	CAPE BRETON I	DUNCAN HEAD	46-14.20	60-29.00	14362.58	42232.96	
	CAPE BRETON I	SOUTHWEST BREAKWATER	47-00.20	60-28.10	14547.32	41996.76	
	CAPE BRETON I	BRIGHTON COVE RANGE	46-26.70	60-27.70	14414.56	42165.87	
	CAPE BRETON I	DINGWALL HARBOUR S LIGHT	46-54.20	60-27.20	14523.87	42023.28	
	CAPE BRETON I	DINGWALL HARBOUR N LIGHT	46-54.30	60-27.20	14524.25	42022.75	
	CAPE BRETON I	KELLY COVE WHARF	46-17.30	60-26.20	14374.07	42201.54	
	CAPE BRETON I	DINGWALL HARBOUR BELL	46-54.20	60-26.00	14522.90	42015.84	
	CAPE BRETON I	BIG BRAS D'OR WHARF	46-17.00	60-25.50	14372.36	42198.70	
	CAPE BRETON I	GREAT BRAS D'OR RANGE	46-17.40	60-25.00	14373.74	42193.80	
	CAPE BRETON I	CAREY POINT RANGE	46-17.70	60-25.00	14375.01	42192.39	
	CAPE BRETON I	GREAT BRAS D'OR LIGHT	46-18.00	60-24.40	14375.90	42187.34	
	CAPE BRETON I	GREAT BRAS D'OR ENTR	46-18.40	60-24.00	14377.34	42183.04	
	CAPE BRETON I	BLACK ROCK POINT	46-18.30	60-23.50	14376.60	42180.48	
	CAPE BRETON I	CAPE NORTH	47-01.70	60-23.50	14549.09	41960.04	
	CAPE BRETON I	INGONISH HARBOUR ENTR	46-38.00	60-23.30	14457.50	42083.07	
	CAPE BRETON I	CAREY BEACH BELL	46-19.00	60-23.20	14379.37	42175.35	
	CAPE BRETON I	CIBOUX ISLAND	46-23.10	60-22.50	14396.09	42151.56	
	CAPE BRETON I	THE POINT	46-41.30	60-21.50	14469.29	42055.28	
	CAPE BRETON I	WHITE POINT BRKWTR	46-52.50	60-21.30	14512.66	41995.80	
	CAPE BRETON I	CAPE SMOKY WHISTLE	46-38.40	60-19.70	14456.47	42059.02	
	CAPE BRETON I	NEIL HARBOUR ENTRANCE	46-48.40	60-19.20	14495.29	42004.45	
	CAPE BRETON I	NEW HAVEN WHISTLE	46-49.30	60-18.40	14498.14	41994.82	
	CAPE BRETON I	NEIL HARBOUR BELL BUOY	46-47.70	60-18.20	14491.82	42001.98	
	CAPE BRETON I	LITTLE BRAS D'OR RANGE	46-18.70	60-17.30	14374.40	42141.14	
	CAPE BRETON I	ALDER POINT BUOY	46-19.00	60-17.10	14375.53	42138.51	
	CAPE BRETON I	LITTLE BRAS D'OR ENTR	46-19.50	60-16.60	14377.30	42133.12	
	CAPE BRETON I	SYDNEY RANGE	46-10.80	60-15.10	14339.74	42164.99	

PASSES

BODY OF WATER	PROV/STATE	NAME	LAT	LON	TD#1	TD#2	CHART
	CAPE BRETON I	BALLAST GROUNDS	46-12.40	60-15.00	14346.48	42156.96	
	CAPE BRETON I	POINT ACONI	46-21.50	60-14.90	14384.55	42113.30	
	CAPE BRETON I	FOURCHU HARBOUR PIER	45-43.20	60-14.70	14218.52	42284.29	
	CAPE BRETON I	FOURCHU HEAD	45-43.10	60-13.80	14217.71	42279.45	
	CAPE BRETON I	SYDNEY BAR	46-12.30	60-13.20	14345.01	42146.66	
	CAPE BRETON I	FOURCHU WHISTLE BUOY	45-42.20	60-12.90	14213.30	42277.96	
	CAPE BRETON I	SYDNEY SOUTH RANGE	46-09.50	60-12.30	14332.62	42154.29	
	CAPE BRETON I	SYDNEY INNER HARB BELL	46-14.60	60-11.40	14353.65	42125.13	
	CAPE BRETON I	ST PAUL ISLAND S POINT	47-11.00	60-09.70	14571.43	41823.31	
	CAPE BRETON I	GABARUS COVE	45-50.60	60-09.00	14249.10	42219.38	
	CAPE BRETON I	NORTH POINT	47-13.60	60-08.40	14579.54	41800.63	
	CAPE BRETON I	ROUSE POINT	45-50.60	60-08.00	14248.66	42213.52	
	CAPE BRETON I	SYDNEY HARBOUR WHISTLE	46-18.40	60-07.80	14367.34	42085.59	
	CAPE BRETON I	LOW POINT	46-16.00	60-07.60	14357.27	42095.82	
	CAPE BRETON I	GUYON ISLAND	45-46.00	60-06.80	14227.84	42226.31	
	CAPE BRETON I	LINGAN RANGE	46-13.70	60-02.80	14344.93	42078.18	
	CAPE BRETON I	GUYON ISLAND WHISTLE	45-46.10	60-02.70	14226.62	42202.03	
	CAPE BRETON I	LOUISBOURG RANGE	45-54.10	59-59.40	14260.11	42147.94	
	CAPE BRETON I	LOUISBOURG NE ARM RANGE	45-55.30	59-58.10	14264.69	42135.03	
	CAPE BRETON I	LOUISBOURG HARBOUR ENTR	45-54.40	59-57.50	14260.55	42135.54	
	CAPE BRETON I	GLACE BAY ENTRANCE	46-11.80	59-57.00	14333.82	42052.89	
	CAPE BRETON I	GLACE BAY BRKWTR	46-12.00	59-57.00	14334.65	42051.94	
	CAPE BRETON I	GLACE BAY BELL	46-13.60	59-55.60	14340.49	42036.11	
	CAPE BRETON I	LOUISBOURG WHISTLE BUOY	45-52.60	59-54.10	14251.32	42123.79	
	CAPE BRETON I	MORIEN BRKWTR	46-08.00	59-52.20	14315.51	42042.57	
	CAPE BRETON I	LITTLE LORRAINE ENTR	45-57.00	59-51.60	14269.01	42089.62	
	CAPE BRETON I	BALEINE BELL BUOY	45-56.40	59-50.80	14266.11	42087.68	
	CAPE BRETON I	BATTERY POINT	46-00.30	59-50.50	14282.46	42068.26	
	CAPE BRETON I	MAIN A DIEU HARBOUR	46-00.20	59-50.40	14282.00	42068.13	
	CAPE BRETON I	MOQUE HEAD FOG SIGNAL	46-00.40	59-49.50	14282.42	42062.00	
	CAPE BRETON I	MAD DOG ROCK BELL	45-60.00	59-49.40	14280.69	42063.24	
	CAPE BRETON I	MAIN A DIEU POINT	46-00.20	59-47.70	14280.74	42052.47	
	CAPE BRETON I	FLINT ISLAND	46-10.80	59-46.30	14324.00	41994.92	
	CAPE BRETON I	PORTNOVA ISLANDS WHISTLE	45-55.70	59-46.20	14261.11	42064.25	
	CAPE BRETON I	SCATARIE POINT	46-02.10	59-40.60	14285.36	42002.69	
ST LAWRENCE GULF	MAGDALEN ISLANDS	DEADMAN ISLAND WHISTLE "Y"	47-15.40	62-13.20	14709.90	42596.72	
ST LAWRENCE GULF	MAGDALEN ISLANDS	AMHERST ISLAND, S CAPE	47-12.80	61-58.30	14682.64	42510.95	
ST LAWRENCE GULF	MAGDALEN ISLANDS	BREAKWATER	47-22.30	61-57.70	14717.69	42454.82	
ST LAWRENCE GULF	MAGDALEN ISLANDS	GRINDSTONE	47-23.10	61-57.60	14720.51	42449.69	
ST LAWRENCE GULF	MAGDALEN ISLANDS	ESTANG DU NORD RANGE	47-22.30	61-57.50	14717.46	42453.48	
ST LAWRENCE GULF	MAGDALEN ISLANDS	CAP-AUX-MEULES W BRKWTR	47-22.60	61-51.50	14711.70	42411.79	
ST LAWRENCE GULF	MAGDALEN ISLANDS	CAP-AUX-MEULES WHARF	47-22.60	61-51.30	14711.47	42410.46	
ST LAWRENCE GULF	MAGDALEN ISLANDS	CAP-AUX-MEULES BRKWTR	47-22.50	61-51.20	14711.00	42410.36	
ST LAWRENCE GULF	MAGDALEN ISLANDS	HOUSE HARBOUR	47-24.40	61-50.40	14717.00	42394.37	

PASSES

BODY OF WATER	PROV/STATE	NAME	LAT	LON	TD#1	TD#2	CHART
ST LAWRENCE GULF	MAGDALEN ISLANDS	AMHERST WHARF LIGHT	47-13.70	61-50.00	14676.80	42450.86	
ST LAWRENCE GULF	MAGDALEN ISLANDS	POINTE BASSE, ALRIGHT I	47-23.40	61-47.50	14710.10	42380.71	
ST LAWRENCE GULF	MAGDALEN ISLANDS	CAPE ALRIGHT	47-23.50	61-46.50	14709.34	42373.50	
ST LAWRENCE GULF	MAGDALEN ISLANDS	ENTRY ISLAND WHARF	47-16.60	61-43.20	14680.27	42389.97	
ST LAWRENCE GULF	MAGDALEN ISLANDS	ENTRY ISLAND	47-16.10	61-42.30	14677.41	42386.77	
ST LAWRENCE GULF	MAGDALEN ISLANDS	ENTRY ISLAND	47-17.30	61-41.50	14681.02	42374.88	
ST LAWRENCE GULF	MAGDALEN ISLANDS	PEARL REEF BELL "Y16"	47-19.50	61-34.40	14681.47	42315.86	
ST LAWRENCE GULF	MAGDALEN ISLANDS	GRAND ENTRY HARBOUR ENTR	47-33.40	61-33.80	14730.18	42232.82	
ST LAWRENCE GULF	MAGDALEN ISLANDS	BRION ISLAND BELL "YJ"	47-47.00	61-32.80	14774.23	42145.59	
ST LAWRENCE GULF	MAGDALEN ISLANDS	BRION ISLAND	47-47.00	61-30.50	14771.67	42130.40	
ST LAWRENCE GULF	MAGDALEN ISLANDS	OLD HARRY HEAD BELL "Y8"	47-31.10	61-26.80	14714.62	42200.04	
ST LAWRENCE GULF	MAGDALEN ISLANDS	EAST POINT	47-37.40	61-23.70	14732.74	42142.90	
ST LAWRENCE GULF	MAGDALEN ISLANDS	EAST POINT WHISTLE "YY"	47-36.80	61-19.70	14726.43	42120.20	
ST LAWRENCE GULF	MAGDALEN ISLANDS	BIRD ROCKS	47-50.30	61-08.70	14758.56	41967.29	
ST LAWRENCE GULF	NEW BRUNSWICK	MIDDLE RIVER RANGE	47-37.50	68-39.70	15164.45	44797.12	
ST LAWRENCE GULF	NEW BRUNSWICK	DALHOUSIE ISLAND	48-04.30	66-22.20	15222.40	43978.67	
ST LAWRENCE GULF	NEW BRUNSWICK	CHALEUR BAY RANGE	48-04.30	66-22.20	15222.40	43978.67	
ST LAWRENCE GULF	NEW BRUNSWICK	DALHOUSIE HARBOUR RANGE	48-04.30	66-22.00	15222.17	43977.46	
ST LAWRENCE GULF	NEW BRUNSWICK	DALHOUSIE WHARF	48-04.30	66-21.70	15221.83	43975.65	
ST LAWRENCE GULF	NEW BRUNSWICK	INCH ARRAN POINT RANGE	48-03.70	66-21.10	15220.50	43977.02	
ST LAWRENCE GULF	NEW BRUNSWICK	NEW MILLS	47-58.50	66-11.40	15201.99	43959.62	
ST LAWRENCE GULF	NEW BRUNSWICK	HERON ISLAND	47-60.00	66-08.20	15199.78	43927.43	
ST LAWRENCE GULF	NEW BRUNSWICK	JACQUET RIVER ENTRANCE	47-55.40	66-02.00	15184.11	43924.17	
ST LAWRENCE GULF	NEW BRUNSWICK	BELLEDUNE POINT BRKWTR	47-54.80	65-50.40	15165.70	43853.14	
ST LAWRENCE GULF	NEW BRUNSWICK	BELLEDUNE POINT	47-54.40	65-50.00	15164.34	43853.53	
ST LAWRENCE GULF	NEW BRUNSWICK	GREEN POINT BREAKWATER	47-51.70	65-45.80	15152.52	43845.88	
ST LAWRENCE GULF	NEW BRUNSWICK	PETIT-ROCHER BRKWTR	47-46.90	65-42.50	15136.88	43858.76	
ST LAWRENCE GULF	NEW BRUNSWICK	WEST BATHURST RANGE	47-38.10	65-39.20	15109.61	43897.93	
ST LAWRENCE GULF	NEW BRUNSWICK	NEPISGUIT RIVER RANGE	47-37.10	65-38.70	15106.03	43901.28	
ST LAWRENCE GULF	NEW BRUNSWICK	BATHURST HARBOUR RANGE	47-39.10	65-37.40	15109.05	43878.67	
ST LAWRENCE GULF	NEW BRUNSWICK	BATHURST HARBOUR "EP2"	47-41.10	65-36.00	15111.78	43855.29	
ST LAWRENCE GULF	NEW BRUNSWICK	SALMON BEACH	47-40.10	65-33.30	15104.43	43843.55	
ST LAWRENCE GULF	NEW BRUNSWICK	WRITE BANK RANGE	47-01.00	65-32.80	14963.36	44072.81	
ST LAWRENCE GULF	NEW BRUNSWICK	CHATHAM BRIDGE PIER	47-01.70	65-28.90	14958.63	44041.04	
ST LAWRENCE GULF	NEW BRUNSWICK	MILLBANK RANGE	47-03.40	65-27.60	14963.72	44023.06	
ST LAWRENCE GULF	NEW BRUNSWICK	ST ANDREWS BANK RANGE	47-04.20	65-25.20	14962.48	44001.61	
ST LAWRENCE GULF	NEW BRUNSWICK	LOWER NEWCASTLE RANGE	47-04.50	65-24.60	14962.61	43995.73	
ST LAWRENCE GULF	NEW BRUNSWICK	LEGGETT SHOAL RANGE	47-04.70	65-24.00	14962.30	43990.36	
ST LAWRENCE GULF	NEW BRUNSWICK	GRANTS BEACH RANGE	47-05.00	65-22.50	14960.63	43977.98	
ST LAWRENCE GULF	NEW BRUNSWICK	STONEHAVEN WHARF	47-45.20	65-22.00	15098.13	43730.81	
ST LAWRENCE GULF	NEW BRUNSWICK	EAST POINT RANGE	47-04.40	65-20.00	14953.00	43962.98	
ST LAWRENCE GULF	NEW BRUNSWICK	MOODY POINT RANGE	47-06.00	65-19.50	14959.08	43951.13	
ST LAWRENCE GULF	NEW BRUNSWICK	OAK CHANNEL RANGE	47-04.30	65-19.20	14950.97	43957.71	
ST LAWRENCE GULF	NEW BRUNSWICK	GRAND DUNE FLATS	47-08.40	65-13.70	14958.09	43896.75	

PASSES

BODY OF WATER	PROV/STATE	NAME	LAT	LON	TD#1	TD#2	CHART
ST LAWRENCE GULF	NEW BRUNSWICK	GRANDE-ANSE RANGE	47-49.10	65-10.60	15088.95	43625.71	
ST LAWRENCE GULF	NEW BRUNSWICK	BURNT CHURCH WHARF	47-11.40	65-08.20	14960.10	43841.18	
ST LAWRENCE GULF	NEW BRUNSWICK	BAY DU VIN ISLAND	47-05.30	65-06.10	14930.01	43858.10	
ST LAWRENCE GULF	NEW BRUNSWICK	ANSE-BLUE WHARF	47-50.00	65-04.80	15081.67	43579.69	
ST LAWRENCE GULF	NEW BRUNSWICK	BLUE COVE RANGE	47-49.90	65-04.80	15081.41	43580.37	
ST LAWRENCE GULF	NEW BRUNSWICK	NEGUAC WHARF	47-14.40	65-04.50	14965.29	43798.28	
ST LAWRENCE GULF	NEW BRUNSWICK	LOWER NEGUAC WHARF RANGE	47-15.40	65-03.30	14967.02	43784.15	
ST LAWRENCE GULF	NEW BRUNSWICK	PORTAGE CHANNEL RANGE	47-07.80	65-02.30	14933.72	43817.85	
ST LAWRENCE GULF	NEW BRUNSWICK	PORTAGE ISLAND RANGE	47-09.50	65-02.00	14940.42	43806.77	
ST LAWRENCE GULF	NEW BRUNSWICK	PORTAGE GULLY BELL	47-10.80	65-00.50	14943.07	43789.10	
ST LAWRENCE GULF	NEW BRUNSWICK	MAISONNETTE POINT	47-50.30	65-00.30	15075.05	43546.68	
ST LAWRENCE GULF	NEW BRUNSWICK	MAISONNETTE POINT WHARF	47-50.10	64-59.00	15072.39	43539.08	
ST LAWRENCE GULF	NEW BRUNSWICK	HUCKLEBERRY GULLY RANGE	47-03.10	64-58.40	14905.66	43813.80	
ST LAWRENCE GULF	NEW BRUNSWICK	YOUNGS WHARF WEST	47-48.00	64-55.80	15061.51	43531.07	
ST LAWRENCE GULF	NEW BRUNSWICK	YOUNGS WHARF	47-47.80	64-55.60	15060.63	43531.02	
ST LAWRENCE GULF	NEW BRUNSWICK	PRESTON BEACH RANGE	47-04.70	64-54.70	14905.97	43779.16	
ST LAWRENCE GULF	NEW BRUNSWICK	KOUCHIBOUGUAC, L'LE GULLY	46-50.80	64-54.60	14839.64	43844.65	
ST LAWRENCE GULF	NEW BRUNSWICK	NORTH TRACADIE WHARF	47-31.50	64-54.50	15009.50	43627.55	
ST LAWRENCE GULF	NEW BRUNSWICK	CARAQUET ISLAND	47-49.40	64-54.30	15062.82	43511.35	
ST LAWRENCE GULF	NEW BRUNSWICK	CARAQUET WEST RANGE	47-48.00	64-54.10	15058.70	43519.31	
ST LAWRENCE GULF	NEW BRUNSWICK	BLACKLANDS GULLY RANGE	46-46.50	64-53.20	14814.93	43853.39	
ST LAWRENCE GULF	NEW BRUNSWICK	VAL COMEAU WHARF	47-28.00	64-53.00	14994.93	43638.11	
ST LAWRENCE GULF	NEW BRUNSWICK	BLACKLANDS GULLY	46-45.80	64-52.80	14810.53	43853.50	
ST LAWRENCE GULF	NEW BRUNSWICK	SOUTH TRACADIE	47-28.50	64-52.50	14995.78	43631.58	
ST LAWRENCE GULF	NEW BRUNSWICK	MIDDLE CARAQUET WHARF	47-48.20	64-52.40	15056.44	43506.21	
ST LAWRENCE GULF	NEW BRUNSWICK	MIDDLE CARAQUET WHARF	47-48.20	64-52.40	15056.44	43506.21	
ST LAWRENCE GULF	NEW BRUNSWICK	NORTH TRACADIE APPR	47-30.80	64-52.00	15002.74	43614.16	
ST LAWRENCE GULF	NEW BRUNSWICK	RICHIBUCTO TOWN RANGE	46-40.90	64-51.80	14782.39	43866.66	
ST LAWRENCE GULF	NEW BRUNSWICK	SOUTH TRACADIE BUOY "Z"	47-28.70	64-51.00	14993.81	43619.76	
ST LAWRENCE GULF	NEW BRUNSWICK	CARAQUET ISLAND RANGE	47-48.50	64-50.50	15054.14	43491.07	
ST LAWRENCE GULF	NEW BRUNSWICK	POINT SAPIN	46-57.70	64-50.00	14865.17	43779.80	
ST LAWRENCE GULF	NEW BRUNSWICK	POINT SAPIN BRKWTR	46-57.80	64-49.80	14865.28	43777.89	
ST LAWRENCE GULF	NEW BRUNSWICK	RICHIBUCTO CHANNEL RANGE	46-43.00	64-49.50	14789.80	43841.65	
ST LAWRENCE GULF	NEW BRUNSWICK	POKEMOUCHE GULLY WHARF	47-40.20	64-48.70	15027.13	43532.48	
ST LAWRENCE GULF	NEW BRUNSWICK	FAGAN POINT RANGE	46-42.60	64-48.10	14785.22	43833.32	
ST LAWRENCE GULF	NEW BRUNSWICK	POINT ESCUMINAC	47-04.40	64-48.00	14892.39	43732.61	
ST LAWRENCE GULF	NEW BRUNSWICK	PILE SHEET RANGE	46-43.10	64-48.00	14787.73	43830.53	
ST LAWRENCE GULF	NEW BRUNSWICK	POKEMOUCHE GULLY RANGE	47-40.10	64-47.40	15024.62	43524.02	
ST LAWRENCE GULF	NEW BRUNSWICK	POINT ESCUMINAC BELL	47-07.20	64-47.10	14903.08	43711.90	
ST LAWRENCE GULF	NEW BRUNSWICK	POKESUDIE ISLAND	47-49.20	64-45.30	15047.56	43450.42	
ST LAWRENCE GULF	NEW BRUNSWICK	POINTE A MARCELLE RANGE	47-47.20	64-45.00	15041.48	43461.50	
ST LAWRENCE GULF	NEW BRUNSWICK	SAPIN LEDGE BUOY	46-58.40	64-44.70	14858.96	43738.46	
ST LAWRENCE GULF	NEW BRUNSWICK	RICHIBUCTO BELL	46-43.50	64-44.20	14783.32	43801.76	
ST LAWRENCE GULF	NEW BRUNSWICK	LITTLE POKEMOUCHE WHARF	47-41.30	64-44.10	15022.70	43493.32	

PASSES

BODY OF WATER	PROV/STATE	NAME	LAT	LON	TD#1	TD#2	CHART
ST LAWRENCE GULF	NEW BRUNSWICK	CHOCKPISH RANGE	46-34.90	64-43.40	14734.68	43830.55	
ST LAWRENCE GULF	NEW BRUNSWICK	POINTE A BERNACHE RANGE	47-45.50	64-43.30	15033.81	43460.75	
ST LAWRENCE GULF	NEW BRUNSWICK	CHOCKPISH, BRKWTR	46-35.00	64-43.20	14734.92	43828.75	
ST LAWRENCE GULF	NEW BRUNSWICK	RICHIBUCTO HEAD	46-40.30	64-42.60	14763.37	43803.56	
ST LAWRENCE GULF	NEW BRUNSWICK	RICHIBUCTO CAPE BRKWTR	46-40.50	64-42.50	14764.29	43802.03	
ST LAWRENCE GULF	NEW BRUNSWICK	POINTE DE LAMEQUE RANGE	47-49.00	64-42.30	15042.12	43430.95	
ST LAWRENCE GULF	NEW BRUNSWICK	BIG SHIPPAGAN WHARF	47-44.80	64-42.20	15029.96	43457.63	
ST LAWRENCE GULF	NEW BRUNSWICK	PAINT POINT RANGE	47-45.80	64-41.70	15032.04	43447.68	
ST LAWRENCE GULF	NEW BRUNSWICK	ST EDWARD DE KENT WHARF	46-32.50	64-41.50	13334.57	44078.85	
ST LAWRENCE GULF	NEW BRUNSWICK	BUCTOUCHE RIVER RANGE	46-29.20	64-40.80	14697.59	43833.46	
ST LAWRENCE GULF	NEW BRUNSWICK	BIG SHIPPEGAN BRKWTR	47-43.10	64-40.00	15021.28	43453.20	
ST LAWRENCE GULF	NEW BRUNSWICK	BIG SHIPPEGAN ENTR	47-43.30	64-39.70	15021.38	43449.84	
ST LAWRENCE GULF	NEW BRUNSWICK	ST THOMAS DE KENT WHARF	46-26.90	64-38.20	14679.96	43823.45	
ST LAWRENCE GULF	NEW BRUNSWICK	BLACK POINT	47-53.10	64-37.50	15045.64	43370.63	
ST LAWRENCE GULF	NEW BRUNSWICK	COCAGNE RIVER RANGE	46-20.30	64-37.00	14638.25	43837.75	
ST LAWRENCE GULF	NEW BRUNSWICK	COCAGNE BAR WHARF	46-24.50	64-36.80	14663.50	43822.08	
ST LAWRENCE GULF	NEW BRUNSWICK	BUCTOUCHE BAR	46-27.70	64-36.80	14682.53	43810.75	
ST LAWRENCE GULF	NEW BRUNSWICK	COTE d'OR WHARF	46-21.00	64-36.80	14642.26	43834.02	
ST LAWRENCE GULF	NEW BRUNSWICK	STE MARIE-SUR MAR RANGE	47-47.00	64-34.10	15023.10	43387.05	
ST LAWRENCE GULF	NEW BRUNSWICK	STE MARIE-SUR-MER	47-46.80	64-34.00	15022.36	43387.65	
ST LAWRENCE GULF	NEW BRUNSWICK	COOK POINT BUOY	46-23.50	64-33.20	14652.10	43800.39	
ST LAWRENCE GULF	NEW BRUNSWICK	BUCTOUCHE BAR BELL"X17"	46-31.60	64-32.90	14699.07	43768.95	
ST LAWRENCE GULF	NEW BRUNSWICK	MISCOU ISLAND WHISTLE "E1"	48-02.00	64-32.80	15061.27	43278.31	
ST LAWRENCE GULF	NEW BRUNSWICK	POINTE DU CHENE RANGE	46-14.50	64-31.80	14594.75	43820.49	
ST LAWRENCE GULF	NEW BRUNSWICK	CAISSIE POINT	46-19.20	64-30.80	14622.54	43798.31	
ST LAWRENCE GULF	NEW BRUNSWICK	POINTE DU CHENE RANGE	46-14.50	64-30.70	14593.24	43812.90	
ST LAWRENCE GULF	NEW BRUNSWICK	HEAD OF BREAKWATER	46-18.80	64-30.60	14619.80	43798.25	
ST LAWRENCE GULF	NEW BRUNSWICK	PIGEON HILL WHARF	47-52.70	64-30.50	15033.45	43324.90	
ST LAWRENCE GULF	NEW BRUNSWICK	FOX DENS GULLY	47-53.20	64-30.30	15034.51	43320.22	
ST LAWRENCE GULF	NEW BRUNSWICK	SHEDIAC HARBOUR BELL "XN"	46-17.00	64-30.10	14608.00	43800.72	
ST LAWRENCE GULF	NEW BRUNSWICK	ISCOU GULLY	47-55.00	64-29.70	15038.45	43304.17	
ST LAWRENCE GULF	NEW BRUNSWICK	MISCOU ISLAND BIRCH POINT	48-00.60	64-29.60	15052.90	43265.92	
ST LAWRENCE GULF	NEW BRUNSWICK	ROBICHAUD	46-13.40	64-23.00	14576.00	43763.37	
ST LAWRENCE GULF	NEW BRUNSWICK	HARSHMANS BROOK WHARF	46-14.00	64-18.00	14573.11	43727.06	
ST LAWRENCE GULF	NEW BRUNSWICK	CAPE L'ABOITEAU	46-14.00	64-18.00	14573.11	43727.06	
ST LAWRENCE GULF	NEW BRUNSWICK	CAPE BALD WHARF	46-14.10	64-15.70	14570.72	43710.93	
ST LAWRENCE GULF	NEW BRUNSWICK	BAS CAP PELE	46-14.10	64-15.70	14570.72	43710.93	
ST LAWRENCE GULF	NEW BRUNSWICK	LITTLE CAPE BRKWTR	46-11.90	64-09.80	14549.72	43677.71	
ST LAWRENCE GULF	NEW BRUNSWICK	LITTLE CAPE OUTER BRKWTR	46-11.90	64-09.70	14549.60	43677.03	
ST LAWRENCE GULF	NEW BRUNSWICK	SHEMOGUE RANGE	46-10.00	64-08.90	14536.95	43677.73	
ST LAWRENCE GULF	NEW BRUNSWICK	FORT MONCTON POINT	46-02.60	64-04.30	14485.45	43669.69	
ST LAWRENCE GULF	NEW BRUNSWICK	BOTSFORD BRKWTR	46-10.20	63-56.00	14522.61	43589.26	
ST LAWRENCE GULF	NEW BRUNSWICK	JOURIMAIN ISLAND	46-09.50	63-48.50	14509.69	43540.73	
ST LAWRENCE GULF	NEW BRUNSWICK	CAPE TORMINTINE ENTR	46-07.60	63-47.10	14496.79	43537.64	

PASSES

BODY OF WATER	PROV/STATE	NAME	LAT	LON	TD#1	TD#2	CHART
ST LAWRENCE GULF	NEW BRUNSWICK	CAPE TORMINTINE WHARF	46-08.00	63-46.70	14498.72	43533.60	
ST LAWRENCE GULF	NEW BRUNSWICK	INDIAN POINT N RANGE	46-06.50	63-46.50	14489.54	43537.24	
ST LAWRENCE GULF	NEW BRUNSWICK	CAPE TORMINTINE WHARF	46-08.10	63-46.40	14498.98	43531.23	
ST LAWRENCE GULF	NEW BRUNSWICK	CAPE TORMINTINE BRKWTR	46-08.00	63-46.40	14498.38	43531.57	
ST LAWRENCE GULF	NEW BRUNSWICK	INDIAN POINT RANGE	46-06.50	63-46.40	14489.43	43536.56	
ST LAWRENCE GULF	NEW BRUNSWICK	CAPE TORMINTINE HARBOUR	46-08.10	63-46.20	14498.75	43529.88	
ST LAWRENCE GULF	NEW BRUNSWICK	CAPE TORMINTINE APPR	46-08.60	63-45.00	14500.37	43520.09	
ST LAWRENCE GULF	NEW BRUNSWICK	TORMINTINE REEFS BELL "X5"	46-06.60	63-41.10	14484.20	43500.52	
	NEW BRUNSWICK	MARK POINT	45-10.20	67-12.70	14131.43	44840.34	
	NEW BRUNSWICK	SPRUCE POINT	45-10.10	67-11.20	14131.50	44833.88	
	NEW BRUNSWICK	ST ANDREWS WEST CHANNEL	45-04.30	67-04.10	14071.75	44796.07	
	NEW BRUNSWICK	ST ANDREWS/NORTH POINT	45-04.10	67-02.90	14070.46	44790.63	
	NEW BRUNSWICK	CHAMCOOK CHANNEL BUOY	45-07.20	67-02.80	14105.19	44793.95	
	NEW BRUNSWICK	TONGUE SHOAL	45-03.80	67-00.80	14068.73	44781.10	
	NEW BRUNSWICK	FAIRHAVEN WHARF	44-57.90	67-00.60	14003.20	44773.21	
	NEW BRUNSWICK	DEER POINT	44-55.50	66-59.10	13977.84	44763.90	
	NEW BRUNSWICK	ROOSEVELT MEMORIAL BRIDGE	44-52.00	66-59.00	13939.10	44759.35	
	NEW BRUNSWICK	CHOCOLATE COVE WHARF	44-56.80	66-58.50	13992.79	44762.84	
	NEW BRUNSWICK	CHERRY ISLET	44-55.10	66-58.10	13974.30	44759.13	
	NEW BRUNSWICK	OUT HEAD OF WHARF	44-53.40	66-57.50	13956.02	44754.56	
	NEW BRUNSWICK	LEONARDVILLE HARBOUR	44-58.20	66-57.40	14009.23	44759.66	
	NEW BRUNSWICK	LORDS COVE RANGE	45-00.40	66-56.90	14033.97	44759.98	
	NEW BRUNSWICK	LORDS COVE GOVT WHARF	45-00.40	66-56.90	14033.97	44759.98	
	NEW BRUNSWICK	RICHARDSON WHARF	44-59.70	66-56.80	14026.31	44758.75	
	NEW BRUNSWICK	POMPEY LEDGE	44-58.80	66-56.70	14016.43	44757.28	
	NEW BRUNSWICK	BULL ROCK WHISTLE "XA1"	44-30.20	66-56.60	13701.29	44723.88	
	NEW BRUNSWICK	MALLOCH BEACH GOVT WHARF	44-55.00	66-56.50	13974.60	44752.07	
	NEW BRUNSWICK	CURRY COVE WHARF	44-55.70	66-56.40	13982.42	44752.43	
	NEW BRUNSWICK	TWO HOUR ROCK	45-01.80	66-56.20	14049.96	44758.46	
	NEW BRUNSWICK	LITTLE PETITE PASSAGE	45-02.10	66-55.60	14053.71	44756.12	
	NEW BRUNSWICK	SOUTHWEST HEAD/GULL CLIFF	44-30.20	66-54.40	13704.19	44714.93	
	NEW BRUNSWICK	LETITE HARBOUR LEDGE	45-02.90	66-54.10	14063.57	44750.27	
	NEW BRUNSWICK	HEAD HARBOUR	44-57.50	66-54.10	14004.17	44744.34	
	NEW BRUNSWICK	MATTHEWS LEDGE	45-03.10	66-53.80	14065.98	44749.13	
	NEW BRUNSWICK	LETITE PASSAGE	45-02.30	66-53.60	14057.32	44747.36	
	NEW BRUNSWICK	MORGAN LEDGE	45-02.20	66-53.60	14056.22	44747.25	
	NEW BRUNSWICK	BACK BAY BREAKWATER	45-03.20	66-51.80	14068.40	44740.14	
	NEW BRUNSWICK	FUNDY ENTR WHISTLE "M"	44-13.30	66-51.70	13525.47	44683.21	
	NEW BRUNSWICK	BLISS ISLAND	45-01.10	66-51.10	14045.87	44734.75	
	NEW BRUNSWICK	SEAL COVE OUTER BRKWTR	44-38.80	66-50.40	13802.86	44707.78	
	NEW BRUNSWICK	ROARING BULL	45-02.40	66-48.80	14061.56	44725.55	
	NEW BRUNSWICK	PEA POINT/PEA ISLET	45-02.40	66-48.60	14061.68	44724.63	
	NEW BRUNSWICK	WHITE HORSE ISLET	44-36.20	66-48.50	13776.74	44696.90	
	NEW BRUNSWICK	BLACKS HARBOUR ENTRANCE	45-02.80	66-48.50	14066.09	44724.57	

PASSES

BODY OF WATER	PROV/STATE	NAME	LAT	LON	TD#1	TD#2	CHART
	NEW BRUNSWICK	LONG EDDY POINT	44-48.00	66-47.00	13906.33	44702.74	
	NEW BRUNSWICK	GANNET ROCK/GRAND MANAN	44-30.60	66-46.90	13718.03	44684.20	
	NEW BRUNSWICK	INGALLS HEAD BRKWTR	44-39.70	66-45.30	13818.12	44686.77	
	NEW BRUNSWICK	NORTH HEAD HARBOUR WHARF	44-45.80	66-45.10	13884.23	44692.08	
	NEW BRUNSWICK	NET ROCKS LEDGES "XV6"	44-45.30	66-44.50	13879.38	44688.91	
	NEW BRUNSWICK	BEAVER HARBOUR BRKWTR	45-04.20	66-44.40	14083.60	44706.75	
	NEW BRUNSWICK	DREWS HEAD	45-03.80	66-44.10	14079.44	44704.97	
	NEW BRUNSWICK	SW WOLF ISLAND	44-56.20	66-44.10	13997.43	44697.80	
	NEW BRUNSWICK	SWALLOW TAIL ISLAND	44-45.90	66-44.00	13886.31	44687.28	
	NEW BRUNSWICK	GULL ISLET	44-41.20	66-43.80	13835.83	44681.72	
	NEW BRUNSWICK	HALF TIDE ROCK/CHENEY	44-39.30	66-43.70	13815.46	44679.38	
	NEW BRUNSWICK	FARMER LEDGE	44-43.40	66-43.60	13859.73	44683.03	
	NEW BRUNSWICK	BEAVER HARB BELL "KEA"	45-02.30	66-43.40	14063.66	44700.28	
	NEW BRUNSWICK	EDMUNDS ROCK	44-40.40	66-43.30	13827.71	44678.72	
	NEW BRUNSWICK	LONG POINT	44-36.90	66-42.60	13790.80	44672.18	
	NEW BRUNSWICK	THE WOLVES WHISTLE "KE"	45-00.50	66-42.50	14044.80	44694.39	
	NEW BRUNSWICK	GREAT DUCK ISLAND	44-41.10	66-41.70	13836.82	44672.35	
	NEW BRUNSWICK	BRAZIL SHOAL BELL	44-35.30	66-41.30	13775.04	44664.93	
	NEW BRUNSWICK	PRANGLE POINT BELL "XP3"	44-38.50	66-40.70	13809.94	44665.40	
	NEW BRUNSWICK	OLD PROPRIETOR LEDGE BELL	44-33.00	66-39.70	13752.22	44655.71	
	NEW BRUNSWICK	OLD PROPRIETOR SHOAL	44-32.20	66-39.40	13744.02	44653.64	
	NOVA SCOTIA	LURCHER SHOAL NK	43-47.50	66-37.00	13278.91	44600.66	
	NOVA SCOTIA	LURCHER SHOAL WHISTLE	43-49.80	66-30.00	13315.50	44574.83	
	NEW BRUNSWICK	MACES BAY WHARF	45-07.10	66-28.80	14120.66	44632.69	
	NEW BRUNSWICK	POINT LEPREAU WHISTLE	45-02.50	66-27.90	14073.01	44625.20	
	NEW BRUNSWICK	POINT LEPREAU	45-03.50	66-27.60	14083.54	44624.35	
	NOVA SCOTIA	SW LEDGE WHISTLE "M2"	44-10.30	66-27.20	13529.97	44581.09	
	NOVA SCOTIA	LURCHER SHOAL	43-53.00	66-26.20	13354.76	44562.10	
	NOVA SCOTIA	NW LEDGE WHISTLE BUOY	44-18.30	66-26.00	13614.16	44582.60	
	NEW BRUNSWICK	DIPPER HARBOUR WHARF	45-05.80	66-24.90	14108.25	44612.11	
	NOVA SCOTIA	BRIER ISLAND	44-15.00	66-23.60	13583.29	44569.38	
	NOVA SCOTIA	GULL ROCK BELL BUOY	44-12.00	66-23.20	13553.06	44565.22	
	NOVA SCOTIA	WESTPORT WHARF	44-15.80	66-21.00	13594.88	44558.55	
	NEW BRUNSWICK	CHANCE HARBOUR/REEF PT	45-07.10	66-20.90	14122.57	44592.25	
	NOVA SCOTIA	NORTH POINT/BRIER I	44-17.20	66-20.60	13609.71	44557.86	
	NOVA SCOTIA	PETER ISLAND ENTR	44-15.40	66-20.40	13591.56	44555.59	
	NOVA SCOTIA	COW LEDGE SHOAL BELL	44-17.10	66-20.30	13609.06	44556.45	
	NOVA SCOTIA	FREEPORT WHARF	44-16.50	66-20.30	13602.93	44555.99	
	NOVA SCOTIA	DARTMOUTH POINT BELL	44-14.80	66-20.00	13585.96	44553.36	
	NOVA SCOTIA	GRAND PASSAGE BRKWTR	44-16.00	66-19.80	13598.46	44553.39	
	NOVA SCOTIA	TRINITY LEDGE WHISTLE	43-58.80	66-18.50	13426.10	44534.52	
	NEW BRUNSWICK	FIVE FATHOM HOLE WHARF	45-11.20	66-15.50	14164.89	44565.56	
	NEW BRUNSWICK	SPLIT ROCK BELL BUOY	45-07.10	66-14.60	14123.67	44559.32	
	NEW BRUNSWICK	MUSQUASH ENTRANCE	45-08.60	66-14.30	14138.82	44558.27	

PASSES

BODY OF WATER	PROV/STATE	NAME	LAT	LON	TD#1	TD#2	CHART
	NOVA SCOTIA	YARMOUTH SOUND WHISTLE	43-45.50	66-14.20	13301.21	44506.21	
	NOVA SCOTIA	BOARS HEAD/PETIT PASS	44-24.20	66-13.10	13689.61	44528.78	
	NOVA SCOTIA	TIVERTON BREAKWATER	44-23.60	66-12.80	13683.86	44527.00	
	NOVA SCOTIA	CAPE ST MARY BAY BUOY	44-04.20	66-12.60	13489.13	44512.92	
	NOVA SCOTIA	CAPE ST MARY BAY	44-05.20	66-12.60	13499.12	44513.63	
	NOVA SCOTIA	CAPE ST MARY BRKWTR	44-05.10	66-12.40	13498.40	44512.67	
	NOVA SCOTIA	PETIT PASSAGE BELL	44-22.30	66-12.20	13671.39	44523.38	
	NOVA SCOTIA	METEGHAN BELL BUOY	44-12.20	66-11.80	13570.27	44514.88	
	NOVA SCOTIA	SANDFORD BELL BUOY	43-55.80	66-10.90	13408.29	44499.61	
	NOVA SCOTIA	CHEGOGGIN BELL "NQ2"	43-50.50	66-10.70	13356.42	44495.02	
	NOVA SCOTIA	WHALE COVE WHARF	44-26.20	66-10.70	13712.28	44518.86	
	NOVA SCOTIA	PORT MAITLAND BELL BUOY	43-59.60	66-10.30	13446.80	44499.63	
	NOVA SCOTIA	METEGHAN OUTER BRKWTR	44-11.70	66-10.10	13567.45	44506.88	
	NOVA SCOTIA	CHEGOGGIN POINT BRKWTR	43-51.00	66-09.70	13363.00	44491.08	
	NOVA SCOTIA	PORT MAITLAND BRKWTR	43-59.10	66-09.60	13442.92	44496.22	
	NOVA SCOTIA	CAT ROCK BELL "Y3"	43-47.00	66-09.50	13324.21	44487.44	
	NOVA SCOTIA	SANDFORD HARBOUR RANGE	43-55.10	66-09.40	13403.77	44492.62	
	NOVA SCOTIA	CAPE FOURCHU/EAST CAPE	43-47.60	66-09.40	13330.25	44487.43	
	NOVA SCOTIA	YARMOUTH BAR BRKWTR	43-49.00	66-09.20	13344.26	44487.55	
	NEW BRUNSWICK	LORNEVILLE BRKWTR	45-11.60	66-08.90	14169.04	44530.11	
	NOVA SCOTIA	SHIPS STERN	43-48.50	66-08.80	13340.06	44485.49	
	NOVA SCOTIA	GREEN ISLAND	43-41.20	66-08.70	13269.29	44480.00	
	NOVA SCOTIA	METEGHAN RIVER BRKWTR	44-13.20	66-08.70	13584.20	44501.50	
	NOVA SCOTIA	EDGE OF SHOAL	43-48.80	66-08.60	13343.33	44484.84	
	NOVA SCOTIA	COMEAUVILLE WHARF	44-17.50	66-08.00	13627.94	44500.98	
	NOVA SCOTIA	LITTLE RIVER WHARF	44-26.60	66-07.70	13719.27	44504.97	
	NOVA SCOTIA	CHEBOGUE POINT BELL	43-43.60	66-07.50	13294.69	44476.59	
	NEW BRUNSWICK	MARBLE COVE ENTRANCE	45-16.30	66-05.30	14214.95	44510.95	
	NOVA SCOTIA	EAST SANDY COVE WHARF	44-29.20	66-05.20	13747.60	44494.49	
	NEW BRUNSWICK	MARBLE COVE	45-16.30	66-05.10	14214.92	44509.84	
	NEW BRUNSWICK	ST JOHN HARBOUR RANGE	45-16.40	66-04.20	14215.75	44504.82	
	NEW BRUNSWICK	W ST JOHN NO 14	45-15.50	66-03.70	14206.92	44501.99	
	NEW BRUNSWICK	ST JOHN PIER NO 12	45-15.60	66-03.70	14207.89	44501.99	
	NEW BRUNSWICK	PARTRIDGE ISLAND	45-14.40	66-03.30	14196.16	44499.70	
	NEW BRUNSWICK	ST ANDREWS WHARF	45-04.30	66-03.30	14097.30	44498.36	
	NOVA SCOTIA	PINKNEY POINT	43-42.20	66-03.20	13288.88	44457.33	
	NOVA SCOTIA	CANDLEBOX ISLAND ENTR	43-39.70	66-02.80	13265.68	44454.01	
	NEW BRUNSWICK	ST JOHN HARB WHISTLE J	45-12.90	66-02.70	14181.50	44496.27	
	NEW BRUNSWICK	COURTENAY BAY BRKWTR	45-16.40	66-02.40	14215.45	44494.74	
	NEW BRUNSWICK	COURTENAY BAY RANGE	45-16.40	66-02.40	14215.45	44494.74	
	NOVA SCOTIA	CENTREVILLE BELL BUOY	44-33.10	66-02.20	13788.93	44481.89	
	NOVA SCOTIA	BIG COOK ISLAND	43-42.60	66-02.10	13294.67	44452.87	
	NOVA SCOTIA	RAN ISLAND LEDGE	43-42.10	66-02.05	13289.17	44454.27	
	NOVA SCOTIA	LITTLE RIVER HARBOUR	43-42.70	66-01.90	13295.98	44452.07	

PASSES

BODY OF WATER	PROV/STATE	NAME	LAT	LON	TD#1	TD#2	CHART
	NOVA SCOTIA	PEASE ISLAND S POINT	43-37.70	66-01.60	13248.83	44447.63	
	NOVA SCOTIA	THE WEST SLUICE	43-40.20	66-01.10	13273.53	44447.07	
	NOVA SCOTIA	WEYMOUTH HARBOUR ENTR	44-26.40	66-01.10	13723.56	44473.39	
	NOVA SCOTIA	FRENCHMANS POINT	43-38.10	66-01.00	13253.74	44445.33	
	NOVA SCOTIA	SEAL ISLAND	43-23.70	66-00.80	13118.79	44435.34	
	NEW BRUNSWICK	BLACK POINT	45-13.00	66-00.50	14182.26	44484.06	
	NOVA SCOTIA	BLONDE ROCK WHISTLE "N4"	43-18.60	66-00.10	13073.12	44429.19	
	NOVA SCOTIA	THE EAST SLUICE	43-40.20	66-00.10	13275.33	44442.79	
	NOVA SCOTIA	BANTAM BELL BUOY	43-43.20	65-58.10	13307.40	44435.97	
	NOVA SCOTIA	TUSKET WEDGE	43-42.80	65-58.00	13303.76	44435.30	
	NOVA SCOTIA	TUSKET RIVER/BIG FISH I	43-42.20	65-57.10	13299.64	44431.05	
	NOVA SCOTIA	ST MARYS BAY	44-34.80	65-56.10	13810.33	44452.50	
	NEW BRUNSWICK	CAPE SPENCER	45-11.70	65-54.60	14169.11	44451.12	
	NOVA SCOTIA	CAMP COVE WHARF	43-43.30	65-50.50	13321.30	44402.76	
	NOVA SCOTIA	DEEP COVE WHARF	44-39.90	65-50.00	13863.88	44423.21	
	NOVA SCOTIA	ABBOT HARBOUR	43-39.60	65-49.20	13288.96	44395.14	
	NEW BRUNSWICK	BLACK RIVER WHARF	45-15.40	65-48.70	14203.09	44417.08	
	NOVA SCOTIA	PRIM POINT/DIGBY GUT	44-41.50	65-47.20	13880.82	44409.11	
	NOVA SCOTIA	DENIS POINT WHARF	43-36.70	65-47.20	13265.58	44384.91	
	NOVA SCOTIA	PUBNICO HARBOUR ENTR	43-35.90	65-47.00	13258.55	44383.63	
	NOVA SCOTIA	LOWER E PUBNICO WHARF	43-36.40	65-46.70	13263.70	44382.57	
	NOVA SCOTIA	PRIM POINT WHISTLE	44-26.60	65-46.40	13738.42	44401.58	
	NOVA SCOTIA	VIGNEAU LEDGE	43-32.20	65-46.20	13225.99	44378.31	
	NOVA SCOTIA	DIGBY GUT ENTRANCE	44-41.30	65-45.60	13879.74	44400.78	
	NOVA SCOTIA	VICTORIA BEACH	44-40.60	65-45.30	13873.20	44399.11	
	NOVA SCOTIA	DIGBY PIER	44-37.60	65-45.10	13844.65	44397.58	
	NOVA SCOTIA	WESTERN WAY LEDGE	43-31.70	65-45.10	13223.45	44373.28	
	NOVA SCOTIA	WOODS HARBOUR/BIG LEDGE	43-31.20	65-44.80	13219.44	44371.73	
	NOVA SCOTIA	OUTER ISLAND S POINT	43-27.40	65-44.70	13185.04	44369.45	
	NOVA SCOTIA	THE FALLS LEDGE	43-32.10	65-44.70	13227.84	44371.73	
	NOVA SCOTIA	FALLS POINT WHARF	43-31.80	65-44.50	13225.46	44370.72	
	NOVA SCOTIA	LOWER WOODS HARB WHARF	43-31.30	65-44.30	13221.27	44369.61	
	NOVA SCOTIA	STODDART ISLAND POINT	43-28.60	65-43.20	13198.78	44363.54	
	NOVA SCOTIA	PROSPECT POINT BRKWTR	43-29.40	65-43.20	13206.04	44363.92	
	NOVA SCOTIA	PIQUET ROCK	43-29.40	65-43.00	13206.41	44363.05	
	NOVA SCOTIA	PORT WADE	44-40.60	65-42.70	13874.56	44385.61	
	NOVA SCOTIA	SHAG HARBOUR WHARF	43-29.60	65-42.40	13209.35	44360.53	
	NOVA SCOTIA	WINCHESTER POINT	44-37.00	65-41.10	13841.28	44376.86	
	NOVA SCOTIA	BEAR POINT WHARF	43-29.20	65-39.40	13211.32	44347.25	
	NOVA SCOTIA	WEST HEAD/CAPE SABLE I	43-27.40	65-39.30	13195.32	44346.02	
	NOVA SCOTIA	FISH ISLAND	43-25.70	65-39.30	13180.07	44345.27	
	NOVA SCOTIA	WEST HEAD BRKWTR	43-27.60	65-39.30	13197.11	44346.11	
	NOVA SCOTIA	CLARK'S HARBOUR WHARF	43-26.50	65-38.20	13189.32	44340.84	
	NOVA SCOTIA	NEWELLTON NEW PIER	43-28.40	65-38.10	13206.54	44341.21	

PASSES

BODY OF WATER	PROV/STATE	NAME	LAT	LON	TD#1	TD#2	CHART
	NOVA SCOTIA	SWIM POINT	43-26.00	65-38.00	13185.23	44339.75	
	NOVA SCOTIA	CAPE SABLE	43-23.40	65-37.30	13163.40	44335.58	
	NOVA SCOTIA	SCHAFNER POINT	44-42.60	65-37.20	13896.06	44356.85	
	NOVA SCOTIA	DONALD HEAD BRKWTR	43-26.90	65-35.20	13198.53	44327.87	
	NOVA SCOTIA	WHITE KNOLL LEDGE BELL	43-25.20	65-34.40	13184.93	44323.68	
	NOVA SCOTIA	PARKERS COVE BRKWTR	44-49.00	65-32.40	13957.40	44330.73	
	NEW BRUNSWICK	QUACO HEAD	45-19.40	65-32.20	14234.35	44318.80	
	NEW BRUNSWICK	ST MARTINS BRKWTR	45-21.30	65-32.00	14251.17	44316.39	
	NOVA SCOTIA	ANNAPOLIS GOVT PIER	44-44.70	65-31.20	13918.03	44324.73	
	NOVA SCOTIA	BACCARO POINT ENTRANCE	43-27.00	65-28.30	13212.13	44297.41	
	NOVA SCOTIA	UPPER PORT LA TOUR BRKWTR	43-30.30	65-28.20	13241.37	44298.05	
	NOVA SCOTIA	PORT LA TOUR BRKWTR	43-30.00	65-28.20	13238.73	44297.95	
	NOVA SCOTIA	CROW NECK ISLAND/GATE ROCK	43-28.70	65-27.20	13229.05	44293.05	
	NOVA SCOTIA	WHALEBACK ROCK	43-29.60	65-27.00	13237.32	44292.44	
	NOVA SCOTIA	BRAZIL ROCK WHISTLE	43-21.00	65-26.80	13162.51	44288.75	
	NOVA SCOTIA	PORT LA TOUR WHISTLE	43-26.50	65-24.20	13215.17	44278.95	
	NOVA SCOTIA	THE SALVAGES	43-28.10	65-22.80	13231.60	44273.12	
	NEW BRUNSWICK	QUACO LEDGE BELL K16	45-14.70	65-22.20	14189.16	44262.43	
	NOVA SCOTIA	INGOMAR WHARF	43-33.80	65-21.80	13283.12	44270.09	
	NOVA SCOTIA	HAMPTON/CHUTE COVE	44-54.30	65-21.20	14007.86	44267.50	
	NOVA SCOTIA	CAPE NEGRO ISLAND	43-30.50	65-20.80	13255.98	44264.71	
	NOVA SCOTIA	GUNNING COVE WHARF	43-40.80	65-20.40	13346.88	44265.23	
	NOVA SCOTIA	GUNNING COVE	43-40.90	65-20.10	13348.22	44263.86	
	NOVA SCOTIA	SURF POINT RANGE	43-40.80	65-20.00	13347.49	44263.37	
	NOVA SCOTIA	SANDY POINT ENTRANCE	43-41.50	65-19.60	13354.27	44261.64	
	NOVA SCOTIA	NEGRO HARBOUR WHISTLE	43-31.00	65-18.90	13263.56	44256.18	
	NOVA SCOTIA	LOWER SANDY PT BRKWTR	43-40.80	65-18.20	13350.23	44254.98	
	NOVA SCOTIA	PORT LORNE PIER	44-57.00	65-16.00	14032.29	44236.93	
	NOVA SCOTIA	CAPE ROSEWAY/McNUTT I	43-37.40	65-15.90	13324.07	44243.65	
	NOVA SCOTIA	LOWER JORDAN BAY WHARF	43-40.90	65-14.40	13356.83	44237.19	
	NOVA SCOTIA	PORT GEORGE PIER	45-00.40	65-09.40	14061.97	44197.06	
	NOVA SCOTIA	BULL ROCK BELL BUOY	43-37.50	65-08.30	13336.64	44208.09	
	NOVA SCOTIA	LOCKEPORT RANGE WHARF	43-42.10	65-06.70	13378.47	44200.85	
	NOVA SCOTIA	OSBORNE HARBOUR WHARF	43-42.90	65-06.60	13385.48	44200.41	
	NOVA SCOTIA	CARTER I INNER BRKWTR	43-42.10	65-06.60	13378.61	44200.38	
	NOVA SCOTIA	CARTER ISLAND/N BRKWTR	43-42.10	65-06.50	13378.75	44199.89	
	NOVA SCOTIA	CARTER ISLAND	43-42.30	65-06.10	13381.04	44198.00	
	NOVA SCOTIA	GULL ROCK ENTRANCE	43-39.30	65-06.00	13355.48	44197.36	
	NOVA SCOTIA	MARGARETSVILLE BRKWTR	45-03.00	65-04.00	14083.82	44163.73	
	NOVA SCOTIA	LOCKEPORT WHISTLE BUOY	43-36.70	65-02.30	13338.86	44179.69	
	NOVA SCOTIA	LITTLE HARBOUR WHARF	43-43.00	65-01.80	13393.06	44177.39	
	NOVA SCOTIA	ISLE HAUTE	45-15.10	65-00.40	14184.73	44131.05	
	NOVA SCOTIA	LITTLE HARBOUR WHISTLE	43-42.40	64-59.90	13390.59	44168.25	
	NEW BRUNSWICK	ALMA PUBLIC WHARF	45-36.00	64-56.70	14351.16	44079.98	

P A S S E S

BODY OF WATER	PROV/STATE	NAME	LAT	LON	TD#1	TD#2	CHAR
	NOVA SCOTIA	PORT HEBERT/EAST SIDE	43-49.10	64-55.80	13452.72	44147.87	
	NOVA SCOTIA	PORT HEBERT/SHINGLE PT	43-48.70	64-55.50	13449.71	44146.44	
	NOVA SCOTIA	PORT HEBERT WHISTLE	43-46.30	64-54.80	13430.36	44143.25	
	NOVA SCOTIA	PORT JOLI WHARF	43-50.40	64-51.80	13468.58	44127.94	
	NOVA SCOTIA	APPLE RIVER ENTRANCE	45-28.40	64-51.40	14287.61	44058.20	
	NOVA SCOTIA	CENTRAL PORT MOUTON	43-55.20	64-50.60	13510.31	44121.08	
	NOVA SCOTIA	LITTLE HOPE SHOAL BELL	43-47.30	64-49.90	13444.95	44119.03	
	NOVA SCOTIA	HARBORVILLE PIER	45-09.10	64-48.60	14131.45	44066.30	
	NOVA SCOTIA	PORT MOUTON/SPECTACLE I	43-55.10	64-48.30	13512.02	44109.54	
	NOVA SCOTIA	LITTLE HOPE ISLAND	43-48.60	64-47.40	13458.85	44106.41	
	NOVA SCOTIA	ADVOCATE HARBOUR	45-19.20	64-47.10	14212.25	44044.56	
	NOVA SCOTIA	LITTLE HOPE I WHISTLE	43-47.40	64-46.90	13449.50	44104.17	
	NEW BRUNSWICK	CAPE ENRAGE	45-35.60	64-46.80	14340.13	44017.12	
	NOVA SCOTIA	CAPE D'OR	45-17.50	64-46.50	14198.42	44043.14	
	NOVA SCOTIA	HUNTS LANDING BRKWTR	43-57.10	64-46.20	13531.00	44098.43	
	NOVA SCOTIA	HUNTS LANDING FOG SIGNAL	43-57.10	64-46.10	13531.10	44097.91	
	NOVA SCOTIA	BLACK ROCK	45-10.20	64-45.80	14139.54	44048.10	
	NOVA SCOTIA	MOUTON HEAD BELL	43-51.20	64-45.70	13482.46	44097.38	
	NOVA SCOTIA	WHITE POINT ROCK BELL	43-55.60	64-43.10	13521.83	44083.12	
	NOVA SCOTIA	PORT MOUTON WHISTLE	43-53.50	64-42.60	13505.01	44081.20	
	NOVA SCOTIA	FORT POINT	44-02.60	64-42.50	13580.47	44077.79	
	NOVA SCOTIA	BROOKLYN PIER BRKWTR	44-02.80	64-41.50	13583.07	44072.55	
	NOVA SCOTIA	MOOSE HARBOUR FOG SIGNAL	44-01.10	64-40.00	13570.44	44065.44	
	NOVA SCOTIA	MOOSE POINT BRKWTR	44-01.20	64-39.80	13571.46	44064.38	
	NOVA SCOTIA	WESTERN HEAD ENTRANCE	43-59.40	64-39.80	13556.62	44065.04	
	NOVA SCOTIA	LIVERPOOL BAY APPROACH	44-01.60	64-38.90	13575.61	44059.58	
	NOVA SCOTIA	COFFIN ISLAND	44-02.00	64-37.70	13580.03	44053.21	
	NEW BRUNSWICK	GRINDSTONE ISLAND	45-43.30	64-37.30	14389.42	43940.58	
	NOVA SCOTIA	HALLS HARBOUR BRKWTR	45-12.10	64-36.80	14151.69	43990.92	
	NOVA SCOTIA	MEDWAY BREAKWATER	44-08.00	64-34.60	13631.93	44034.32	
	NOVA SCOTIA	PORT GREVILLE BELL BUOY	45-23.00	64-33.10	14234.58	43951.60	
	NOVA SCOTIA	PORT GREVILLE	45-24.60	64-33.00	14246.72	43948.30	
	NOVA SCOTIA	VOGLERS COVE	44-09.20	64-32.80	13643.18	44024.21	
	NOVA SCOTIA	MEDWAY HEAD ENTRANCE	44-06.20	64-32.50	13618.99	44024.18	
	NOVA SCOTIA	MEDWAY WHISTLE	44-05.00	64-31.50	13610.08	44019.54	
	NOVA SCOTIA	RAGGED POINT WHARF	45-39.60	64-29.30	14355.47	43896.19	
	NOVA SCOTIA	CHERRY COVE	44-09.50	64-29.00	13648.57	44003.91	
	NOVA SCOTIA	APPLE COVE BELL	44-08.30	64-28.70	13639.10	44003.00	
	NOVA SCOTIA	LITTLE HARBOUR BELL	44-09.60	64-28.30	13649.91	44000.13	
	NOVA SCOTIA	CAPE SHARP ENTRANCE	45-21.90	64-23.60	14221.06	43893.86	
	NOVA SCOTIA	MINAS BASIN WHARF	45-12.10	64-22.80	14146.64	43905.10	
	NOVA SCOTIA	UPPER PEREAU	45-12.10	64-22.80	14146.64	43905.10	
	NOVA SCOTIA	BUSH ISLAND WHARF	44-14.00	64-22.40	13689.44	43965.70	
	NOVA SCOTIA	INDIAN ISLAND WHISTLE	44-09.30	64-22.30	13652.03	43968.36	

PASSES

BODY OF WATER	PROV/STATE	NAME	LAT	LON	TD#1	TD#2	CHART
	NOVA SCOTIA	MAHONE HARBOUR	44-26.80	64-22.10	13791.66	43954.16	
	NOVA SCOTIA	DUBLIN SHORE WHARF	44-16.00	64-22.00	13705.65	43962.11	
	NOVA SCOTIA	LA HAVE/FORT POINT	44-17.30	64-21.10	13716.55	43956.26	
	NOVA SCOTIA	WESTHAVER ISLAND	44-26.20	64-20.30	13787.69	43944.68	
	NOVA SCOTIA	PARRSBORO GOVT WHARF	45-23.40	64-19.20	14229.79	43863.49	
	NOVA SCOTIA	PARRSBORO HARBOUR ENTR	45-23.20	64-19.10	14228.26	43863.23	
	NOVA SCOTIA	MOSHER ISLAND	44-14.20	64-19.00	13693.27	43947.19	
	NOVA SCOTIA	LUNENBURG HARBOUR WHARF	44-22.50	64-18.50	13759.25	43937.88	
	NOVA SCOTIA	BEACON SHOAL	44-28.80	64-18.00	13809.22	43929.53	
	NOVA SCOTIA	BREAKWATER NEAR HEAD	44-21.60	64-17.80	13752.49	43934.77	
	NOVA SCOTIA	FELTZEN SOUTH BRKWTR	44-19.80	64-17.00	13738.72	43931.88	
	NOVA SCOTIA	KAULBACH ISLAND	44-28.20	64-17.00	13804.90	43924.50	
	NOVA SCOTIA	WEST IRONBOUND ISLAND	44-13.70	64-16.50	13690.94	43934.04	
	NOVA SCOTIA	LA HAVE WHISTLE BUOY	44-10.50	64-16.10	13666.02	43934.29	
	NOVA SCOTIA	POLLOCK SHOAL BELL	44-14.60	64-14.50	13699.30	43922.48	
	NOVA SCOTIA	QUAKER ISLAND	44-31.00	64-14.00	13827.98	43904.95	
	NOVA SCOTIA	EAST POINT ISLAND	44-21.00	64-12.80	13750.37	43907.74	
	NOVA SCOTIA	TANNER ISLAND	44-22.10	64-12.10	13759.31	43902.88	
	NOVA SCOTIA	TANNER PASS WHISTLE	44-22.10	64-11.60	13759.55	43900.11	
	NOVA SCOTIA	LUNENBURG BAY BELL	44-20.40	64-11.20	13746.51	43899.45	
	NOVA SCOTIA	LUNENBURG BAY WHISTLE	44-17.50	64-11.10	13723.99	43901.49	
	NOVA SCOTIA	SUMMERVILLE WHARF	45-05.60	64-10.40	14093.67	43839.52	
	NOVA SCOTIA	BIG TANCOOK I WHARF	44-28.00	64-10.30	13805.99	43887.16	
	NOVA SCOTIA	CROSS ISLAND	44-18.70	64-10.20	13733.83	43895.48	
	NOVA SCOTIA	HANTSPORT WHARF	45-04.10	64-10.20	14082.38	43840.67	
	NOVA SCOTIA	MITCHNER POINT	45-02.60	64-08.80	14070.82	43834.54	
	NOVA SCOTIA	LITTLE TANCOOK I WHARF	44-28.30	64-08.50	13809.00	43876.75	
	NOVA SCOTIA	NEW HARBOUR/MAHONE BAY	44-28.40	64-05.60	13810.86	43860.33	
	NOVA SCOTIA	EAST IRONBOUND I WHARF	44-26.40	64-05.00	13795.74	43859.09	
	NOVA SCOTIA	FIVE ISLANDS/EAST RIVER	45-24.10	64-04.10	14226.38	43766.80	
	NOVA SCOTIA	HUBBARDS COVE/GREEN COVE	44-37.30	64-03.30	13879.53	43837.05	
	NOVA SCOTIA	PEARL ISLAND WHISTLE	44-21.40	64-02.20	13758.71	43848.66	
	NOVA SCOTIA	NORTHWEST COVE WHARF	44-32.00	64-01.50	13839.72	43833.10	
	NOVA SCOTIA	NORTHEAST SHOAL BELL	44-25.00	64-01.40	13786.52	43840.41	
	NOVA SCOTIA	HORSESHOE LEDGE WHISTLE	44-28.30	63-58.40	13812.70	43819.84	
	NOVA SCOTIA	CROUCHER ISLAND	44-38.40	63-57.50	13889.00	43802.27	
	NOVA SCOTIA	INDIAN HARBOUR	44-31.30	63-56.80	13835.84	43807.21	
	NOVA SCOTIA	YANKEE COVE	44-31.00	63-56.30	13833.74	43804.73	
	NOVA SCOTIA	PEGGYS POINT BELL	44-28.50	63-55.80	13815.12	43804.90	
	NOVA SCOTIA	PEGGYS POINT	44-29.50	63-55.20	13822.83	43800.30	
	NOVA SCOTIA	PEGGYS COVE WHARF	44-29.60	63-55.00	13823.64	43799.05	
	NOVA SCOTIA	DOVER WEST WHARF	44-29.70	63-52.40	13825.23	43784.16	

PASSES

BODY OF WATER	PROV/STATE	NAME	LAT	LON	TD#1	TD#2	CHAR
	NOVA SCOTIA	PORT DOVER	44-29.40	63-51.70	13823.22	43780.57	
	NOVA SCOTIA	EAST DOVER PUBLIC WHARF	44-29.70	63-50.80	13825.74	43775.07	
	NOVA SCOTIA	SAULS ISLAND	44-28.10	63-47.00	13815.13	43755.54	
	NOVA SCOTIA	PROSPECT PUBLIC WHARF	44-28.20	63-47.00	13815.87	43755.41	
	NOVA SCOTIA	GETTY ISLAND/BRIG POINT	44-26.30	63-46.10	13802.18	43752.75	
	NOVA SCOTIA	LOWER PROSPECT	44-27.10	63-43.60	13808.93	43737.55	
	NOVA SCOTIA	GOVT WHARF	44-28.10	63-42.90	13816.48	43732.26	
	NOVA SCOTIA	BERGEMAN POINT RANGE	45-51.70	63-42.50	14395.35	43557.99	
	NOVA SCOTIA	TERENCE BAY/SHIPLEY HEAD	44-27.60	63-42.40	13812.99	43730.09	
	NOVA SCOTIA	FISHING PT OUTER RANGE	45-51.30	63-41.00	14391.46	43549.27	
	NOVA SCOTIA	FISHING POINT	45-52.30	63-40.80	14397.54	43544.97	
	NOVA SCOTIA	TERENCE BAY BELL	44-26.90	63-40.70	13808.46	43721.38	
	NOVA SCOTIA	FISHING POINT RANGE	45-52.20	63-40.50	14396.65	43543.29	
	NOVA SCOTIA	STEVEWN POINT RANGE	45-51.90	63-40.10	14394.40	43541.54	
	NOVA SCOTIA	PENNANT WHISTLE BUOY	44-23.90	63-39.80	13786.97	43720.27	
	NOVA SCOTIA	PENNANT POINT BELL	44-25.60	63-39.20	13799.54	43714.63	
	NOVA SCOTIA	PENNANT HARBOUR ENTRANCE	44-28.30	63-38.10	13819.47	43704.69	
	NOVA SCOTIA	BEDFORD INSTITUTE WHARF	44-40.90	63-36.80	13910.43	43678.45	
	NOVA SCOTIA	BULL POINT/SAMBRO HARB	44-28.50	63-35.80	13821.62	43691.30	
	NOVA SCOTIA	INNER SAMBRO FAIRWAY BELL	44-27.10	63-35.80	13811.54	43693.28	
	NOVA SCOTIA	SAMBRO	44-26.20	63-33.80	13805.74	43683.18	
	NOVA SCOTIA	INNER RANGE	44-38.40	63-33.70	13893.00	43664.36	
	NOVA SCOTIA	SAMBRO HARBOUR WHISTLE	44-24.50	63-33.60	13793.62	43684.44	
	NOVA SCOTIA	HALIFAX TERMINALS BRKWTR	44-37.60	63-33.60	13887.31	43665.04	
	NOVA SCOTIA	HERRING COVE BREAKWATER	44-34.20	63-33.50	13863.08	43669.72	
	NOVA SCOTIA	HERRING COVE	44-34.00	63-33.40	13861.67	43669.45	
	NOVA SCOTIA	SANDWICH POINT RANGE	44-35.00	63-33.00	13868.89	43665.61	
	NOVA SCOTIA	KETCH HARBOUR BUOY	44-28.30	63-32.30	13821.25	43671.64	
	NOVA SCOTIA	SANDWICH POINT MID RANGE	44-36.80	63-32.20	13881.85	43658.18	
	NOVA SCOTIA	MAUGHER BEACH	44-36.10	63-32.10	13876.90	43658.70	
	NOVA SCOTIA	THE SISTERS BELL BUOY	44-26.20	63-31.50	13806.51	43670.13	
	NOVA SCOTIA	CHEBUCTO HEAD	44-30.50	63-31.40	13837.20	43663.25	
	NOVA SCOTIA	BELL ROCK BELL	44-29.00	63-31.10	13826.60	43663.76	
	NOVA SCOTIA	EASTERN PASSAGE/LOWLOR I	44-36.30	63-29.80	13878.73	43645.06	
	NOVA SCOTIA	MACFARLANE POINT RANGE	45-48.80	63-27.80	14364.33	43469.88	
	NOVA SCOTIA	HALIFAX APPROACH "HB"	44-26.60	63-27.60	13810.63	43647.37	
	NOVA SCOTIA	DEVILS ISLAND	44-34.80	63-27.50	13868.57	43634.15	
	NOVA SCOTIA	MULLINS POINT RANGE	45-49.50	63-25.50	14366.69	43452.68	
	NOVA SCOTIA	HALIFAX APPROACH "HA"	44-21.80	63-24.30	13777.90	43635.74	
	NOVA SCOTIA	BEAR COVE BELL H6	44-32.60	63-21.40	13854.44	43602.51	
	NOVA SCOTIA	RAT ROCK	44-37.60	63-16.20	13889.97	43563.91	
	NOVA SCOTIA	AMET ISLAND	45-50.10	63-10.70	14358.00	43353.96	
	NOVA SCOTIA	MUSQUODOBOIT HARBOUR	44-41.70	63-04.70	13919.00	43489.12	
	NOVA SCOTIA	SKINNER COVE BRKWTR	45-47.60	63-02.80	14336.94	43310.51	

PASSES

BODY OF WATER	PROV/STATE	NAME	LAT	LON	TD#1	TD#2	CHART
	NOVA SCOTIA	JEDDORE ROCK	44-39.80	63-00.70	13906.69	43469.41	
	NOVA SCOTIA	TONEY RIVER WHARF	45-46.50	62-53.50	14323.51	43253.84	
	NOVA SCOTIA	WHITEHEAD ISLAND	43-39.70	62-52.10	13511.76	43518.50	
	NOVA SCOTIA	EGG ISLAND	44-39.90	62-51.80	13908.20	43417.19	
	NOVA SCOTIA	OWLS HEAD	44-43.20	62-48.00	13929.86	43388.03	
	NOVA SCOTIA	SHIP HARBOUR/WOLF POINT	44-45.00	62-45.40	13941.51	43368.85	
	NOVA SCOTIA	NORWAY POINT RANGE	45-40.30	62-43.40	14280.54	43208.98	
	NOVA SCOTIA	PICTOU ISLAND TOWN PT	45-40.40	62-42.20	14280.35	43201.00	
	NOVA SCOTIA	CARIBOU HARBOUR MID RANGE	45-44.10	62-42.20	14301.66	43188.97	
	NOVA SCOTIA	CARIBOU HARBOUR RANGE	45-44.40	62-41.30	14302.76	43182.21	
	NOVA SCOTIA	CARIBOU POINT	45-45.90	62-40.90	14311.04	43174.66	
	NOVA SCOTIA	PICTOU ISLAND ENTR	45-41.30	62-40.80	14284.64	43189.16	
	NOVA SCOTIA	GULL ROCK BELL	45-46.50	62-40.50	14314.17	43170.09	
	NOVA SCOTIA	CARIBOU HARBOUR BELL	45-45.10	62-39.90	14305.79	43170.91	
	NOVA SCOTIA	PICTOU BAR	45-41.20	62-39.90	14283.48	43183.74	
	NOVA SCOTIA	POPES HARBOUR	44-47.70	62-39.20	13958.70	43326.23	
	NOVA SCOTIA	EAST RIVER RANGE	45-37.40	62-39.00	14260.98	43190.22	
	NOVA SCOTIA	SKINNER REEF BELL	45-44.80	62-37.20	14302.24	43154.61	
	NOVA SCOTIA	PICTOU ISLAND W END	45-48.20	62-36.20	14320.71	43136.70	
	NOVA SCOTIA	SPRY BAY RANGE	44-49.40	62-36.00	13969.30	43303.36	
	NOVA SCOTIA	PICTOU ISLAND SW	45-48.20	62-35.20	14320.00	43130.27	
	NOVA SCOTIA	PICTOU ISLAND	45-48.90	62-30.90	14320.86	43100.25	
	NOVA SCOTIA	PICTOU ISLAND BRKWTR	45-49.30	62-30.60	14322.86	43096.93	
	NOVA SCOTIA	GEDDES SHOAL WHISTLE	44-44.50	62-28.20	13938.76	43268.84	
	NOVA SCOTIA	SHEET HARBOUR PASSAGE	44-51.50	62-27.00	13981.88	43244.98	
	NOVA SCOTIA	BEAVER ISLAND	44-49.60	62-20.70	13969.97	43212.39	
	NOVA SCOTIA	BEAVER ISLAND WHISTLE	44-49.60	62-19.90	13969.94	43207.66	
	NOVA SCOTIA	BAILLE BROOK RANGE	45-42.50	62-16.50	14276.06	43030.67	
	NOVA SCOTIA	BASSOON REEFS BELL	44-50.60	62-13.60	13975.69	43167.95	
	NOVA SCOTIA	BOWEN LEDGE BELL	44-52.00	62-10.60	13983.86	43146.61	
	NOVA SCOTIA	ARISAIG HARBOUR RANGE	45-45.60	62-10.20	14289.03	42979.95	
	NOVA SCOTIA	THRUMCAP ISLAND	44-57.40	62-02.40	14014.81	43083.54	
	NOVA SCOTIA	SMITH ROCK BELL	44-53.80	62-01.50	13993.78	43088.06	
	NOVA SCOTIA	LISCOMB ISLAND	44-59.20	61-58.00	14024.64	43052.37	
	NOVA SCOTIA	BALLANTYNES COVE WHARF	45-51.50	61-55.10	14310.56	42862.86	
	NOVA SCOTIA	CAPE GEORGE	45-52.50	61-54.10	14315.07	42852.76	
	NOVA SCOTIA	CRIBBEAN HEAD WHARF	45-45.30	61-53.80	14277.43	42877.71	
	NOVA SCOTIA	ST MARYS RIVER	45-03.10	61-53.80	14046.24	43016.16	
	NOVA SCOTIA	LISCOMB FAIRWAY WHISTLE	44-55.00	61-53.60	14000.02	43038.12	
	NOVA SCOTIA	AMHERST HARB BUOY YK22	47-22.60	61-51.30	14712.45	42410.96	
	NOVA SCOTIA	CAP AUX MEULES RANGE	47-22.60	61-51.30	14712.45	42410.96	
	NOVA SCOTIA	ST MARYS RIVER BELL	44-59.60	61-49.70	14025.76	43001.97	
	NOVA SCOTIA	BAYFIELD WHARF	45-38.70	61-45.20	14238.03	42848.04	
	NOVA SCOTIA	POMQUET ISLAND	45-39.50	61-45.00	14242.12	42843.91	

PASSES

BODY OF WATER	PROV/STATE	NAME	LAT	LON	TD#1	TD#2	CHART
	NOVA SCOTIA	MOUTON HARBOUR RANGE	45-05.50	61-43.90	14057.86	42950.00	
	NOVA SCOTIA	MOUTON HARBOUR RANGE	45-05.70	61-43.60	14058.91	42947.61	
	NOVA SCOTIA	MOUTON HARBOUR	45-05.70	61-43.50	14058.89	42947.02	
	NOVA SCOTIA	PORT BICKERTON E RANGE	45-06.30	61-43.40	14062.20	42944.59	
	NOVA SCOTIA	PORT BICKERTON	45-05.40	61-42.10	14056.95	42939.59	
	NOVA SCOTIA	PORT BICKERTON ENTRANCE	45-04.80	61-41.70	14053.55	42939.04	
	NOVA SCOTIA	FISHERMANS HARBOUR	45-06.70	61-40.70	14063.86	42927.27	
	NOVA SCOTIA	ISAAC HARBOUR	45-10.00	61-39.30	14081.68	42908.65	
	NOVA SCOTIA	PORT BECKERTON BELL	45-01.20	61-39.20	14033.20	42935.09	
	NOVA SCOTIA	BARRIOS BEACH BRKWTR	45-38.80	61-37.60	14234.68	42800.67	
	NOVA SCOTIA	ROSE SHOAL BELL	45-04.60	61-37.40	14051.66	42914.11	
	NOVA SCOTIA	DRUMHEAD BRKWTR	45-08.70	61-36.20	14073.86	42894.24	
	NOVA SCOTIA	SOUTH EASTER BELL	45-02.90	61-35.50	14041.99	42908.07	
	NOVA SCOTIA	TOM COD SHOALS BELL	45-04.50	61-33.10	14050.33	42888.94	
	NOVA SCOTIA	ISAAC'S HARBOUR WHISTLE	45-02.20	61-32.70	14037.71	42893.66	
	NOVA SCOTIA	COUNTRY ISLAND	45-06.60	61-32.60	14061.67	42879.43	
	NOVA SCOTIA	HAVRE BOUCHER RANGE	45-41.00	61-31.70	14243.00	42756.17	
	NOVA SCOTIA	CODDLE HARBOUR	45-09.40	61-31.10	14076.52	42861.66	
	NOVA SCOTIA	GUYSBOROUGH ENTRANCE	45-22.50	61-29.50	14145.99	42808.78	
	NOVA SCOTIA	NORTH CANSO ENTRANCE	45-41.50	61-29.30	14244.32	42739.51	
	NOVA SCOTIA	GUYSBOROUGH BELL	45-22.40	61-28.00	14144.94	42800.07	
	NOVA SCOTIA	NEW HARBOUR COVE BRKWTR	45-10.20	61-27.10	14079.92	42835.30	
	NOVA SCOTIA	AULD COVE RANGE	45-38.90	61-26.20	14229.57	42730.17	
	NOVA SCOTIA	SHOAL POINT WHISTLE	45-09.00	61-25.50	14073.14	42829.68	
	NOVA SCOTIA	CANSO CANAL ANCHORAGE	45-39.20	61-25.30	14230.65	42723.54	
	NOVA SCOTIA	CAPE PORCUPINE RANGE	45-38.70	61-25.10	14228.02	42724.18	
	NOVA SCOTIA	BALACHE POINT RANGE	45-39.00	61-25.00	14229.49	42722.45	
	NOVA SCOTIA	CANSO CANAL ANCHORAGE	45-38.80	61-24.60	14228.29	42720.74	
	NOVA SCOTIA	POINT TUPPER ENTR	45-36.50	61-22.50	14215.63	42716.45	
	NOVA SCOTIA	LARRY'S RIVER	45-13.00	61-22.20	14093.64	42797.01	
	NOVA SCOTIA	LARRY'S RIVER BRKWTR	45-13.00	61-22.20	14093.64	42797.01	
	NOVA SCOTIA	PEEBLES POINT WHARF	45-35.20	61-21.30	14208.49	42713.94	
	NOVA SCOTIA	PEEBLES POINT WHARF	45-35.10	61-21.30	14207.98	42714.31	
	NOVA SCOTIA	CAHIL ROCK RANGE	45-34.20	61-21.30	14203.40	42717.62	
	NOVA SCOTIA	CHARLOS HARBOUR RANGE	45-14.60	61-20.10	14101.54	42779.19	
	NOVA SCOTIA	SHIP POINT	45-33.90	61-19.90	14201.27	42710.21	
	NOVA SCOTIA	PARK POINT RANGE	45-32.60	61-19.30	14194.41	42711.33	
	NOVA SCOTIA	MIDDLE MELFORD RANGE	45-32.40	61-19.00	14193.26	42710.24	
	NOVA SCOTIA	TORBAY/BERRY HEAD	45-11.50	61-18.70	14084.88	42781.20	
	NOVA SCOTIA	BEAR HEAD	45-33.00	61-17.30	14195.59	42697.74	
	NOVA SCOTIA	PORT MALCOLM RANGE	45-34.50	61-17.30	14203.19	42692.20	
	NOVA SCOTIA	COLE HARBOUR ENTR RANGE	45-15.60	61-17.20	14106.01	42758.57	
	NOVA SCOTIA	QUEENSPORT/ROOK ISLAND	45-21.00	61-16.40	14133.83	42735.25	
	NOVA SCOTIA	COLE HARBOUR SE SIDE	45-15.60	61-16.20	14105.74	42752.62	

PASSES

BODY OF WATER	PROV/STATE	NAME	LAT	LON	TD#1	TD#2	CHART
	NOVA SCOTIA	EDDY POINT RANGE	45-31.20	61-15.20	14185.61	42691.63	
	NOVA SCOTIA	EDDY POINT	45-31.30	61-15.00	14186.04	42690.05	
	NOVA SCOTIA	CAPE ARGOS	45-29.20	61-14.00	14175.00	42691.68	
	NOVA SCOTIA	JANURIN ISLAND RANGE	45-29.20	61-14.00	14175.00	42691.68	
	NOVA SCOTIA	FLYING POINT SHOALS	45-12.00	61-13.20	14086.22	42746.99	
	NOVA SCOTIA	PORT FELIX	45-13.70	61-13.20	14095.08	42741.26	
	NOVA SCOTIA	THREE TOP ISLAND	45-12.50	61-09.60	14087.98	42724.05	
	NOVA SCOTIA	WHITE HEAD ISLAND	45-11.80	61-08.20	14084.04	42718.16	
	NOVA SCOTIA	CHEDABUCTO BAY BUOY "CF"	45-24.00	61-03.10	14144.86	42645.25	
	NOVA SCOTIA	ROCK ISLAND	45-17.00	61-01.80	14109.11	42662.48	
	NOVA SCOTIA	DURELL ISLAND RANGE	45-21.20	61-01.30	14130.21	42644.63	
	NOVA SCOTIA	LITTLE DOVER HARBOUR	45-16.70	61-01.20	14107.43	42660.00	
	NOVA SCOTIA	HOME SHOAL BELL	45-15.30	61-01.00	14100.27	42663.71	
	NOVA SCOTIA	DOVER BAY/GULF ROCK	45-16.80	61-01.00	14107.88	42658.46	
	NOVA SCOTIA	LITTLE DOVER RUN	45-16.60	61-00.30	14106.69	42655.04	
	NOVA SCOTIA	CANSO HARBOUR WHISTLE	45-22.10	60-59.90	14134.31	42633.10	
	NOVA SCOTIA	HART ISLAND RANGE	45-20.60	60-59.50	14126.65	42636.12	
	NOVA SCOTIA	PISCATIQUI ISLAND	45-20.60	60-59.20	14126.56	42634.35	
	NOVA SCOTIA	GRAVES ISLAND BRKWTR	45-20.20	60-59.10	14124.53	42635.19	
	NOVA SCOTIA	LANIGAN BEACH RANGE	45-20.00	60-58.80	14123.43	42634.13	
	NOVA SCOTIA	CHEDABUCTO BAY BUOY "CE"	45-24.00	60-58.80	14143.47	42619.69	
	NOVA SCOTIA	WHITE PT LEDGES WHISTLE	45-13.50	60-58.60	14090.55	42655.88	
	NOVA SCOTIA	MAN OF WAR ROCK BELL	45-19.70	60-57.00	14121.42	42624.57	
	NOVA SCOTIA	CRANBERRY ISLAND	45-19.50	60-55.70	14120.05	42617.63	
	NOVA SCOTIA	CHEDABUCTO BAY BUOY "CD"	45-24.00	60-54.60	14142.14	42594.80	
	NOVA SCOTIA	CAPE BREAKER BELL	45-18.10	60-54.20	14112.63	42613.81	
	NOVA SCOTIA	GRIME SHOAL WHISTLE	45-21.10	60-50.80	14126.63	42582.97	
	NOVA SCOTIA	CHEDABUCTO BAY WHISTLE "CA"	45-23.90	60-41.70	14137.70	42519.15	
	NOVA SCOTIA	SABLE ISLAND	43-56.00	60-01.40	13708.22	42581.18	
	NOVA SCOTIA	SABLE ISLAND EAST SIDE	43-57.60	59-47.50	13721.52	42504.62	
	PRINCE EDWARD I	WEST POINT WHISTLE	46-40.10	64-30.10	14741.66	43715.68	
	PRINCE EDWARD I	WEST POINT	46-37.20	64-23.30	14715.21	43679.46	
	PRINCE EDWARD I	SEAL POINT WHARF	46-44.40	64-22.80	14752.50	43645.93	
	PRINCE EDWARD I	HOWARD COVE @ SEAL PT	46-44.40	64-22.70	14752.34	43645.22	
	PRINCE EDWARD I	WEST POINT RANGE	46-22.30	64-22.30	14629.11	43728.65	
	PRINCE EDWARD I	MIMINEGASH BELL "44N"	46-54.00	64-14.20	14786.30	43541.99	
	PRINCE EDWARD I	MIMINEGASH RANGE	46-52.80	64-14.20	14780.54	43547.56	
	PRINCE EDWARD I	FISHING COVE BRKWTR	46-24.10	64-08.10	14619.72	43623.64	
	PRINCE EDWARD I	FISHING COVE W BRKWTR	46-24.40	64-08.10	14621.44	43622.54	
	PRINCE EDWARD I	CAPE EGMONT	46-24.10	64-08.10	14619.72	43623.64	
	PRINCE EDWARD I	SKINNERS POND BRKWTR	46-58.00	64-07.60	14794.48	43476.34	
	PRINCE EDWARD I	CANOE GULLY RANGE	46-26.90	64-06.40	14633.25	43601.41	
	PRINCE EDWARD I	NORTHPORT RANGE WHARF	46-47.70	64-03.60	14739.03	43495.97	
	PRINCE EDWARD I	ALBERTON INNER RANGE	46-48.30	64-03.30	14741.52	43491.16	

PASSES

BODY OF WATER	PROV/STATE	NAME	LAT	LON	TD#1	TD#2	CHART
	PRINCE EDWARD I	CASCUMPEQUE ENTRANCE	46-48.00	64-02.20	14738.36	43484.77	
	PRINCE EDWARD I	ALBERTON RANGE	46-48.30	64-01.90	14739.38	43481.31	
	PRINCE EDWARD I	NORTH POINT REEF WHISTLE	47-05.00	64-00.10	14813.96	43388.86	
	PRINCE EDWARD I	CASCUMPEQUE BELL "JV2"	46-47.70	63-60.00	14733.54	43470.66	
	PRINCE EDWARD I	NORTH POINT	47-03.50	63-60.00	14807.22	43395.68	
	PRINCE EDWARD I	TIGNISH HARBOUR BRKWTR	46-57.00	63-59.70	14777.43	43425.39	
	PRINCE EDWARD I	NORTH POINT BRKWTR	47-01.80	63-59.40	14798.74	43399.91	
	PRINCE EDWARD I	CONWAY INLET	46-39.30	63-52.70	14680.54	43456.26	
	PRINCE EDWARD I	PORT HILL WHARF	46-35.60	63-52.10	14660.49	43467.59	
	PRINCE EDWARD I	MISCOUCHE SHOAL BELL	46-19.90	63-51.40	14573.67	43523.92	
	PRINCE EDWARD I	SUMMERSIDE HARBOUR ENTR	46-49.10	63-49.10	14724.09	43387.91	
	PRINCE EDWARD I	SEACOW HEAD RANGE	46-19.00	63-48.60	14565.03	43508.03	
	PRINCE EDWARD I	INDIAN HEAD RANGE	46-23.20	63-47.40	14587.14	43484.18	
	PRINCE EDWARD I	DARNLEY PT OUTER RANGE	46-34.60	63-42.80	14642.45	43407.22	
	PRINCE EDWARD I	DARNLEY PT INNER RANGE	46-34.40	63-42.80	14641.41	43408.05	
	PRINCE EDWARD I	PORT BORDON PIER	46-14.70	63-42.00	14532.47	43478.54	
	PRINCE EDWARD I	DETACHED BREAKWATER	46-14.70	63-42.00	14532.47	43478.54	
	PRINCE EDWARD I	PORT BORDON RANGE	46-15.00	63-41.70	14533.83	43475.43	
	PRINCE EDWARD I	DARNLEY BASIN RANGE	46-32.30	63-39.70	14626.28	43395.29	
	PRINCE EDWARD I	DARNLEY POINT RANGE	46-33.80	63-39.10	14633.32	43384.96	
	PRINCE EDWARD I	MALPEQUE BELL "JP2"	46-35.00	63-37.20	14637.00	43366.84	
	PRINCE EDWARD I	TRYON SHOALS BELL	46-08.80	63-32.00	14487.18	43431.75	
	PRINCE EDWARD I	CAPE TRYON	46-32.00	63-30.40	14612.60	43332.49	
	PRINCE EDWARD I	WRIGHTS RANGE	46-12.30	63-30.00	14505.04	43405.88	
	PRINCE EDWARD I	LEARDS RANGE	46-12.80	63-29.40	14507.20	43400.03	
	PRINCE EDWARD I	PALMERS WHARF	46-12.80	63-29.40	14507.20	43400.03	
	PRINCE EDWARD I	NEW LONDON, GRENVILLE	46-30.80	63-29.20	14604.83	43329.20	
	PRINCE EDWARD I	NEW LONDON BELL "JM1"	46-31.80	63-28.20	14608.76	43318.21	
	PRINCE EDWARD I	NORTH RUSTICO HARBOUR	46-27.30	63-17.60	14572.31	43264.26	
	PRINCE EDWARD I	N RUSTICO INNER BRKWTR	46-27.20	63-17.50	14571.68	43263.98	
	PRINCE EDWARD I	NORTHERN BREAKWATER	46-27.40	63-17.30	14572.48	43261.81	
	PRINCE EDWARD I	NORTH RUSTICO BELL "JK2"	46-27.80	63-16.80	14573.96	43256.77	
	PRINCE EDWARD I	NINE MILE CREEK WHARF	46-08.90	63-13.10	14467.89	43304.71	
	PRINCE EDWARD I	ST PETERS ISLAND	46-07.00	63-10.90	14455.04	43296.90	
	PRINCE EDWARD I	COVEHEAD RANGE	46-25.50	63-09.00	14552.88	43213.22	
	PRINCE EDWARD I	BRIGHTON BEACH RANGE	46-13.80	63-09.00	14490.68	43259.15	
	PRINCE EDWARD I	COVEHEAD BRIDGE	46-25.80	63-08.80	14554.21	43210.64	
	PRINCE EDWARD I	COVEHEAD HARBOUR	46-25.80	63-08.70	14554.09	43209.97	
	PRINCE EDWARD I	COVEHEAD APPROACH "JJ1"	46-26.90	63-08.30	14559.31	43202.75	
	PRINCE EDWARD I	WARREN COVE RANGE	46-12.00	63-08.30	14480.12	43261.22	
	PRINCE EDWARD I	CHARLOTTETOWN AVIATION LT	46-17.00	63-08.00	14506.92	43240.21	
	PRINCE EDWARD I	BLOCKHOUSE POINT	46-11.50	63-07.80	14476.87	43259.74	
	PRINCE EDWARD I	PRIM REEFS WHISTLE	46-02.70	63-07.00	14427.05	43286.31	
	PRINCE EDWARD I	FITZROY ROCK BELL	46-07.10	63-06.70	14451.46	43268.60	

PASSES

BODY OF WATER	PROV/STATE	NAME	LAT	LON	TD#1	TD#2	CHART
	PRINCE EDWARD I	HAZZARD POINT ENTR	46-11.70	63-04.50	14474.59	43236.97	
	PRINCE EDWARD I	TRACADIE HARBOUR ENTR	46-24.60	63-02.50	14540.87	43172.98	
	PRINCE EDWARD I	PRIM POINT	46-03.00	63-02.40	14424.45	43254.83	
	PRINCE EDWARD I	N TRACADIE BELL "JH1"	46-26.10	63-02.00	14548.01	43163.45	
	PRINCE EDWARD I	GRAND TRACADIE WHARF	46-24.20	63-01.70	14537.91	43169.22	
	PRINCE EDWARD I	PINETTE RIVER RANGE	46-03.30	62-57.40	14421.51	43220.76	
	PRINCE EDWARD I	BELLE RIVER BRKWTR	45-58.40	62-51.00	14388.59	43196.22	
	PRINCE EDWARD I	SAVAGE HARBOUR	46-26.00	62-50.00	14534.24	43083.13	
	PRINCE EDWARD I	SAVAGE HARBOUR BELL	46-26.80	62-49.50	14537.71	43076.41	
	PRINCE EDWARD I	INDIAN ROCKS WHISTLE	45-55.00	62-49.20	14368.05	43196.38	
	PRINCE EDWARD I	WOOD ISLAND HARBOUR RANGE	45-57.00	62-45.10	14375.87	43162.67	
	PRINCE EDWARD I	ST PETERS HARBOUR, BRKWTR	46-26.50	62-44.90	14531.26	43046.85	
	PRINCE EDWARD I	WOOD ISLAND	45-57.00	62-44.80	14375.62	43160.72	
	PRINCE EDWARD I	ST PETERS HARBOUR RANGE	46-26.30	62-44.50	14529.83	43045.02	
	PRINCE EDWARD I	ST PETERS BELL "JD1"	46-28.10	62-44.30	14538.56	43036.04	
	PRINCE EDWARD I	LITTLE SANDS BRKWTR	45-57.70	62-38.70	14374.51	43118.54	
	PRINCE EDWARD I	LOWER MONTAGUE WHARF	46-10.20	62-33.80	14437.09	43039.54	
	PRINCE EDWARD I	ST ANDREW POINT	46-09.80	62-31.80	14433.21	43027.99	
	PRINCE EDWARD I	BEACH POINT BRKWTR	46-01.00	62-29.30	14384.70	43045.36	
	PRINCE EDWARD I	MURRAY HARBOUR RANGE	46-01.30	62-28.70	14385.81	43040.35	
	PRINCE EDWARD I	PANMURE HEAD	46-08.70	62-28.00	14424.12	43007.43	
	PRINCE EDWARD I	CAPE BEAR	46-00.20	62-27.70	14379.14	43037.98	
	PRINCE EDWARD I	GRAHAM POND S BRKWTR	46-05.80	62-27.20	14408.31	43013.48	
	PRINCE EDWARD I	MURRAY HARBOUR BELL "NM"	46-02.10	62-27.20	14388.83	43027.60	
	PRINCE EDWARD I	GRAHAM POND BREAKWATER	46-05.80	62-27.10	14408.23	43012.83	
	PRINCE EDWARD I	SHIPWRECK POINT	46-28.20	62-25.50	14519.38	42910.31	
	PRINCE EDWARD I	ANNANDALE RANGE	46-15.50	62-25.40	14456.60	42963.22	
	PRINCE EDWARD I	NAUFRAGE WEST BRKWTR	46-28.20	62-25.10	14518.97	42907.66	
	PRINCE EDWARD I	NAUFRAGE EAST BRKWTR	46-28.10	62-25.00	14518.39	42907.43	
	PRINCE EDWARD I	LAUNCHING POND BOAT HARB	46-13.20	62-24.60	14444.21	42967.31	
	PRINCE EDWARD I	BEAR REEF WHISTE "N4"	46-00.60	62-24.30	14378.55	43014.46	
	PRINCE EDWARD I	FORTUNE BAY N RANGE	46-19.70	62-21.10	14473.57	42917.60	
	PRINCE EDWARD I	SOURIS HARBOUR WHISTLE "NA"	46-19.80	62-15.50	14468.84	42880.44	
	PRINCE EDWARD I	KNIGHT POINT BRKWTR	46-20.80	62-15.30	14473.54	42874.89	
	PRINCE EDWARD I	KNIGHT POINT	46-20.80	62-15.00	14473.26	42872.93	
	PRINCE EDWARD I	BASIN HEAD HARBOUR BRKWTR	46-22.60	62-06.60	14474.20	42810.24	
	PRINCE EDWARD I	WEST BREAKWATER	46-28.10	62-04.40	14498.21	42771.69	
	PRINCE EDWARD I	NORTH LAKE HARBOUR RANGE	46-28.10	62-04.10	14497.92	42769.73	
	PRINCE EDWARD I	EAST POINT	46-27.10	61-58.30	14487.83	42736.29	
	PRINCE EDWARD I	EAST PT WHISTLE "NDN"	46-28.10	61-56.30	14490.64	42718.78	
ST LAWRENCE GULF	QUEBEC	MILNE POINT RANGE	50-13.30	60-18.90	15028.6	40669.5	
ST LAWRENCE GULF	QUEBEC	CAIRNTORR ROCK "C64"	50-07.30	60-18.60	15019.2	40709.9	
ST LAWRENCE GULF	QUEBEC	CORMORANT ROCKS	50-07.30	60-03.70	15007.0	40613.5	
ST LAWRENCE GULF	QUEBEC	ST MARY ISLANDS	50-18.30	59-39.40	15004.7	40378.7	

PASSES

BODY OF WATER	PROV/STATE	NAME	LAT	LON	TD#1	TD#2	CHART
ST LAWRENCE GULF	QUEBEC	NETAGAMU RIVER	50-28.20	59-36.50	15017.3	40289.7	
ST LAWRENCE GULF	QUEBEC	HARRINGTON HARBOUR ENTR	50-29.60	59-29.10	15013.7	40232.1	
ST LAWRENCE GULF	QUEBEC	ENTRY ISLAND	50-29.60	59-28.20	15013.0	40226.3	
ST LAWRENCE GULF	QUEBEC	ENTRY CLIFF	50-29.30	59-27.70	15012.2	40225.2	
ST LAWRENCE GULF	QUEBEC	CAPE AIREY	50-28.20	59-27.50	15010.5	40231.8	
ST LAWRENCE GULF	QUEBEC	ILE DU GRAND RIGOLET	50-40.80	59-14.60	15019.1	40059.6	
ST LAWRENCE GULF	QUEBEC	WHALE HEAD ANCHORAGE	50-39.60	59-12.00	15015.5	40051.4	
ST LAWRENCE GULF	QUEBEC	MUTTON BAY	50-46.20	59-02.10	15017.6	39941.2	
ST LAWRENCE GULF	QUEBEC	ENTRANCE ISLAND	50-44.10	59-00.50	15013.5	39945.8	
ST LAWRENCE GULF	QUEBEC	BAIE DE LA TABATIERE	50-50.60	58-58.50	15021.2	39887.1	
ST LAWRENCE GULF	QUEBEC	ILE CORMANDIERE	50-51.50	58-55.90	15020.6	39864.1	
ST LAWRENCE GULF	QUEBEC	INNER ISLAND	51-08.80	58-53.70	15041.8	39730.9	
ST LAWRENCE GULF	QUEBEC	ILE DU GUET	50-55.80	58-52.80	15024.2	39814.1	
ST LAWRENCE GULF	QUEBEC	LA BOULE ISLAND	50-50.20	58-52.60	15016.5	39582.1	
ST LAWRENCE GULF	QUEBEC	ILE PLAT	50-45.10	58-45.40	15004.2	39842.4	
ST LAWRENCE GULF	QUEBEC	ST AUGUSTIN RIVER	51-13.30	58-38.70	15037.4	39602.7	
ST LAWRENCE GULF	QUEBEC	ROBIN ISLAND	51-08.90	58-33.40	15028.3	39598.2	
ST LAWRENCE GULF	QUEBEC	TICKLE ISLAND	51-10.40	58-31.50	15029.0	39575.6	
ST LAWRENCE GULF	QUEBEC	ILE PAUL NADEAU	51-10.70	58-27.80	15026.9	39549.6	
ST LAWRENCE GULF	QUEBEC	NORTHEAST POINT	51-10.60	58-25.70	15025.4	39536.8	
ST LAWRENCE GULF	QUEBEC	MISTANOQUE ISLAND	51-15.30	58-12.60	15022.9	39420.0	
ST LAWRENCE GULF	QUEBEC	MERMOT ISLAND	51-19.20	57-50.60	15014.0	38251.5	
ST LAWRENCE GULF	QUEBEC	OLD FORT BAY	51-25.30	57-48.70	15020.6	39198.8	
ST LAWRENCE GULF	QUEBEC	CHENAL DU VIEUX FORT	51-23.90	57-48.30	15018.5	39204.6	
ST LAWRENCE GULF	QUEBEC	ILE DES ESQUIMAUX	51-25.20	57-42.40	15016.5	39158.0	
ST LAWRENCE GULF	QUEBEC	ST PAUL RIVER ENTR	51-25.20	57-42.00	15016.2	39155.4	
ST LAWRENCE GULF	QUEBEC	WHALE ISLAND	51-21.40	57-41.60	15011.1	39179.7	
ST LAWRENCE GULF	QUEBEC	BAIE AU SAUMON	51-25.80	57-39.20	15015.2	39133.4	
ST LAWRENCE GULF	QUEBEC	PIGEON ISLAND	51-28.30	57-15.50	15004.0	38967.4	
ST LAWRENCE GULF	QUEBEC	BRADORE BAY	51-29.50	57-15.00	15005.2	38955.5	
ST LAWRENCE GULF	QUEBEC	LOURDES DE BLANC SABLON	51-24.70	57-11.90	14997.1	38972.2	
ST LAWRENCE GULF	QUEBEC	GREENLY ISLAND	51-22.50	57-11.50	14994.0	38986.4	
ST LAWRENCE GULF	QUEBEC	L'ANSE AU CLAIR WHARF	51-25.60	57-03.90	14993.5	38917.6	
ST LAWRENCE RIVER	NEW BRUNSWICK	CAMPBELLTON PIER	48-00.70	66-40.10	15238.18	31632.78	
ST LAWRENCE RIVER	NEW BRUNSWICK	CAMPBELLTON WHARF	48-00.80	66-39.90	15238.07	31631.00	
ST LAWRENCE RIVER	QUEBEC	BUTTERNUT ISLAND RANGE	45-05.60	74-29.40	14527.81	60134.53	1413
ST LAWRENCE RIVER	QUEBEC	LANCASTER BAR D41	45-07.40	74-27.00	14498.64	60133.48	1413
ST LAWRENCE RIVER	QUEBEC	SOUTH GULBY RANGE	45-07.30	74-26.20	14494.07	60134.84	
ST LAWRENCE RIVER	QUEBEC	POINTE NADIEAUS	45-09.70	74-25.20	14469.81	60130.36	1412
ST LAWRENCE RIVER	QUEBEC	POINTE DUPUIS RANGE	45-07.70	74-24.60	14480.49	60136.08	1412
ST LAWRENCE RIVER	QUEBEC	ST ANCIENT SHOAL D27	45-09.40	74-22.00	14450.74	60135.52	1412
ST LAWRENCE RIVER	QUEBEC	ILE CHRETIEN RANGE	45-10.00	74-20.00	14433.01	60136.79	1412
ST LAWRENCE RIVER	QUEBEC	POINTE BEAUDETTE RANGE	45-12.10	74-19.00	14411.05	60133.09	1412
ST LAWRENCE RIVER	QUEBEC	ST ANICET EAST RANGE	45-11.20	74-18.50	14414.25	60135.93	1412

PASSES

BODY OF WATER	PROV/STATE	NAME	LAT	LON	TD#1	TD#2	CHART
ST LAWRENCE RIVER	QUEBEC	BUOY D17	45-12.20	74-18.00	14403.64	60134.21	1412
ST LAWRENCE RIVER	QUEBEC	BUOY D18	45-12.50	74-18.00	14401.47	60133.49	1412
ST LAWRENCE RIVER	QUEBEC	BUOY D14	45-12.80	74-17.30	14394.62	60133.72	1412
ST LAWRENCE RIVER	QUEBEC	BUOY D13	45-12.60	74-17.10	14394.72	60134.47	1412
ST LAWRENCE RIVER	QUEBEC	ST ZOTIQUE ANCH "DJ"	45-12.60	74-16.70	14392.05	60135.00	1412
ST LAWRENCE RIVER	QUEBEC	HAT POINTE RANGE	45-13.40	74-16.60	14385.59	60133.22	
ST LAWRENCE RIVER	QUEBEC	BUOY D12	45-13.20	74-16.30	14385.02	60134.10	1412
ST LAWRENCE RIVER	QUEBEC	ST ZOTIQUE ANCH "DD"	45-13.20	74-15.50	14379.67	60135.17	1412
ST LAWRENCE RIVER	QUEBEC	BUOY D10	45-13.70	74-15.30	14374.71	60134.25	1412
ST LAWRENCE RIVER	QUEBEC	BUOY D9	45-13.50	74-14.90	14373.48	60135.26	1412
ST LAWRENCE RIVER	QUEBEC	ST ZOTIQUE ANCH "DH"	45-14.00	74-14.30	14365.84	60134.87	1412
ST LAWRENCE RIVER	QUEBEC	ST ZOTIQUE ANCH "DA"	45-13.80	74-13.60	14362.59	60136.27	1412
ST LAWRENCE RIVER	QUEBEC	ST ZOTIQUE BUOY "DE"	45-13.50	74-13.60	14364.75	60136.98	1412
ST LAWRENCE RIVER	QUEBEC	ST ZOTIQUE ANCH "DC"	45-14.20	74-13.60	14359.71	60135.32	1412
ST LAWRENCE RIVER	QUEBEC	BUOY D8	45-13.70	74-13.50	14362.64	60136.63	1412
ST LAWRENCE RIVER	QUEBEC	BUOY D6	45-13.80	74-13.00	14358.56	60137.06	1412
ST LAWRENCE RIVER	QUEBEC	BUOY D5	45-13.70	74-12.60	14356.59	60137.82	
ST LAWRENCE RIVER	QUEBEC	BUOY D3	45-13.80	74-11.40	14347.79	60139.15	1412
ST LAWRENCE RIVER	QUEBEC	BUOY D4	45-13.90	74-11.40	14347.07	60138.91	1412
ST LAWRENCE RIVER	QUEBEC	BEAUHARNOIS CANAL C49	45-14.00	74-09.60	14334.21	60141.00	1411
ST LAWRENCE RIVER	QUEBEC	BEAUHARNOIS CANAL C48	45-14.10	74-09.30	14331.47	60141.15	1411
ST LAWRENCE RIVER	QUEBEC	BEAUHARNOIS CANAL C46	45-14.00	74-08.70	14328.13	60142.15	1411
ST LAWRENCE RIVER	QUEBEC	WEST ENTRANCE RANGE	45-14.10	74-08.50	14326.06	60142.17	1411
ST LAWRENCE RIVER	QUEBEC	BEAUHARNOIS ANCH "CN"	45-13.60	74-08.30	14328.29	60143.59	1411
ST LAWRENCE RIVER	QUEBEC	BEAUHARNOIS CANAL C45	45-13.80	74-08.30	14326.86	60143.12	1411
ST LAWRENCE RIVER	QUEBEC	BEAUHARNOIS CANAL C44	45-14.00	74-08.10	14324.08	60142.91	1411
ST LAWRENCE RIVER	QUEBEC	BEAUHARNOIS ANCH "CM"	45-13.30	74-07.20	14323.00	60145.66	1411
ST LAWRENCE RIVER	QUEBEC	BEAUHARNOIS CANAL C38	45-13.40	74-06.00	14314.14	60146.93	1411
ST LAWRENCE RIVER	QUEBEC	BEAUHARNOIS CANAL C39	45-13.30	74-06.00	14314.85	60147.16	1411
ST LAWRENCE RIVER	QUEBEC	BEAUHARNOIS CANAL C37	45-13.20	74-05.60	14312.85	60147.89	1411
ST LAWRENCE RIVER	QUEBEC	BEAUHARNOIS CANAL C34	45-13.30	74-05.40	14310.78	60147.91	1411
ST LAWRENCE RIVER	QUEBEC	BEAUHARNOIS CANAL C30	45-13.30	74-04.50	14304.66	60149.01	1411
ST LAWRENCE RIVER	QUEBEC	BEAUHARNOIS CANAL C29	45-13.20	74-04.50	14305.37	60149.24	1411
ST LAWRENCE RIVER	QUEBEC	DUCK FRONT RANGE	45-13.00	74-04.00	14303.39	60150.31	1411
ST LAWRENCE RIVER	QUEBEC	VALLEYFIELD RANGE	45-13.00	74-04.00	14303.39	60150.31	1411
ST LAWRENCE RIVER	QUEBEC	BEAUHARNOIS CANAL C28	45-13.30	74-03.70	14299.21	60149.99	1411
ST LAWRENCE RIVER	QUEBEC	BEAUHARNOIS CANAL C27	45-13.20	74-03.70	14299.92	60150.22	1411
ST LAWRENCE RIVER	QUEBEC	BEAUHARNOIS CANAL C25	45-13.20	74-03.00	14295.15	60151.07	1411
ST LAWRENCE RIVER	QUEBEC	BEAUHARNOIS CANAL C24	45-13.30	74-03.00	14294.44	60150.84	1411
ST LAWRENCE RIVER	QUEBEC	BEAUHARNOIS CANAL C23	45-13.20	74-02.50	14291.74	60151.68	1411
ST LAWRENCE RIVER	QUEBEC	BEAUHARNOIS CANAL C22	45-13.40	74-02.20	14288.27	60151.59	1411
ST LAWRENCE RIVER	QUEBEC	BEAUHARNOIS CANAL C21	45-13.40	74-01.80	14285.54	60152.07	1411
ST LAWRENCE RIVER	QUEBEC	BEAUHARNOIS ANCH "CK"	45-13.30	74-01.70	14285.57	60152.41	1411
ST LAWRENCE RIVER	QUEBEC	CAMPSITE RANGE	43-13.30	74-01.00	15090.28	60322.29	

PASSES

BODY OF WATER	PROV/STATE	NAME	LAT	LON	TD#1	TD#2	CHART
ST LAWRENCE RIVER	QUEBEC	BEAUHARNOIS CANAL C20	45-13.80	74-00.80	14275.86	60152.36	1411
ST LAWRENCE RIVER	QUEBEC	BEAUHARNOIS ANCH "CJ"	45-13.70	74-00.30	14273.15	60153.19	1411
ST LAWRENCE RIVER	QUEBEC	ST LOUIS DIRECTIONAL, E	45-14.00	74-00.20	14270.34	60152.63	1412
ST LAWRENCE RIVER	QUEBEC	BEAUHARNOIS CANAL C14	45-14.30	73-59.70	14264.79	60152.55	1411
ST LAWRENCE RIVER	QUEBEC	BEAUHARNOIS CANAL C13	45-14.20	73-59.50	14264.12	60153.02	1411
ST LAWRENCE RIVER	QUEBEC	BEAUHARNOIS CANAL C10	45-14.70	73-59.10	14257.84	60152.36	1411
ST LAWRENCE RIVER	QUEBEC	BEAUHARNOIS CANAL C11	45-14.60	73-59.00	14257.86	60152.71	1411
ST LAWRENCE RIVER	QUEBEC	BEAUHARNOIS CANAL C8	45-15.40	73-58.00	14245.35	60152.10	1411
ST LAWRENCE RIVER	QUEBEC	ST LOUIS BRIDGE RANGE	45-15.00	73-57.70	14246.13	60153.35	1411
ST LAWRENCE RIVER	QUEBEC	BEAUHARNOIS CANAL C7	45-15.60	73-57.50	14240.50	60152.24	1411
ST LAWRENCE RIVER	QUEBEC	BEAUHARNOIS ANCH "CE"	45-15.60	73-57.30	14239.13	60152.48	1411
ST LAWRENCE RIVER	QUEBEC	BEAUHARNOIS CANAL C6	45-46.20	73-57.20	14026.03	60082.04	
ST LAWRENCE RIVER	QUEBEC	BEAUHARNOIS ANCH "CD"	45-16.00	73-57.00	14234.25	60151.94	1411
ST LAWRENCE RIVER	QUEBEC	MELOCHEVILLE RANGE	45-19.20	73-56.60	14208.92	60145.22	1410
ST LAWRENCE RIVER	QUEBEC	BEAUHARNOIS CANAL C2	45-17.00	73-56.50	14223.76	60150.29	1411
ST LAWRENCE RIVER	QUEBEC	BEAUHARNOIS ANCH "CA"	45-17.00	73-56.20	14221.70	60150.65	1411
ST LAWRENCE RIVER	QUEBEC	SOUTH WALL APPROACH	45-17.60	73-56.00	14216.10	60149.54	1411
ST LAWRENCE RIVER	QUEBEC	POWERHOUSE RANGE	45-16.70	73-56.00	14222.45	60151.55	1411
ST LAWRENCE RIVER	QUEBEC	BEAUHARNOIS CANAL LOCK	45-18.00	73-55.70	14211.22	60149.00	1411
ST LAWRENCE RIVER	QUEBEC	BEAUHARNOIS ANCH "B"	45-20.00	73-55.00	14192.35	60145.34	1410
ST LAWRENCE RIVER	QUEBEC	BEAUHARNOIS ANCH "A"	45-20.40	73-54.30	14184.75	60145.29	1410
ST LAWRENCE RIVER	QUEBEC	POINTE FORTIER	45-21.20	73-54.00	14177.09	60143.85	1410
ST LAWRENCE RIVER	QUEBEC	LAKE ST LOUIS A51	45-20.50	73-53.00	14175.15	60146.61	1410
ST LAWRENCE RIVER	QUEBEC	LAKE ST LOUIS A52	45-20.60	73-53.00	14174.45	60146.39	1410
ST LAWRENCE RIVER	QUEBEC	LAKE ST LOUIS A46	45-21.00	73-52.10	14165.48	60146.56	1410
ST LAWRENCE RIVER	QUEBEC	LAKE ST LOUIS A45	45-20.90	73-52.00	14165.49	60146.90	1410
ST LAWRENCE RIVER	QUEBEC	LAKE ST LOUIS A40	45-21.40	73-51.00	14155.13	60146.97	1410
ST LAWRENCE RIVER	QUEBEC	LAKE ST LOUIS A39	45-21.40	73-50.60	14152.39	60147.43	1410
ST LAWRENCE RIVER	QUEBEC	LAKE ST LOUIS A38	45-21.60	73-50.50	14150.30	60147.11	1410
ST LAWRENCE RIVER	QUEBEC	LAKE ST LOUIS A34	45-22.30	73-49.60	14139.24	60146.61	1410
ST LAWRENCE RIVER	QUEBEC	LAKE ST LOUIS A28	45-23.10	73-48.50	14126.11	60146.13	1410
ST LAWRENCE RIVER	QUEBEC	LAKE ST LOUIS A27	45-23.00	73-48.40	14126.12	60146.47	1410
ST LAWRENCE RIVER	QUEBEC	CAUGHNAWAGA RANGE	45-24.20	73-47.80	14113.64	60144.51	1409
ST LAWRENCE RIVER	QUEBEC	LAKE ST LOUIS A22	45-24.00	73-47.40	14112.28	60145.42	1410
ST LAWRENCE RIVER	QUEBEC	LAKE ST LOUIS A21	45-24.00	73-47.20	14110.91	60145.65	1410
ST LAWRENCE RIVER	QUEBEC	LAKE ST LOUIS A18	45-24.30	73-47.00	14107.46	60145.23	1410
ST LAWRENCE RIVER	QUEBEC	LAKE ST LOUIS A17	45-24.10	73-46.80	14107.46	60145.90	1410
ST LAWRENCE RIVER	QUEBEC	LALE ST LOUIS A13	45-24.20	73-46.40	14104.02	60146.14	1410
ST LAWRENCE RIVER	QUEBEC	LACHINE BUOY A	45-24.30	73-46.10	14101.26	60146.27	1410
ST LAWRENCE RIVER	QUEBEC	ILE DORVAL RANGE	45-25.10	73-45.60	14092.28	60145.09	
ST LAWRENCE RIVER	QUEBEC	LAKE ST LOUIS A9	45-24.20	73-45.40	14097.13	60147.30	1410
ST LAWRENCE RIVER	QUEBEC	LAKE ST LOUIS A10	45-24.30	73-45.40	14096.44	60147.08	1410
ST LAWRENCE RIVER	QUEBEC	POINTE JOHNSON	45-24.00	73-44.80	14094.38	60148.42	1410
ST LAWRENCE RIVER	QUEBEC	LAKE ST LOUIS A8	45-24.40	73-44.50	14089.55	60147.89	1410

PASSES

BODY OF WATER	PROV/STATE	NAME	LAT	LON	TD#1	TD#2	CHART
ST LAWRENCE RIVER	QUEBEC	LAKE ST LOUIS A7	45-24.30	73-44.50	14090.24	60148.11	1410
ST LAWRENCE RIVER	QUEBEC	LAKE ST LOUIS A5	45-24.30	73-44.20	14088.17	60148.45	1410
ST LAWRENCE RIVER	QUEBEC	LAKE ST LOUIS A4	45-24.40	73-44.00	14086.10	60148.47	1409
ST LAWRENCE RIVER	QUEBEC	LAKE ST LOUIS A3	45-24.30	73-43.80	14085.41	60148.91	1409
ST LAWRENCE RIVER	QUEBEC	LAKE ST LOUIS W DYKE	45-24.50	73-43.30	14080.58	60149.04	1409
ST LAWRENCE RIVER	QUEBEC	LAKE ST LOUIS A1	45-24.40	73-43.20	14080.58	60149.38	1409
ST LAWRENCE RIVER	QUEBEC	HONORE MERCIER BRIDGE	45-25.00	73-40.00	14054.31	60151.67	
ST LAWRENCE RIVER	QUEBEC	TURNING BASIN NO 2	45-24.00	73-33.00	14012.49	60161.38	1410
ST LAWRENCE RIVER	QUEBEC	PTE DU HAVRE BUOY M203	45-30.50	73-32.70	13966.04	60147.97	
ST LAWRENCE RIVER	QUEBEC	JACQUES CARTIER BRIDGE	45-31.30	73-32.60	13959.92	60146.37	
ST LAWRENCE RIVER	QUEBEC	ILE STE HELENE BUOY	45-32.10	73-32.00	13950.32	60145.32	
ST LAWRENCE RIVER	QUEBEC	LONGUEUIL M187	45-33.10	73-31.10	13937.31	60144.19	
ST LAWRENCE RIVER	QUEBEC	TETREAULTVILLE RANGE	45-35.80	73-30.70	13916.34	60138.86	
ST LAWRENCE RIVER	QUEBEC	POULIER A GAGNON M177	45-34.00	73-30.60	13927.76	60142.82	
ST LAWRENCE RIVER	QUEBEC	MONTREAL HARB "A"	45-34.60	73-30.40	13922.33	60141.77	
ST LAWRENCE RIVER	QUEBEC	MONTREAL HARB "B"	45-34.40	73-30.40	13923.68	60142.19	
ST LAWRENCE RIVER	QUEBEC	POULIER A GAGNON M175	45-34.60	73-30.20	13920.95	60141.98	
ST LAWRENCE RIVER	QUEBEC	POINTE-AUX-TREMBLES M167	45-36.00	73-30.20	13911.52	60139.00	
ST LAWRENCE RIVER	QUEBEC	POINTE-AUX-TREMBLES M163	45-36.60	73-30.10	13906.80	60137.82	
ST LAWRENCE RIVER	QUEBEC	TURNING BASIN NO 1	45-27.00	73-30.00	13971.04	60158.26	
ST LAWRENCE RIVER	QUEBEC	POINTE-AUX-TREMBLES M159	45-37.20	73-29.70	13900.00	60136.99	
ST LAWRENCE RIVER	QUEBEC	LONGUE POINTE TRAV RANGE	45-33.70	73-29.70	13923.54	60144.45	
ST LAWRENCE RIVER	QUEBEC	GR BATTURES TRAILHANDLIER	45-35.70	73-29.60	13909.38	60140.31	
ST LAWRENCE RIVER	QUEBEC	POINTE-AUX-TRENBLES M157	45-37.80	73-29.30	13893.21	60136.16	
ST LAWRENCE RIVER	QUEBEC	ST PATRICE "PAT"	45-39.10	73-28.70	13880.36	60134.05	
ST LAWRENCE RIVER	QUEBEC	POINTE-AUX-TREMBLES M151	45-03.80	73-28.60	14120.94	60206.24	
ST LAWRENCE RIVER	QUEBEC	ILE AUX VACHES TRAV M147	45-39.20	73-28.30	13876.92	60134.29	
ST LAWRENCE RIVER	QUEBEC	ILE STE THERESE RANGE	45-39.90	73-28.00	13870.17	60133.13	
ST LAWRENCE RIVER	QUEBEC	VARENNES BUOY M143	45-40.00	73-27.70	13867.43	60133.25	
ST LAWRENCE RIVER	QUEBEC	ILE STE THERESE RANGE	45-41.10	73-27.60	13859.42	60131.01	
ST LAWRENCE RIVER	QUEBEC	ILE A L'AIGLE RANGE	45-40.00	73-27.50	13866.05	60133.48	
ST LAWRENCE RIVER	QUEBEC	VARENNES CURVE M133	45-41.20	73-27.10	13855.29	60131.36	
ST LAWRENCE RIVER	QUEBEC	VARENNES CURVE M129	45-41.80	73-27.00	13850.62	60130.19	
ST LAWRENCE RIVER	QUEBEC	VARENNES BUOY "V"	45-42.00	73-27.00	13849.29	60129.76	
ST LAWRENCE RIVER	QUEBEC	VARENNES BUOY	45-41.70	73-27.00	13851.28	60130.40	
ST LAWRENCE RIVER	QUEBEC	ILE DESLAURIERS M124	45-42.20	73-26.70	13845.89	60129.67	
ST LAWRENCE RIVER	QUEBEC	VARENNES RANGE	45-41.20	73-26.50	13851.14	60132.04	
ST LAWRENCE RIVER	QUEBEC	ILE LEBEL RANGE	45-44.40	73-26.40	13829.26	60125.30	
ST LAWRENCE RIVER	QUEBEC	ILE DESLAURIERS RANGE	45-42.80	73-26.40	13839.83	60128.73	
ST LAWRENCE RIVER	QUEBEC	ILE DESLAURIERS M118	45-43.20	73-26.10	13835.11	60128.21	
ST LAWRENCE RIVER	QUEBEC	CAP ST MICHEL BUOY	45-43.00	73-26.00	13835.75	60128.75	
ST LAWRENCE RIVER	QUEBEC	CAP ST MICHEL M119	45-42.90	73-26.00	13836.41	60128.97	
ST LAWRENCE RIVER	QUEBEC	CAP ST MICHEL M117	45-43.20	73-25.80	13833.03	60128.56	
ST LAWRENCE RIVER	QUEBEC	ILE BELLEGARDE M116	45-44.10	73-25.10	13822.25	60127.42	

PASSES

BODY OF WATER	PROV/STATE	NAME	LAT	LON	TD#1	TD#2	CHA
ST LAWRENCE RIVER	QUEBEC	POULIER D'TROIS BOUEES M103	45-45.00	73-24.00	13808.70	60126.75	
ST LAWRENCE RIVER	QUEBEC	LAKE ST LOUIS A25	45-23.40	73-23.40	13949.21	60172.38	141
ST LAWRENCE RIVER	QUEBEC	VERCHERES COURSE M89	45-46.40	73-22.30	13787.74	60125.69	
ST LAWRENCE RIVER	QUEBEC	ST SULPICE TRAV RANGE	45-49.00	73-22.30	13770.75	60120.14	
ST LAWRENCE RIVER	QUEBEC	ST SULPICE COURSE RANGE	45-49.70	73-21.00	13757.21	60120.13	
ST LAWRENCE RIVER	QUEBEC	BOUCHARD PENINSULA RANGE	45-49.00	73-21.00	13761.76	60121.63	
ST LAWRENCE RIVER	QUEBEC	ILE BOUCHARD RANGE	45-47.90	73-20.70	13766.85	60124.31	
ST LAWRENCE RIVER	QUEBEC	ILE AUX PRUNES M82	45-47.40	73-20.70	13770.11	60125.37	
ST LAWRENCE RIVER	QUEBEC	VERCHERES TRAV RANGE	45-47.80	73-19.70	13760.57	60125.65	
ST LAWRENCE RIVER	QUEBEC	ILE AUX BOEUFS M79	45-48.20	73-19.50	13756.57	60125.02	
ST LAWRENCE RIVER	QUEBEC	MOUSSEAU RANGE	45-50.20	73-18.30	13735.26	60122.14	
ST LAWRENCE RIVER	QUEBEC	CONTRECOEUR TRAV RANGE	45-50.00	73-17.00	13727.54	60124.02	
ST LAWRENCE RIVER	QUEBEC	CONTRECOEUR BUOY M45	45-51.60	73-16.00	13710.26	60121.77	
ST LAWRENCE RIVER	QUEBEC	LAVALTRIE RANGE	45-53.00	73-15.90	13700.56	60118.92	
ST LAWRENCE RIVER	QUEBEC	CONTRECOEUR/VERCHERES RANGE	45-52.00	73-15.10	13701.44	60121.93	
ST LAWRENCE RIVER	QUEBEC	CONTRECOEUR BUOY M37	45-52.50	73-15.10	13698.22	60120.88	
ST LAWRENCE RIVER	QUEBEC	CONTRECOEUR M33	45-53.10	73-14.50	13690.20	60120.29	
ST LAWRENCE RIVER	QUEBEC	CONTRECOEUR M29	45-53.60	73-14.00	13683.53	60119.79	
ST LAWRENCE RIVER	QUEBEC	ILE ST OURS, S	45-54.30	73-13.50	13675.58	60118.88	
ST LAWRENCE RIVER	QUEBEC	BELLMOUTH CURVE M20	45-54.50	73-13.10	13671.52	60118.91	
ST LAWRENCE RIVER	QUEBEC	ILE ST OURS BUOY	45-56.80	73-13.00	13656.18	60114.17	
ST LAWRENCE RIVER	QUEBEC	ILE ST OURS M16	45-55.00	73-13.00	13667.64	60117.97	
ST LAWRENCE RIVER	QUEBEC	ILE ST OURS RANGE	45-53.10	73-13.00	13679.78	60121.96	
ST LAWRENCE RIVER	QUEBEC	ILE ST OURS COURSE	45-58.00	73-12.70	13646.49	60111.98	
ST LAWRENCE RIVER	QUEBEC	ILE ST OURS COURSE M5	45-57.00	73-12.60	13652.14	60114.20	
ST LAWRENCE RIVER	QUEBEC	CONTRECOEUR COURSE RANGE	45-55.30	73-12.60	13662.95	60117.79	
ST LAWRENCE RIVER	QUEBEC	BELLMOUTH CURVE	45-55.20	73-12.50	13662.89	60118.11	
ST LAWRENCE RIVER	QUEBEC	PETITE TRAV RANGE	45-54.70	73-12.50	13666.08	60119.16	
ST LAWRENCE RIVER	QUEBEC	VERCHERES VILLAGE RANGE	45-46.80	73-12.40	13716.22	60135.74	
ST LAWRENCE RIVER	QUEBEC	ILE AUX FOINS M1	46-02.10	73-10.00	13602.00	60106.40	
ST LAWRENCE RIVER	QUEBEC	LAKE ST PETER S154	43-02.50	73-09.90	14754.14	60315.29	
ST LAWRENCE RIVER	QUEBEC	ILE DUPAS RANGE	46-03.50	73-09.40	13589.12	60104.13	
ST LAWRENCE RIVER	QUEBEC	SOREL BASIN RANGE	46-02.90	73-06.90	13575.52	60108.24	
ST LAWRENCE RIVER	QUEBEC	NEPIGON SHOAL S146	46-03.70	73-05.60	13561.53	60108.03	
ST LAWRENCE RIVER	QUEBEC	LAKE ST PETER S141	46-03.50	73-05.00	13557.98	60108.91	
ST LAWRENCE RIVER	QUEBEC	STE ANNE DE SOREL RANGE	46-03.50	73-03.40	13547.47	60110.91	
ST LAWRENCE RIVER	QUEBEC	ILE DE GRACE S139	46-03.80	73-03.00	13542.83	60110.73	
ST LAWRENCE RIVER	QUEBEC	ILE DE GRACE RANGE	46-04.10	73-03.00	13540.98	60110.10	
ST LAWRENCE RIVER	QUEBEC	ILE DE GRACE S136	46-04.00	73-02.90	13540.90	60110.42	
ST LAWRENCE RIVER	QUEBEC	LAKE ST PETER S130	46-04.20	73-02.30	13535.49	60110.67	
ST LAWRENCE RIVER	QUEBEC	ILE DE GRACE S129	46-04.10	73-02.10	13534.71	60111.10	
ST LAWRENCE RIVER	QUEBEC	ILE DU MOINE RANGE	46-04.00	73-01.50	13531.15	60111.97	
ST LAWRENCE RIVER	QUEBEC	ILE LA PIERRE S126	46-05.00	73-01.00	13521.50	60110.45	
ST LAWRENCE RIVER	QUEBEC	ILE DES BARQUES S123	46-04.90	73-00.70	13520.03	60110.99	

PASSES

BODY OF WATER	PROV/STATE	NAME	LAT	LON	TD#1	TD#2	CHART
ST LAWRENCE RIVER	QUEBEC	ISLE DES BARQUES RANGE	46-05.30	72-59.70	13510.59	60111.26	
ST LAWRENCE RIVER	QUEBEC	ILE LA PIERRE S120	46-05.90	72-59.30	13504.12	60110.46	
ST LAWRENCE RIVER	QUEBEC	LAKE ST PETER S117	46-06.00	72-58.80	13500.02	60110.81	
ST LAWRENCE RIVER	QUEBEC	LAKE ST PETER S116	46-06.30	72-58.60	13496.80	60110.41	
ST LAWRENCE RIVER	QUEBEC	ILE AUX RAISIN CANAL SN2	46-06.20	72-58.40	13496.01	60110.83	
ST LAWRENCE RIVER	QUEBEC	LAKE ST PETER S114	46-06.80	72-58.10	13490.25	60109.92	
ST LAWRENCE RIVER	QUEBEC	ILE AUX RAISIN RANGE	46-06.20	72-58.00	13493.21	60111.27	
ST LAWRENCE RIVER	QUEBEC	LAKE ST PETER S113	46-06.70	72-58.00	13490.16	60110.24	
ST LAWRENCE RIVER	QUEBEC	LAKE ST PETER S110	46-07.60	72-57.50	13481.19	60108.93	
ST LAWRENCE RIVER	QUEBEC	LAKE ST PETER S111	46-07.10	72-57.50	13484.23	60109.96	
ST LAWRENCE RIVER	QUEBEC	LAKE ST PETER S108	46-08.40	72-57.30	13474.93	60107.51	
ST LAWRENCE RIVER	QUEBEC	LAKE ST PETER S107	46-08.00	72-57.20	13476.67	60108.44	
ST LAWRENCE RIVER	QUEBEC	LAKE ST PETER S102	46-09.10	72-57.10	13469.30	60106.29	
ST LAWRENCE RIVER	QUEBEC	LAKE ST PETER S103	46-08.90	72-57.00	13469.81	60106.81	
ST LAWRENCE RIVER	QUEBEC	LAKE ST PETER S101	46-09.40	72-56.60	13463.99	60106.22	
ST LAWRENCE RIVER	QUEBEC	LAKE ST PETER S100	46-09.80	72-56.50	13460.88	60105.50	
ST LAWRENCE RIVER	QUEBEC	LAKE ST PETER LIGHT	46-09.40	72-56.50	13463.30	60106.33	
ST LAWRENCE RIVER	QUEBEC	LAKE ST PETER S97	46-10.00	72-56.00	13456.19	60105.65	
ST LAWRENCE RIVER	QUEBEC	LAKE ST PETER S92	46-10.50	72-55.60	13450.38	60105.06	
ST LAWRENCE RIVER	QUEBEC	LAKE ST PETER S91	46-10.40	72-55.50	13450.29	60105.37	
ST LAWRENCE RIVER	QUEBEC	LOUISVILLE RANGE	46-13.30	72-55.50	13432.90	60099.40	
ST LAWRENCE RIVER	QUEBEC	LAKE ST PETER CURVE	46-11.20	72-55.00	13441.99	60104.28	
ST LAWRENCE RIVER	QUEBEC	LAKE ST PETER S87	46-10.70	72-55.00	13444.99	60105.31	
ST LAWRENCE RIVER	QUEBEC	LAKE ST PETER S86	46-11.10	72-54.80	13441.19	60104.70	
ST LAWRENCE RIVER	QUEBEC	LAKE ST PETER S81	46-11.10	72-54.40	13438.40	60105.14	
ST LAWRENCE RIVER	QUEBEC	LAKE ST PETER S82	46-11.40	72-54.20	13435.21	60104.75	
ST LAWRENCE RIVER	QUEBEC	LAKE ST PETER S79	46-11.30	72-53.70	13432.32	60105.50	
ST LAWRENCE RIVER	QUEBEC	LAKE ST PETER S80	46-11.60	72-53.50	13429.12	60105.10	
ST LAWRENCE RIVER	QUEBEC	LAKE ST PETER S77	46-11.60	72-53.10	13426.33	60105.54	
ST LAWRENCE RIVER	QUEBEC	LAKE ST PETER S74	46-12.00	72-52.00	13416.25	60105.92	
ST LAWRENCE RIVER	QUEBEC	LAKE ST PETER S73	46-12.00	72-52.00	13416.25	60105.92	
ST LAWRENCE RIVER	QUEBEC	LAKE ST PETER S67	46-12.20	72-51.00	13408.06	60106.59	
ST LAWRENCE RIVER	QUEBEC	LAKE ST PETER S68	46-12.30	72-51.00	13407.47	60106.39	
ST LAWRENCE RIVER	QUEBEC	LAKE ST PETER S62	46-12.50	72-50.00	13399.28	60107.06	
ST LAWRENCE RIVER	QUEBEC	LAKE ST PETER CURVE	46-12.30	72-50.00	13400.47	60107.47	
ST LAWRENCE RIVER	QUEBEC	LAKE ST PETER S63	46-12.50	72-50.00	13399.28	60107.06	
ST LAWRENCE RIVER	QUEBEC	YAMACHICHE BUOY C	46-12.30	72-49.30	13395.57	60108.22	
ST LAWRENCE RIVER	QUEBEC	YAMACHICHE BEND	46-13.00	72-49.20	13390.71	60106.91	
ST LAWRENCE RIVER	QUEBEC	LAKE ST PETER C58	46-12.80	72-49.20	13391.90	60107.31	
ST LAWRENCE RIVER	QUEBEC	YAMACHICHE BUOY B	46-12.50	72-49.00	13392.28	60108.14	
ST LAWRENCE RIVER	QUEBEC	YAMACHICHE BUOY A	46-12.70	72-48.50	13387.59	60108.27	
ST LAWRENCE RIVER	QUEBEC	YAMACHICHE BEND S51	46-13.00	72-48.40	13385.11	60107.77	
ST LAWRENCE RIVER	QUEBEC	YAMACHICHE BEND S54	46-13.10	72-48.30	13383.81	60107.67	
ST LAWRENCE RIVER	QUEBEC	LAKE ST PETER S44	46-13.80	72-47.00	13370.56	60107.65	

PASSES

BODY OF WATER	PROV/STATE	NAME	LAT	LON	TD#1	TD#2	CHAR
ST LAWRENCE RIVER	QUEBEC	LAKE ST PETER S43	46-13.70	72-46.80	13369.74	60108.06	
ST LAWRENCE RIVER	QUEBEC	LAKE ST PETER S41	46-14.30	72-45.60	13357.79	60108.12	
ST LAWRENCE RIVER	QUEBEC	LAKE ST PETER S42	46-14.60	72-45.50	13355.32	60107.63	
ST LAWRENCE RIVER	QUEBEC	BAIEVILLE LIGHT	46-09.60	72-45.30	13383.57	60117.87	
ST LAWRENCE RIVER	QUEBEC	LAKE ST PETER S32	46-15.10	72-44.10	13342.55	60108.10	
ST LAWRENCE RIVER	QUEBEC	LAKE ST PETER S31	46-15.00	72-44.00	13342.43	60108.41	
ST LAWRENCE RIVER	QUEBEC	LAKE ST PETER C27	46-15.60	72-43.00	13331.89	60108.26	
ST LAWRENCE RIVER	QUEBEC	LAKE ST PETER C26	46-16.00	72-42.70	13327.45	60107.77	
ST LAWRENCE RIVER	QUEBEC	LAKE ST PETER C25	46-15.60	72-42.50	13328.38	60108.79	
ST LAWRENCE RIVER	QUEBEC	LAKE ST PETER C22	46-16.00	72-42.10	13323.23	60108.40	
ST LAWRENCE RIVER	QUEBEC	LAKE ST PETER C21	46-15.80	72-42.00	13323.69	60108.91	
ST LAWRENCE RIVER	QUEBEC	POINTE DU-LAC BUOY	46-16.00	72-41.70	13320.42	60108.82	
ST LAWRENCE RIVER	QUEBEC	LAKE ST PETER S16	46-16.00	72-41.50	13319.01	60109.03	
ST LAWRENCE RIVER	QUEBEC	LAKE ST PETER S17	46-15.70	72-41.20	13318.65	60109.95	
ST LAWRENCE RIVER	QUEBEC	LAKE ST PETER S12	46-15.90	72-40.70	13313.96	60110.07	
ST LAWRENCE RIVER	QUEBEC	LAKE ST PETER S13	46-15.80	72-40.60	13313.84	60110.37	
ST LAWRENCE RIVER	QUEBEC	LAKE ST PETER S10	46-15.80	72-40.00	13309.62	60110.99	
ST LAWRENCE RIVER	QUEBEC	BANC DES ANGLAIS S9	46-15.50	72-39.60	13308.55	60112.00	
ST LAWRENCE RIVER	QUEBEC	LAKE ST PETER S8	46-15.80	72-39.30	13304.68	60111.72	
ST LAWRENCE RIVER	QUEBEC	LAKE ST PETER PIER	46-15.50	72-39.10	13305.02	60112.52	
ST LAWRENCE RIVER	QUEBEC	LAKE ST PETER S6	46-16.00	72-38.80	13299.99	60111.84	
ST LAWRENCE RIVER	QUEBEC	BATTURE LAFORCE S4	46-16.10	72-38.10	13294.47	60112.36	
ST LAWRENCE RIVER	QUEBEC	BATTURE LAFORCE S3	46-16.00	72-38.00	13294.35	60112.66	
ST LAWRENCE RIVER	QUEBEC	PORT ST FRANCOIS WHARF	46-16.40	72-37.20	13286.38	60112.69	
ST LAWRENCE RIVER	QUEBEC	STE ANGELE RANGE	46-18.80	72-34.00	13249.94	60111.22	
ST LAWRENCE RIVER	QUEBEC	TROIS RIVIERES BRIDGE	46-18.50	72-33.80	13250.24	60112.02	
ST LAWRENCE RIVER	QUEBEC	TROIS RIVIERES BRIDGE	46-18.40	72-33.70	13250.11	60112.32	
ST LAWRENCE RIVER	QUEBEC	PTE DES CHERNAUX C61	46-19.80	72-32.30	13232.20	60110.99	
ST LAWRENCE RIVER	QUEBEC	PTE DES CHERNAUX C52	46-20.70	72-31.60	13222.14	60109.93	
ST LAWRENCE RIVER	QUEBEC	PTE DES CHERNAUX C53	46-20.50	72-31.10	13219.74	60110.83	
ST LAWRENCE RIVER	QUEBEC	PTE DES CHERNAUX C48	46-21.30	72-30.60	13211.67	60109.77	
ST LAWRENCE RIVER	QUEBEC	PTE DES CHERNAUX	46-21.30	72-30.50	13210.96	60109.87	
ST LAWRENCE RIVER	QUEBEC	PTE DES CHERNAUX C49	46-21.10	72-30.40	13211.38	60110.36	
ST LAWRENCE RIVER	QUEBEC	CAP DE LA MADELEINE C47	46-21.80	72-29.80	13203.18	60109.60	
ST LAWRENCE RIVER	QUEBEC	CAP DE LA MADELEINE WHARF	46-22.00	72-29.80	13202.05	60109.21	
ST LAWRENCE RIVER	QUEBEC	CAP DE LA MADELEINE C46	46-22.20	72-29.40	13198.09	60109.22	
ST LAWRENCE RIVER	QUEBEC	CAP DE LA MADELEINE C45	46-22.00	72-29.30	13198.51	60109.72	
ST LAWRENCE RIVER	QUEBEC	CAP DE LA MADELEINE C43	46-22.20	72-29.00	13195.26	60109.63	
ST LAWRENCE RIVER	QUEBEC	BECANCOUR TRAV C40	46-22.50	72-29.00	13193.57	60109.04	
ST LAWRENCE RIVER	QUEBEC	CAP DE LA MADELEINE C41	46-22.40	72-28.40	13189.89	60109.84	
ST LAWRENCE RIVER	QUEBEC	BECANCOUR BEND C36	46-22.70	72-27.70	13183.25	60109.96	
ST LAWRENCE RIVER	QUEBEC	BECANCOUR TRAV C39	46-22.60	72-27.70	13183.81	60110.16	
ST LAWRENCE RIVER	QUEBEC	BECANCOUR BEND C34	46-23.00	72-26.70	13174.48	60110.38	
ST LAWRENCE RIVER	QUEBEC	BECAVCOUR BEND C33	46-22.80	72-26.60	13174.90	60110.87	

PASSES

BODY OF WATER	PROV/STATE	NAME	LAT	LON	TD#1	TD#2	CHART
ST LAWRENCE RIVER	QUEBEC	BECANCOUR BEND C30	46-23.00	72-26.10	13170.23	60110.98	
ST LAWRENCE RIVER	QUEBEC	BATTURE FRANCOCEUR C28	46-23.30	72-25.70	13165.72	60110.80	
ST LAWRENCE RIVER	QUEBEC	BATTURE PROVENCHER C27	46-23.10	72-25.50	13165.42	60111.38	
ST LAWRENCE RIVER	QUEBEC	BECANCOUR U TRAV RANGE	46-23.30	72-23.80	13152.24	60112.68	
ST LAWRENCE RIVER	QUEBEC	BECANCOUR COURSE C23	46-24.30	72-23.60	13145.25	60110.95	
ST LAWRENCE RIVER	QUEBEC	POINTE A BIGOT	46-25.00	72-23.00	13137.11	60110.19	
ST LAWRENCE RIVER	QUEBEC	POINTE A BIGOT BAY C20	46-25.10	72-22.50	13133.01	60110.49	
ST LAWRENCE RIVER	QUEBEC	BIGOT BAY C21	46-25.00	72-22.40	13132.85	60110.78	
ST LAWRENCE RIVER	QUEBEC	POULIER DUBORD C19	46-25.60	72-21.50	13123.15	60110.52	
ST LAWRENCE RIVER	QUEBEC	CHAMPLAIN RANGE	46-26.10	72-21.50	13120.40	60109.55	
ST LAWRENCE RIVER	QUEBEC	POULIER DUBORD C18	46-26.00	72-21.20	13118.82	60110.04	
ST LAWRENCE RIVER	QUEBEC	POULIER DUBORD C17	46-26.00	72-21.20	13118.82	60110.04	
ST LAWRENCE RIVER	QUEBEC	POULIER CARPENTIER C16	46-26.20	72-20.70	13114.17	60110.15	
ST LAWRENCE RIVER	QUEBEC	CHAMPLAIN @ CHURCH	46-26.40	72-20.70	13113.07	60109.76	
ST LAWRENCE RIVER	QUEBEC	POULIER CARPENTIER C15	46-26.00	72-20.60	13114.56	60110.63	
ST LAWRENCE RIVER	QUEBEC	POULIER CARPENTIER C14	46-26.30	72-20.10	13109.36	60110.55	
ST LAWRENCE RIVER	QUEBEC	CHAMPLAIN TRAV C13	46-26.10	72-20.00	13109.75	60111.03	
ST LAWRENCE RIVER	QUEBEC	CHAMPLAIN TRAV C7	46-26.30	72-17.90	13093.71	60112.70	
ST LAWRENCE RIVER	QUEBEC	CHAMPLAIN TRAV C4	46-26.50	72-17.10	13086.92	60113.09	
ST LAWRENCE RIVER	QUEBEC	PTE A LA CITROUILLE C2	46-26.60	72-16.50	13082.10	60113.48	
ST LAWRENCE RIVER	QUEBEC	PTE A LA CITROUILLE C3	46-26.40	72-16.40	13082.48	60113.96	
ST LAWRENCE RIVER	QUEBEC	PTE A LA CITROUILLE	46-27.10	72-16.10	13076.53	60112.91	
ST LAWRENCE RIVER	QUEBEC	PTE A LA CITROUILLE D90	46-26.80	72-16.10	13078.16	60113.49	
ST LAWRENCE RIVER	QUEBEC	PTE A LA CITROUILLE D88	46-27.10	72-15.80	13074.39	60113.21	
ST LAWRENCE RIVER	QUEBEC	PTE A LA CITROUILLE D87	46-27.00	72-15.50	13072.79	60113.68	
ST LAWRENCE RIVER	QUEBEC	BATISCAN WHARF	46-30.00	72-14.80	13051.60	60108.65	
ST LAWRENCE RIVER	QUEBEC	BATTURE PERRON D82	46-28.40	72-14.70	13059.51	60111.79	
ST LAWRENCE RIVER	QUEBEC	BATISCAN RIVER	46-30.60	72-14.40	13045.54	60107.89	
ST LAWRENCE RIVER	QUEBEC	BATTURE PERRON D77	46-29.00	72-14.20	13052.70	60111.13	
ST LAWRENCE RIVER	QUEBEC	BATISCAN ST PIERRE D71	46-30.00	72-13.80	13044.48	60109.62	
ST LAWRENCE RIVER	QUEBEC	BATISCAN TRAV D62	46-31.20	72-13.00	13032.38	60108.11	
ST LAWRENCE RIVER	QUEBEC	BATTURE ST PIERRE D67	46-30.50	72-12.80	13034.68	60109.63	
ST LAWRENCE RIVER	QUEBEC	BATTURE ST PIERRE D63	46-31.00	72-12.80	13032.02	60108.68	
ST LAWRENCE RIVER	QUEBEC	GENTILLY RANGE	46-25.80	72-12.80	13060.05	60118.54	
ST LAWRENCE RIVER	QUEBEC	LES BECQUETS WHARF	46-30.50	72-12.40	13031.84	60110.02	
ST LAWRENCE RIVER	QUEBEC	BATISCAN TRAV D60	46-31.50	72-12.30	13025.80	60108.22	
ST LAWRENCE RIVER	QUEBEC	BATISCAN COURSE D59	46-31.40	72-12.20	13025.62	60108.50	
ST LAWRENCE RIVER	QUEBEC	BATISCAN TRAV D56	46-32.00	72-11.30	13016.02	60108.23	
ST LAWRENCE RIVER	QUEBEC	CAP LEVRARD D54	46-32.10	72-10.80	13011.93	60108.52	
ST LAWRENCE RIVER	QUEBEC	BATISCAN TRAV D53	46-32.00	72-10.70	13011.75	60108.81	
ST LAWRENCE RIVER	QUEBEC	LA PERADE	46-34.10	72-10.40	12998.56	60105.11	
ST LAWRENCE RIVER	QUEBEC	CAP LEVRARD D52	46-32.30	72-10.40	13008.03	60108.53	
ST LAWRENCE RIVER	QUEBEC	CAP LEVRARD D49	46-32.40	72-10.00	13004.65	60108.73	
ST LAWRENCE RIVER	QUEBEC	CAP LEVRARD D42	46-33.20	72-09.00	12993.31	60108.18	

PASSES

BODY OF WATER	PROV/STATE	NAME	LAT	LON	TD#1	TD#2	CHAR
ST LAWRENCE RIVER	QUEBEC	CAP LEVRARD D41	46-33.10	72-08.90	12993.13	60108.46	
ST LAWRENCE RIVER	QUEBEC	CAP A LA ROCHE D40	46-33.50	72-08.50	12988.18	60108.09	
ST LAWRENCE RIVER	QUEBEC	CAP A LA ROCHE D37	46-33.60	72-08.00	12984.09	60108.38	
ST LAWRENCE RIVER	QUEBEC	CAP A LA ROCHE D38	46-33.70	72-08.00	12983.56	60108.19	
ST LAWRENCE RIVER	QUEBEC	CAP A LA ROCHE D36	46-33.80	72-07.50	12979.48	60108.43	
ST LAWRENCE RIVER	QUEBEC	CAP A LA ROCHE D35	46-33.70	72-07.40	12979.29	60108.76	
ST LAWRENCE RIVER	QUEBEC	CAP A LA ROCHE CURVE D32	46-34.00	72-06.90	12974.15	60108.68	
ST LAWRENCE RIVER	QUEBEC	CAP A LA ROCHE CURVE D31	46-33.80	72-06.80	12974.48	60109.15	
ST LAWRENCE RIVER	QUEBEC	DESCHAILLONS WHARF	46-33.70	72-06.40	12972.15	60109.72	
ST LAWRENCE RIVER	QUEBEC	CAP A LA ROCHE CURVE D29	46-33.80	72-06.20	12970.20	60109.72	
ST LAWRENCE RIVER	QUEBEC	POULIER RAYER D30	46-34.00	72-06.20	12969.16	60109.34	
ST LAWRENCE RIVER	QUEBEC	CAP CHARLES	46-33.40	72-05.20	12965.14	60111.42	
ST LAWRENCE RIVER	QUEBEC	CAP CHARLES COURSE D24	46-34.00	72-04.80	12959.16	60110.67	
ST LAWRENCE RIVER	QUEBEC	POINTE DES GRONDINES RANGE	46-34.70	72-04.20	12951.24	60109.93	
ST LAWRENCE RIVER	QUEBEC	POULIER DU CALVAIRE D23	46-33.90	72-04.10	12954.67	60111.52	
ST LAWRENCE RIVER	QUEBEC	BATTURE A CADIEUX D18	46-34.20	72-03.50	12948.82	60111.52	
ST LAWRENCE RIVER	QUEBEC	BATTURE A CADIEUX D15	46-34.10	72-03.30	12947.91	60111.90	
ST LAWRENCE RIVER	QUEBEC	BATTURE DU CHENE D9	46-34.80	72-01.60	12932.12	60112.18	
ST LAWRENCE RIVER	QUEBEC	BATTURE SIMON BAY D4	46-35.50	72-00.50	12920.64	60111.90	
ST LAWRENCE RIVER	QUEBEC	POINTE LANGLOIS	46-35.00	71-59.40	12915.33	60113.85	
ST LAWRENCE RIVER	QUEBEC	GRONDINES EST Q84	46-36.30	71-59.30	12907.95	60111.53	
ST LAWRENCE RIVER	QUEBEC	ILET MAYRAND Q83	46-36.50	71-58.50	12901.20	60111.99	
ST LAWRENCE RIVER	QUEBEC	ILET MAYRAND Q80	46-37.10	71-58.10	12895.29	60111.16	
ST LAWRENCE RIVER	QUEBEC	VIELLE ENGLISE RANGE	46-36.70	71-57.60	12893.70	60112.37	
ST LAWRENCE RIVER	QUEBEC	LOTHINIERE	46-36.70	71-57.40	12892.30	60112.55	
ST LAWRENCE RIVER	QUEBEC	BARRE A BOULARD Q75	46-37.40	71-56.70	12883.73	60111.90	
ST LAWRENCE RIVER	QUEBEC	BARRE A BOULARD Q76	46-37.60	71-56.70	12882.72	60111.53	
ST LAWRENCE RIVER	QUEBEC	ILE RICHELIEU Q73	46-38.10	71-55.50	12871.59	60111.72	
ST LAWRENCE RIVER	QUEBEC	ILE RICHELIEU Q70	46-38.50	71-55.20	12867.44	60111.25	
ST LAWRENCE RIVER	QUEBEC	ILE RICHELIEU	46-38.60	71-54.60	12862.63	60111.62	
ST LAWRENCE RIVER	QUEBEC	RAPIDES RICHELIEU Q68	46-39.20	71-54.20	12856.76	60110.88	
ST LAWRENCE RIVER	QUEBEC	PORTNEUF BUOY Q66	46-39.80	71-53.80	12850.91	60110.15	
ST LAWRENCE RIVER	QUEBEC	PORTNEUF/LOTHINERE Q67	46-39.50	71-53.60	12850.96	60110.88	
ST LAWRENCE RIVER	QUEBEC	PORTNEUF BUOY Q65	46-40.10	71-53.10	12844.40	60110.23	
ST LAWRENCE RIVER	QUEBEC	PORTNEUF RIVER ENTR	46-41.40	71-52.60	12834.40	60108.30	
ST LAWRENCE RIVER	QUEBEC	PORTNEUF WHARF	46-40.90	71-52.60	12836.86	60109.22	
ST LAWRENCE RIVER	QUEBEC	BARRE A BOULARD RANGE	46-39.60	71-52.60	12843.29	60111.61	
ST LAWRENCE RIVER	QUEBEC	POINTE AU PLATON Q63	46-40.50	71-52.50	12838.11	60110.05	
ST LAWRENCE RIVER	QUEBEC	POINTE AU PLATON Q61	46-40.70	71-51.10	12827.08	60110.96	
ST LAWRENCE RIVER	QUEBEC	POINTE AU PLATON	46-40.20	71-51.00	12828.83	60111.97	
ST LAWRENCE RIVER	QUEBEC	CAP SANTE TRAVERSE Q57	46-40.10	71-49.00	12814.95	60113.96	
ST LAWRENCE RIVER	QUEBEC	CAP SANTE TRAVERSE Q57	46-40.10	71-49.00	12814.95	60113.96	
ST LAWRENCE RIVER	QUEBEC	CAP SANTE TRAVERSE Q55	46-39.70	71-48.00	12809.72	60115.59	
ST LAWRENCE RIVER	QUEBEC	CAP SANTE TRAVERSE Q56	46-39.80	71-47.80	12807.79	60115.59	

PASSES

BODY OF WATER	PROV/STATE	NAME	LAT	LON	TD#1	TD#2	CHART
ST LAWRENCE RIVER	QUEBEC	CAP SANTE TRAVERSE Q53	46-39.10	71-46.40	12801.15	60118.10	
ST LAWRENCE RIVER	QUEBEC	CAP SANTE TRAVERSE Q54	46-39.30	71-46.30	12799.44	60117.83	
ST LAWRENCE RIVER	QUEBEC	BARRE STE CROIX Q51	46-38.60	71-45.00	12793.5	60120.2	
ST LAWRENCE RIVER	QUEBEC	STE CROIX Q50	46-38.60	71-44.30	12788.5	60120.9	
ST LAWRENCE RIVER	QUEBEC	STE CROIX	46-37.70	71-44.00	12790.7	60122.7	
ST LAWRENCE RIVER	QUEBEC	BARRE STE CROIX Q50	46-38.50	71-44.00	12786.8	60121.3	
ST LAWRENCE RIVER	QUEBEC	STE CROIX Q48	46-38.50	71-42.80	12778.1	60122.3	
ST LAWRENCE RIVER	QUEBEC	STE CROIX RANGE	46-37.70	71-42.00	12776.3	60124.5	
ST LAWRENCE RIVER	QUEBEC	STE ANTOINE Q42	46-39.00	71-39.90	12754.6	60123.9	
ST LAWRENCE RIVER	QUEBEC	STE CROIX EST	46-38.40	71-38.20	12745.3	60126.5	
ST LAWRENCE RIVER	QUEBEC	POINTE STE ANTOINE Q38	46-40.10	71-36.90	12727.5	60124.5	
ST LAWRENCE RIVER	QUEBEC	POINTE STE ANTOINE Q37	46-39.90	71-36.50	12725.6	60125.2	
ST LAWRENCE RIVER	QUEBEC	STE ANTOINE TRAV RANGE	46-40.00	71-34.90	12713.5	60125.4	
ST LAWRENCE RIVER	QUEBEC	PTE AUX TREMBLES Q3	46-40.70	71-34.60	12707.9	60125.4	
ST LAWRENCE RIVER	QUEBEC	POINTE-AUX-TREMBLES	46-41.80	71-34.50	12701.9	60123.6	
ST LAWRENCE RIVER	QUEBEC	VAUQUELIN CLUB, CENTER	46-41.80	71-34.50	12701.9	60123.6	
ST LAWRENCE RIVER	QUEBEC	VAUQUELIN CLUB NAUTIQUE	46-41.80	71-34.40	12701.2	60123.7	
ST LAWRENCE RIVER	QUEBEC	VAUQUELIN CLUB WHARF	46-42.00	71-34.00	12697.3	60123.6	
ST LAWRENCE RIVER	QUEBEC	TREMBLES SHOAL Q32	46-41.20	71-33.20	12695.3	60125.7	
ST LAWRENCE RIVER	QUEBEC	BANC DE ST ANTOINE Q31	46-41.20	71-32.80	12692.4	60126.1	
ST LAWRENCE RIVER	QUEBEC	BANC DE ST ANTOINE Q29	46-41.50	71-31.80	12683.7	60126.4	
ST LAWRENCE RIVER	QUEBEC	POINTE AUBIN Q27	46-42.00	71-30.30	12670.4	60126.7	
ST LAWRENCE RIVER	QUEBEC	HAUT-FOND ST AUGUSTIN Q23	46-42.40	71-28.80	12657.6	60127.3	
ST LAWRENCE RIVER	QUEBEC	HAUT-FOND ST AUGUSTIN Q22	46-42.50	71-28.60	12655.7	60127.3	
ST LAWRENCE RIVER	QUEBEC	HAUT-FOND ST AUGUSTIN Q20	46-42.70	71-27.80	12648.9	60127.6	
ST LAWRENCE RIVER	QUEBEC	POINTE ST NICHOLAS	46-42.10	71-26.80	12644.5	60129.5	
ST LAWRENCE RIVER	QUEBEC	QUEBEC BUOY Q18	46-42.80	71-26.80	12641.2	60128.2	
ST LAWRENCE RIVER	QUEBEC	POINTE ST NICHOLAS Q20	46-42.70	71-26.70	12640.9	60128.5	
ST LAWRENCE RIVER	QUEBEC	QUEBEC BUOY Q16	46-43.00	71-25.40	12630.0	60129.0	
ST LAWRENCE RIVER	QUEBEC	POINTE A BASILE RANGE	46-43.80	71-19.80	12585.4	60132.2	
ST LAWRENCE RIVER	QUEBEC	LE SAULT BRIDGE	46-44.80	71-17.30	12562.5	60132.5	
ST LAWRENCE RIVER	QUEBEC	PIERRE-LAPORTE BRIDGE	46-44.80	71-17.30	12562.5	60132.5	
ST LAWRENCE RIVER	QUEBEC	POINTE A PUISEAUX	46-46.30	71-14.60	12526.0	60132.0	
ST LAWRENCE RIVER	QUEBEC	ST RUMUALD Q11	46-45.90	71-14.50	12537.0	60132.8	
ST LAWRENCE RIVER	QUEBEC	QUEBEC YACHT CLUB	46-47.00	71-14.30	12530.6	60131.1	
ST LAWRENCE RIVER	QUEBEC	W MARINA @ BRKWTR	46-47.00	71-14.10	12529.2	60131.2	
ST LAWRENCE RIVER	QUEBEC	E MARINA @ BRKWTR	46-47.00	71-14.10	12529.2	60131.2	
ST LAWRENCE RIVER	QUEBEC	WOLFE COVE Q6	46-47.20	71-13.50	12523.9	60131.4	
ST LAWRENCE RIVER	QUEBEC	ANSE FRECHETTE Q7	46-46.70	71-13.00	12522.5	60132.6	
ST LAWRENCE RIVER	QUEBEC	WOLFE COVE Q4	46-47.80	71-12.80	12516.1	60130.9	
ST LAWRENCE RIVER	QUEBEC	ST CHARLES RIVER	46-49.40	71-12.40	12506.2	60128.5	
ST LAWRENCE RIVER	QUEBEC	QUEENS WHARF, Quebec	46-48.60	71-12.20	12508.2	60130.0	
ST LAWRENCE RIVER	QUEBEC	LEVIS MARINA, Quebec	46-47.50	71-12.00	12511.6	60132.0	
ST LAWRENCE RIVER	QUEBEC	ST CHARLES RIVER KP-2	46-50.00	71-11.30	12495.5	60128.4	

PASSES

BODY OF WATER	PROV/STATE	NAME	LAT	LON	TD#1	TD#2	CHART
ST LAWRENCE RIVER	QUEBEC	POINTE LEVY SHOAL K165	46-49.30	71-11.10	12497.1	60129.7	
ST LAWRENCE RIVER	QUEBEC	BEAUPORT BANK K166	46-50.30	71-11.00	12492.0	60128.1	
ST LAWRENCE RIVER	QUEBEC	ORLEANS ISLAND CH V159	46-50.30	71-09.00	12477.4	60129.7	
ST LAWRENCE RIVER	QUEBEC	ORLEANS ISLAND CH V34	46-52.50	71-08.50	12464.4	60126.3	
ST LAWRENCE RIVER	QUEBEC	ORLEANS ISLAND CH V35	46-52.50	71-08.10	12461.5	60126.6	
ST LAWRENCE RIVER	QUEBEC	PTE DU BOUT DE L'ILE	46-50.70	71-07.90	12467.6	60129.8	
ST LAWRENCE RIVER	QUEBEC	ORLEANS ISLAND CH V31	46-53.20	71-07.60	12454.9	60125.9	
ST LAWRENCE RIVER	QUEBEC	L'ANGE GARDIEN RANGE	46-53.90	71-07.30	12449.8	60124.9	
ST LAWRENCE RIVER	QUEBEC	PTE DE LA MARTINIERE	46-49.70	71-07.00	12465.3	60132.2	
ST LAWRENCE RIVER	QUEBEC	CAP CHARLES D22	46-34.00	71-04.10	12515.9	60160.2	
ST LAWRENCE RIVER	QUEBEC	PRICE MONUMENT RANGE	48-25.80	71-02.60	12184.9	59965.8	
ST LAWRENCE RIVER	QUEBEC	POINTE ST PIERRE	46-55.60	71-02.50	12407.8	60125.8	
ST LAWRENCE RIVER	QUEBEC	ORLEANS ISLAND V-22	46-56.60	71-01.50	12396.5	60124.9	
ST LAWRENCE RIVER	QUEBEC	RIVIERE DU MOULIN	48-26.10	71-01.50	12178.1	59966.4	
ST LAWRENCE RIVER	QUEBEC	SAGUENAY	48-27.00	71-01.20	12175.3	59965.1	
ST LAWRENCE RIVER	QUEBEC	RIVIERE DU CARIBOU RANGE	48-27.40	71-00.60	12171.4	59965.0	
ST LAWRENCE RIVER	QUEBEC	ORLEANS ISLAND V-19	46-57.20	71-00.50	12386.8	60124.7	
ST LAWRENCE RIVER	QUEBEC	BEAUMONT REEFS K-147	46-50.90	70-60.00	12408.8	60135.6	
ST LAWRENCE RIVER	QUEBEC	POINTE A L'ILLET	48-27.00	70-59.30	12164.3	59967.1	
ST LAWRENCE RIVER	QUEBEC	POINTE A L'ILLET, E	48-27.00	70-59.10	12163.2	59967.3	
ST LAWRENCE RIVER	QUEBEC	POSTE ST MARTIN RANGE	48-26.60	70-59.00	12163.0	59968.2	
ST LAWRENCE RIVER	QUEBEC	RIVIERE VALIN RANGE	48-27.60	70-58.90	12161.3	59966.5	
ST LAWRENCE RIVER	QUEBEC	STE FAMILLE	46-57.90	70-58.60	12370.2	60125.0	
ST LAWRENCE RIVER	QUEBEC	BATTURE AUX LOUPS MAR	48-25.50	70-55.70	12145.1	59973.6	
ST LAWRENCE RIVER	QUEBEC	STE-ANNE-D'BEAUPRE WHARF	47-01.20	70-55.70	12336.4	60121.7	
ST LAWRENCE RIVER	QUEBEC	STE-MICHEL-D'BELLECHASSE	46-52.50	70-55.00	12365.4	60136.7	
ST LAWRENCE RIVER	QUEBEC	STE JEAN D'ORLEANS WHARF	46-54.90	70-53.80	12346.9	60133.6	
ST LAWRENCE RIVER	QUEBEC	ORLEANS ISLAND V-13	47-01.70	70-53.60	12319.3	60122.5	
ST LAWRENCE RIVER	QUEBEC	ANSE A'PHILIPPE	48-21.20	70-52.80	12133.0	59984.3	
ST LAWRENCE RIVER	QUEBEC	BAGOTVILLE WHARF	48-20.70	70-52.70	12133.0	59985.3	
ST LAWRENCE RIVER	QUEBEC	PORT ALFRED RANGE	48-20.10	70-52.50	12132.5	59986.6	
ST LAWRENCE RIVER	QUEBEC	EASTERN NARROWS K-136	46-55.50	70-52.30	12333.5	60133.8	
ST LAWRENCE RIVER	QUEBEC	ORLEANS ISLAND V-8	47-02.20	70-51.90	12305.0	60123.0	
ST LAWRENCE RIVER	QUEBEC	MADAME ISLAND REEF	46-55.90	70-50.50	12318.7	60134.4	
ST LAWRENCE RIVER	QUEBEC	EASTERN NARROWS K-128	46-57.70	70-50.20	12309.5	60131.7	
ST LAWRENCE RIVER	QUEBEC	EASTERN NARROWS K-127	46-57.60	70-50.00	12308.4	60132.0	
ST LAWRENCE RIVER	QUEBEC	POINTE AUX PINS	48-25.10	70-49.90	12111.9	59980.3	
ST LAWRENCE RIVER	QUEBEC	DOMAINE, NE	47-01.10	70-49.70	12293.0	60126.5	
ST LAWRENCE RIVER	QUEBEC	EASTERN NARROWS K-124	46-59.00	70-49.00	12295.8	60130.5	
ST LAWRENCE RIVER	QUEBEC	EASTERN NARROWS K-123	46-58.90	70-48.60	12293.2	60130.9	
ST LAWRENCE RIVER	QUEBEC	ST FRANCOIS WHARF	46-59.80	70-48.50	12289.1	60129.5	
ST LAWRENCE RIVER	QUEBEC	PTE ARGENTENAGE RANGE	47-00.50	70-48.30	12285.0	60128.5	
ST LAWRENCE RIVER	QUEBEC	EASTERN NARROWS K-120	47-00.20	70-47.80	12282.5	60129.4	
ST LAWRENCE RIVER	QUEBEC	EASTERN NARROWS K-119	47-00.10	70-47.60	12281.4	60129.7	

PASSES

BODY OF WATER	PROV/STATE	NAME	LAT	LON	TD#1	TD#2	CHART
ST LAWRENCE RIVER	QUEBEC	SEMINAIRE SPIT V-6	47-03.00	70-47.00	12266.5	60125.4	
ST LAWRENCE RIVER	QUEBEC	EASTERN NARROWS K-116	47-01.40	70-46.70	12270.0	60128.3	
ST LAWRENCE RIVER	QUEBEC	EASTERN NARROWS K-115	47-01.30	70-46.50	12268.9	60128.6	
ST LAWRENCE RIVER	QUEBEC	ILE DE BELLECHASSE	46-56.00	70-46.10	14524.10	32498.83	
ST LAWRENCE RIVER	QUEBEC	EASTERN NARROWS K-112	47-02.60	70-45.50	12256.9	60127.2	
ST LAWRENCE RIVER	QUEBEC	EASTERN NARROWS K-111	47-02.50	70-45.30	12255.8	60127.5	
ST LAWRENCE RIVER	QUEBEC	EASTERN NARROWS K-107	47-03.80	70-44.10	12242.5	60126.3	
ST LAWRENCE RIVER	QUEBEC	CAP ROUGE K-104	47-05.20	70-43.40	12232.5	60124.5	
ST LAWRENCE RIVER	QUEBEC	CAP ROUGE K-103	47-05.20	70-43.20	12231.1	60124.6	
ST LAWRENCE RIVER	QUEBEC	CAP BRULE, S	47-06.50	70-43.00	12225.2	60122.7	
ST LAWRENCE RIVER	QUEBEC	BRULE BANK RANGE	47-05.40	70-42.70	12226.7	60124.7	
ST LAWRENCE RIVER	QUEBEC	CAP EST	48-22.60	70-42.40	12070.7	59992.2	
ST LAWRENCE RIVER	QUEBEC	BRULE BANK RANGE	47-05.80	70-42.20	12221.8	60124.4	
ST LAWRENCE RIVER	QUEBEC	CAP ROUGE RANGE	47-07.50	70-42.10	12215.3	60121.7	
ST LAWRENCE RIVER	QUEBEC	CAP GRIBANE RANGE	47-08.50	70-41.20	12205.5	60120.7	
ST LAWRENCE RIVER	QUEBEC	LONGUE POINTE K-95	47-08.20	70-40.70	12202.9	60121.6	
ST LAWRENCE RIVER	QUEBEC	LONGUE POINTE K-96	47-08.70	70-40.50	12199.8	60120.9	
ST LAWRENCE RIVER	QUEBEC	SAULT AU COCHON	47-11.80	70-38.30	12174.1	60117.5	
ST LAWRENCE RIVER	QUEBEC	WYE ROCK BUOY H121	46-60.00	70-38.00	14578.03	32494.90	
ST LAWRENCE RIVER	QUEBEC	POINTE AUX PINS	47-02.40	70-34.50	14604.88	32492.09	
ST LAWRENCE RIVER	QUEBEC	ANSE AUX ERABLES	48-21.50	70-34.30	12024.4	60002.0	
ST LAWRENCE RIVER	QUEBEC	PETITE RIVIERE WHARF	47-18.20	70-33.70	12122.6	60110.5	
ST LAWRENCE RIVER	QUEBEC	MONTMAGNY HEAD WHARF	46-59.20	70-33.20	14592.11	32495.79	
ST LAWRENCE RIVER	QUEBEC	CAP ROUGE	48-22.50	70-32.20	12011.5	60002.2	
ST LAWRENCE RIVER	QUEBEC	ILE AUX GRUES	47-03.30	70-32.00	14619.48	32490.92	
ST LAWRENCE RIVER	QUEBEC	BEAUJEU CHANNEL	47-04.20	70-31.00	14628.23	32489.72	
ST LAWRENCE RIVER	QUEBEC	ILE AUX COUDRES K-70	47-22.10	70-29.70	12084.0	60107.2	
ST LAWRENCE RIVER	QUEBEC	HOSPITAL ROCK RANGE	47-08.00	70-28.00	14659.85	32484.16	
ST LAWRENCE RIVER	QUEBEC	ILE AUX COUDRES K-65	47-24.60	70-26.10	12052.7	60105.8	
ST LAWRENCE RIVER	QUEBEC	POINTE DE LA PRAIRIE	47-24.60	70-25.90	12051.3	60106.0	
ST LAWRENCE RIVER	QUEBEC	ILE AUX COUDRES, SW	47-22.20	70-25.80	12056.3	60110.0	
ST LAWRENCE RIVER	QUEBEC	ILE AUX CORBEAUX RANGE	47-26.10	70-25.70	12046.5	60103.7	
ST LAWRENCE RIVER	QUEBEC	ILE AUX COUDRES WHARF	47-25.20	70-23.60	12033.8	60106.7	
ST LAWRENCE RIVER	QUEBEC	GOOSE CAPE WHARF	47-26.90	70-21.90	12018.2	60105.3	
ST LAWRENCE RIVER	QUEBEC	STONE PILLAR	47-12.30	70-21.60	14706.25	32476.57	
ST LAWRENCE RIVER	QUEBEC	LA ROCHE A VEILLON H98	47-12.00	70-21.20	14706.37	32477.07	
ST LAWRENCE RIVER	QUEBEC	TRINITY BAY	48-21.20	70-20.70	11945.8	60015.2	
ST LAWRENCE RIVER	QUEBEC	ST ROCHE SHOAL H89	47-16.80	70-18.10	14740.99	32467.51	
ST LAWRENCE RIVER	QUEBEC	ST JEAN PORT JOLI WHARF	47-12.90	70-16.50	14729.14	32474.98	
ST LAWRENCE RIVER	QUEBEC	LOWER TRAV BELL H79	47-21.30	70-15.30	14771.61	32457.25	
ST LAWRENCE RIVER	QUEBEC	ST ROCHE ENTRANCE H72	47-22.80	70-14.60	14780.61	32453.59	
ST LAWRENCE RIVER	QUEBEC	GOOSE CAPE	47-29.30	70-14.00	11958.5	60107.3	
ST LAWRENCE RIVER	QUEBEC	POINTE AU BOEUF	48-16.30	70-12.20	11898.7	60031.1	
ST LAWRENCE RIVER	QUEBEC	L'ANSE ST JEAN	48-14.70	70-10.80	11891.7	60035.0	

PASSES

BODY OF WATER	PROV/STATE	NAME	LAT	LON	TD#1	TD#2
ST LAWRENCE RIVER	QUEBEC	POINTE AU PIC	47-37.40	70-08.50	11907.7	60098.4
ST LAWRENCE RIVER	QUEBEC	MURRAY BELL K-64	47-37.40	70-08.10	11905.0	60098.7
ST LAWRENCE RIVER	QUEBEC	POINTE CLAVEAU	48-15.60	70-06.90	11868.2	60036.8
ST LAWRENCE RIVER	QUEBEC	CAP A L'AIGLE MARINA	47-39.80	70-05.80	11886.4	60096.5
ST LAWRENCE RIVER	QUEBEC	CAP A L'AIGLE	47-39.70	70-05.80	11886.6	60096.7
ST LAWRENCE RIVER	QUEBEC	MORIN SHOAL BELL	47-36.10	70-02.30	14876.19	32412.58
ST LAWRENCE RIVER	QUEBEC	ILE ST LOUIS, N	48-15.10	70-01.20	11835.3	60042.4
ST LAWRENCE RIVER	QUEBEC	CAPE SALMON	47-46.10	69-54.30	11804.8	60095.0
ST LAWRENCE RIVER	QUEBEC	ANSE A PIERROT, E	48-14.10	69-53.70	11792.3	60050.3
ST LAWRENCE RIVER	QUEBEC	POINTE AUX CREPES	48-13.00	69-53.70	11792.3	60052.1
ST LAWRENCE RIVER	QUEBEC	HARE ISLAND H64	47-38.60	69-53.30	14916.74	32399.47
ST LAWRENCE RIVER	QUEBEC	HARE ISLAND K61	47-41.70	69-53.00	14926.78	32388.51
ST LAWRENCE RIVER	QUEBEC	HARE ISLAND BANK K-61	47-41.70	69-52.90	11799.1	60103.0
ST LAWRENCE RIVER	QUEBEC	ANSE DE ROCHE	48-13.10	69-52.60	11785.9	60052.8
ST LAWRENCE RIVER	QUEBEC	GRANDE ILE	47-37.30	69-51.80	14918.29	32402.99
ST LAWRENCE RIVER	QUEBEC	CAPE DOGS	47-54.60	69-48.30	11762.6	60085.9
ST LAWRENCE RIVER	QUEBEC	CAP DE LA BOULE, N	48-08.90	69-48.30	11761.0	60063.0
ST LAWRENCE RIVER	QUEBEC	ILE AUX LIEVRES ENTR	47-47.20	69-47.20	14961.49	32363.86
ST LAWRENCE RIVER	QUEBEC	HARE ISLAND	47-48.00	69-46.50	14965.83	32360.18
ST LAWRENCE RIVER	QUEBEC	ILE AUX LIEVRES	47-48.00	69-46.00	11750.6	60098.0
ST LAWRENCE RIVER	QUEBEC	LONG PILGRIM	47-43.00	69-44.90	14958.88	32377.93
ST LAWRENCE RIVER	QUEBEC	ANSE DU PORTAGE WHARF	48-07.60	69-43.90	11735.3	60068.5
ST LAWRENCE RIVER	QUEBEC	PILGRIM SHOAL H63	47-45.80	69-43.80	14969.72	32366.38
ST LAWRENCE RIVER	QUEBEC	ANSE A L'EAU WHARF	48-08.30	69-43.70	11734.3	60067.5
ST LAWRENCE RIVER	QUEBEC	BAIE STE CATHERINE	48-06.90	69-43.30	11731.8	60070.1
ST LAWRENCE RIVER	QUEBEC	POINTE NOIRE RANGE	48-07.40	69-43.10	11730.7	60069.4
ST LAWRENCE RIVER	QUEBEC	POINTE DE L'ISLET	48-08.10	69-43.00	11730.2	60068.4
ST LAWRENCE RIVER	QUEBEC	TADOUSSAC WHARF	48-08.30	69-42.90	11729.7	60068.2
ST LAWRENCE RIVER	QUEBEC	MIDDLE BANK BUOY H60	47-48.30	69-42.60	14979.74	32355.53
ST LAWRENCE RIVER	QUEBEC	BRANDYPOT	47-52.30	69-41.00	14993.91	32337.78
ST LAWRENCE RIVER	QUEBEC	LARK REEF S-7	48-07.20	69-40.50	11715.6	60071.7
ST LAWRENCE RIVER	QUEBEC	T AUX VACHES REEF S-8	48-07.50	69-40.30	11714.5	60071.4
ST LAWRENCE RIVER	QUEBEC	BAR REEF S-5	48-06.90	69-39.10	11707.5	60073.3
ST LAWRENCE RIVER	QUEBEC	DEMERS ROCK BUOY H58	47-51.40	69-39.00	14998.57	32339.45
ST LAWRENCE RIVER	QUEBEC	LARK REEF K-58	48-04.60	69-38.60	11704.1	60077.3
ST LAWRENCE RIVER	QUEBEC	VACHES SHOAL S-4	48-07.40	69-38.00	11701.3	60073.3
ST LAWRENCE RIVER	QUEBEC	WHITE ISLAND REEF K59	47-59.10	69-38.00	15016.85	32305.60
ST LAWRENCE RIVER	QUEBEC	VACHES SHOAL S-3	48-06.80	69-37.90	11700.5	60074.3
ST LAWRENCE RIVER	QUEBEC	WHITE ISLAND REEF	47-54.60	69-37.80	11698.2	60093.6
ST LAWRENCE RIVER	QUEBEC	LARK REEF K-56	48-04.60	69-37.60	11698.3	60078.0
ST LAWRENCE RIVER	QUEBEC	BARRETT LEDGE BUOY H56	47-53.00	69-37.20	15007.73	32330.85
ST LAWRENCE RIVER	QUEBEC	PRINCE SHOAL	48-06.50	69-36.90	11694.7	60075.5
ST LAWRENCE RIVER	QUEBEC	PRINCE SHOAL BELL	48-07.10	69-36.10	11690.3	60075.2
ST LAWRENCE RIVER	QUEBEC	ROCHERS DU SAGUENAT K-54	48-07.80	69-35.90	11689.4	60074.2

PASSES

BODY OF WATER	PROV/STATE	NAME	LAT	LON	TD#1	TD#2	CHART
ST LAWRENCE RIVER	QUEBEC	PTE DE LA RIVIERE DU LUOP	47-50.90	69-34.30	15012.95	32336.57	
ST LAWRENCE RIVER	QUEBEC	RED ISLET H-55	48-05.60	69-34.00	11677.8	60079.1	
ST LAWRENCE RIVER	QUEBEC	ROCHE PERCEE BUOY H55	47-55.00	69-33.50	15023.44	32318.06	
ST LAWRENCE RIVER	QUEBEC	GRS BERGERRONNES KJ-2	48-13.50	69-33.30	11677.3	60067.2	
ST LAWRENCE RIVER	QUEBEC	RED ISLET ENTRANCE	48-04.20	69-33.30	11673.3	60081.8	
ST LAWRENCE RIVER	QUEBEC	RED ISLET H-52	48-04.50	69-31.70	11664.2	60082.5	
ST LAWRENCE RIVER	QUEBEC	RED ISLET H-51	48-06.90	69-31.10	11661.8	60079.2	
ST LAWRENCE RIVER	QUEBEC	RED ISLET H-50	48-06.40	69-29.60	11653.1	60081.1	
ST LAWRENCE RIVER	QUEBEC	CAP BON DESIR	48-16.30	69-28.20	11651.1	60066.6	
ST LAWRENCE RIVER	QUEBEC	ILE VERTE WHARF	47-60.00	69-27.80	15049.53	32288.37	
ST LAWRENCE RIVER	QUEBEC	CACAUNA WHARF	47-60.00	69-26.00	15054.92	32285.84	
ST LAWRENCE RIVER	QUEBEC	ANSE AU BASQUES	48-19.10	69-24.80	11635.1	60064.7	
ST LAWRENCE RIVER	QUEBEC	LES ESCOUMINS WHARF	48-20.80	69-23.40	11629.1	60063.1	
ST LAWRENCE RIVER	QUEBEC	ILE AUX BASQUES	48-09.20	69-14.30	15099.31	32223.53	
ST LAWRENCE RIVER	QUEBEC	TROIS PISTOLES RANGE	48-08.10	69-11.20	15106.57	32222.32	
ST LAWRENCE RIVER	QUEBEC	POINTE AU BOISVERT	48-33.90	69-08.50	11569.2	60053.7	
ST LAWRENCE RIVER	QUEBEC	PORTNEUF SANDS K-48	48-33.00	69-07.30	11562.5	60056.0	
ST LAWRENCE RIVER	QUEBEC	BAIE VERTE BRKWTR	48-44.30	69-02.90	11557.4	60041.7	
ST LAWRENCE RIVER	QUEBEC	POINTE ROCHEUSE	48-44.30	69-02.90	11557.4	60041.7	
ST LAWRENCE RIVER	QUEBEC	CAP A LA CARRE BELL	48-20.00	69-01.00	15140.70	32139.35	
ST LAWRENCE RIVER	QUEBEC	FORESTVILLE BUOY K-38	48-44.50	68-58.50	15157.2	44239.0	
ST LAWRENCE RIVER	QUEBEC	RECIF DU NORD-QUEST H47	48-24.10	68-57.40	15150.80	32108.98	
ST LAWRENCE RIVER	QUEBEC	ALCIDE ROCL BUOY	48-20.20	68-56.00	15151.82	32126.49	
ST LAWRENCE RIVER	QUEBEC	ILE BICQUETTE	48-25.00	68-53.60	15159.11	32094.69	
ST LAWRENCE RIVER	QUEBEC	ILE DU BIC	48-23.20	68-53.40	15158.74	32103.91	
ST LAWRENCE RIVER	QUEBEC	CAPE COLOMBIER	48-49.20	68-52.60	15169.2	44184.5	
ST LAWRENCE RIVER	QUEBEC	ST SIMEON	57-50.60	68-52.60	11791.1	60089.1	
ST LAWRENCE RIVER	QUEBEC	ANSE DE SABLE	48-09.10	68-51.30	15156.3	44536.0	
ST LAWRENCE RIVER	QUEBEC	POINTE A MICHEL	48-53.90	68-39.60	15190.8	44110.4	
ST LAWRENCE RIVER	QUEBEC	RIMOUSKI BUOY HT2	48-29.50	68-31.20	15200.95	32006.35	
ST LAWRENCE RIVER	QUEBEC	RIMOUSKI HARB WHARF	48-29.00	68-31.10	15201.06	32008.84	
ST LAWRENCE RIVER	QUEBEC	RIMOUSKI HARBOUR RANGE	48-28.10	68-31.10	15200.96	32013.90	
ST LAWRENCE RIVER	QUEBEC	RIMOUSKI ROADS BELL H41	48-30.50	68-31.10	15201.21	32000.42	
ST LAWRENCE RIVER	QUEBEC	POINTE-AU-PERE	48-31.10	68-28.10	15205.88	31987.49	
ST LAWRENCE RIVER	QUEBEC	POINTE DE MANICUAGAN	49-06.10	68-11.60	15225.2	43917.8	
ST LAWRENCE RIVER	QUEBEC	ANSE DU MOULIN E	49-14.90	68-08.30	15228.3	43827.9	
ST LAWRENCE RIVER	QUEBEC	MANICUAGAN SHOAL K-30	49-03.80	68-08.30	15229.2	43927.6	
ST LAWRENCE RIVER	QUEBEC	BAIE COMEAU FERRY	49-14.10	68-07.90	15228.7	43833.7	
ST LAWRENCE RIVER	QUEBEC	BAIE DES ANGLAIS RANGE	49-16.10	68-07.80	15228.6	43815.5	
ST LAWRENCE RIVER	QUEBEC	BAIE COMEAU WHARF	49-14.10	68-07.70	15228.9	43833.0	
ST LAWRENCE RIVER	QUEBEC	POINTE ST PANCRACE, W	49-15.20	68-05.30	15231.0	43815.0	
ST LAWRENCE RIVER	QUEBEC	POINTE ST PANCRACE	49-15.20	68-04.70	15231.5	43812.9	
ST LAWRENCE RIVER	QUEBEC	RIVIERE MANICAUAGAN KD-14	49-12.10	68-03.40	15233.0	43836.2	
ST LAWRENCE RIVER	QUEBEC	POINTE MITIS	48-40.80	68-02.10	15237.43	31839.71	

PASSES

BODY OF WATER	PROV/STATE	NAME	LAT	LON	TD#1	TD#2	CHAR
ST LAWRENCE RIVER	QUEBEC	POINTE A LA CROIX	49-16.20	67-49.10	15243.7	43747.9	
ST LAWRENCE RIVER	QUEBEC	GODBOUT BUOY K-14	49-17.80	67-36.20	15251.3	43683.8	
ST LAWRENCE RIVER	QUEBEC	GODBOUT WHARF	49-19.30	67-35.50	15251.5	43667.6	
ST LAWRENCE RIVER	QUEBEC	GODBOUT	49-19.40	67-35.40	15251.5	43666.3	
ST LAWRENCE RIVER	QUEBEC	MATANE W BREAKWATER	48-50.90	67-34.70	15255.49	31667.77	
ST LAWRENCE RIVER	QUEBEC	MATANE E BREAKWATER	48-50.80	67-34.60	15255.55	31667.86	
ST LAWRENCE RIVER	QUEBEC	RAILWAY WHARF	48-50.60	67-34.50	15255.62	31668.49	
ST LAWRENCE RIVER	QUEBEC	MATANE RANGE	48-50.70	67-31.50	15256.95	31654.24	
ST LAWRENCE RIVER	QUEBEC	POINTE DES MONTS	49-19.00	67-22.90	15257.1	43618.7	
ST LAWRENCE RIVER	QUEBEC	EGG ISLAND	49-37.30	67-10.60	15259.1	43404.6	
ST LAWRENCE RIVER	QUEBEC	GREAT CAWEE ISLAND	49-49.60	67-00.40	15260.4	43253.2	
ST LAWRENCE RIVER	QUEBEC	LE GROS MECHINS WHARF	49-00.40	66-58.60	15262.71	31442.07	
ST LAWRENCE RIVER	QUEBEC	LES MECHINS EAST	49-00.30	66-58.50	15262.71	31442.05	
ST LAWRENCE RIVER	QUEBEC	PORT CARTIER ENTR BELL	50-00.20	66-47.80	15261.8	43105.7	
ST LAWRENCE RIVER	QUEBEC	PORT CARTIER ENTR, W	50-01.70	66-46.90	15261.8	43088.9	
ST LAWRENCE RIVER	QUEBEC	CAP CHAT	49-05.30	66-44.30	15261.72	31342.27	
ST LAWRENCE RIVER	QUEBEC	POINTE AUX JAMBONS	50-02.50	66-44.10	15262.1	43069.2	
ST LAWRENCE RIVER	QUEBEC	OAK POINT RANGE	48-02.40	66-36.60	15236.08	31601.74	
ST LAWRENCE RIVER	QUEBEC	STE ANNE DES MONTS WHARF	49-08.10	66-29.20	15258.66	31246.11	
ST LAWRENCE RIVER	QUEBEC	NOIRE ORE TERMINAL	50-09.90	66-28.90	15262.7	42935.6	
ST LAWRENCE RIVER	QUEBEC	POINTE A LA CHASSE	50-07.70	66-27.20	15262.7	42945.7	
ST LAWRENCE RIVER	QUEBEC	WEST ROCKS	50-07.30	66-26.00	15262.7	42943.2	
ST LAWRENCE RIVER	QUEBEC	POINTE AU CORBEAU	50-09.10	66-25.50	15262.7	42925.9	
ST LAWRENCE RIVER	QUEBEC	IMPERIAL OIL WHARF	50-11.80	66-22.90	15262.7	42890.9	
ST LAWRENCE RIVER	QUEBEC	ILE GRANDE-BASQUE	50-09.20	66-22.70	15262.6	42911.4	
ST LAWRENCE RIVER	QUEBEC	BAY OF SEVEN ISLANDS	50-11.70	66-22.60	15262.7	42890.3	
ST LAWRENCE RIVER	QUEBEC	ILE DU COROSSOL	50-05.30	66-22.60	15262.5	42943.2	
ST LAWRENCE RIVER	QUEBEC	GRANDE TOURELLE RANGE	49-10.00	66-22.50	15256.87	31199.65	
ST LAWRENCE RIVER	QUEBEC	IRON ORE CO WHARF	50-11.40	66-22.30	15262.6	42891.3	
ST LAWRENCE RIVER	QUEBEC	BASQUE REEF BELL D-6	50-10.90	66-22.00	15262.6	42894.0	
ST LAWRENCE RIVER	QUEBEC	MIGUASHA WHARF	48-06.00	66-21.00	15222.77	31480.86	
ST LAWRENCE RIVER	QUEBEC	STE MARTHE DE GASPE	49-12.40	66-10.30	15252.67	31118.91	
ST LAWRENCE RIVER	QUEBEC	CARLETON WHARF	48-06.00	66-07.90	15207.25	31390.32	
ST LAWRENCE RIVER	QUEBEC	POINTE TRACADIGACHE	48-05.20	66-07.50	15205.75	31390.74	
ST LAWRENCE RIVER	QUEBEC	BLACK CAPE GOVT PIER	48-08.20	65-50.30	15187.54	31256.84	
ST LAWRENCE RIVER	QUEBEC	MONT LOUIS RANGE	49-13.80	65-43.90	15239.05	30955.40	
ST LAWRENCE RIVER	QUEBEC	RUISSEAU LEBLANC	48-04.60	65-37.00	15163.38	31172.62	
ST LAWRENCE RIVER	QUEBEC	BONAVENTURA RANGE	48-02.20	65-29.00	15147.28	31120.86	
ST LAWRENCE RIVER	QUEBEC	POINTE BONAVENTURA	48-00.20	65-27.00	15140.36	31112.05	
ST LAWRENCE RIVER	QUEBEC	CAP DE LA MADELEINE	49-15.00	65-20.00	15223.12	30801.54	
ST LAWRENCE RIVER	QUEBEC	PASPEBIAC BREAKWATER	48-01.10	65-15.60	15124.79	31022.79	
ST LAWRENCE RIVER	QUEBEC	PASPEBIAC WEST WHARF	48-01.10	65-15.50	15124.64	31022.02	
ST LAWRENCE RIVER	QUEBEC	PASPEBIAC POINT	48-00.90	65-14.90	15123.30	31018.02	
ST LAWRENCE RIVER	QUEBEC	GRANDE VALLEE RANGE	49-13.80	65-08.10	15212.81	30729.36	

PASSES

BODY OF WATER	PROV/STATE	NAME	LAT	LON	TD#1	TD#2	CHART
ST LAWRENCE RIVER	QUEBEC	GRANDE VALLEE RANGE	49-13.50	65-07.90	15212.41	30729.10	
ST LAWRENCE RIVER	QUEBEC	ST GODEFROI WHARF	48-04.40	65-07.00	15118.68	30947.76	
ST LAWRENCE RIVER	QUEBEC	WEST POINTE	48-09.10	64-57.00	15113.63	30858.51	
ST LAWRENCE RIVER	QUEBEC	SHELDRAKE RIVER	50-15.80	64-54.60	15239.0	42390.5	
ST LAWRENCE RIVER	QUEBEC	RUISSEAU CHAPADOS WHARF	48-11.50	64-51.70	15110.86	30811.68	
ST LAWRENCE RIVER	QUEBEC	CLORIDORME RANGE	49-11.20	64-50.90	15195.54	30624.84	
ST LAWRENCE RIVER	QUEBEC	CLORIDORME RANGE	49-10.80	64-50.90	15195.16	30626.13	
ST LAWRENCE RIVER	QUEBEC	RIVIERE-AU-TONNERE	50-16.40	64-46.90	15235.4	42341.8	
ST LAWRENCE RIVER	QUEBEC	THUNDER RIVER	50-16.60	64-46.80	15235.4	42339.7	
ST LAWRENCE RIVER	QUEBEC	MAQUEREAU POINT	48-12.40	64-46.50	15105.21	30769.72	
ST LAWRENCE RIVER	QUEBEC	NEWPORT WHARF	48-17.10	64-43.30	15110.21	30732.99	
ST LAWRENCE RIVER	QUEBEC	NEWPORT POINT	48-17.17	64-43.10	15110.07	30731.30	
ST LAWRENCE RIVER	QUEBEC	POINTE DU GRAND-PABOS	48-18.20	64-42.00	15110.58	30720.25	
ST LAWRENCE RIVER	QUEBEC	CHANDLER RANGE	48-20.80	64-40.50	15113.57	30702.03	
ST LAWRENCE RIVER	QUEBEC	ILE DUPUIS	48-20.40	64-40.20	15112.38	30700.84	
ST LAWRENCE RIVER	QUEBEC	CHANDLER EAST	48-20.50	64-39.50	15111.62	30695.30	
ST LAWRENCE RIVER	QUEBEC	L'ANSE A VALLEAU	49-05.30	64-33.60	15172.57	30525.72	
ST LAWRENCE RIVER	QUEBEC	L'ANSE A VALLEAU EAST	49-04.80	64-32.70	15171.07	30520.99	
ST LAWRENCE RIVER	QUEBEC	WEST POINT	49-51.80	64-31.40	15212.5	42441.6	
ST LAWRENCE RIVER	QUEBEC	GRANDE RIVIERE RANGE	48-23.80	64-30.20	15105.34	30616.71	
ST LAWRENCE RIVER	QUEBEC	GRANDE RIVIERE HAR RANGE	48-23.60	64-29.60	15104.14	30612.70	
ST LAWRENCE RIVER	QUEBEC	MARINA DE GASPE ENTR	48-49.70	64-28.50	15146.75	30534.75	
ST LAWRENCE RIVER	QUEBEC	MARINA DE GASPE BRKWTR	48-49.70	64-28.50	15146.75	30534.75	
ST LAWRENCE RIVER	QUEBEC	GOVERNMENT WHARF	48-49.50	64-26.30	15143.93	30519.55	
ST LAWRENCE RIVER	QUEBEC	PENOUILLE PENINSULA	48-51.10	64-25.50	15145.34	30509.42	
ST LAWRENCE RIVER	QUEBEC	LITTLE RIVER JETTY	48-24.90	64-23.60	15098.59	30564.21	
ST LAWRENCE RIVER	QUEBEC	FOX RIVER RANGE	48-59.70	64-23.20	15154.69	30469.33	
ST LAWRENCE RIVER	QUEBEC	FOX RIVER WHARF	48-59.90	64-22.90	15154.64	30466.67	
ST LAWRENCE RIVER	QUEBEC	FOX RIVER BELL H16	49-00.10	64-22.80	15154.79	30465.41	
ST LAWRENCE RIVER	QUEBEC	ELLIS BAY "PM5"	49-46.10	64-21.30	15200.9	42424.7	
ST LAWRENCE RIVER	QUEBEC	CAP D'ESOIR	48-25.10	64-19.10	15092.93	30529.72	
ST LAWRENCE RIVER	QUEBEC	GROS CAP AUX OS	48-49.50	64-19.00	15135.47	30467.06	
ST LAWRENCE RIVER	QUEBEC	ANSE AU BEAUFILS RANGE	48-28.20	64-18.60	15098.35	30518.44	
ST LAWRENCE RIVER	QUEBEC	GRIFFON COVE RANGE	48-56.20	64-18.40	15144.63	30444.91	
ST LAWRENCE RIVER	QUEBEC	L'ANSE A BRILLANT RANGE	48-43.20	64-17.50	15123.72	30472.62	
ST LAWRENCE RIVER	QUEBEC	GRANDE GREVE RANGE	48-47.50	64-13.60	15126.02	30433.17	
ST LAWRENCE RIVER	QUEBEC	PERCE	48-30.10	64-13.20	15094.92	30473.25	
ST LAWRENCE RIVER	QUEBEC	CAP DES ROSIERS EAST	48-50.30	64-12.80	15129.48	30420.20	
ST LAWRENCE RIVER	QUEBEC	PERCE BREAKWATER	48-31.20	64-12.70	15096.38	30466.87	
ST LAWRENCE RIVER	QUEBEC	PERROQUET ISLANDS	50-13.20	64-12.40	15213.6	42163.7	
ST LAWRENCE RIVER	QUEBEC	CAP DES ROSIERS	48-51.40	64-12.10	15130.37	30412.33	
ST LAWRENCE RIVER	QUEBEC	MAL BAIE WHARF	48-37.20	64-12.00	15106.60	30447.15	
ST LAWRENCE RIVER	QUEBEC	CAP DE GASPE	48-45.10	64-09.80	15117.56	30411.48	
ST LAWRENCE RIVER	QUEBEC	ILE PLATE	48-37.60	64-09.50	15104.18	30427.61	

PASSES

BODY OF WATER	PROV/STATE	NAME	LAT	LON	TD#1	TD#2	CHART
ST LAWRENCE RIVER	QUEBEC	CAP DE RABAST	49-57.10	64-08.90	15200.1	42264.8	
ST LAWRENCE RIVER	QUEBEC	MINGAN HARB, E ENTR	50-17.40	64-01.30	15209.1	42065.3	
ST LAWRENCE RIVER	QUEBEC	MINGAN HARB, W ENTR	50-17.40	64-00.70	15208.7	42061.7	
ST LAWRENCE RIVER	QUEBEC	FRIGHT ISLAND "CM10"	50-11.90	63-59.90	15204.5	42098.0	
ST LAWRENCE RIVER	QUEBEC	MINGAN ISLANDS	50-09.50	63-44.60	15191.9	42022.3	
ST LAWRENCE RIVER	QUEBEC	FRIGHT ISLAND	50-12.20	63-41.30	15191.6	41981.9	
ST LAWRENCE RIVER	QUEBEC	FRIGHT ISLAND "CM12"	50-12.70	63-39.90	15191.0	41969.6	
ST LAWRENCE RIVER	QUEBEC	FRIGHT ISLAND CHANNEL	50-15.40	63-39.30	15192.7	41945.9	
ST LAWRENCE RIVER	QUEBEC	OUTARDS BAY K-32	48-53.50	63-38.00	15094.1	42545.5	
ST LAWRENCE RIVER	QUEBEC	ESKIMO POINT RANGE	50-14.30	63-36.80	15190.0	41938.6	
ST LAWRENCE RIVER	QUEBEC	SOUTHEAST POINT	49-23.50	63-35.70	15136.8	42309.7	
ST LAWRENCE RIVER	QUEBEC	HARVE-ST PIERRE "CM5"	50-13.70	63-35.60	15188.7	41935.6	
ST LAWRENCE RIVER	QUEBEC	PETITE ILE DU MARTEAU	50-12.20	63-33.60	15186.0	41934.2	
ST LAWRENCE RIVER	QUEBEC	LA GRANDE POINT	50-12.20	63-26.90	15181.0	41892.5	
ST LAWRENCE RIVER	QUEBEC	COLLINS SHOAL "C84"	50-10.30	63-04.10	15161.6	41763.0	
ST LAWRENCE RIVER	QUEBEC	CARLTON POINT	49-43.90	62-56.60	15125.6	41907.3	
ST LAWRENCE RIVER	QUEBEC	JOHAN BEETZ BAY	50-17.00	62-47.90	15155.4	41611.7	
ST LAWRENCE RIVER	QUEBEC	BAGOT BLUFF, NW	49-03.90	62-15.60	15020.3	41924.9	
ST LAWRENCE RIVER	QUEBEC	AQUANISH RIVER	50-13.10	62-05.10	15116.5	41364.1	
ST LAWRENCE RIVER	QUEBEC	TABLE HEAD	49-21.10	61-53.80	15029.4	41659.6	
ST LAWRENCE RIVER	QUEBEC	NATASQUAN POINT	50-05.10	61-44.30	15088.7	41285.2	
ST LAWRENCE RIVER	QUEBEC	HEALTH POINT	49-05.10	61-42.10	14987.0	41694.6	
ST LAWRENCE RIVER	QUEBEC	KEGASHKA POINT	50-10.50	61-16.00	15072.0	41062.1	
ST LAWRENCE RIVER	QUEBEC	KEGASHKA WHARF	50-11.10	61-15.90	15072.7	41057.2	
ST LAWRENCE RIVER	QUEBEC	KEGASHKA BAY	50-11.80	61-15.60	15073.4	41050.4	
ST LAWRENCE RIVER	QUEBEC	TREBLE ISLAND	50-10.10	60-41.90	15042.8	40841.9	
ST LAWRENCE RIVER	QUEBEC	MACKENZIE POINT	50-12.80	60-41.90	15046.8	40823.0	
ST LAWRENCE RIVER	QUEBEC	LITTLE LAKE POINT	50-12.80	60-41.40	15046.3	40819.7	
ST LAWRENCE RIVER	QUEBEC	GETHSEMANI HARBOUR	50-12.50	60-41.30	15045.8	40821.1	
ST LAWRENCE RIVER	QUEBEC	GETHSEMANI ANCHORAGE	50-12.20	60-40.20	15044.5	40816.1	
ST LAWRENCE RIVER	QUEBEC	SAFE ANCHORGE	50-12.20	60-40.20	15044.5	40816.1	
ST LAWRENCE SEAWAY		TIBBETTS POINT BUOY	44-06.00	76-24.40	15699.7	60076.9	14767
ST LAWRENCE SEAWAY		WOLFE ISLAND S LIGHT	44-07.60	76-23.20	15679.6	60074.9	14767
ST LAWRENCE SEAWAY		TIBBETTS POINT LIGHT	44-06.00	76-22.20	15688.8	60083.7	14767
ST LAWRENCE SEAWAY		POINT ALEXANDRIA LIGHT	44-08.10	76-21.30	15665.7	60078.9	14767
ST LAWRENCE SEAWAY		ST LAWRENCE SEAWAY NO 243	44-07.80	76-20.70	15665.3	60081.8	14767
ST LAWRENCE SEAWAY		BAYFIELD ISLAND RANGE	44-11.70	76-19.70	15625.9	60071.1	14767
ST LAWRENCE SEAWAY		CARLETON ISLAND LIGHT	44-10.20	76-18.70	15634.1	60079.3	14767
ST LAWRENCE SEAWAY		IRVINE POINT RANGE	44-12.30	76-18.60	15615.1	60072.3	14767
ST LAWRENCE SEAWAY		BANFORD POINT LIGHT	44-12.50	76-14.30	15591.3	60084.0	14767
ST LAWRENCE SEAWAY		ST LAWRENCE SEAWAY NO 231	44-12.30	76-12.40	15583.1	60090.0	14767
ST LAWRENCE SEAWAY		WOLFE ISLAND LIGHT	44-14.30	76-11.10	15558.8	60086.8	14767
ST LAWRENCE SEAWAY		WOLFE ISLAND CUT "PV2"	44-14.00	76-10.50	15558.3	60089.4	14766
ST LAWRENCE SEAWAY		ST LAWRENCE SEAWAY NO 229	44-13.20	76-09.60	15560.4	60094.6	14766

PASSES

BODY OF WATER	PROV/STATE	NAME	LAT	LON	TD#1	TD#2	CHART
ST LAWRENCE SEAWAY		ST LAWRENCE SEAWAY NO 227	44-14.40	76-06.50	15533.3	60098.8	14766
ST LAWRENCE SEAWAY		CLAYTON MUNICIPAL BRKWTR	44-14.20	76-05.50	15529.6	60102.1	14766
ST LAWRENCE SEAWAY		ST LAWRENCE SEAWAY NO 217A	44-15.60	76-03.90	15508.8	60101.5	14766
ST LAWRENCE SEAWAY		ST LAWRENCE SEAWAY NO 213	44-16.90	76-00.90	15481.1	60104.7	14766
ST LAWRENCE SEAWAY		ST LAWRENCE SEAWAY NO 210	44-17.70	75-59.90	15468.7	60104.5	14766
ST LAWRENCE SEAWAY		ST LAWRENCE SEAWAY NO 209	44-17.90	75-59.20	15463.1	60105.6	14766
ST LAWRENCE SEAWAY		ST LAWRENCE SEAWAY NO 206	44-18.60	75-58.20	15451.6	60105.7	14766
ST LAWRENCE SEAWAY		KEEWAYDIN STATE P BRKWTR	44-19.40	75-56.20	15433.5	60108.0	14766
ST LAWRENCE SEAWAY		ST LAWRENCE SEAWAY NO 194	44-20.10	75-55.80	15174.0	60010.0	14766
ST LAWRENCE SEAWAY		ST LAWRENCE SEAWAY NO 183	44-22.40	75-53.10	15390.6	60105.6	14765
ST LAWRENCE SEAWAY		ST LAWRENCE SEAWAY NO 180	44-23.80	75-51.40	15369.1	60105.1	14765
ST LAWRENCE SEAWAY		HAFFIE SHOAL LIGHT	44-27.50	75-50.70	15334.0	60094.9	14765
ST LAWRENCE SEAWAY		CHIMNEY ISLAND LIGHT	44-28.00	75-50.00	15325.8	60094.9	14765
ST LAWRENCE SEAWAY		HASKELL LIGHT NO 173	44-26.20	75-49.40	15337.5	60102.0	14765
ST LAWRENCE SEAWAY		ST LAWRENCE SEAWAY NO 168	44-27.00	75-48.80	15327.3	60100.9	14765
ST LAWRENCE SEAWAY		BAY STATE ANCH "PE"	44-30.40	75-47.20	15289.8	60093.8	14765
ST LAWRENCE SEAWAY		ST LAWRENCE SEAWAY NO 160	44-29.80	75-46.60	15291.3	60097.0	14765
ST LAWRENCE SEAWAY		BAY STATE ANCH "PC"	44-31.10	75-46.50	15279.9	60093.2	14765
ST LAWRENCE SEAWAY		ST LAWRENCE SEAWAY NO 159	44-29.88	75-46.40	15108.1	60156.3	14765
ST LAWRENCE SEAWAY		ST LAWRENCE SEAWAY NO 157	44-30.30	75-46.30	15285.4	60096.1	14765
ST LAWRENCE SEAWAY		ST LAWRENCE SEAWAY NO 153	44-30.60	75-46.20	15282.4	60095.4	14765
ST LAWRENCE SEAWAY		ST LAWRENCE SEAWAY NO 152	44-31.10	75-46.00	15277.0	60094.3	14765
ST LAWRENCE SEAWAY		ST LAWRENCE SEAWAY NO 151	44-31.40	75-45.50	15271.7	60094.5	14765
ST LAWRENCE SEAWAY		ST LAWRENCE SEAWAY NO 150	44-31.80	75-45.30	15267.2	60093.7	14765
ST LAWRENCE SEAWAY		DEWATTEVILLE ISLAND RANGE	44-32.90	75-44.99	15250.6	60093.2	14765
ST LAWRENCE SEAWAY		ST LAWRENCE SEAWAY NO 147A	44-32.20	75-44.60	15259.8	60094.0	14765
ST LAWRENCE SEAWAY		ST LAWRENCE SEAWAY NO 147	44-32.50	75-44.20	15255.0	60094.0	14765
ST LAWRENCE SEAWAY		ST LAWRENCE SEAWAY NO 145	44-33.60	75-42.90	15238.4	60093.5	14765
ST LAWRENCE SEAWAY		ST LAWRENCE SEAWAY NO 143A	44-33.70	75-42.70	15236.4	60093.6	14765
ST LAWRENCE SEAWAY		ST LAWRENCE SEAWAY NO 143	44-34.00	75-42.40	15232.2	60093.3	14765
ST LAWRENCE SEAWAY		SMITH ISLAND NO 140	44-34.30	75-42.10	15228.0	60093.1	14764
ST LAWRENCE SEAWAY		REFUGEE ISLAND NO 139A	44-34.20	75-42.00	15228.2	60093.6	14764
ST LAWRENCE SEAWAY		S McNAIR ISLAND NO 137A	44-35.60	75-40.00	15205.0	60093.7	14764
ST LAWRENCE SEAWAY		McNAIR ISLAND NO 137	44-35.70	75-39.90	15203.6	60093.6	14764
ST LAWRENCE SEAWAY		MAITLAND LIGHTED BUOY	44-37.80	75-36.40	15165.9	60094.8	14764
ST LAWRENCE SEAWAY		ST LAWRENCE SEAWAY NO 132A	44-47.10	75-29.90	15052.0	60080.5	14763
ST LAWRENCE SEAWAY		ST LAWRENCE SEAWAY NO 132	44-43.10	75-29.10	15079.5	60094.1	14764
ST LAWRENCE SEAWAY		OGDENSBURG HARBOR NO 1	44-42.80	75-28.50	15078.3	60096.2	14764
ST LAWRENCE SEAWAY		ST LAWRENCE SEAWAY NO 131A	44-43.70	75-28.00	15068.1	60094.6	14763
ST LAWRENCE SEAWAY		ST LAWRENCE SEAWAY NO 131	44-44.30	75-27.10	15057.9	60094.6	14763
ST LAWRENCE SEAWAY		SPENCER I PIER LIGHT	44-44.60	75-26.90	15054.2	60094.1	14763
ST LAWRENCE SEAWAY		ST LAWRENCE SEAWAY NO 130	44-44.60	75-26.60	15052.4	60094.8	14763
ST LAWRENCE SEAWAY		CHIMNEY ISLAND LIGHT	44-44.50	75-26.40	15052.0	60095.5	14763
ST LAWRENCE SEAWAY		ST LAWRENCE SEAWAY NO 128	44-44.80	75-26.20	15048.4	60095.0	14763

PASSES

BODY OF WATER	PROV/STATE	NAME	LAT	LON	TD#1	TD#2	CHAR
ST LAWRENCE SEAWAY		ST LAWRENCE SEAWAY NO 129	44-44.80	75-25.90	15046.6	60095.6	1476.
ST LAWRENCE SEAWAY		DRUMMOND ISLAND RANGE	44-45.50	75-25.60	15039.2	60094.1	1476.
ST LAWRENCE SEAWAY		GALOP ISLAND RANGE	44-45.20	75-25.20	15039.2	60095.8	1476.
ST LAWRENCE SEAWAY		GALOP ISLAND N RANGE	44-46.60	75-22.90	15014.1	60096.3	1476.
ST LAWRENCE SEAWAY		ST LAWRENCE SEAWAY NO 120	44-46.90	75-22.70	15010.5	60095.8	1476.
ST LAWRENCE SEAWAY		ST LAWRENCE SEAWAY NO 118	44-47.10	75-22.20	15005.9	60096.2	1476
ST LAWRENCE SEAWAY		SPARROWHAWK POINT LIGHT	44-48.10	75-20.00	14984.5	60097.6	1476.
ST LAWRENCE SEAWAY		TOUSSAINT I WEST LIGHT	44-48.70	75-20.00	14979.8	60095.9	1476.
ST LAWRENCE SEAWAY		ST LAWRENCE SEAWAY NO 114	44-48.80	75-19.80	14977.8	60096.0	1476
ST LAWRENCE SEAWAY		ST LAWRENCE SEAWAY NO 112	44-49.00	75-19.50	14974.4	60096.0	1476.
ST LAWRENCE SEAWAY		ST LAWRENCE SEAWAY NO 113	44-48.90	75-19.30	14973.9	60096.7	1476.
ST LAWRENCE SEAWAY		IROQUOIS LOCK LIGHT	44-49.30	75-19.20	14970.1	60095.7	1476.
ST LAWRENCE SEAWAY		ST LAWRENCE SEAWAY NO 108	44-50.40	75-18.50	14957.2	60093.9	1476.
ST LAWRENCE SEAWAY		IROQUOIS LOCK RANGE	44-50.70	75-18.20	14953.0	60093.6	1476
ST LAWRENCE SEAWAY		ST LAWRENCE SEAWAY NO 106	44-50.90	75-17.50	14947.1	60094.4	1476
ST LAWRENCE SEAWAY		ST LAWRENCE SEAWAY NO 104	44-51.30	75-16.40	14937.2	60095.3	1476
ST LAWRENCE SEAWAY		ST LAWRENCE SEAWAY NO 100	44-51.60	75-15.70	14928.1	60096.6	1476
ST LAWRENCE SEAWAY		ST LAWRENCE SEAWAY NO 102	44-51.50	75-15.70	14931.4	60096.1	1476
ST LAWRENCE SEAWAY		ST LAWRENCE SEAWAY NO 96A	44-52.30	75-14.00	14914.6	60097.0	1476
ST LAWRENCE SEAWAY		MARIATOWN APPROACH RANGE	44-52.60	75-13.70	14910.4	60096.8	1476
ST LAWRENCE SEAWAY		ST LAWRENCE SEAWAY NO 95	44-52.80	75-12.60	14906.7	60097.9	1476
ST LAWRENCE SEAWAY		MARIATOWN RANGE LIGHT	44-53.00	75-12.60	14900.5	60097.7	1476
ST LAWRENCE SEAWAY		ST LAWRENCE SEAWAY NO 92	44-52.90	75-12.20	14898.8	60098.7	1476
ST LAWRENCE SEAWAY		OGDEN ISLAND RANGE	44-52.80	75-11.70	14896.5	60099.9	1476
ST LAWRENCE SEAWAY		ST LAWRENCE SEAWAY NO 88	44-53.10	75-11.40	14892.3	60099.6	1476
ST LAWRENCE SEAWAY		ST LAWRENCE SEAWAY NO 86	44-53.20	75-11.00	14889.1	60100.1	1476
ST LAWRENCE SEAWAY		CANADA ISLAND ANCH "XJ"	44-53.60	75-10.50	14882.8	60099.9	1476
ST LAWRENCE SEAWAY		ST LAWRENCE SEAWAY NO 85	44-53.60	75-09.90	14879.1	60101.0	1476
ST LAWRENCE SEAWAY		CANADA ISLAND ANCH XE	44-53.80	75-09.80	14876.9	60100.6	1476
ST LAWRENCE SEAWAY		ST LAWRENCE SEAWAY NO 82	44-54.10	75-09.20	14870.9	60100.9	1476
ST LAWRENCE SEAWAY		ST LAWRENCE SEAWAY NO 81	44-54.00	75-09.00	14870.4	60101.5	1476
ST LAWRENCE SEAWAY		GOOSE NECK ISLAND SHOALS	44-54.90	75-08.80	14862.1	60099.4	1476
ST LAWRENCE SEAWAY		WEAVER SHOAL RANGE	44-55.50	75-07.90	14851.9	60099.3	1476
ST LAWRENCE SEAWAY		DORAN SHOAL RANGE LIGHT	44-56.00	75-06.80	14841.1	60099.9	1476
ST LAWRENCE SEAWAY		ST LAWRENCE SEAWAY NO 74	44-55.40	75-06.60	14844.6	60102.0	1467
ST LAWRENCE SEAWAY		ST LAWRENCE SEAWAY 73	44-55.60	75-05.80	14838.03	60102.83	1415
ST LAWRENCE SEAWAY		ST LAWRENCE SEAWAY NO 72	44-55.80	75-05.50	14834.6	60102.8	1476
ST LAWRENCE SEAWAY		ST LAWRENCE SEAWAY NO 70	44-55.80	75-04.80	14830.2	60104.1	1476
ST LAWRENCE SEAWAY		WEAVER SHOAL ANCH "XC"	44-56.50	75-03.40	14810.1	60105.3	1476
ST LAWRENCE SEAWAY		WEAVER SHOAL ANCH "XA"	44-56.70	75-02.70	14810.1	60105.3	1476
ST LAWRENCE SEAWAY		FISHER LANDING LIGHT	44-16.70	75-00.60	15107.3	60213.7	1476
ST LAWRENCE SEAWAY		CAT ISLAND LIGHT	44-57.20	75-00.40	14791.8	60107.9	1476
ST LAWRENCE SEAWAY		WILSON HILL RANGE LIGHT	44-57.00	74-59.70	14788.9	60109.7	1476
ST LAWRENCE SEAWAY		ST LAWRENCE SEAWAY NO 55	44-57.50	74-58.10	14774.9	60111.0	1476

PASSES

BODY OF WATER	PROV/STATE	NAME	LAT	LON	TD#1	TD#2	CHART
ST LAWRENCE SEAWAY		ST LAWRENCE SEAWAY NO 34	44-58.90	74-50.50	14715.7	60119.8	14761
ST LAWRENCE SEAWAY		POLLYS GUT DIKE A "C"	44-59.50	74-45.80	14680.9	60125.7	14761
ST LAWRENCE SEAWAY		ST LAWRENCE SEAWAY 14A	44-59.40	74-44.40	14672.53	60128.11	
ST LAWRENCE SEAWAY		ST LAWRENCE SEAWAY 15	44-59.40	74-43.70	14667.98	60129.18	1414
ST LAWRENCE SEAWAY		SINGLE STATION NO 13	44-59.60	74-43.40	14664.5	60129.1	14761
ST LAWRENCE SEAWAY		ST LAWRENCE SEAWAY 13	44-59.60	74-43.40	14664.51	60129.12	1414
ST LAWRENCE SEAWAY		RAQUETTE POINT LT 11	44-60.00	74-43.10	14659.54	60128.55	
ST LAWRENCE SEAWAY		SINGLE STATION NO 11	44-59.80	74-43.10	14661.1	60129.1	14761
ST LAWRENCE SEAWAY		ST LAWRENCE SEAWAY 10	45-00.10	74-42.90	14657.49	60128.60	1413
ST LAWRENCE SEAWAY		SINGLE STATION NO 10	45-00.10	74-42.80	14656.8	60128.8	14761
ST LAWRENCE SEAWAY		ST LAWRENCE SEAWAY 9	44-60.00	74-42.70	14656.94	60129.16	1413
ST LAWRENCE SEAWAY		ST LAWRENCE SEAWAY 7	44-60.00	74-42.10	14653.03	60130.07	1413
ST LAWRENCE SEAWAY		ST LAWRENCE SEAWAY 8	45-00.10	74-42.10	14652.28	60129.81	1413
ST LAWRENCE SEAWAY		ST LAWRENCE SEAWAY 5B	44-60.00	74-41.80	14651.07	60130.52	1413
ST LAWRENCE SEAWAY		ST LAWRENCE SEAWAY NO 5B	44-60.00	74-41.80	14651.1	60130.5	14761
ST LAWRENCE SEAWAY		ST LAWRENCE SEAWAY 6	44-60.00	74-41.40	14648.46	60131.12	1413
ST LAWRENCE SEAWAY		ST LAWRENCE SEAWAY NO 5A	44-59.90	74-41.40	14649.2	60131.4	14761
ST LAWRENCE SEAWAY		ST LAWRENCE SEAWAY 5A	44-60.00	74-41.40	14648.46	60131.12	1413
ST LAWRENCE SEAWAY		CORNWALL ISLAND LT 4	44-60.00	74-41.00	14645.85	60131.72	
ST LAWRENCE SEAWAY		ST LAWRENCE SEAWAY 5	44-60.00	74-41.00	14645.85	60131.72	1413
ST LAWRENCE SEAWAY		ST LAWRENCE SEAWAY NO 4	45-00.10	74-41.00	14645.1	60131.5	14761
ST LAWRENCE SEAWAY		ST LAWRENCE SEAWAY NO 5	44-59.90	74-41.00	14646.6	60132.0	14761
ST LAWRENCE SEAWAY		ST LAWRENCE SEAWAY 3	44-60.00	74-40.50	14642.58	60132.47	1413
ST LAWRENCE SEAWAY		CORNWALL ISLAND BUOY 2	45-00.20	74-40.50	14641.08	60131.95	
ST LAWRENCE SEAWAY		ST LAWRENCE SEAWAY NO 2	45-00.20	74-40.50	14641.1	60132.0	14761
ST LAWRENCE SEAWAY		ST LAWRENCE SEAWAY 1	45-00.20	74-40.10	14638.46	60132.55	1413
ST LAWRENCE SEAWAY		ST LAWRENCE SEAWAY D96	45-00.40	74-40.10	14636.96	60132.04	1413
ST LAWRENCE SEAWAY		ST LAWRENCE SEAWAY NO 1	45-00.20	74-40.10	14638.5	60132.6	1413
ST LAWRENCE SEAWAY		ST LAWRENCE SEAWAY D95	45-00.40	74-40.00	14636.31	60132.19	1413
ST LAWRENCE SEAWAY		CORNWALL ISLAND RANGE	45-00.90	74-39.90	14631.90	60131.07	1413
ST LAWRENCE SEAWAY		ST LAWRENCE SEAWAY D92	45-00.90	74-39.70	14630.59	60131.37	1413
ST LAWRENCE SEAWAY		ST LAWRENCE SEAWAY D93	45-00.80	74-39.60	14630.69	60131.77	1413
ST LAWRENCE SEAWAY		ST LAWRENCE SEAWAY D90	45-01.00	74-39.50	14628.53	60131.41	1413
ST LAWRENCE SEAWAY		ST LAWRENCE SEAWAY D91	45-01.00	74-39.50	14628.53	60131.41	1413
ST LAWRENCE SEAWAY		THIRD CRAB ISLAND	45-01.40	74-39.30	14624.22	60130.69	
ST LAWRENCE SEAWAY		ST LAWRENCE SEAWAY D89	45-01.00	74-39.30	14627.22	60131.71	1413
ST LAWRENCE SEAWAY		CORNWALL ISLAND "DCB1413	45-01.20	74-39.10	14624.42	60131.50	
ST LAWRENCE SEAWAY		ST LAWRENCE SEAWAY D88	45-01.40	74-38.70	14620.30	60131.58	1413
ST LAWRENCE SEAWAY		ST LAWRENCE SEAWAY D87	45-01.50	74-38.40	14617.58	60131.77	1413
ST LAWRENCE SEAWAY		SOUTHWEST ANCH "DQ"	45-01.70	74-37.50	14610.18	60132.59	1413
ST LAWRENCE SEAWAY		ILE ST REGIS ANCH "DN"	45-02.00	74-37.10	14605.32	60132.43	1413
ST LAWRENCE SEAWAY		ST LAWRENCE SEAWAY D84	45-02.10	74-37.00	14603.91	60132.32	1413
ST LAWRENCE SEAWAY		ST LAWRENCE SEAWAY D82	45-02.20	74-36.60	14600.54	60132.65	1413
ST LAWRENCE SEAWAY		McGIBBONS POINT D80	45-02.40	74-36.50	14598.39	60132.30	1413

PASSES

BODY OF WATER	PROV/STATE	NAME	LAT	LON	TD#1	TD#2	CHA
ST LAWRENCE SEAWAY		ST LAWRENCE SEAWAY D81	45-02.20	74-36.40	14599.23	60132.95	141
ST LAWRENCE SEAWAY		ST LAWRENCE SEAWAT D77	45-02.30	74-36.00	14595.85	60133.28	141
ST LAWRENCE SEAWAY		ST LAWRENCE SEAWAY D76	45-02.50	74-36.00	14594.36	60132.77	141
ST LAWRENCE SEAWAY		SOUTH ANCH "DM"	45-02.20	74-35.80	14595.28	60133.82	141
ST LAWRENCE SEAWAY		DANIS POINT ANCH "DX"	45-02.60	74-35.70	14591.64	60132.96	141
ST LAWRENCE SEAWAY		DICKERSON I ANCH "DK"	45-02.30	74-35.30	14591.25	60134.30	141
ST LAWRENCE SEAWAY		ST LAWRENCE SEAWAY D74	45-02.70	74-34.60	14583.66	60134.31	141
ST LAWRENCE SEAWAY		ST LAWRENCE SEAWAY D73	45-02.60	74-34.50	14583.75	60134.70	141
ST LAWRENCE SEAWAY		ST LAWRENCE SEAWAY D72	45-02.70	74-34.30	14581.68	60134.74	141
ST LAWRENCE SEAWAY		ST LAWRENCE SEAWAY D69	45-02.80	74-34.00	14578.96	60134.92	141
ST LAWRENCE SEAWAY		CLARK ISLAND D70	45-02.90	74-34.00	14578.22	60134.67	
ST LAWRENCE SEAWAY		STANLEY CRAB DIR LIGHT	45-02.70	74-33.60	14577.07	60135.75	141
ST LAWRENCE SEAWAY		ST LAWRENCE SEAWAY D68	45-03.10	74-33.40	14572.77	60135.04	141
ST LAWRENCE SEAWAY		STANLEY ISLAND D67	45-03.10	74-33.30	14572.11	60135.18	141
ST LAWRENCE SEAWAY		ST LAWRENCE SEAWAY D65	45-03.20	74-33.00	14569.39	60135.36	141
ST LAWRENCE SEAWAY		STANLEY ISLAND LIGHT	45-03.00	74-33.00	14570.88	60135.86	141
ST LAWRENCE SEAWAY		RENSHAW ISLAND D66	45-03.30	74-33.00	14568.65	60135.11	141
ST LAWRENCE SEAWAY		ST LAWRENCE SEAWAY D64	45-03.50	74-32.50	14563.86	60135.33	141
ST LAWRENCE SEAWAY		ST LAWRENCE SEAWAY D63	45-03.50	74-32.20	14561.88	60135.75	141
ST LAWRENCE SEAWAY		ST LAWRENCE SEAWAY D62	45-03.70	74-32.10	14559.74	60135.40	141
ST LAWRENCE SEAWAY		ST LAWRENCE SEAWAY D60	45-04.00	74-31.80	14555.53	60135.08	141
ST LAWRENCE SEAWAY		ST LAWRENCE SEAWAY D59	45-03.90	74-31.70	14555.61	60135.47	141
ST LAWRENCE SEAWAY		ST LAWRENCE SEAWAY D58	45-04.20	74-31.40	14551.40	60135.16	141
ST LAWRENCE SEAWAY		ST LAWRENCE SEAWAY D57	45-04.20	74-31.30	14550.74	60135.30	141
ST LAWRENCE SEAWAY		THOMPSON ISLAND RANGE	45-04.10	74-31.10	14550.16	60135.83	141
ST LAWRENCE SEAWAY		ST LAWRENCE SEAWAY D56	45-04.80	74-30.50	14541.01	60134.95	141
ST LAWRENCE SEAWAY		ST LAWRENCE SEAWAY D55	45-04.70	74-30.50	14541.75	60135.20	141
ST LAWRENCE SEAWAY		THOMPSON ISLAND RANGE	45-04.60	74-30.30	14541.16	60135.73	141
ST LAWRENCE SEAWAY		ST LAWRENCE SEAWAY D54	45-05.10	74-30.00	14535.48	60134.91	141
ST LAWRENCE SEAWAY		ST LAWRENCE SEAWAY D53	45-05.20	74-29.70	14532.75	60135.09	141
ST LAWRENCE SEAWAY		ST LAWRENCE SEAWAY D52	45-05.50	74-29.70	14530.54	60134.35	141
ST LAWRENCE SEAWAY		ST LAWRENCE SEAWAY D48	45-06.40	74-29.10	14519.92	60132.98	141
ST LAWRENCE SEAWAY		ST LAWRENCE SEAWAY D49	45-06.10	74-29.10	14522.13	60133.72	141
ST LAWRENCE SEAWAY		ST LAWRENCE SEAWAY D47	45-06.40	74-28.80	14517.93	60133.40	141
ST LAWRENCE SEAWAY		ST LAWRENCE SEAWAY D46	45-06.60	74-28.70	14515.79	60133.05	141
ST LAWRENCE SEAWAY		ST LAWRENCE SEAWAT D44	45-07.10	74-27.80	14506.15	60133.09	141
ST LAWRENCE SEAWAY		ST LAWRENCE SEAWAY D45	45-07.10	74-27.70	14505.49	60133.23	141
ST LAWRENCE SEAWAY		ST LAWRENCE SEAWAY D43	45-07.30	74-27.30	14501.36	60133.30	141
ST LAWRENCE SEAWAY		ST LAWRENCE SEAWAY D42	45-07.40	74-27.30	14500.63	60133.06	141
ST LAWRENCE SEAWAY		ST LAWRENCE SEAWAY D40	45-07.60	74-27.10	14497.83	60132.84	141
ST LAWRENCE SEAWAY		ST LAWRENCE SEAWAY D39	45-07.50	74-26.60	14495.25	60133.79	141
ST LAWRENCE SEAWAY		ST LAWRENCE SEAWAY D38	45-07.60	74-26.60	14494.52	60133.54	141
ST LAWRENCE SEAWAY		ST LAWRENCE SEAWAY D36	45-07.60	74-26.00	14490.53	60134.38	141
ST LAWRENCE SEAWAY		ST LAWRENCE SEAWAY D37	45-07.60	74-26.00	14490.53	60134.38	141

PASSES

BODY OF WATER	PROV/STATE	NAME	LAT	LON	TD#1	TD#2	CHART
ST LAWRENCE SEAWAY		ST LAWRENCE SEAWAY D35	45-07.60	74-25.40	14486.55	60135.22	1412
ST LAWRENCE SEAWAY		ST LAWRENCE SEAWAY D34	45-07.80	74-25.40	14485.08	60134.73	1412
ST LAWRENCE SEAWAY		ST LAWRENCE SEAWAY D31	45-08.30	74-24.10	14472.77	60135.31	1412
ST LAWRENCE SEAWAY		ST LAWRENCE SEAWAY D30	45-08.70	74-23.50	14465.85	60135.16	1412
ST LAWRENCE SEAWAY		ST LAWRENCE SEAWAY D28	45-09.30	74-22.40	14454.13	60135.22	1412
ST LAWRENCE SEAWAY		ST LAWRENCE SEAWAY D25	45-10.10	74-20.60	14436.29	60135.74	1412
ST LAWRENCE SEAWAY		ST LAWRENCE SEAWAY D24	45-10.60	74-20.00	14428.64	60135.35	1412
ST LAWRENCE SEAWAY		ST LAWRENCE SEAWAY D22	45-11.00	74-19.20	14420.38	60135.47	1412
ST LAWRENCE SEAWAY		ST LAWRENCE SEAWAY D20	45-11.20	74-19.00	14417.59	60135.26	1412
ST LAWRENCE SEAWAY		ST LAWRENCE SEAWAY D21	45-10.80	74-19.00	14420.50	60136.22	1412
ST LAWRENCE SEAWAY		ST LAWRENCE SEAWAY V33	45-24.30	73-39.00	14052.20	60154.29	1409
ST LAWRENCE SEAWAY		ST LAWRENCE SEAWAY V32	45-24.30	73-38.70	14050.12	60154.61	1409
ST LAWRENCE SEAWAY		ST LAWRENCE SEAWAY V29	45-24.10	73-38.50	14050.10	60155.26	1409
ST LAWRENCE SEAWAY		ST LAWRENCE RIVER M209	45-30.00	73-32.70	13969.44	60149.03	
ST LAWRENCE SEAWAY		ST LAWRENCE RIVER M201	45-30.70	73-32.60	13963.99	60147.65	
ST LAWRENCE SEAWAY		ST LAWRENCE RIVER M199	46-31.00	73-32.60	13579.05	60013.48	
ST LAWRENCE SEAWAY		ST LAWRENCE RIVER M191	45-32.10	73-31.70	13948.24	60145.66	
ST LAWRENCE SEAWAY		ST LAWRENCE RIVER M189	45-33.00	73-31.30	13939.38	60144.18	
ST LAWRENCE SEAWAY		ST LAWRENCE RIVER M144	45-40.00	73-28.00	13869.51	60132.91	
ST LAWRENCE SEAWAY		ST LAWRENCE RIVER M140	45-40.60	73-27.50	13862.05	60132.19	
ST LAWRENCE SEAWAY		ST LAWRENCE RIVER M138	45-40.90	73-27.40	13859.36	60131.66	
ST LAWRENCE SEAWAY		ST LAWRENCE RIVER M132	45-41.40	73-27.30	13855.35	60130.71	
ST LAWRENCE SEAWAY		ST LAWRENCE RIVER M139	45-40.70	73-27.20	13859.31	60132.32	
ST LAWRENCE SEAWAY		ST LAWRENCE RIVER M130	45-41.70	73-27.10	13851.97	60130.29	
ST LAWRENCE SEAWAY		ST LAWRENCE RIVER M123	45-42.30	73-26.40	13843.15	60129.80	
ST LAWRENCE SEAWAY		ST LAWRENCE RIVER M122	45-42.50	73-26.40	13841.82	60129.37	
ST LAWRENCE SEAWAY		ST LAWRENCE RIVER M104	45-45.00	73-24.00	13808.70	60126.75	
ST LAWRENCE SEAWAY		ST LAWRENCE RIVER M88	45-46.60	73-22.30	13786.43	60125.27	
ST LAWRENCE SEAWAY		ST LAWRENCE RIVER M87	45-46.70	73-22.00	13783.70	60125.39	
ST LAWRENCE SEAWAY		ST LAWRENCE RIVER M84	45-47.10	73-21.20	13775.54	60125.45	
ST LAWRENCE SEAWAY		ST LAWRENCE RIVER M78	45-48.80	73-19.00	13749.21	60124.32	
ST LAWRENCE SEAWAY		ST LAWRENCE RIVER M76	45-50.20	73-17.30	13728.32	60123.27	
ST LAWRENCE SEAWAY		ST LAWRENCE RIVER M54	45-50.60	73-17.00	13723.66	60122.75	
ST LAWRENCE SEAWAY		ST LAWRENCE RIVER M57	45-50.50	73-16.80	13722.92	60123.19	
ST LAWRENCE SEAWAY		ST LAWRENCE RIVER M52	45-51.00	73-16.60	13718.30	60122.36	
ST LAWRENCE SEAWAY		ST LAWRENCE RIVER M51	45-50.80	73-16.40	13718.20	60123.01	
ST LAWRENCE SEAWAY		ST LAWRENCE RIVER M50	45-51.20	73-16.30	13714.92	60122.27	
ST LAWRENCE SEAWAY		ST LAWRENCE RIVER M49	45-51.20	73-16.20	13714.23	60122.38	
ST LAWRENCE SEAWAY		ST LAWRENCE RIVER M46	45-51.60	73-16.10	13710.96	60121.65	
ST LAWRENCE SEAWAY		ST LAWRENCE RIVER M41	45-52.00	73-15.60	13704.91	60121.37	
ST LAWRENCE SEAWAY		ST LAWRENCE RIVER M38	45-52.60	73-15.20	13698.27	60120.56	
ST LAWRENCE SEAWAY		ST LAWRENCE RIVER M32	45-53.50	73-14.50	13687.64	60119.44	
ST LAWRENCE SEAWAY		ST LAWRENCE RIVER M26	45-54.00	73-13.60	13678.19	60119.40	
ST LAWRENCE SEAWAY		ST LAWRENCE RIVER M23	45-54.10	73-13.10	13674.08	60119.75	

PASSES

BODY OF WATER	PROV/STATE	NAME	LAT	LON	TD#1	TD#2	CHAR
ST LAWRENCE SEAWAY		ST LAWRENCE RIVER M10	45-55.80	73-13.00	13662.54	60116.28	
ST LAWRENCE SEAWAY		ST LAWRENCE RIVER M7	45-56.50	73-12.70	13656.01	60115.15	
ST LAWRENCE SEAWAY		ST LAWRENCE RIVER M9	45-55.80	73-12.70	13660.46	60116.62	
ST LAWRENCE SEAWAY		ST LAWRENCE RIVER S2	47-16.50	72-37.40	12980.45	59989.90	
ST LAWRENCE SEAWAY		ST LAWRENCE RIVER C72	46-17.60	72-35.50	13267.43	60112.06	
ST LAWRENCE SEAWAY		ST LAWRENCE RIVER C71	46-17.40	72-35.00	13265.06	60112.96	
ST LAWRENCE SEAWAY		ST LAWRENCE RIVER C70	46-18.10	72-34.60	13258.20	60111.99	
ST LAWRENCE SEAWAY		ST LAWRENCE RIVER C68	46-18.40	72-34.00	13252.23	60112.01	
ST LAWRENCE SEAWAY		ST LAWRENCE RIVER C67	46-18.30	72-33.70	13250.69	60112.51	
ST LAWRENCE SEAWAY		ST LAWRENCE RIVER C66	46-18.70	72-33.50	13246.98	60111.93	
ST LAWRENCE SEAWAY		ST LAWRENCE RIVER C65	46-18.60	72-33.30	13246.13	60112.33	
ST LAWRENCE SEAWAY		ST LAWRENCE RIVER C63	46-20.10	72-31.70	13226.25	60111.01	
ST LAWRENCE SEAWAY		ST LAWRENCE BAY WHISTLE	47-01.00	60-28.50	14550.65	41994.93	
ST LAWRENCE SEAWAY		ST LAWRENCE BAY	47-00.20	60-28.10	14547.32	41996.76	

CHAPTER 7

HEAVENLY HAVENS

The controlling coordinates in this chapter and those that follow — the coordinates to use when you input waypoints — are the TDs, not the latitudes and longitudes. Each pair of TDs in Chapters 7 through 13 was measured on site with the ASF function disabled, and if you track them down the same way (ASF function off) you should find pretty near the exact spot whose coordinates we recorded. The "local alignment" process described near the end of Chapter 3 isn't necessary when you're working with raw TDs in this fashion. You can, conceivably, jump aboard your freshly chartered or just-arrived boat in the marina, punch in the TDs for an anchorage 10 miles down the bay, and expect the loran to guide you to it with good precision.

Many loran receiver models, when operated in Lat/Lon mode, will automatically sift through and override available secondaries based on such variables as crossing angles and SNRs (see Chapter 3) to get the best fix. With these lorans, you may choose to navigate to the approximate waypoint in the Lat/Lon mode, then switch to TDs for the final zeroing in.

When giving the coordinates for havens, we offer no guarantees of privacy, solitude, quiet, or fine neighbors. When you find one or more of these, consider yourself in hog heaven and then hope for a good bottom.

Coordinates for these havens are included to provide a convenient listing of some of the places we have stayed and enjoyed. While the list is only rudimentary, it may serve a useful purpose to those who want to know what makes for a good "gunkhole."

Coordinates in this chapter are listed by province, body of water, description, latitude, longitude, time delay one, and time delay two. Since most of the havens are quite shallow (four to five feet), you should verify them each time you want to slip into one of these gunkholes. Review an updated chart of the area along with a local tide table whenever it is necessary to know for sure the high/low mean or actual water depth at any of these havens.

FOOD, FUN, FRIENDSHIP
People at most places will tolerate just about any legal activity around a boat and appreciate that a vacation is a time for fun. We have learned over the years that the nicest people can be found around boats, and there is no better time than evenings to spread good will and happiness around.

Share your catch with another boater and you're sure to meet some of the nicest people in the world. We often arrange to offer the meat for dinner if our new-found friends will bring the salad. (We have found that it is easier to procure fresh fish than fresh vegetables for salads.)

We share our bounty and catches with people we meet freely and encourage them to join in our fun. Look for the boat Sancho, with Captain Rod and First Mate Susie. Offer us a handshake and we will have fun from then on.

HAVENS

BODY OF WATER	PROV/STATE	NAME	LAT	LON	TD#1	TD#2	CHART
LABRADOR SEA	NEWFOUNDLAND	WESTPORT COVE	49-47.00	56-37.00	Suggest	GPS	
LABRADOR SEA	NEWFOUNDLAND	SEAL COVE	49-55.80	56-22.90	Suggest	GPS	
LABRADOR SEA	NEWFOUNDLAND	SULEY ANN COVE FERRY	49-38.00	55-48.00	Suggest	GPS	
LABRADOR SEA	NEWFOUNDLAND	GOOSE COVE	51-19.00	55-39.00	Suggest	GPS	
LABRADOR SEA	NEWFOUNDLAND	MOUSE ISLAND	51-19.00	55-39.00	Suggest	GPS	
LABRADOR SEA	NEWFOUNDLAND	BULL POINT/COOMBS COVE	47-27.00	55-38.00	Suggest	GPS	
LABRADOR SEA	NEWFOUNDLAND	COTTRELLS COVE POINT	49-29.00	55-18.00	Suggest	GPS	
LABRADOR SEA	NEWFOUNDLAND	COTTRELLS COVE WHARF	49-30.00	55-17.00	Suggest	GPS	
LABRADOR SEA	NEWFOUNDLAND	STURGEON COVE HEAD	49-31.00	55-07.00	Suggest	GPS	
LABRADOR SEA	NEWFOUNDLAND	TIDES COVE POINT	47-07.00	55-04.00	Suggest	GPS	
LABRADOR SEA	NEWFOUNDLAND	VICTORIA COVE	49-21.00	54-28.00	Suggest	GPS	
LABRADOR SEA	NEWFOUNDLAND	MAN OF WAR COVE	49-34.00	54-18.00	Suggest	GPS	
LABRADOR SEA	NEWFOUNDLAND	SEAL COVE	49-43.00	54-17.00	Suggest	GPS	
LABRADOR SEA	NEWFOUNDLAND	ROCKY BAY	49-26.90	54-13.80	Suggest	GPS	
LABRADOR SEA	NEWFOUNDLAND	BURNT PT, SELDOM COVE	49-36.00	54-09.00	Suggest	GPS	
LABRADOR SEA	NEWFOUNDLAND	PENNGS COVE	48-50.10	53-41.20	Suggest	GPS	
LABRADOR SEA	NEWFOUNDLAND	CANDLE COVE ROCKS	49-06.00	53-36.00	Suggest	GPS	
LABRADOR SEA	NEWFOUNDLAND	SHOE COVE POINT	49-02.00	53-36.00	Suggest	GPS	
LABRADOR SEA	NEWFOUNDLAND	POUND COVE	49-10.00	53-32.00	Suggest	GPS	
LABRADOR SEA	NEWFOUNDLAND	KINGS COVE	48-35.00	53-19.00	Suggest	GPS	
LABRADOR SEA	NEWFOUNDLAND	NEWMANS COVE	48-35.10	53-11.70	Suggest	GPS	
LABRADOR SEA	NEWFOUNDLAND	SALMON COVE POINT	47-28.00	53-09.00	Suggest	GPS	
LABRADOR SEA	NEWFOUNDLAND	BEAR COVE POINT	46-56.40	52-53.60	Suggest	GPS	
LABRADOR SEA	NEWFOUNDLAND	PORTUGAL COVE	47-37.60	52-51.60	Suggest	GPS	
LAKE HURON		PROVIDENCE BAY WHARF	45-39.50	82-16.10	30397.76	48466.92	2266
ST LAWRENCE GULF	NEW BRUNSWICK	BLUE COVE RANGE	47-49.90	65-04.80	15081.41	43580.37	
ST LAWRENCE GULF	NOVA SCOTIA	CANSO CANAL ANCHORAGE	45-39.20	61-25.30	14230.65	42723.54	
ST LAWRENCE GULF	NOVA SCOTIA	CANSO CANAL ANCHORAGE	45-38.80	61-24.60	14228.29	42720.74	
ST LAWRENCE GULF	PRINCE EDWARD I	HOWARD COVE @ SEAL PT	46-44.40	64-22.70	14752.34	43645.22	
ST LAWRENCE GULF	PRINCE EDWARD I	FISHING COVE W BRKWTR	46-24.40	64-08.10	14621.44	43622.54	
ST LAWRENCE GULF	PRINCE EDWARD I	FISHING COVE BRKWTR	46-24.10	64-08.10	14619.72	43623.64	
ST LAWRENCE GULF	PRINCE EDWARD I	COVEHEAD RANGE	46-25.50	63-09.00	14552.88	43213.22	
ST LAWRENCE GULF	PRINCE EDWARD I	COVEHEAD BRIDGE	46-25.80	63-08.80	14554.21	43210.64	
ST LAWRENCE GULF	PRINCE EDWARD I	COVEHEAD HARBOUR	46-25.80	63-08.70	14554.09	43209.97	
ST LAWRENCE GULF	PRINCE EDWARD I	COVEHEAD APPROACH "JJ1"	46-26.90	63-08.30	14559.31	43202.75	
ST LAWRENCE GULF	PRINCE EDWARD I	WARREN COVE RANGE	46-12.00	63-08.30	14480.12	43261.22	
ST LAWRENCE GULF	QUEBEC	WHALE HEAD ANCHORAGE	50-39.60	59-12.00	15015.5	40051.4	
ST LAWRENCE RIVER	QUEBEC	ST ZOTIQUE ANCH "DJ"	45-12.60	74-16.70	14392.05	60135.00	1412
ST LAWRENCE RIVER	QUEBEC	ST ZOTIQUE ANCH "DD"	45-13.20	74-15.50	14379.67	60135.17	1412
ST LAWRENCE RIVER	QUEBEC	ST ZOTIQUE ANCH "DH"	45-14.00	74-14.30	14365.84	60134.87	1412
ST LAWRENCE RIVER	QUEBEC	ST ZOTIQUE ANCH "DC"	45-14.20	74-13.60	14359.71	60135.32	1412
ST LAWRENCE RIVER	QUEBEC	ST ZOTIQUE ANCH "DA"	45-13.80	74-13.60	14362.59	60136.27	1412
ST LAWRENCE RIVER	QUEBEC	BEAUHARNOIS ANCH "CN"	45-13.60	74-08.30	14328.29	60143.59	1411
ST LAWRENCE RIVER	QUEBEC	BEAUHARNOIS ANCH "CM"	45-13.30	74-07.20	14323.00	60145.66	1411

HAVENS

BODY OF WATER	PROV/STATE	NAME	LAT	LON	TD#1	TD#2	CHART
ST LAWRENCE RIVER	QUEBEC	BEAUHARNOIS ANCH "CK"	45-13.30	74-01.70	14285.57	60152.41	1411
ST LAWRENCE RIVER	QUEBEC	BEAUHARNOIS ANCH "CJ"	45-13.70	74-00.30	14273.15	60153.19	1411
ST LAWRENCE RIVER	QUEBEC	BEAUHARNOIS ANCH "CE"	45-15.60	73-57.30	14239.13	60152.48	1411
ST LAWRENCE RIVER	QUEBEC	BEAUHARNOIS ANCH "CD"	45-16.00	73-57.00	14234.25	60151.94	1411
ST LAWRENCE RIVER	QUEBEC	BEAUHARNOIS ANCH "CA"	45-17.00	73-56.20	14221.70	60150.65	1411
ST LAWRENCE RIVER	QUEBEC	BEAUHARNOIS ANCH "B"	45-20.00	73-55.00	14192.35	60145.34	1410
ST LAWRENCE RIVER	QUEBEC	BEAUHARNOIS ANCH "A"	45-20.40	73-54.30	14184.75	60145.29	1410
ST LAWRENCE RIVER	QUEBEC	PORTNEUF RIVER ENTR	46-41.40	71-52.60	12834.40	60108.30	
ST LAWRENCE RIVER	QUEBEC	WOLFE COVE Q6	46-47.20	71-13.50	12523.9	60131.4	
ST LAWRENCE RIVER	QUEBEC	WOLFE COVE Q4	46-47.80	71-12.80	12516.1	60130.9	
ST LAWRENCE RIVER	QUEBEC	GRIFFON COVE RANGE	48-56.20	64-18.40	15144.63	30444.91	
ST LAWRENCE RIVER	QUEBEC	SAFE ANCHORGE	50-12.20	60-40.20	15044.5	40816.1	
ST LAWRENCE RIVER	QUEBEC	GETHSEMANI ANCHORAGE	50-12.20	60-40.20	15044.5	40816.1	
ST LAWRENCE SEAWAY	NY/QUEBEC	SOUTHWEST ANCH "DQ"	45-01.70	74-37.50	14610.18	60132.59	1413
ST LAWRENCE SEAWAY	NY/QUEBEC	ILE ST REGIS ANCH "DN"	45-02.00	74-37.10	14605.32	60132.43	1413
ST LAWRENCE SEAWAY	NY/QUEBEC	SOUTH ANCH "DM"	45-02.20	74-35.80	14595.28	60133.82	1413
ST LAWRENCE SEAWAY	NY/QUEBEC	DANIS POINT ANCH "DX"	45-02.60	74-35.70	14591.64	60132.96	1413
ST LAWRENCE SEAWAY	NY/QUEBEC	DICKERSON I ANCH "DK"	45-02.30	74-35.30	14591.25	60134.30	1413

CHAPTER 8
PLENTIFUL PORTS

To us, a port is a place where a boater can get major services for his boat, with restaurants, shopping malls, and grocery stores nearby. Obviously, diesel, gasoline, and mechanical services must likewise be available.

Here are listings of places that we have been to and places that have been sent to us for publication. Of course, this list is not exhaustive, and should you have a place you would like to see published for others to enjoy, or for your own convenience, turn your ASF off and send us your time delay and latitude/longitude readings, along with the name of the port, marina, or gas dock. There is no charge for publishing this information, and we do not presume or assume anything about the convenience of any facility contained herein.

Coordinates for the ports' sea buoys are included for convenience, along with body of water or province, county, description, latitude, longitude, time delay one, and time delay two coordinates.

Please review the first two paragraphs of Chapter 7 for tips on using these coordinates.

HELPFUL HINT
Lots of polish on the deck makes for a pretty boat, teaches everyone the value of yoga, and provides quick lessons in aerobic exercise.

WIT & WISDOM

Captain Jack Bolack of Gulfwind Marine regularly delivers boats from the greater Tampa Bay area to Mobile, Alabama. On one of our more memorable trips together, we came face to face with fate and luck, but allowed a basic lack of faith in the tales of years gone by to cloud our eyes to the opportunity of a lifetime.

As Captain Jack and I headed west from Steinhatchee, Florida, early one morning, we found ourselves contentedly discussing the previous evening's dinner and the size of the fine steak we devoured. Just about the time our conversation settled to a couple of yeps, we came upon a small squall line that actually followed our course as far as we could see.

About three or four miles ahead, we could see small whitecaps and rain obscuring the horizon. Wet gear in place, we ran up on the rain about the same time the sun peeked over the horizon, casting its rays into the rain and thereby painting a beautiful rainbow within our grasp. As we drove under the rainbow, we could actually see its ends touching the water.

Immediately, I took the loran numbers down and pleaded for an opportunity to stop to dive for our pots of gold, but Captain Jack kept on going, muttering something about bilge water, authors, dreamers, and fairy tales.

I have the loran listings of the rainbow's end if anyone is still in the pursuit of a dream and a legend of love and luck. On a nice day, you might even find Sancho there, searching for the impossible dream.

PORTS

BODY OF WATER	PROV/STATE	NAME	LAT	LON	TD#1	TD#2	CHART
GEORGIAN BAY	ONTARIO	BRUCE MINES WHARF	46-17.83	83-47.39	30845.49	48001.66	2250
GEORGIAN BAY	ONTARIO	NORTH KEPPEL WHARF	44-47.67	80-56.80	29945.52	48931.83	2282
GEORGIAN BAY	ONTARIO	OWEN SOUND PIER	44-34.84	80-56.35	29954.03	49022.52	2282
GEORGIAN BAY	ONTARIO	PENETANG NORTH WHARF	44-46.45	79-56.40	29533.41	48977.13	2218
LABRADOR SEA	NEWFOUNDLAND	GREAT HARBOUR DEEP	50-22.90	56-24.80	Suggest	GPS	
LABRADOR SEA	NEWFOUNDLAND	FOURCHE HARBOUR	50-31.00	56-15.00	Suggest	GPS	
LABRADOR SEA	NEWFOUNDLAND	WHITE POINT HARBOUR	50-43.30	56-07.00	Suggest	GPS	
LABRADOR SEA	NEWFOUNDLAND	COACHMANS HARBOUR	50-03.30	56-05.70	Suggest	GPS	
LABRADOR SEA	NEWFOUNDLAND	FLEUR-DE-LYS HARBOUR	50-07.40	56-04.80	Suggest	GPS	
LABRADOR SEA	NEWFOUNDLAND	SPRINGDALE WHARF	49-29.90	56-03.80	Suggest	GPS	
LABRADOR SEA	NEWFOUNDLAND	MAIN BROOK WHARF	51-10.00	56-00.00	Suggest	GPS	
LABRADOR SEA	NEWFOUNDLAND	SMITH HARBOUR	49-44.40	55-57.70	Suggest	GPS	
LABRADOR SEA	NEWFOUNDLAND	GAULTOIS HARBOUR	47-36.00	55-54.00	Suggest	GPS	
LABRADOR SEA	NEWFOUNDLAND	BEACHSIDE WHARF	49-38.60	55-53.40	Suggest	GPS	
LABRADOR SEA	NEWFOUNDLAND	PACQUET HARBOUR	49-59.00	55-51.00	Suggest	GPS	
LABRADOR SEA	NEWFOUNDLAND	WESTERN BREAKWATER	47-05.00	55-50.00	Suggest	GPS	
LABRADOR SEA	NEWFOUNDLAND	FORTUNE HARBOURBUOY	47-05.00	55-50.00	Suggest	GPS	
LABRADOR SEA	NEWFOUNDLAND	GRAND BANK BRKWTR	47-06.00	55-45.00	Suggest	GPS	
LABRADOR SEA	NEWFOUNDLAND	PILLYS ISLAND FERRY WHARF	49-34.00	55-44.00	Suggest	GPS	
LABRADOR SEA	NEWFOUNDLAND	HARBOUR ROCK	51-22.00	55-34.00	Suggest	GPS	
LABRADOR SEA	NEWFOUNDLAND	ANTHONY HARBOUR ENTR	51-22.00	55-34.00	Suggest	GPS	
LABRADOR SEA	NEWFOUNDLAND	ENGLISH HARBOUR WEST	47-27.00	55-30.00	Suggest	GPS	
LABRADOR SEA	NEWFOUNDLAND	GRIQUET HARBOUR	51-33.00	55-27.00	Suggest	GPS	
LABRADOR SEA	NEWFOUNDLAND	QUIRPON HARBOUR, NE	51-36.00	55-27.00	Suggest	GPS	
LABRADOR SEA	NEWFOUNDLAND	BELLARAM HARBOUR	47-31.00	55-25.00	Suggest	GPS	
LABRADOR SEA	NEWFOUNDLAND	LEAMINGTON PT WHARF	49-21.00	55-23.00	Suggest	GPS	
LABRADOR SEA	NEWFOUNDLAND	COTTRELLS COVE WHARF	49-30.00	55-17.00	Suggest	GPS	
LABRADOR SEA	NEWFOUNDLAND	CORBIN HARBOUR LG PT	46-57.00	55-14.00	Suggest	GPS	
LABRADOR SEA	NEWFOUNDLAND	CABBAGE HARBOUR	49-20.00	55-13.00	Suggest	GPS	
LABRADOR SEA	NEWFOUNDLAND	LONG HARBOUR POINT	47-35.00	55-08.00	Suggest	GPS	
LABRADOR SEA	NEWFOUNDLAND	RED HARBOUR HEAD	47-17.00	54-59.00	Suggest	GPS	
LABRADOR SEA	NEWFOUNDLAND	ST BERNARDS BRKWTR	47-32.00	54-58.00	Suggest	GPS	
LABRADOR SEA	NEWFOUNDLAND	MORETONS HARBOUR	49-35.00	54-52.00	Suggest	GPS	
LABRADOR SEA	NEWFOUNDLAND	MORETONS HARBOUR	49-35.00	54-51.00	Suggest	GPS	
LABRADOR SEA	NEWFOUNDLAND	ODERIN HARBOUR ENTR	47-18.00	54-49.00	Suggest	GPS	
LABRADOR SEA	NEWFOUNDLAND	SUMMERFORD WHARF	49-30.00	54-47.00	Suggest	GPS	
LABRADOR SEA	NEWFOUNDLAND	TWILLINGATE WHARF	49-40.00	54-46.00	Suggest	GPS	
LABRADOR SEA	NEWFOUNDLAND	TERRENCEVILLE WHARF	47-40.00	54-44.00	Suggest	GPS	
LABRADOR SEA	NEWFOUNDLAND	PETIT FORTE HARBOUR	47-23.00	54-40.00	Suggest	GPS	
LABRADOR SEA	NEWFOUNDLAND	FAREWELL HARBOUR F WHARF	49-33.00	54-29.00	Suggest	GPS	
LABRADOR SEA	NEWFOUNDLAND	STAG HARBOUR	49-33.00	54-18.00	Suggest	GPS	
LABRADOR SEA	NEWFOUNDLAND	CARMENVILLE WHARF	49-24.00	54-17.00	Suggest	GPS	
LABRADOR SEA	NEWFOUNDLAND	FOGO ISLAND HARBOUR	49-44.00	54-16.00	Suggest	GPS	
LABRADOR SEA	NEWFOUNDLAND	CANN ISLAND, SELDOM HARB	49-35.00	54-11.00	Suggest	GPS	

PORTS

BODY OF WATER	PROV/STATE	NAME	LAT	LON	TD#1	TD#2	CHART
LABRADOR SEA	NEWFOUNDLAND	PUBLIC WHARF	49-44.00	54-10.00	Suggest	GPS	
LABRADOR SEA	NEWFOUNDLAND	RED ISLAND HARBOUR	47-24.00	54-09.00	Suggest	GPS	
LABRADOR SEA	NEWFOUNDLAND	NORTH HARBOUR POINT	47-49.00	54-06.00	Suggest	GPS	
LABRADOR SEA	NEWFOUNDLAND	TILTON HARBOUR, W	49-42.00	54-04.00	Suggest	GPS	
LABRADOR SEA	NEWFOUNDLAND	MUSGRAVE HARBOUR	49-28.00	53-58.00	Suggest	GPS	
LABRADOR SEA	NEWFOUNDLAND	BRACH WEST BRKWTR	46-53.00	53-57.00	Suggest	GPS	
LABRADOR SEA	NEWFOUNDLAND	FOX HARBOUR	47-19.30	53-54.60	Suggest	GPS	
LABRADOR SEA	NEWFOUNDLAND	FISHERMANS WHARF	49-01.10	53-52.70	Suggest	GPS	
LABRADOR SEA	NEWFOUNDLAND	SALVAGE HARBOUR	48-41.00	53-38.00	Suggest	GPS	
LABRADOR SEA	NEWFOUNDLAND	GOOSEBERRY HARBOUR	48-53.00	53-37.00	Suggest	GPS	
LABRADOR SEA	NEWFOUNDLAND	WESLEYVILLE HARBOUR	49-08.00	53-34.00	Suggest	GPS	
LABRADOR SEA	NEWFOUNDLAND	GREENSPOND HARBOUR	49-04.00	53-34.00	Suggest	GPS	
LABRADOR SEA	NEWFOUNDLAND	HEARTS CONTENT HARBOUR	47-53.00	53-23.00	Suggest	GPS	
LABRADOR SEA	NEWFOUNDLAND	FORT POINT, TRINITY HARB	48-22.00	53-21.00	Suggest	GPS	
LABRADOR SEA	NEWFOUNDLAND	HANTS HARBOUR	48-01.00	53-15.00	Suggest	GPS	
LABRADOR SEA	NEWFOUNDLAND	PORT DE GRAVE, N BRKWTR	47-35.30	53-12.60	Suggest	GPS	
LABRADOR SEA	NEWFOUNDLAND	CONCEPTION HARBOUR	47-26.40	53-12.60	Suggest	GPS	
LABRADOR SEA	NEWFOUNDLAND	PORT DE GRAVE, S BRKWTR	47-35.20	53-12.60	Suggest	GPS	
LABRADOR SEA	NEWFOUNDLAND	HARBOUR GRACE ISLANDS	47-43.00	53-09.00	Suggest	GPS	
LABRADOR SEA	NEWFOUNDLAND	BONAVISTA BRKWTR	48-38.90	53-07.10	Suggest	GPS	
LABRADOR SEA	NEWFOUNDLAND	CATALINA HARBOUR	48-31.00	53-05.00	Suggest	GPS	
LABRADOR SEA	NEWFOUNDLAND	OUTER BREAKWATER	48-05.20	53-00.70	Suggest	GPS	
LABRADOR SEA	NEWFOUNDLAND	INNER BREAKWATER	48-05.20	53-00.50	Suggest	GPS	
LABRADOR SEA	NEWFOUNDLAND	ST PIERRE HARB ENTR	46-46.70	46-10.10	Suggest	GPS	
LABRADOR SEA	NEWFOUNDLAND	TREPASSEY HARBOUR	46-43.00	43-23.00	Suggest	GPS	
LAKE ERIE		LUNA PIER MARINA NO 1	41-48.70	83-26.40	43666.03	56661.40	14846
LAKE ERIE		LUNA PIER MARINA NO 2	41-48.70	83-26.40	43666.03	56661.40	14846
LAKE ERIE		TOLEDO BEACH MARINA RANGE	41-49.70	83-24.80	43676.07	56679.50	14846
LAKE ERIE		BOLLES HARB ENTR NO 15	41-52.30	83-22.80	43697.55	56708.20	14846
LAKE ERIE		BOLLES HARB ENTR NO 10A	41-52.10	83-22.60	43696.67	56708.99	14846
LAKE ERIE		SANDY CREEK ENTR NO 1	41-55.40	83-19.50	43725.15	56750.06	14846
LAKE ERIE		TOLEDO HARBOR ENTR NO 2	41-49.40	83-11.90	43701.97	56787.73	14847
LAKE ERIE		METRO PARK MARINA RANGE	42-03.20	83-11.60	43793.73	56851.42	14848
LAKE ERIE		FORD YACHT CLUB NO 1	42-05.30	83-10.20	43810.51	56872.45	14848
LAKE ERIE		GROSSE ILE YACHT CLUB	42-05.30	83-09.00	43813.27	56882.54	14848
LAKE ERIE		DETROIT RIVER PIER NO 30	42-01.50	83-08.10	43790.68	56873.43	14848
LAKE ERIE		BAR POINT PIER "33D"	42-02.40	83-08.10	43796.55	56877.38	14848
LAKE ERIE		BAR POINT PIER D33	42-02.40	83-08.05	16448.83	56877.80	2123
LAKE ERIE		LIVINGSTON CHANNEL ENTR	42-08.20	83-07.30	43835.88	56909.52	14848
LAKE ERIE		GREEN COVE MARINA NO 1	41-36.80	83-06.20	43628.03	56781.02	14846
LAKE ERIE		RIVERFRONT S ENTR NO 2	42-19.40	83-03.30	43916.09	56991.42	14848
LAKE ERIE		RIVERFRONT S ENTR NO 1	42-19.30	83-03.30	43915.47	56990.99	14848
LAKE ERIE		RIVERFRONT N ENTR NO 1	42-19.40	83-03.20	43916.33	56992.25	14848
LAKE ERIE		RIVERFRONT N ENTR NO 2	42-19.40	83-03.10	43916.57	56993.09	14848

PORTS

BODY OF WATER	PROV/STATE	NAME	LAT	LON	TD#1	TD#2	CHART
LAKE ERIE		NUGENTS CANAL PT W ENTR	41-30.60	82-59.80	43597.94	56809.38	14846
LAKE ERIE		DETROIT BOAT CLUB LIGHT	42-20.50	82-59.10	43933.13	57031.06	14848
LAKE ERIE		MEMORIAL PARK MARINA	42-21.00	82-59.00	43936.48	57034.01	14848
LAKE ERIE		LAKE FRONT MARINA RANGE	41-31.50	82-58.40	43607.33	56825.42	14846
LAKE ERIE		LAKE FRONT MARINA W LIGHT	41-31.50	82-58.30	43607.55	56826.30	14846
LAKE ERIE		COLONY CLUB MARINA LIGHT	41-33.20	82-51.40	43634.60	56893.52	14844
LAKE ERIE		MARINE CITY DOCK LIGHT	41-32.00	82-48.00	43633.44	56917.93	14842
LAKE ERIE		CHANNEL GROVE MARINA	41-32.20	82-47.20	43636.64	56925.73	14842
LAKE ERIE		EAST HARBOR ENTR NO 2	41-32.60	82-47.00	43639.96	56929.18	14842
LAKE ERIE		LAKEVIEW E ENTR LIGHT	41-32.40	82-46.40	43639.84	56933.54	14842
LAKE ERIE		SCHROCKS MARINA E BRKWTR	41-32.60	82-46.10	43641.95	56937.02	14842
LAKE ERIE		KINGSVILLE WEST PIER	42-01.45	82-43.85	16462.75	57079.13	2181
LAKE ERIE		STANDARD SLAG DOCK	41-32.70	82-43.80	43647.77	56957.45	14842
LAKE ERIE		BAY POINT MARINA LIGHT	41-30.20	82-43.00	43631.43	56953.78	14842
LAKE ERIE		PATTERY PK MARINA S ENTR	41-27.80	82-42.10	43615.89	56951.44	14845
LAKE ERIE		SANDUSKY HARBOR PIER	41-30.00	82-40.50	43635.50	56974.72	14845
LAKE ERIE		SCUDDER INNER WHARF	41-48.80	82-39.52	16487.15	57062.89	2181
LAKE ERIE		SAWMILL CREEK ENTR	41-25.00	82-36.00	43608.64	56992.88	14830
LAKE ERIE		SAWMILL CREEK ENTR	41-25.00	82-35.60	43609.52	56996.38	14830
LAKE ERIE		HURON HARBOR ENTR NO 1	41-24.50	82-32.20	43613.31	57024.01	14843
LAKE ERIE		VERMILLION W PIER NO 4	41-25.70	82-21.90	43645.46	57119.19	14826
LAKE ERIE		RONDEAU EAST PIER	42-15.36	81-54.46	16461.08	57558.29	2181
LAKE ERIE		CLEVELAND HARB W PIER	41-30.50	81-43.10	43775.54	57478.99	14839
LAKE ERIE		EAST 55TH ST MARINA ENTR	41-31.90	81-39.20	43796.38	57518.90	14839
LAKE ERIE		CLEVELAND HARB E ENTR	41-32.60	81-39.10	43802.09	57522.64	14839
LAKE ERIE		NE YACHT CLUB OUTER LIGHT	41-34.40	81-35.10	43826.45	57565.04	14826
LAKE ERIE		EUCLID BEACH PIER	41-35.50	81-34.20	43837.35	57577.40	14826
LAKE ERIE		WILDWOOD E PIER	41-35.30	81-34.00	43836.32	57578.34	14826
LAKE ERIE		CHAGRIN W PIER LIGHT	41-40.60	81-26.30	43897.90	57667.26	14825
LAKE ERIE		CHAGRIN E PIER LIGHT	41-40.60	81-26.20	43898.17	57668.13	14825
LAKE ERIE		MENTOR HARB YACHT CLUB	41-43.50	81-21.00	43934.77	57725.33	14825
LAKE ERIE		FAIRPORT HARB W PIER	41-45.70	81-16.80	43963.39	57770.89	14825
LAKE ERIE		FAIRPORT HARB E PIER	41-45.70	81-16.80	43963.39	57770.89	14825
LAKE ERIE		PORT BURWELL E PIER	42-38.40	80-48.45	16442.94	58207.33	2181
LAKE ERIE		PORT DOVER E PIER	42-46.87	80-12.08	16439.38	58546.12	2181
LAKE ERIE		PORT DOVER MARINA	42-46.84	80-11.69	16439.69	58549.42	2181
LAKE ERIE		ERIE YACHT CLUB RANGE	42-07.00	80-08.00	44340.66	58455.84	14835
LAKE ERIE		ERIE HARB ENTR NO 12	42-08.80	80-05.30	44363.56	58486.12	14835
LAKE ERIE		ERIE HARB ENTR NO 10	42-08.90	80-05.30	44364.32	58486.48	14835
LAKE ERIE		ERIE HARB ENTR RANGE	42-09.10	80-04.90	44367.21	58490.71	14835
LAKE ERIE		JOHN E LAMPE MARINA NO 1	42-08.90	80-04.50	44367.08	58493.50	14835
LAKE ERIE		JOHN E LAMPE MARINA NO 2	42-08.90	80-04.40	44367.43	58494.38	14835
LAKE ERIE		ERIE HARBOR PIER LIGHT	42-09.40	80-04.30	44371.55	58497.07	14835
LAKE ERIE		ERIE HARBOR ENTR NO 2	42-09.80	80-03.20	44378.37	58508.18	14835

PORTS

BODY OF WATER	PROV/STATE	NAME	LAT	LON	TD#1	TD#2	CHART
LAKE ERIE		WILLIS DISTR CO DOCK	42-10.50	80-00.60	44392.69	58533.53	14823
LAKE ERIE		PORT MAITLAND E PIER	42-51.19	79-34.71	16447.15	58880.88	2140
LAKE ERIE		LA SALLE YACHT CLUB	43-04.40	78-59.30	44971.15	59210.09	14832
LAKE ERIE		BEAVER I ST PARK E ENTR	42-57.50	78-57.30	44944.21	59217.86	14832
LAKE ERIE		EAST RIVER MARINA N ENTR	42-58.10	78-56.00	44952.63	59230.04	14832
LAKE ERIE		JAFCO MARINA S LIGHT	42-56.60	78-54.60	44950.41	59239.91	14832
LAKE ERIE		JAFCO MARINA N LIGHT	42-56.60	78-54.60	44950.41	59239.91	14832
LAKE ERIE		SMITH BOYS MARINA N LIGHT	43-01.80	78-52.90	44984.04	59261.90	14832
LAKE ERIE		GENERAL MILLS DOCK NO 2	42-52.30	78-52.60	44935.14	59250.25	14833
LAKE ERIE		LACKAWANNA W PIER LIGHT	42-49.80	78-51.70	44924.68	59253.57	14833
LAKE ERIE		LACKAWANNA E PIER LIGHT	42-49.90	78-51.70	44925.25	59253.76	14833
LAKE HURON		PICKEREL CHAN ENTR NO 2	45-24.90	84-47.70	31325.37	48307.62	14886
LAKE HURON		CHEBOYGAN RIVER ENTR NO 2	45-39.90	84-27.40	31164.00	48223.58	14881
LAKE HURON		LES CHENEAUXS W ENTR NO 1	45-57.80	84-27.10	31109.32	48073.25	14885
LAKE HURON		CANADIAN CANAL ENTR "QM1"	46-30.50	84-20.50	30987.69	47822.13	14884
LAKE HURON		SAULT STE MARIE WHARF	46-30.20	84-19.70	30984.38	47826.54	14884
LAKE HURON		HAMMOND BAY HARBOR LIGHT	45-35.60	84-09.70	31077.56	48298.32	14881
LAKE HURON		RAINS WHARF RANGE LIGHT	46-15.30	84-05.70	30948.69	47979.99	14883
LAKE HURON		DETOUR HARBOR ENTR NO 2	45-59.70	83-54.00	30924.39	48132.41	14882
LAKE HURON		ROGERS CITY HARBOR NO 2	45-25.50	83-48.40	30983.02	48425.15	14864
LAKE HURON		ROGERS CITY HARBOR NO 1	45-25.50	83-48.40	30983.02	48425.15	14864
LAKE HURON		OAKHURST PARK MARINA	43-37.80	83-37.10	31271.40	49357.13	14863
LAKE HURON		PRESQUE ISLE HARBOR RANGE	45-20.30	83-29.40	30883.37	48502.24	14864
LAKE HURON		SEBEWAING YACHT CLUB LIGHT	43-44.30	83-27.80	31178.94	49309.14	14863
LAKE HURON		PARTRIDGE POINT MARINA	45-01.10	83-27.20	30922.15	48664.31	14864
LAKE HURON		JERRYS MARINA RANGE	44-15.70	83-26.30	31056.51	49045.49	14863
LAKE HURON		AU SABLE N PIERHEAD	44-24.40	83-19.00	30978.18	48980.84	14863
LAKE HURON		HARRISVILLE W BRKWTR	44-39.60	83-17.00	30918.26	48856.97	14864
LAKE HURON		CASEVILLE HARBOR BRKWTR	43-56.90	82-17.10	30616.46	49254.71	14863
LAKE HURON		GODERICH S BRKWTR	43-44.72	81-44.18	30397.05	49361.30	2291
LAKE HURON		BAYFIELD WHARF	43-34.20	81-42.50	30410.50	49439.02	2260
LAKE HURON		STOKES BAY ENTR "VK"	44-56.75	81-28.10	30149.21	48841.39	2292
LAKE HURON		PORT ELGIN S BRKWTR	44-24.36	81-24.37	30168.35	49080.30	2291
LAKE HURON		PORT ELGIN N BRKWTR	44-26.71	81-24.35	30164.54	49063.22	2291
LAKE MICHIGAN		STOCKBRIDGE HARB ENTR NO 2	44-04.00	88-20.10	32731.46	48496.01	14916
LAKE MICHIGAN		SUAMICO RIVER ENTR NO 3	44-37.80	88-00.50	32474.46	48207.85	14910
LAKE MICHIGAN		GREEN BAY HARB DISPOSAL	44-32.30	88-00.20	32501.78	48266.43	14918
LAKE MICHIGAN		GREEN BAY HARB ENTR NO 29	44-33.50	87-59.60	32493.13	48255.98	14918
LAKE MICHIGAN		GREEN BAY HARBOR RANGE	44-34.80	87-59.00	32483.98	48244.50	14918
LAKE MICHIGAN		GREEN BAY HARBOR RANGE	44-35.40	87-57.50	32474.85	48243.52	14918
LAKE MICHIGAN		GREEN BAY HARB ENTR LIGHT	44-39.20	87-54.10	32441.54	48215.87	14918
LAKE MICHIGAN		PENSAUKEE HARBOR LIGHT	44-49.30	87-53.90	32389.57	48112.02	14910
LAKE MICHIGAN		MILWAUKEE N ENTR NO 1	43-02.60	87-52.80	32988.13	49258.95	14924
LAKE MICHIGAN		MILWAUKEE N ENTR NO 2	43-02.70	87-52.80	32987.50	49257.84	14924

PORTS

BODY OF WATER	PROV/STATE	NAME	LAT	LON	TD#1	TD#2	CHART
LAKE MICHIGAN		MILWAUKEE S ENTR NO 2	43-00.50	87-52.60	33000.58	49282.79	14924
LAKE MICHIGAN		MILWAUKEE S ENTR LIGHT	43-00.50	87-52.60	33000.58	49282.79	14924
LAKE MICHIGAN		GREAT LAKES HARB RANGE	42-18.60	87-49.90	33265.71	49758.31	14905
LAKE MICHIGAN		OCONTO HARBOR S PIER LIGHT	44-53.90	87-49.30	32348.01	48081.05	14910
LAKE MICHIGAN		WAUKEGAN S HARB MARINA NO 1	42-21.40	87-49.30	33244.14	49728.73	14904
LAKE MICHIGAN		WAUKEGAN S HARB MARINA NO 2	42-21.40	87-49.20	33243.73	49729.04	14904
LAKE MICHIGAN		RUNAWAY BAY ENTR N LIGHT	42-29.60	87-48.50	33185.36	49639.33	14904
LAKE MICHIGAN		KENOSHA HARBOR ENTR NO 1	42-35.30	87-47.70	33143.95	49578.09	14904
LAKE MICHIGAN		RACINE LAUNCH BASIN ENTR	42-43.70	87-46.60	33083.91	49487.86	14925
LAKE MICHIGAN		RACINE E ENTR LIGHT	42-44.00	87-46.20	33080.27	49485.75	14925
LAKE MICHIGAN		WILMETTE HARBOR PIER LIGHT	42-04.80	87-40.80	33323.75	49940.86	14905
LAKE MICHIGAN		MANITOWOC HARB JUNCTION	44-05.60	87-39.00	32557.22	48619.89	14922
LAKE MICHIGAN		MANITOWOC HARBOR NO 5	44-05.70	87-38.90	32556.24	48619.15	14922
LAKE MICHIGAN		MANITOWOC HARBOR NO 4	44-06.70	87-38.90	32550.73	48608.55	14922
LAKE MICHIGAN		MANITOWOC HARBOR BUOY	44-05.60	87-38.80	32556.36	48620.54	14922
LAKE MICHIGAN		MANITOWOC HARBOR NO 2	44-05.60	87-38.80	32556.36	48620.54	14922
LAKE MICHIGAN		BELMONT HARBOR LIGHT	41-56.50	87-38.00	33370.66	50042.54	14927
LAKE MICHIGAN		DIVERSEY HARB ENTR S BRKWTR	41-55.90	87-37.90	33374.52	50049.60	14928
LAKE MICHIGAN		DIVERSEY HARB ENTR N BRKWTR	41-55.90	87-37.80	33374.09	50049.88	14928
LAKE MICHIGAN		DIVERSEY YACHT HARB RANGE	41-55.90	87-37.80	33374.09	50049.88	14928
LAKE MICHIGAN		BURNHAM PARK HARBOR LIGHT	41-51.10	87-36.60	33403.40	50107.52	14928
LAKE MICHIGAN		CHICAGO HARB S BRKWTR NO 1	41-52.50	87-36.60	33393.30	50091.68	14928
LAKE MICHIGAN		CHICAGO HARBOR LIGHT	41-53.30	87-35.40	33382.33	50085.94	14928
LAKE MICHIGAN		MENOMINEE ENTRANCE NO 2	45-06.00	87-34.70	32228.83	48009.36	14917
LAKE MICHIGAN		CHICAGO HARBOR NO 1	41-53.20	87-34.30	33378.21	50090.07	14928
LAKE MICHIGAN		CALUMET RIVER ENTR LIGHT	41-43.90	87-31.80	33434.61	50202.04	14929
LAKE MICHIGAN		CALUMET HARBOR DISP AREA	41-43.90	87-31.40	33432.82	50203.08	14929
LAKE MICHIGAN		INDIANA HARBOR NO 7	41-43.80	87-31.00	33431.76	50205.26	14929
LAKE MICHIGAN		INDIANA HARBOR LIGHT	41-44.30	87-30.50	33425.85	50200.89	14929
LAKE MICHIGAN		INDIANA HARBOR NO 1	41-43.10	87-29.70	33431.02	50216.55	14929
LAKE MICHIGAN		INDIANA HARB BRKWTR	41-43.50	87-29.60	33427.63	50212.28	14929
LAKE MICHIGAN		INDIANA HARBOR NO 2	41-41.10	87-26.80	33432.42	50246.52	14929
LAKE MICHIGAN		INDIANA HARBOR NO 1	41-41.20	87-26.60	33430.76	50245.89	14929
LAKE MICHIGAN		INDIANA HARBOR E BRKWTR	41-40.90	87-26.50	33432.50	50249.54	14929
LAKE MICHIGAN		INDIANA HARBOR S BULKHEAD	41-39.60	87-25.20	33436.02	50267.44	14929
LAKE MICHIGAN		BUFFINGTON HARBOR RANGE	41-38.50	87-25.10	33443.67	50280.14	14927
LAKE MICHIGAN		STURGEON BAY ENTR LIGHT	44-52.10	87-24.90	32254.06	48183.03	14919
LAKE MICHIGAN		BAILEYS HARBOR DIR LIGHT	45-04.20	87-07.20	32117.86	48119.63	14909
LAKE MICHIGAN		BAILEYS HARBOR NO 1	45-02.80	87-06.90	32123.08	48134.51	14909
LAKE MICHIGAN		DETROIT HARBOR NO 11	45-20.50	86-56.20	31993.99	47995.30	14909
LAKE MICHIGAN		DETROIT HARBOR ENTR LIGHT	45-19.90	86-56.20	31996.66	48001.12	14909
LAKE MICHIGAN		SHIPYARD I MARINA NO 2	45-20.50	86-55.70	31991.73	47996.92	14909
LAKE MICHIGAN		PORT DES MORTS ENTR	45-13.80	86-53.90	32013.48	48067.85	14909
LAKE MICHIGAN		JACKSON HARBOR LIGHT	45-24.20	86-51.00	31954.13	47976.36	14909

PORTS

BODY OF WATER	PROV/STATE	NAME	LAT	LON	TD#1	TD#2	CHART
LAKE MICHIGAN		JACKSON HARBOR NO 1	45-25.20	86-50.90	31949.32	47967.06	14909
LAKE MICHIGAN		NEW BUFFALO HARBOR NO 1	41-48.10	86-45.00	33162.09	50249.41	14905
LAKE MICHIGAN		MANISTEE HARB N PIER LIGHT	44-15.10	86-20.80	32132.19	48745.61	14938
LAKE MICHIGAN		HARBOUR TOWNE ENTR NO 2	43-13.70	86-19.50	32461.05	49378.56	14934
LAKE MICHIGAN		HARBOUR TOWNE ENTR NO 1	43-13.70	86-19.50	32461.05	49378.56	14934
LAKE MICHIGAN		BEAR LAKE ENTR W LIGHT	43-14.40	86-17.90	32447.86	49374.42	14934
LAKE MICHIGAN		ARCADIA ENTR BUOY	44-29.00	86-15.40	32034.89	48620.33	14907
LAKE MICHIGAN		GRAND HAVEN S PIER ENTR	43-03.50	86-15.40	32497.84	49492.63	14933
LAKE MICHIGAN		SAUGATUCK HARB OLD NO 1	42-39.90	86-13.00	32627.44	49743.04	14934
LAKE MICHIGAN		LELAND HARBOR NO 1	45-01.40	85-45.80	31731.68	48382.16	14912
LAKE MICHIGAN		CUTTY SARK HARB N BRKWTR	44-46.10	85-30.40	31713.31	48563.86	14913
LAKE MICHIGAN		CUTTY SARK HARB S BRKWTR	44-46.00	85-30.40	31713.74	48564.80	14913
LAKE MICHIGAN		ST JAMES HARBOR NO 1	45-44.00	85-29.80	31482.21	48033.40	14911
LAKE MICHIGAN		NW MARINE YACHT BASIN NO 3	45-18.40	85-14.70	31496.98	48302.24	14942
LAKE MICHIGAN		HARBORAGE MARINA ENTR NO 2	45-12.60	85-01.40	31445.56	48385.87	14942
LAKE MICHIGAN		HARBOR SPRINGS ANCH "B"	45-25.60	84-59.10	31385.77	48275.03	14913
LAKE MICHIGAN		HARBOR SPRINGS ANCH "A"	45-25.60	84-58.40	31381.95	48276.68	14913
LAKE MICHIGAN		HOLLAND HARBOR N BRKWTR	42-46.40	82-12.90	30806.92	49789.06	14932
LAKE ONTARIO		PORT WELLER ENTR RANGE	43-13.40	79-13.00	16368.94	59102.57	14822
LAKE ONTARIO		PORT WELLER E BRKWTR	43-14.70	79-12.90	16363.03	59104.73	14822
LAKE ONTARIO		WILSON HARBOR NO 2	43-19.20	78-50.20	16347.61	59297.28	14806
LAKE ONTARIO		BRADDOCK BAY ENTR LIGHT	43-18.70	77-42.60	16346.88	59839.95	14805
LAKE ONTARIO		ROCHESTER HARBOR LIGHT	43-15.80	77-36.00	16364.27	59895.04	14815
LAKE ONTARIO		PULTNEYVILLE YACHT CLUB	43-17.10	77-11.10	16323.69	60062.77	14804
LAKE ONTARIO		DAVENPORT MARINE DOCK	43-13.50	76-55.60	16317.78	60162.70	14814
LAKE ONTARIO		PORT BAY ENTR NO 1	43-18.30	76-50.20	16253.62	60167.91	14804
LAKE ONTARIO		FAIR HAVEN BRKWTR NO 2	43-21.00	76-42.50	16196.50	60187.41	14803
LAKE ONTARIO		WEST PIER HEAD LIGHT	43-28.40	76-31.00	16072.52	60195.83	14813
LAKE ONTARIO		MEXICO PT B LAUNCH NO 2	43-31.60	76-15.50	15958.23	60223.46	14803
LAKE ONTARIO		MEXICO PT B LAUNCH NO 1	43-31.50	76-15.40	15958.52	60224.02	14803
LAKE ONTARIO		HENDERSON HARB ANCH "A"	43-51.10	76-12.20	15767.86	60164.00	14811
LAKE ONTARIO		SACKETS HARBOR LIGHT	43-56.60	76-08.70	15700.16	60153.72	14811
LAKE ONTARIO		NAVY PT MARINE DOCK 4	43-57.00	76-07.30	15688.81	60155.77	14811
LAKE ONTARIO		BLACK RIVER ENTR NO 1	43-59.20	76-04.70	15655.00	60154.54	14811
LAKE ONTARIO		BLACK RIVER ENTR NO 2	43-59.10	76-04.60	15655.30	60155.12	14811
LAKE ST CLAIR	MICH/ONT	GROSSE POINT PIER	42-23.00	82-54.00	31240.02	49974.04	14853
LAKE ST CLAIR	MICH/ONT	CLUB DOCK LIGHT	42-23.00	82-53.80	31238.36	49973.97	14853
LAKE ST CLAIR	MICH/ONT	CRESCENT SAIL YACHT CLUB	42-24.10	82-53.10	31227.94	49965.40	14853
LAKE ST CLAIR	MICH/ONT	MARATHON OIL CO LIGHT	42-28.30	82-52.80	31208.02	49933.38	14853
LAKE ST CLAIR	MICH/ONT	SALT RIVER ENTR E LIGHT	42-39.20	82-47.10	31116.67	49848.84	14853
LAKE ST CLAIR	MICH/ONT	SALT RIVER ENTR W LIGHT	42-39.20	82-47.10	31116.67	49848.84	14853
LAKE ST CLAIR	MICH/ONT	HURON POINTE YACHT CLUB	42-35.60	82-46.90	31129.48	49876.32	14853
LAKE ST CLAIR	MICH/ONT	LOTTIVUE ENTR NO 2	42-39.30	82-45.70	31104.78	49847.86	14853
LAKE ST CLAIR	MICH/ONT	N CHANNEL ENTR NO 1	42-32.30	82-41.60	31098.88	49900.12	14852

PORTS

BODY OF WATER	PROV/STATE	NAME	LAT	LON	TD#1	TD#2	CHART
LAKE ST CLAIR	MICH/ONT	BELVEDERE BOAT CLUB	42-38.00	82-39.50	31058.86	49856.63	14852
LAKE ST CLAIR	MICH/ONT	FAIR HAVEN ENTR NO 1	42-39.90	82-39.00	31047.28	49842.16	14853
LAKE ST CLAIR	MICH/ONT	N CHANNEL YACHT CLUB NO 2	42-37.70	82-38.90	31055.09	49858.77	14852
LAKE ST CLAIR	MICH/ONT	WALPOLE I FERRY BRKWTR	42-36.90	82-30.90	30991.93	49863.03	14852
LAKE ST CLAIR	MICH/ONT	STOKES POINT WHARF	42-44.10	82-28.70	30946.17	49808.79	14852
LAKE ST CLAIR	MICH/ONT	HARTS LANDING NO A46	42-47.30	82-28.30	30930.84	49784.73	14852
LAKE ST CLAIR	MICH/ONT	RECORS POINT DOCK	42-45.50	82-28.30	30937.59	49798.24	14852
LAKE ST CLAIR	MICH/ONT	DUPONT LIGHTED BUOY	42-54.00	82-27.50	30899.49	49734.18	14852
LAKE ST CLAIR	MICH/ONT	PORT HURON CAR FERRY	42-57.90	82-25.40	30868.24	49704.64	14852
LAKE SUPERIOR		ALLQUES ORE DOCK NO 3	46-42.10	96-01.10	33003.57	45123.09	14975
LAKE SUPERIOR		BUFFALO POINT MARINA ENTR	49-02.50	95-13.70	32481.86	44007.78	14999
LAKE SUPERIOR		NAMAKAN ISLAND "N"	48-27.10	92-42.80	32323.79	44733.38	14993
LAKE SUPERIOR		DULUTH HARBOR BASIN NO 5	46-46.10	92-05.80	32609.70	45824.31	14975
LAKE SUPERIOR		HARBOR COVE MARINA NO 1	46-46.30	92-05.60	32608.49	45823.23	14975
LAKE SUPERIOR		DULUTH HARB N PIER LIGHT	46-46.90	92-05.30	32605.52	45818.58	14975
LAKE SUPERIOR		BARKERS ISLAND MARINA NO 5	46-42.80	92-02.90	32616.35	45871.58	14975
LAKE SUPERIOR		SUPERIOR HARB BASIN NO 1	46-42.30	92-01.00	32614.21	45885.68	14975
LAKE SUPERIOR		SUPERIOR INNER S PIER	46-42.40	92-00.80	32613.39	45885.61	14975
LAKE SUPERIOR		SUPERIOR INNER N PIER	46-42.50	92-00.80	32613.00	45884.59	14975
LAKE SUPERIOR		SUPERIOR ENTRY S BRKWTR	46-42.80	92-00.40	32611.74	45885.48	14975
LAKE SUPERIOR		KNIFE RIVER HARB ENTR	46-56.60	91-46.70	32527.06	45812.10	14966
LAKE SUPERIOR		TACONITE HARB E PIER NO 2	47-31.60	91-34.40	32367.18	45548.66	14967
LAKE SUPERIOR		PORT WING E PIER LIGHT	46-47.60	91-23.20	32507.78	46015.25	14966
LAKE SUPERIOR		CORNUCOPIA E PIER LIGHT	46-51.60	91-06.30	32451.11	46059.38	14966
LAKE SUPERIOR		ASHLAND HARB B RAMP NO 2	46-36.00	90-53.20	32480.41	46273.79	14974
LAKE SUPERIOR		ASHLAND HARB B RAMP NO 1	46-36.00	90-53.20	32480.41	46273.79	14974
LAKE SUPERIOR		CENTRAL AVE DOCK LIGHT	46-40.10	90-53.00	32463.40	46234.86	14974
LAKE SUPERIOR		BAYFIELD HARB S BRKWTR	46-48.50	90-48.70	32418.93	46175.06	14973
LAKE SUPERIOR		BAYFIELD HARB N BRKWTR	46-48.60	90-48.70	32418.53	46174.11	14973
LAKE SUPERIOR		LA POINTE HARBOR W BRKWTR	46-46.70	90-47.40	32422.71	46198.52	14973
LAKE SUPERIOR		STOCKTON I HARB E ENTR	46-54.90	90-33.10	32352.84	46191.02	14973
LAKE SUPERIOR		GRAND MARINA NO 1	47-44.60	90-20.40	32132.95	45824.58	14967
LAKE SUPERIOR		GRAND MARINA HARB NO 7	47-44.60	90-20.10	32132.13	45826.10	14967
LAKE SUPERIOR		GRAND PORTAGE PIER	47-57.60	89-40.90	31976.71	45921.77	14967
LAKE SUPERIOR		GRAND PORTAGE BAY ENTR	47-57.20	89-38.30	31970.51	45937.46	14967
LAKE SUPERIOR		ONOTONAGON HARB W PIER	46-52.80	89-19.80	32148.93	46558.04	14965
LAKE SUPERIOR		ONOTONAGON HARB E PIER	46-52.70	89-19.70	32149.00	46559.39	14965
LAKE SUPERIOR		MISSION RIVER ENTR A14	48-21.33	89-13.05	31816.68	45887.34	2314
LAKE SUPERIOR		MISSION RIVER ENTR BRKWTR	48-21.23	89-13.02	31816.90	45888.16	2314
LAKE SUPERIOR		KAMINISTIQUIA OLD WHARF	48-23.63	89-12.90	31808.96	45872.55	2314
LAKE SUPERIOR		KAMINISTIQUIA R ENTR S	48-23.53	89-12.83	31809.07	45873.55	2314
LAKE SUPERIOR		KAMINISTIQUIA R TERM ENTR D7	48-23.58	89-12.67	31808.43	45873.97	2314
LAKE SUPERIOR		THUNDER BAY S ENTR	48-24.73	89-12.35	31803.86	45867.79	2314
LAKE SUPERIOR		MISSION CHANNEL ENTRANCE	48-21.00	89-12.07	31814.80	45894.21	2314

P O R T S

BODY OF WATER	PROV/STATE	NAME	LAT	LON	TD#1	TD#2	CHART
LAKE SUPERIOR		KAMINISTIQUIA RIVER ENTR	48-23.88	89-12.00	31805.49	45875.13	2314
LAKE SUPERIOR		KAMINISTIQUIA RIVER ENTR D1	48-23.76	89-11.94	31805.69	45876.22	2314
LAKE SUPERIOR		THUNDER BAY CENTRAL ENTR	48-25.90	89-11.87	31798.76	45862.27	2314
LAKE SUPERIOR		THUNDER BAY N ENTR	48-26.63	89-10.63	31792.78	45863.29	2314
LAKE SUPERIOR		KEWEENAW UPPER ENTR LIGHT	47-14.10	88-37.80	31932.89	46562.60	14972
LAKE SUPERIOR		KEWEENAW UPPER ENTR NO 72	47-13.60	88-37.50	31933.70	46568.12	14972
LAKE SUPERIOR		ROCK HARBOR W ENTR	48-05.70	88-34.40	31746.62	46175.29	14976
LAKE SUPERIOR		KEWEENAW W ENTR LIGHT	46-58.10	88-25.90	31951.15	46750.92	14972
LAKE SUPERIOR		COPPER HARB ENT "CH"	47-28.70	87-51.80	31723.04	46641.30	14964
LAKE SUPERIOR		ROSSPORT HARBOUR ENTR	48-49.53	87-31.37	31413.05	46154.37	2312
LAKE SUPERIOR		ROSSPORT WHARF	48-50.02	87-31.20	31411.21	46152.03	2312
LAKE SUPERIOR		PRESQUE ISLE HARB BRKWTR	46-34.40	87-22.40	31804.11	47215.81	14970
LAKE SUPERIOR		LITTLE LAKE HARBOR NO 2	46-43.10	85-21.80	31252.16	47551.24	14962
LAKE SUPERIOR		LITTLE LAKE HARBOR NO 3	46-43.00	85-21.80	31252.45	47552.06	14962
LAKE SUPERIOR		MICHIPICOTEN HARBOUR	47-56.55	84-54.45	30950.04	47076.77	2315
LAKE SUPERIOR		MICHIPICOTEN RIVER ENTR	47-55.99	84-51.12	30937.18	47090.99	2315
LAKE SUPERIOR		MAMAINSE HARBOUR	47-02.25	84-47.19	31039.57	47500.20	2315
ST LAWRENCE GULF	CAPE BRETON I	MABOU HARBOUR	46-05.10	61-27.90	14359.98	42637.21	
ST LAWRENCE GULF	CAPE BRETON I	INVERNESS HARBOUR BRKWTR	46-13.70	61-19.60	14394.48	42548.11	
ST LAWRENCE GULF	CAPE BRETON I	INVERNESS HARBOUR RANGE	46-13.60	61-19.20	14393.73	42546.03	
ST LAWRENCE GULF	CAPE BRETON I	MARGAREE HARBOUR RANGE	46-26.40	61-06.80	14441.85	42409.90	
ST LAWRENCE GULF	CAPE BRETON I	MARGAREE HARBOUR	46-26.50	61-06.60	14442.13	42408.18	
ST LAWRENCE GULF	CAPE BRETON I	GRAND ETANG HARBOUR	46-33.00	61-02.60	14466.99	42352.11	
ST LAWRENCE GULF	CAPE BRETON I	EASTERN HARBOUR RANGE	46-38.00	61-00.70	14486.54	42315.81	
ST LAWRENCE GULF	CAPE BRETON I	CHETICAMP HARBOUR BUOY	46-38.80	61-00.60	14489.79	42311.25	
ST LAWRENCE GULF	CAPE BRETON I	LITTLE HARBOUR WHARF	45-35.00	60-44.50	14192.21	42493.27	
ST LAWRENCE GULF	CAPE BRETON I	OTTER HARBOUR RANGE	46-13.10	60-31.80	14359.57	42255.02	
ST LAWRENCE GULF	CAPE BRETON I	DINGWALL HARBOUR S LIGHT	46-54.20	60-27.20	14523.87	42023.28	
ST LAWRENCE GULF	CAPE BRETON I	DINGWALL HARBOUR N LIGHT	46-54.30	60-27.20	14524.25	42022.75	
ST LAWRENCE GULF	CAPE BRETON I	DINGWALL HARBOUR BELL	46-54.20	60-26.00	14522.90	42015.84	
ST LAWRENCE GULF	CAPE BRETON I	INGONISH HARBOUR ENTR	46-38.00	60-23.30	14457.50	42083.07	
ST LAWRENCE GULF	CAPE BRETON I	NEIL HARBOUR ENTRANCE	46-48.40	60-19.20	14495.29	42004.45	
ST LAWRENCE GULF	CAPE BRETON I	NEIL HARBOUR BELL BUOY	46-47.70	60-18.20	14491.82	42001.98	
ST LAWRENCE GULF	CAPE BRETON I	FOURCHU HARBOUR PIER	45-43.20	60-14.70	14218.52	42284.29	
ST LAWRENCE GULF	CAPE BRETON I	SYDNEY INNER HARB BELL	46-14.60	60-11.40	14353.65	42125.13	
ST LAWRENCE GULF	CAPE BRETON I	SYDNEY HARBOUR WHISTLE	46-18.40	60-07.80	14367.34	42085.59	
ST LAWRENCE GULF	CAPE BRETON I	LOUISBOURG HARBOUR ENTR	45-54.40	59-57.50	14260.55	42135.54	
ST LAWRENCE GULF	CAPE BRETON I	MAIN A DIEU HARBOUR	46-00.20	59-50.40	14282.00	42068.13	
ST LAWRENCE GULF	MAGDALEN ISLANDS	BREAKWATER	47-22.30	61-57.70	14717.69	42454.82	
ST LAWRENCE GULF	MAGDALEN ISLANDS	CAP-AUX-MEULES W BRKWTR	47-22.60	61-51.50	14711.70	42411.79	
ST LAWRENCE GULF	MAGDALEN ISLANDS	CAP-AUX-MEULES WHARF	47-22.60	61-51.30	14711.47	42410.46	
ST LAWRENCE GULF	MAGDALEN ISLANDS	CAP-AUX-MEULES BRKWTR	47-22.50	61-51.20	14711.00	42410.36	
ST LAWRENCE GULF	MAGDALEN ISLANDS	HOUSE HARBOUR	47-24.40	61-50.40	14717.00	42394.37	
ST LAWRENCE GULF	MAGDALEN ISLANDS	AMHERST WHARF LIGHT	47-13.70	61-50.00	14676.80	42450.86	

PORTS

BODY OF WATER	PROV/STATE	NAME	LAT	LON	TD#1	TD#2	CHART
ST LAWRENCE GULF	MAGDALEN ISLANDS	ENTRY ISLAND WHARF	47-16.60	61-43.20	14680.27	42389.97	
ST LAWRENCE GULF	MAGDALEN ISLANDS	ENTRY ISLAND	47-16.10	61-42.30	14677.41	42386.77	
ST LAWRENCE GULF	MAGDALEN ISLANDS	ENTRY ISLAND	47-17.30	61-41.50	14681.02	42374.88	
ST LAWRENCE GULF	MAGDALEN ISLANDS	GRAND ENTRY HARBOUR ENTR	47-33.40	61-33.80	14730.18	42232.82	
ST LAWRENCE GULF	NEW BRUNSWICK	DALHOUSIE HARBOUR RANGE	48-04.30	66-22.00	15222.17	43977.46	
ST LAWRENCE GULF	NEW BRUNSWICK	DALHOUSIE WHARF	48-04.30	66-21.70	15221.83	43975.65	
ST LAWRENCE GULF	NEW BRUNSWICK	JACQUET RIVER ENTRANCE	47-55.40	66-02.00	15184.11	43924.17	
ST LAWRENCE GULF	NEW BRUNSWICK	BELLEDUNE POINT BRKWTR	47-54.80	65-50.40	15165.70	43853.14	
ST LAWRENCE GULF	NEW BRUNSWICK	GREEN POINT BREAKWATER	47-51.70	65-45.80	15152.52	43845.88	
ST LAWRENCE GULF	NEW BRUNSWICK	PETIT-ROCHER BRKWTR	47-46.90	65-42.50	15136.88	43858.76	
ST LAWRENCE GULF	NEW BRUNSWICK	BATHURST HARBOUR RANGE	47-39.10	65-37.40	15109.05	43878.67	
ST LAWRENCE GULF	NEW BRUNSWICK	BATHURST HARBOUR "EP2"	47-41.10	65-36.00	15111.78	43855.29	
ST LAWRENCE GULF	NEW BRUNSWICK	STONEHAVEN WHARF	47-45.20	65-22.00	15098.13	43730.81	
ST LAWRENCE GULF	NEW BRUNSWICK	BURNT CHURCH WHARF	47-11.40	65-08.20	14960.10	43841.18	
ST LAWRENCE GULF	NEW BRUNSWICK	ANSE-BLUE WHARF	47-50.00	65-04.80	15081.67	43579.69	
ST LAWRENCE GULF	NEW BRUNSWICK	NEGUAC WHARF	47-14.40	65-04.50	14965.29	43798.28	
ST LAWRENCE GULF	NEW BRUNSWICK	LOWER NEGUAC WHARF RANGE	47-15.40	65-03.30	14967.02	43784.15	
ST LAWRENCE GULF	NEW BRUNSWICK	MAISONNETTE POINT WHARF	47-50.10	64-59.00	15072.39	43539.08	
ST LAWRENCE GULF	NEW BRUNSWICK	YOUNGS WHARF WEST	47-48.00	64-55.80	15061.51	43531.07	
ST LAWRENCE GULF	NEW BRUNSWICK	YOUNGS WHARF	47-47.80	64-55.60	15060.63	43531.02	
ST LAWRENCE GULF	NEW BRUNSWICK	NORTH TRACADIE WHARF	47-31.50	64-54.50	15009.50	43627.55	
ST LAWRENCE GULF	NEW BRUNSWICK	VAL COMEAU WHARF	47-28.00	64-53.00	14994.93	43638.11	
ST LAWRENCE GULF	NEW BRUNSWICK	MIDDLE CARAQUET WHARF	47-48.20	64-52.40	15056.44	43506.21	
ST LAWRENCE GULF	NEW BRUNSWICK	MIDDLE CARAQUET WHARF	47-48.20	64-52.40	15056.44	43506.21	
ST LAWRENCE GULF	NEW BRUNSWICK	POINT SAPIN BRKWTR	46-57.80	64-49.80	14865.28	43777.89	
ST LAWRENCE GULF	NEW BRUNSWICK	POKEMOUCHE GULLY WHARF	47-40.20	64-48.70	15027.13	43532.48	
ST LAWRENCE GULF	NEW BRUNSWICK	LITTLE POKEMOUCHE WHARF	47-41.30	64-44.10	15022.70	43493.32	
ST LAWRENCE GULF	NEW BRUNSWICK	CHOCKPISH, BRKWTR	46-35.00	64-43.20	14734.92	43828.75	
ST LAWRENCE GULF	NEW BRUNSWICK	RICHIBUCTO CAPE BRKWTR	46-40.50	64-42.50	14764.29	43802.03	
ST LAWRENCE GULF	NEW BRUNSWICK	BIG SHIPPAGAN WHARF	47-44.80	64-42.20	15029.96	43457.63	
ST LAWRENCE GULF	NEW BRUNSWICK	ST EDWARD DE KENT WHARF	46-32.50	64-41.50	13334.57	44078.85	
ST LAWRENCE GULF	NEW BRUNSWICK	BIG SHIPPEGAN BRKWTR	47-43.10	64-40.00	15021.28	43453.20	
ST LAWRENCE GULF	NEW BRUNSWICK	BIG SHIPPEGAN ENTR	47-43.30	64-39.70	15021.38	43449.84	
ST LAWRENCE GULF	NEW BRUNSWICK	ST THOMAS DE KENT WHARF	46-26.90	64-38.20	14679.96	43823.45	
ST LAWRENCE GULF	NEW BRUNSWICK	COCAGNE BAR WHARF	46-24.50	64-36.80	14663.50	43822.08	
ST LAWRENCE GULF	NEW BRUNSWICK	COTE d'OR WHARF	46-21.00	64-36.80	14642.26	43834.02	
ST LAWRENCE GULF	NEW BRUNSWICK	HEAD OF BREAKWATER	46-18.80	64-30.60	14619.80	43798.25	
ST LAWRENCE GULF	NEW BRUNSWICK	PIGEON HILL WHARF	47-52.70	64-30.50	15033.45	43324.90	
ST LAWRENCE GULF	NEW BRUNSWICK	SHEDIAC HARBOUR BELL "XN"	46-17.00	64-30.10	14608.00	43800.72	
ST LAWRENCE GULF	NEW BRUNSWICK	HARSHMANS BROOK WHARF	46-14.00	64-18.00	14573.11	43727.06	
ST LAWRENCE GULF	NEW BRUNSWICK	CAPE BALD WHARF	46-14.10	64-15.70	14570.72	43710.93	
ST LAWRENCE GULF	NEW BRUNSWICK	LITTLE CAPE BRKWTR	46-11.90	64-09.80	14549.72	43677.71	
ST LAWRENCE GULF	NEW BRUNSWICK	LITTLE CAPE OUTER BRKWTR	46-11.90	64-09.70	14549.60	43677.03	
ST LAWRENCE GULF	NEW BRUNSWICK	BOTSFORD BRKWTR	46-10.20	63-56.00	14522.61	43589.26	

PORTS

BODY OF WATER	PROV/STATE	NAME	LAT	LON	TD#1	TD#2	CHAR
ST LAWRENCE GULF	NEW BRUNSWICK	CAPE TORMINTINE ENTR	46-07.60	63-47.10	14496.79	43537.64	
ST LAWRENCE GULF	NEW BRUNSWICK	CAPE TORMINTINE WHARF	46-08.00	63-46.70	14498.72	43533.60	
ST LAWRENCE GULF	NEW BRUNSWICK	CAPE TORMINTINE BRKWTR	46-08.00	63-46.40	14498.38	43531.57	
ST LAWRENCE GULF	NEW BRUNSWICK	CAPE TORMINTINE WHARF	46-08.10	63-46.40	14498.98	43531.23	
ST LAWRENCE GULF	NEW BRUNSWICK	CAPE TORMINTINE HARBOUR	46-08.10	63-46.20	14498.75	43529.88	
	NEW BRUNSWICK	FAIRHAVEN WHARF	44-57.90	67-00.60	14003.20	44773.21	
	NEW BRUNSWICK	CHOCOLATE COVE WHARF	44-56.80	66-58.50	13992.79	44762.84	
	NEW BRUNSWICK	OUT HEAD OF WHARF	44-53.40	66-57.50	13956.02	44754.56	
	NEW BRUNSWICK	LEONARDVILLE HARBOUR	44-58.20	66-57.40	14009.23	44759.66	
	NEW BRUNSWICK	LORDS COVE GOVT WHARF	45-00.40	66-56.90	14033.97	44759.98	
	NEW BRUNSWICK	RICHARDSON WHARF	44-59.70	66-56.80	14026.31	44758.75	
	NEW BRUNSWICK	MALLOCH BEACH GOVT WHARF	44-55.00	66-56.50	13974.60	44752.07	
	NEW BRUNSWICK	CURRY COVE WHARF	44-55.70	66-56.40	13982.42	44752.43	
	NEW BRUNSWICK	HEAD HARBOUR	44-57.50	66-54.10	14004.17	44744.34	
	NEW BRUNSWICK	LETITE HARBOUR LEDGE	45-02.90	66-54.10	14063.57	44750.27	
	NEW BRUNSWICK	BLACKS HARBOUR ENTRANCE	45-02.80	66-48.50	14066.09	44724.57	
	NEW BRUNSWICK	NORTH HEAD HARBOUR WHARF	44-45.80	66-45.10	13884.23	44692.08	
	NEW BRUNSWICK	BEAVER HARBOUR BRKWTR	45-04.20	66-44.40	14083.60	44706.75	
	NEW BRUNSWICK	BEAVER HARB BELL "KEA"	45-02.30	66-43.40	14063.66	44700.28	
	NEW BRUNSWICK	MACES BAY WHARF	45-07.10	66-28.80	14120.66	44632.69	
	NEW BRUNSWICK	DIPPER HARBOUR WHARF	45-05.80	66-24.90	14108.25	44612.11	
	NOVA SCOTIA	WESTPORT WHARF	44-15.80	66-21.00	13594.88	44558.55	
	NEW BRUNSWICK	CHANCE HARBOUR/REEF PT	45-07.10	66-20.90	14122.57	44592.25	
	NOVA SCOTIA	FREEPORT WHARF	44-16.50	66-20.30	13602.93	44555.99	
	NEW BRUNSWICK	FIVE FATHOM HOLE WHARF	45-11.20	66-15.50	14164.89	44565.56	
	NOVA SCOTIA	WHALE COVE WHARF	44-26.20	66-10.70	13712.28	44518.86	
	NOVA SCOTIA	SANDFORD HARBOUR RANGE	43-55.10	66-09.40	13403.77	44492.62	
	NOVA SCOTIA	COMEAUVILLE WHARF	44-17.50	66-08.00	13627.94	44500.98	
	NOVA SCOTIA	LITTLE RIVER WHARF	44-26.60	66-07.70	13719.27	44504.97	
	NOVA SCOTIA	EAST SANDY COVE WHARF	44-29.20	66-05.20	13747.60	44494.49	
	NEW BRUNSWICK	ST JOHN HARBOUR RANGE	45-16.40	66-04.20	14215.75	44504.82	
	NEW BRUNSWICK	ST JOHN PIER NO 12	45-15.60	66-03.70	14207.89	44501.99	
	NEW BRUNSWICK	ST ANDREWS WHARF	45-04.30	66-03.30	14097.30	44498.36	
	NEW BRUNSWICK	ST JOHN HARB WHISTLE J	45-12.90	66-02.70	14181.50	44496.27	
	NOVA SCOTIA	LITTLE RIVER HARBOUR	43-42.70	66-01.90	13295.98	44452.07	
	NOVA SCOTIA	WEYMOUTH HARBOUR ENTR	44-26.40	66-01.10	13723.56	44473.39	
	NOVA SCOTIA	CAMP COVE WHARF	43-43.30	65-50.50	13321.30	44402.76	
	NOVA SCOTIA	DEEP COVE WHARF	44-39.90	65-50.00	13863.88	44423.21	
	NOVA SCOTIA	ABBOT HARBOUR	43-39.60	65-49.20	13288.96	44395.14	
	NEW BRUNSWICK	BLACK RIVER WHARF	45-15.40	65-48.70	14203.09	44417.08	
	NOVA SCOTIA	DENIS POINT WHARF	43-36.70	65-47.20	13265.58	44384.91	
	NOVA SCOTIA	PUBNICO HARBOUR ENTR	43-35.90	65-47.00	13258.55	44383.63	
	NOVA SCOTIA	LOWER E PUBNICO WHARF	43-36.40	65-46.70	13263.70	44382.57	
	NOVA SCOTIA	DIGBY PIER	44-37.60	65-45.10	13844.65	44397.58	

PORTS

BODY OF WATER	PROV/STATE	NAME	LAT	LON	TD#1	TD#2	CHART
	NOVA SCOTIA	WOODS HARBOUR/BIG LEDGE	43-31.20	65-44.80	13219.44	44371.73	
	NOVA SCOTIA	FALLS POINT WHARF	43-31.80	65-44.50	13225.46	44370.72	
	NOVA SCOTIA	LOWER WOODS HARB WHARF	43-31.30	65-44.30	13221.27	44369.61	
	NOVA SCOTIA	SHAG HARBOUR WHARF	43-29.60	65-42.40	13209.35	44360.53	
	NOVA SCOTIA	BEAR POINT WHARF	43-29.20	65-39.40	13211.32	44347.25	
	NOVA SCOTIA	CLARK'S HARBOUR WHARF	43-26.50	65-38.20	13189.32	44340.84	
	NOVA SCOTIA	NEWELLTON NEW PIER	43-28.40	65-38.10	13206.54	44341.21	
	NOVA SCOTIA	ANNAPOLIS GOVT PIER	44-44.70	65-31.20	13918.03	44324.73	
	NOVA SCOTIA	INGOMAR WHARF	43-33.80	65-21.80	13283.12	44270.09	
	NOVA SCOTIA	GUNNING COVE WHARF	43-40.80	65-20.40	13346.88	44265.23	
	NOVA SCOTIA	NEGRO HARBOUR WHISTLE	43-31.00	65-18.90	13263.56	44256.18	
	NOVA SCOTIA	PORT LORNE PIER	44-57.00	65-16.00	14032.29	44236.93	
	NOVA SCOTIA	LOWER JORDAN BAY WHARF	43-40.90	65-14.40	13356.83	44237.19	
	NOVA SCOTIA	PORT GEORGE PIER	45-00.40	65-09.40	14061.97	44197.06	
	NOVA SCOTIA	LOCKEPORT RANGE WHARF	43-42.10	65-06.70	13378.47	44200.85	
	NOVA SCOTIA	OSBORNE HARBOUR WHARF	43-42.90	65-06.60	13385.48	44200.41	
	NOVA SCOTIA	LITTLE HARBOUR WHARF	43-43.00	65-01.80	13393.06	44177.39	
	NOVA SCOTIA	LITTLE HARBOUR WHISTLE	43-42.40	64-59.90	13390.59	44168.25	
	NEW BRUNSWICK	ALMA PUBLIC WHARF	45-36.00	64-56.70	14351.16	44079.98	
	NOVA SCOTIA	PORT JOLI WHARF	43-50.40	64-51.80	13468.58	44127.94	
	NOVA SCOTIA	HARBORVILLE PIER	45-09.10	64-48.60	14131.45	44066.30	
	NOVA SCOTIA	ADVOCATE HARBOUR	45-19.20	64-47.10	14212.25	44044.56	
	NOVA SCOTIA	BROOKLYN PIER BRKWTR	44-02.80	64-41.50	13583.07	44072.55	
	NOVA SCOTIA	MOOSE HARBOUR FOG SIGNAL	44-01.10	64-40.00	13570.44	44065.44	
	NOVA SCOTIA	HALLS HARBOUR BRKWTR	45-12.10	64-36.80	14151.69	43990.92	
	NOVA SCOTIA	RAGGED POINT WHARF	45-39.60	64-29.30	14355.47	43896.19	
	NOVA SCOTIA	LITTLE HARBOUR BELL	44-09.60	64-28.30	13649.91	44000.13	
	NOVA SCOTIA	MINAS BASIN WHARF	45-12.10	64-22.80	14146.64	43905.10	
	NOVA SCOTIA	BUSH ISLAND WHARF	44-14.00	64-22.40	13689.44	43965.70	
	NOVA SCOTIA	MAHONE HARBOUR	44-26.80	64-22.10	13791.66	43954.16	
	NOVA SCOTIA	DUBLIN SHORE WHARF	44-16.00	64-22.00	13705.65	43962.11	
	NOVA SCOTIA	PARRSBORO GOVT WHARF	45-23.40	64-19.20	14229.79	43863.49	
	NOVA SCOTIA	PARRSBORO HARBOUR ENTR	45-23.20	64-19.10	14228.26	43863.23	
	NOVA SCOTIA	LUNENBURG HARBOUR WHARF	44-22.50	64-18.50	13759.25	43937.88	
	NOVA SCOTIA	SUMMERVILLE WHARF	45-05.60	64-10.40	14093.67	43839.52	
	NOVA SCOTIA	BIG TANCOOK I WHARF	44-28.00	64-10.30	13805.99	43887.16	
	NOVA SCOTIA	HANTSPORT WHARF	45-04.10	64-10.20	14082.38	43840.67	
	NOVA SCOTIA	LITTLE TANCOOK I WHARF	44-28.30	64-08.50	13809.00	43876.75	
	NOVA SCOTIA	NEW HARBOUR/MAHONE BAY	44-28.40	64-05.60	13810.86	43860.33	
	NOVA SCOTIA	EAST IRONBOUND I WHARF	44-26.40	64-05.00	13795.74	43859.09	
	NOVA SCOTIA	NORTHWEST COVE WHARF	44-32.00	64-01.50	13839.72	43833.10	
	NOVA SCOTIA	INDIAN HARBOUR	44-31.30	63-56.80	13835.84	43807.21	
	NOVA SCOTIA	PEGGYS COVE WHARF	44-29.60	63-55.00	13823.64	43799.05	
	NOVA SCOTIA	DOVER WEST WHARF	44-29.70	63-52.40	13825.23	43784.16	

PORTS

BODY OF WATER	PROV/STATE	NAME	LAT	LON	TD#1	TD#2	CHART
	NOVA SCOTIA	EAST DOVER PUBLIC WHARF	44-29.70	63-50.80	13825.74	43775.07	
	NOVA SCOTIA	PROSPECT PUBLIC WHARF	44-28.20	63-47.00	13815.87	43755.41	
	NOVA SCOTIA	GOVT WHARF	44-28.10	63-42.90	13816.48	43732.26	
	NOVA SCOTIA	PENNANT HARBOUR ENTRANCE	44-28.30	63-38.10	13819.47	43704.69	
	NOVA SCOTIA	BEDFORD INSTITUTE WHARF	44-40.90	63-36.80	13910.43	43678.45	
	NOVA SCOTIA	BULL POINT/SAMBRO HARB	44-28.50	63-35.80	13821.62	43691.30	
	NOVA SCOTIA	SAMBRO HARBOUR WHISTLE	44-24.50	63-33.60	13793.62	43684.44	
	NOVA SCOTIA	KETCH HARBOUR BUOY	44-28.30	63-32.30	13821.25	43671.64	
	NOVA SCOTIA	MUSQUODOBOIT HARBOUR	44-41.70	63-04.70	13919.00	43489.12	
	NOVA SCOTIA	TONEY RIVER WHARF	45-46.50	62-53.50	14323.51	43253.84	
	NOVA SCOTIA	SHIP HARBOUR/WOLF POINT	44-45.00	62-45.40	13941.51	43368.85	
	NOVA SCOTIA	CARIBOU HARBOUR MID RANGE	45-44.10	62-42.20	14301.66	43188.97	
	NOVA SCOTIA	CARIBOU HARBOUR RANGE	45-44.40	62-41.30	14302.76	43182.21	
	NOVA SCOTIA	CARIBOU HARBOUR BELL	45-45.10	62-39.90	14305.79	43170.91	
	NOVA SCOTIA	POPES HARBOUR	44-47.70	62-39.20	13958.70	43326.23	
	NOVA SCOTIA	SHEET HARBOUR PASSAGE	44-51.50	62-27.00	13981.88	43244.98	
	NOVA SCOTIA	ARISAIG HARBOUR RANGE	45-45.60	62-10.20	14289.03	42979.95	
	NOVA SCOTIA	BALLANTYNES COVE WHARF	45-51.50	61-55.10	14310.56	42862.86	
	NOVA SCOTIA	CRIBBEAN HEAD WHARF	45-45.30	61-53.80	14277.43	42877.71	
	NOVA SCOTIA	AMHERST HARB BUOY YK22	47-22.60	61-51.30	14712.45	42410.96	
	NOVA SCOTIA	BAYFIELD WHARF	45-38.70	61-45.20	14238.03	42848.04	
	NOVA SCOTIA	MOUTON HARBOUR RANGE	45-05.50	61-43.90	14057.86	42950.00	
	NOVA SCOTIA	MOUTON HARBOUR RANGE	45-05.70	61-43.60	14058.91	42947.61	
	NOVA SCOTIA	MOUTON HARBOUR	45-05.70	61-43.50	14058.89	42947.02	
	NOVA SCOTIA	FISHERMANS HARBOUR	45-06.70	61-40.70	14063.86	42927.27	
	NOVA SCOTIA	ISAAC HARBOUR	45-10.00	61-39.30	14081.68	42908.65	
	NOVA SCOTIA	ISAAC'S HARBOUR WHISTLE	45-02.20	61-32.70	14037.71	42893.66	
	NOVA SCOTIA	CODDLE HARBOUR	45-09.40	61-31.10	14076.52	42861.66	
	NOVA SCOTIA	NEW HARBOUR COVE BRKWTR	45-10.20	61-27.10	14079.92	42835.30	
	NOVA SCOTIA	PEEBLES POINT WHARF	45-35.20	61-21.30	14208.49	42713.94	
	NOVA SCOTIA	PEEBLES POINT WHARF	45-35.10	61-21.30	14207.98	42714.31	
	NOVA SCOTIA	CHARLOS HARBOUR RANGE	45-14.60	61-20.10	14101.54	42779.19	
	NOVA SCOTIA	COLE HARBOUR ENTR RANGE	45-15.60	61-17.20	14106.01	42758.57	
	NOVA SCOTIA	COLE HARBOUR SE SIDE	45-15.60	61-16.20	14105.74	42752.62	
	NOVA SCOTIA	LITTLE DOVER HARBOUR	45-16.70	61-01.20	14107.43	42660.00	
	NOVA SCOTIA	CANSO HARBOUR WHISTLE	45-22.10	60-59.90	14134.31	42633.10	
ST LAWRENCE GULF	PRINCE EDWARD I	SEAL POINT WHARF	46-44.40	64-22.80	14752.50	43645.93	
ST LAWRENCE GULF	PRINCE EDWARD I	FISHING COVE BRKWTR	46-24.10	64-08.10	14619.72	43623.64	
ST LAWRENCE GULF	PRINCE EDWARD I	FISHING COVE W BRKWTR	46-24.40	64-08.10	14621.44	43622.54	
ST LAWRENCE GULF	PRINCE EDWARD I	SKINNERS POND BRKWTR	46-58.00	64-07.60	14794.48	43476.34	
ST LAWRENCE GULF	PRINCE EDWARD I	NORTHPORT RANGE WHARF	46-47.70	64-03.60	14739.03	43495.97	
ST LAWRENCE GULF	PRINCE EDWARD I	CASCUMPEQUE ENTRANCE	46-48.00	64-02.20	14738.36	43484.77	
ST LAWRENCE GULF	PRINCE EDWARD I	TIGNISH HARBOUR BRKWTR	46-57.00	63-59.70	14777.43	43425.39	
ST LAWRENCE GULF	PRINCE EDWARD I	NORTH POINT BRKWTR	47-01.80	63-59.40	14798.74	43399.91	

PORTS

BODY OF WATER	PROV/STATE	NAME	LAT	LON	TD#1	TD#2	CHART
ST LAWRENCE GULF	PRINCE EDWARD I	PORT HILL WHARF	46-35.60	63-52.10	14660.49	43467.59	
ST LAWRENCE GULF	PRINCE EDWARD I	SUMMERSIDE HARBOUR ENTR	46-49.10	63-49.10	14724.09	43387.91	
ST LAWRENCE GULF	PRINCE EDWARD I	DETACHED BREAKWATER	46-14.70	63-42.00	14532.47	43478.54	
ST LAWRENCE GULF	PRINCE EDWARD I	PALMERS WHARF	46-12.80	63-29.40	14507.20	43400.03	
ST LAWRENCE GULF	PRINCE EDWARD I	NORTH RUSTICO HARBOUR	46-27.30	63-17.60	14572.31	43264.26	
ST LAWRENCE GULF	PRINCE EDWARD I	N RUSTICO INNER BRKWTR	46-27.20	63-17.50	14571.68	43263.98	
ST LAWRENCE GULF	PRINCE EDWARD I	NORTHERN BREAKWATER	46-27.40	63-17.30	14572.48	43261.81	
ST LAWRENCE GULF	PRINCE EDWARD I	NINE MILE CREEK WHARF	46-08.90	63-13.10	14467.89	43304.71	
ST LAWRENCE GULF	PRINCE EDWARD I	COVEHEAD HARBOUR	46-25.80	63-08.70	14554.09	43209.97	
ST LAWRENCE GULF	PRINCE EDWARD I	HAZZARD POINT ENTR	46-11.70	63-04.50	14474.59	43236.97	
ST LAWRENCE GULF	PRINCE EDWARD I	TRACADIE HARBOUR ENTR	46-24.60	63-02.50	14540.87	43172.98	
ST LAWRENCE GULF	PRINCE EDWARD I	GRAND TRACADIE WHARF	46-24.20	63-01.70	14537.91	43169.22	
ST LAWRENCE GULF	PRINCE EDWARD I	BELLE RIVER BRKWTR	45-58.40	62-51.00	14388.59	43196.22	
ST LAWRENCE GULF	PRINCE EDWARD I	SAVAGE HARBOUR	46-26.00	62-50.00	14534.24	43083.13	
ST LAWRENCE GULF	PRINCE EDWARD I	SAVAGE HARBOUR BELL	46-26.80	62-49.50	14537.71	43076.41	
ST LAWRENCE GULF	PRINCE EDWARD I	WOOD ISLAND HARBOUR RANGE	45-57.00	62-45.10	14375.87	43162.67	
ST LAWRENCE GULF	PRINCE EDWARD I	ST PETERS HARBOUR, BRKWTR	46-26.50	62-44.90	14531.26	43046.85	
ST LAWRENCE GULF	PRINCE EDWARD I	ST PETERS HARBOUR RANGE	46-26.30	62-44.50	14529.83	43045.02	
ST LAWRENCE GULF	PRINCE EDWARD I	LITTLE SANDS BRKWTR	45-57.70	62-38.70	14374.51	43118.54	
ST LAWRENCE GULF	PRINCE EDWARD I	LOWER MONTAGUE WHARF	46-10.20	62-33.80	14437.09	43039.54	
ST LAWRENCE GULF	PRINCE EDWARD I	BEACH POINT BRKWTR	46-01.00	62-29.30	14384.70	43045.36	
ST LAWRENCE GULF	PRINCE EDWARD I	MURRAY HARBOUR RANGE	46-01.30	62-28.70	14385.81	43040.35	
ST LAWRENCE GULF	PRINCE EDWARD I	MURRAY HARBOUR BELL "NM"	46-02.10	62-27.20	14388.83	43027.60	
ST LAWRENCE GULF	PRINCE EDWARD I	GRAHAM POND S BRKWTR	46-05.80	62-27.20	14408.31	43013.48	
ST LAWRENCE GULF	PRINCE EDWARD I	GRAHAM POND BREAKWATER	46-05.80	62-27.10	14408.23	43012.83	
ST LAWRENCE GULF	PRINCE EDWARD I	NAUFRAGE WEST BRKWTR	46-28.20	62-25.10	14518.97	42907.66	
ST LAWRENCE GULF	PRINCE EDWARD I	NAUFRAGE EAST BRKWTR	46-28.10	62-25.00	14518.39	42907.43	
ST LAWRENCE GULF	PRINCE EDWARD I	LAUNCHING POND BOAT HARB	46-13.20	62-24.60	14444.21	42967.31	
ST LAWRENCE GULF	PRINCE EDWARD I	SOURIS HARBOUR WHISTLE "NA"	46-19.80	62-15.50	14468.84	42880.44	
ST LAWRENCE GULF	PRINCE EDWARD I	KNIGHT POINT BRKWTR	46-20.80	62-15.30	14473.54	42874.89	
ST LAWRENCE GULF	PRINCE EDWARD I	BASIN HEAD HARBOUR BRKWTR	46-22.60	62-06.60	14474.20	42810.24	
ST LAWRENCE GULF	PRINCE EDWARD I	WEST BREAKWATER	46-28.10	62-04.40	14498.21	42771.69	
ST LAWRENCE GULF	PRINCE EDWARD I	NORTH LAKE HARBOUR RANGE	46-28.10	62-04.10	14497.92	42769.73	
ST LAWRENCE GULF	QUEBEC	HARRINGTON HARBOUR ENTR	50-29.60	59-29.10	15013.7	40232.1	
ST LAWRENCE GULF	QUEBEC	L'ANSE AU CLAIR WHARF	51-25.60	57-03.90	14993.5	38917.6	
ST LAWRENCE RIVER	NEW BRUNSWICK	CAMPBELLTON PIER	48-00.70	66-40.10	15238.18	31632.78	
ST LAWRENCE RIVER	NEW BRUNSWICK	CAMPBELLTON WHARF	48-00.80	66-39.90	15238.07	31631.00	
ST LAWRENCE RIVER	QUEBEC	ST ZOTIQUE ANCH "DJ"	45-12.60	74-16.70	14392.05	60135.00	1412
ST LAWRENCE RIVER	QUEBEC	ST ZOTIQUE ANCH "DD"	45-13.20	74-15.50	14379.67	60135.17	1412
ST LAWRENCE RIVER	QUEBEC	ST ZOTIQUE ANCH "DH"	45-14.00	74-14.30	14365.84	60134.87	1412
ST LAWRENCE RIVER	QUEBEC	ST ZOTIQUE ANCH "DA"	45-13.80	74-13.60	14362.59	60136.27	1412
ST LAWRENCE RIVER	QUEBEC	ST ZOTIQUE ANCH "DC"	45-14.20	74-13.60	14359.71	60135.32	1412
ST LAWRENCE RIVER	QUEBEC	BEAUHARNOIS ANCH "CN"	45-13.60	74-08.30	14328.29	60143.59	1411
ST LAWRENCE RIVER	QUEBEC	BEAUHARNOIS ANCH "CM"	45-13.30	74-07.20	14323.00	60145.66	1411

PORTS

BODY OF WATER	PROV/STATE	NAME	LAT	LON	TD#1	TD#2	CHART
ST LAWRENCE RIVER	QUEBEC	BEAUHARNOIS ANCH "CK"	45-13.30	74-01.70	14285.57	60152.41	1411
ST LAWRENCE RIVER	QUEBEC	BEAUHARNOIS ANCH "CJ"	45-13.70	74-00.30	14273.15	60153.19	1411
ST LAWRENCE RIVER	QUEBEC	BEAUHARNOIS ANCH "CE"	45-15.60	73-57.30	14239.13	60152.48	1411
ST LAWRENCE RIVER	QUEBEC	BEAUHARNOIS ANCH "CD"	45-16.00	73-57.00	14234.25	60151.94	1411
ST LAWRENCE RIVER	QUEBEC	BEAUHARNOIS ANCH "CA"	45-17.00	73-56.20	14221.70	60150.65	1411
ST LAWRENCE RIVER	QUEBEC	BEAUHARNOIS ANCH "B"	45-20.00	73-55.00	14192.35	60145.34	1410
ST LAWRENCE RIVER	QUEBEC	BEAUHARNOIS ANCH "A"	45-20.40	73-54.30	14184.75	60145.29	1410
ST LAWRENCE RIVER	QUEBEC	LAKE ST LOUIS W DYKE	45-24.50	73-43.30	14080.58	60149.04	1409
ST LAWRENCE RIVER	QUEBEC	TURNING BASIN NO 2	45-24.00	73-33.00	14012.49	60161.38	1410
ST LAWRENCE RIVER	QUEBEC	MONTREAL HARB "B"	45-34.40	73-30.40	13923.68	60142.19	
ST LAWRENCE RIVER	QUEBEC	MONTREAL HARB "A"	45-34.60	73-30.40	13922.33	60141.77	
ST LAWRENCE RIVER	QUEBEC	TURNING BASIN NO 1	45-27.00	73-30.00	13971.04	60158.26	
ST LAWRENCE RIVER	QUEBEC	VERCHERES VILLAGE RANGE	45-46.80	73-12.40	13716.22	60135.74	
ST LAWRENCE RIVER	QUEBEC	LAKE ST PETER PIER	46-15.50	72-39.10	13305.02	60112.52	
ST LAWRENCE RIVER	QUEBEC	PORT ST FRANCOIS WHARF	46-16.40	72-37.20	13286.38	60112.69	
ST LAWRENCE RIVER	QUEBEC	CAP DE LA MADELEINE WHARF	46-22.00	72-29.80	13202.05	60109.21	
ST LAWRENCE RIVER	QUEBEC	BATISCAN WHARF	46-30.00	72-14.80	13051.60	60108.65	
ST LAWRENCE RIVER	QUEBEC	LES BECQUETS WHARF	46-30.50	72-12.40	13031.84	60110.02	
ST LAWRENCE RIVER	QUEBEC	DESCHAILLONS WHARF	46-33.70	72-06.40	12972.15	60109.72	
ST LAWRENCE RIVER	QUEBEC	BATTURE SIMON BAY D4	46-35.50	72-00.50	12920.64	60111.90	
ST LAWRENCE RIVER	QUEBEC	PORTNEUF WHARF	46-40.90	71-52.60	12836.86	60109.22	
ST LAWRENCE RIVER	QUEBEC	VAUQUELIN CLUB NAUTIQUE	46-41.80	71-34.40	12701.2	60123.7	
ST LAWRENCE RIVER	QUEBEC	VAUQUELIN CLUB WHARF	46-42.00	71-34.00	12697.3	60123.6	
ST LAWRENCE RIVER	QUEBEC	QUEBEC YACHT CLUB	46-47.00	71-14.30	12530.6	60131.1	
ST LAWRENCE RIVER	QUEBEC	W MARINA @ BRKWTR	46-47.00	71-14.10	12529.2	60131.2	
ST LAWRENCE RIVER	QUEBEC	E MARINA @ BRKWTR	46-47.00	71-14.10	12529.2	60131.2	
ST LAWRENCE RIVER	QUEBEC	QUEENS WHARF, Quebec	46-48.60	71-12.20	12508.2	60130.0	
ST LAWRENCE RIVER	QUEBEC	LEVIS MARINA, Quebec	46-47.50	71-12.00	12511.6	60132.0	
ST LAWRENCE RIVER	QUEBEC	BATTURE AUX LOUPS MAR	48-25.50	70-55.70	12145.1	59973.6	
ST LAWRENCE RIVER	QUEBEC	STE-ANNE-D'BEAUPRE WHARF	47-01.20	70-55.70	12336.4	60121.7	
ST LAWRENCE RIVER	QUEBEC	STE-MICHEL-D'BELLECHASSE	46-52.50	70-55.00	12365.4	60136.7	
ST LAWRENCE RIVER	QUEBEC	STE JEAN D'ORLEANS WHARF	46-54.90	70-53.80	12346.9	60133.6	
ST LAWRENCE RIVER	QUEBEC	MONTMAGNY HEAD WHARF	46-59.20	70-33.20	14592.11	32495.79	
ST LAWRENCE RIVER	QUEBEC	ILE AUX COUDRES WHARF	47-25.20	70-23.60	12033.8	60106.7	
ST LAWRENCE RIVER	QUEBEC	GOOSE CAPE WHARF	47-26.90	70-21.90	12018.2	60105.3	
ST LAWRENCE RIVER	QUEBEC	ST JEAN PORT JOLI WHARF	47-12.90	70-16.50	14729.14	32474.98	
ST LAWRENCE RIVER	QUEBEC	ST ROCHE ENTRANCE H72	47-22.80	70-14.60	14780.61	32453.59	
ST LAWRENCE RIVER	QUEBEC	CAP A L'AIGLE MARINA	47-39.80	70-05.80	11886.4	60096.5	
ST LAWRENCE RIVER	QUEBEC	ILE AUX LIEVRES ENTR	47-47.20	69-47.20	14961.49	32363.86	
ST LAWRENCE RIVER	QUEBEC	ANSE DU PORTAGE WHARF	48-07.60	69-43.90	11735.3	60068.5	
ST LAWRENCE RIVER	QUEBEC	ANSE A L'EAU WHARF	48-08.30	69-43.70	11734.3	60067.5	
ST LAWRENCE RIVER	QUEBEC	TADOUSSAC WHARF	48-08.30	69-42.90	11729.7	60068.2	
ST LAWRENCE RIVER	QUEBEC	RED ISLET ENTRANCE	48-04.20	69-33.30	11673.3	60081.8	
ST LAWRENCE RIVER	QUEBEC	ILE VERTE WHARF	47-60.00	69-27.80	15049.53	32288.37	

PORTS

BODY OF WATER	PROV/STATE	NAME	LAT	LON	TD#1	TD#2	CHART
ST LAWRENCE RIVER	QUEBEC	CACAUNA WHARF	47-60.00	69-26.00	15054.92	32285.84	
ST LAWRENCE RIVER	QUEBEC	LES ESCOUMINS WHARF	48-20.80	69-23.40	11629.1	60063.1	
ST LAWRENCE RIVER	QUEBEC	PORTNEUF SANDS K-48	48-33.00	69-07.30	11562.5	60056.0	
ST LAWRENCE RIVER	QUEBEC	BAIE VERTE BRKWTR	48-44.30	69-02.90	11557.4	60041.7	
ST LAWRENCE RIVER	QUEBEC	RIMOUSKI HARB WHARF	48-29.00	68-31.10	15201.06	32008.84	
ST LAWRENCE RIVER	QUEBEC	RIMOUSKI HARBOUR RANGE	48-28.10	68-31.10	15200.96	32013.90	
ST LAWRENCE RIVER	QUEBEC	BAIE COMEAU WHARF	49-14.10	68-07.70	15228.9	43833.0	
ST LAWRENCE RIVER	QUEBEC	GODBOUT WHARF	49-19.30	67-35.50	15251.5	43667.6	
ST LAWRENCE RIVER	QUEBEC	MATANE W BREAKWATER	48-50.90	67-34.70	15255.49	31667.77	
ST LAWRENCE RIVER	QUEBEC	MATANE E BREAKWATER	48-50.80	67-34.60	15255.55	31667.86	
ST LAWRENCE RIVER	QUEBEC	RAILWAY WHARF	48-50.60	67-34.50	15255.62	31668.49	
ST LAWRENCE RIVER	QUEBEC	LE GROS MECHINS WHARF	49-00.40	66-58.60	15262.71	31442.07	
ST LAWRENCE RIVER	QUEBEC	STE ANNE DES MONTS WHARF	49-08.10	66-29.20	15258.66	31246.11	
ST LAWRENCE RIVER	QUEBEC	NOIRE ORE TERMINAL	50-09.90	66-28.90	15262.7	42935.6	
ST LAWRENCE RIVER	QUEBEC	IMPERIAL OIL WHARF	50-11.80	66-22.90	15262.7	42890.9	
ST LAWRENCE RIVER	QUEBEC	IRON ORE CO WHARF	50-11.40	66-22.30	15262.6	42891.3	
ST LAWRENCE RIVER	QUEBEC	MIGUASHA WHARF	48-06.00	66-21.00	15222.77	31480.86	
ST LAWRENCE RIVER	QUEBEC	CARLETON WHARF	48-06.00	66-07.90	15207.25	31390.32	
ST LAWRENCE RIVER	QUEBEC	BLACK CAPE GOVT PIER	48-08.20	65-50.30	15187.54	31256.84	
ST LAWRENCE RIVER	QUEBEC	PASPEBIAC BREAKWATER	48-01.10	65-15.60	15124.79	31022.79	
ST LAWRENCE RIVER	QUEBEC	PASPEBIAC WEST WHARF	48-01.10	65-15.50	15124.64	31022.02	
ST LAWRENCE RIVER	QUEBEC	ST GODEFROI WHARF	48-04.40	65-07.00	15118.68	30947.76	
ST LAWRENCE RIVER	QUEBEC	RUISSEAU CHAPADOS WHARF	48-11.50	64-51.70	15110.86	30811.68	
ST LAWRENCE RIVER	QUEBEC	NEWPORT WHARF	48-17.10	64-43.30	15110.21	30732.99	
ST LAWRENCE RIVER	QUEBEC	MARINA DE GASPE BRKWTR	48-49.70	64-28.50	15146.75	30534.75	
ST LAWRENCE RIVER	QUEBEC	MARINA DE GASPE ENTR	48-49.70	64-28.50	15146.75	30534.75	
ST LAWRENCE RIVER	QUEBEC	GOVERNMENT WHARF	48-49.50	64-26.30	15143.93	30519.55	
ST LAWRENCE RIVER	QUEBEC	FOX RIVER WHARF	48-59.90	64-22.90	15154.64	30466.67	
ST LAWRENCE RIVER	QUEBEC	PERCE BREAKWATER	48-31.20	64-12.70	15096.38	30466.87	
ST LAWRENCE RIVER	QUEBEC	MAL BAIE WHARF	48-37.20	64-12.00	15106.60	30447.15	
ST LAWRENCE RIVER	QUEBEC	MINGAN HARB, E ENTR	50-17.40	64-01.30	15209.1	42065.3	
ST LAWRENCE RIVER	QUEBEC	MINGAN HARB, W ENTR	50-17.40	64-00.70	15208.7	42061.7	
ST LAWRENCE RIVER	QUEBEC	KEGASHKA WHARF	50-11.10	61-15.90	15072.7	41057.2	
ST LAWRENCE RIVER	QUEBEC	GETHSEMANI HARBOUR	50-12.50	60-41.30	15045.8	40821.1	

CHAPTER 9
REACHING ROCKS

Coordinates for rocks are included to provide boaters with a comprehensive listing of the rocky bottom structures that are available to them. This is not to be taken as an exhaustive list of all the rocks in a given area; rather, it should provide you with fine examples of substantial habitats that offer excellent fishing opportunities.

Fishing the rocky areas is probably best accomplished by either trolling or drifting. Susie's favorite method is drifting while dangling fresh bait on a three-foot monofilament leader, using a chunk of lead just large enough to keep the line about two feet from the bottom.

When trolling, we like to use leaded jigs sweetened with a piece of cut bait. We also use surgical tubing (blue fish rigs), Chartreuse Bombers, spoons, and — before the day is out — the tackle box. But then, we're south Florida fishermen. Locals know best.

Susie has found the secret to catching fish: keep the bait in the water and concentrate on what you are doing. I tend to fall asleep.

There's something you should know about anchoring in rocky areas: to date we have turned three "Danforth" anchors inside out, and we once broke our teak anchor pulpit completely off trying to get free to go home. While drifting may seem impractical, it sure is a lot cheaper than anchoring.

As usual, coordinates in this chapter are listed by body of water or province, depth, description, latitude, longitude, time delay one, and time delay two. Depths listed as "00," have yet to be confirmed, and if you plan to dive at any of the coordinates, be sure to use the depth-finding equipment on your boat or charter boat to determine water depth prior to making the actual dive. Also, the time delay (TD) numbers are the authority in this case and should be used in lieu of the latitude and longitude listings, as described in the introduction to Chapter 7.

We strongly endorse having up-to-date charts of the area aboard, which should be consulted along with tide tables to determine the proper course of action prior to venturing into unfamiliar waters.

DAFFYNITION
COVE: (1) A quiet indentation within the landmass where sailors and powerboat drivers attempt to anchor their boats for the night so that they can use the phrase "trust me." (2) A place where boats gather to tell lies about their adventures. (3) A haven. (4) A wonderful place to camp on the boat while playing soft music, cooking dinner, relaxing, and making plans for the next day's journey while your neighbor shows off his bigger boat.

HELPFUL HINT
We know that fish must eat something. We have tried every pretty-looking lure, fresh-cut bait, and live bait we could muster and have had only marginal luck with all of them. This year we are going to follow Madison Avenue's approach to baiting; we are going to troll with naked lures.

ROCKS

BODY OF WATER	PROV/STATE	NAME	LAT	LON	TD#1	TD#2	DEPTH
GEORGIAN BAY	ONTARIO	WEST SISTER ROCK	46-18.22	83-54.93	30884.67	47981.51	00
GEORGIAN BAY	ONTARIO	MEREDITH ROCK	45-58.95	82-14.42	30360.58	48323.82	00
GEORGIAN BAY	ONTARIO	ROBERTSON ROCK LIGHT J72	46-03.45	82-13.47	30349.32	48291.98	00
GEORGIAN BAY	ONTARIO	DUNCAN CITY ROCK EE5	46-00.23	81-43.45	30179.53	48361.45	00
GEORGIAN BAY	ONTARIO	CAROLINE ROCKS EE6	46-00.15	81-43.23	30178.32	48362.35	00
GEORGIAN BAY	ONTARIO	CAMPBELL ROCK J12	45-49.62	81-33.23	30128.53	48452.05	00
GEORGIAN BAY	ONTARIO	JACKMAN ROCK NO E1	45-57.98	81-29.63	30101.01	48397.06	00
GEORGIAN BAY	ONTARIO	FLAT ROCK	45-58.98	81-25.58	30076.78	48395.47	00
GEORGIAN BAY	ONTARIO	KEYSTONE ROCK LIGHT H21	45-45.23	80-39.00	29808.18	48547.82	00
GEORGIAN BAY	ONTARIO	TIZARD ROCK LIGHT AL	45-34.08	80-33.30	29774.41	48629.77	00
GEORGIAN BAY	ONTARIO	RED ROCK	45-21.60	80-24.48	29720.08	48722.72	00
GEORGIAN BAY	ONTARIO	FARR ROCK LIGHT NO P7	45-21.42	80-22.77	29709.39	48725.40	00
GEORGIAN BAY	ONTARIO	ARIEL ROCK LIGHT NO P12	45-21.28	80-20.75	29696.78	48728.06	00
GEORGIAN BAY	ONTARIO	ARTHUR ORR ROCK NO P13	45-21.10	80-20.33	29694.15	48729.63	00
GEORGIAN BAY	ONTARIO	HALL ROCK SHOAL NO P16	45-20.47	80-19.56	29689.28	48734.52	00
GEORGIAN BAY	ONTARIO	TELEGRAPH ROCK NO P22	45-20.10	80-18.88	29684.99	48737.58	00
GEORGIAN BAY	ONTARIO	McCLELLAND ROCK P28	45-19.78	80-15.48	29663.72	48742.53	00
GEORGIAN BAY	ONTARIO	CARLING ROCK NO P30	45-20.08	80-14.17	29655.60	48741.58	00
GEORGIAN BAY	ONTARIO	LOCKERBIE ROCK NO TN11	44-32.23	80-13.81	29654.15	49063.11	00
GEORGIAN BAY	ONTARIO	LOTTIE WOLF ROCK NO M2	44-55.75	80-10.41	29628.35	48907.37	00
GEORGIAN BAY	ONTARIO	McKERREL ROCK NO P37	45-20.59	80-03.17	29587.54	48746.95	00
GEORGIAN BAY	ONTARIO	RED ROCK GO HOME BAY	44-58.21	79-57.66	29544.84	48898.88	00
GEORGIAN BAY	ONTARIO	TURNING ROCK HONEY HARBOUR	44-50.93	79-49.53	29488.84	48951.33	00
GEORGIAN BAY	ONTARIO	TURNING ROCK WAUBAUSHENE	44-46.33	79-44.40	29452.82	48983.93	00
GEORGIAN BAY	ONTARIO	MARY ROCKS	44-46.20	79-43.40	29446.08	48985.25	00
LABRADOR SEA	NEWFOUNDLAND	MAQUELON ROCKS BUOY	47-04.00	56-13.00	Suggest	GPS	00
LABRADOR SEA	NEWFOUNDLAND	BAD ROCK	50-47.00	56-10.00	Suggest	GPS	00
LABRADOR SEA	NEWFOUNDLAND	TINKER ROCK	47-37.00	56-03.00	Suggest	GPS	00
LABRADOR SEA	NEWFOUNDLAND	ROCKY POINT, BRETON	47-29.00	55-48.00	Suggest	GPS	00
LABRADOR SEA	NEWFOUNDLAND	GULL ROCK	49-41.00	55-41.00	Suggest	GPS	00
LABRADOR SEA	NEWFOUNDLAND	HARBOUR ROCK	51-22.00	55-34.00	Suggest	GPS	00
LABRADOR SEA	NEWFOUNDLAND	STAG ROCK	47-02.00	55-11.00	Suggest	GPS	00
LABRADOR SEA	NEWFOUNDLAND	DUCK ROCK	47-09.00	55-05.00	Suggest	GPS	00
LABRADOR SEA	NEWFOUNDLAND	STANLEY ROCKS BELL	47-15.00	54-59.00	Suggest	GPS	00
LABRADOR SEA	NEWFOUNDLAND	STEERING ROCK	47-21.00	54-54.00	Suggest	GPS	00
LABRADOR SEA	NEWFOUNDLAND	ROCKY BAY	49-26.90	54-13.80	Suggest	GPS	00
LABRADOR SEA	NEWFOUNDLAND	TINKER ROCK	49-35.00	54-11.00	Suggest	GPS	00
LABRADOR SEA	NEWFOUNDLAND	JOE BATTS ARM ROCKS	49-44.00	54-10.00	Suggest	GPS	00
LABRADOR SEA	NEWFOUNDLAND	IRONSKULL ROCK	47-27.00	54-05.00	Suggest	GPS	00
LABRADOR SEA	NEWFOUNDLAND	SHAG ROCKS	47-25.00	53-55.00	Suggest	GPS	00
LABRADOR SEA	NEWFOUNDLAND	CANDLE COVE ROCKS	49-06.00	53-36.00	Suggest	GPS	00
LABRADOR SEA	NEWFOUNDLAND	BENBURRY ROCK BUOY "JV4"	49-07.00	53-36.00	Suggest	GPS	00
LABRADOR SEA	NEWFOUNDLAND	SEINE ROCK	49-04.00	53-34.30	Suggest	GPS	00
LABRADOR SEA	NEWFOUNDLAND	POUND ROCKS	49-04.00	53-34.00	Suggest	GPS	00

ROCKS

BODY OF WATER	PROV/STATE	NAME	LAT	LON	TD#1	TD#2	DEPTH
LABRADOR SEA	NEWFOUNDLAND	KENNYS ROCKS	49-13.00	53-28.00	Suggest	GPS	00
LABRADOR SEA	NEWFOUNDLAND	CHARGE ROCK WHISTLE "JX"	49-15.00	53-22.00	Suggest	GPS	00
LABRADOR SEA	NEWFOUNDLAND	BAIT ROCKS, COLEYS PT	47-35.00	53-15.00	Suggest	GPS	00
LABRADOR SEA	NEWFOUNDLAND	CHAIN ROCKS	47-34.00	52-41.00	Suggest	GPS	00
LABRADOR SEA	NEWFOUNDLAND	VIRGIN ROCKS WHISTLE	46-29.00	50-46.00	Suggest	GPS	00
LAKE ERIE		FLAT ROCK	41-40.45	83-04.11	43657.00	56815.20	00
LAKE HURON		INKSTER ROCK LIGHT JS5	45-33.12	82-01.10	30315.17	48535.74	00
LAKE SUPERIOR		JARVIS ROCK	48-06.17	89-17.58	31879.20	45971.69	00
LAKE SUPERIOR		BARWIS ROCK LIGHT JC	48-50.22	87-36.95	31429.70	46127.16	00
ST LAWRENCE GULF	MAGDALEN ISLANDS	BIRD ROCKS	47-50.30	61-08.70	14758.56	41967.29	00
	NEW BRUNSWICK	BULL ROCK WHISTLE "XA1"	44-30.20	66-56.60	13701.29	44723.88	00
	NEW BRUNSWICK	TWO HOUR ROCK	45-01.80	66-56.20	14049.96	44758.46	00
	NEW BRUNSWICK	GANNET ROCK/GRAND MANAN	44-30.60	66-46.90	13718.03	44684.20	00
	NEW BRUNSWICK	NET ROCKS LEDGES "XV6"	44-45.30	66-44.50	13879.38	44688.91	00
	NEW BRUNSWICK	HALF TIDE ROCK/CHENEY	44-39.30	66-43.70	13815.46	44679.38	00
	NEW BRUNSWICK	EDMUNDS ROCK	44-40.40	66-43.30	13827.71	44678.72	00
	NEW BRUNSWICK	GULL ROCK BELL BUOY	44-12.00	66-23.20	13553.06	44565.22	00
	NEW BRUNSWICK	SPLIT ROCK BELL BUOY	45-07.10	66-14.60	14123.67	44559.32	00
	NOVA SCOTIA	CAT ROCK BELL "Y3"	43-47.00	66-09.50	13324.21	44487.44	00
	NOVA SCOTIA	BLONDE ROCK WHISTLE "N4"	43-18.60	66-00.10	13073.12	44429.19	00
	NOVA SCOTIA	PIQUET ROCK	43-29.40	65-43.00	13206.41	44363.05	00
	NOVA SCOTIA	CROW NECK ISLAND/GATE ROCK	43-28.70	65-27.20	13229.05	44293.05	00
	NOVA SCOTIA	WHALEBACK ROCK	43-29.60	65-27.00	13237.32	44292.44	00
	NOVA SCOTIA	BRAZIL ROCK WHISTLE	43-21.00	65-26.80	13162.51	44288.75	00
	NOVA SCOTIA	BULL ROCK BELL BUOY	43-37.50	65-08.30	13336.64	44208.09	00
	NOVA SCOTIA	GULL ROCK ENTRANCE	43-39.30	65-06.00	13355.48	44197.36	00
	NOVA SCOTIA	BLACK ROCK	45-10.20	64-45.80	14139.54	44048.10	00
	NOVA SCOTIA	WHITE POINT ROCK BELL	43-55.60	64-43.10	13521.83	44083.12	00
	NOVA SCOTIA	BELL ROCK BELL	44-29.00	63-31.10	13826.60	43663.76	00
	NOVA SCOTIA	RAT ROCK	44-37.60	63-16.20	13889.97	43563.91	00
	NOVA SCOTIA	JEDDORE ROCK	44-39.80	63-00.70	13906.69	43469.41	00
	NOVA SCOTIA	GULL ROCK BELL	45-46.50	62-40.50	14314.17	43170.09	00
	NOVA SCOTIA	SMITH ROCK BELL	44-53.80	62-01.50	13993.78	43088.06	00
	NOVA SCOTIA	CAHIL ROCK RANGE	45-34.20	61-21.30	14203.40	42717.62	00
	NOVA SCOTIA	ROCK ISLAND	45-17.00	61-01.80	14109.11	42662.48	00
	NOVA SCOTIA	DOVER BAY/GULF ROCK	45-16.80	61-01.00	14107.88	42658.46	00
	NOVA SCOTIA	MAN OF WAR ROCK BELL	45-19.70	60-57.00	14121.42	42624.57	00
ST LAWRENCE GULF	PRINCE EDWARD I	FITZROY ROCK BELL	46-07.10	63-06.70	14451.46	43268.60	00
ST LAWRENCE GULF	PRINCE EDWARD I	INDIAN ROCKS WHISTLE	45-55.00	62-49.20	14368.05	43196.38	00
ST LAWRENCE GULF	QUEBEC	CAIRNTORR ROCK "C64"	50-07.30	60-18.60	15019.2	40709.9	00
ST LAWRENCE GULF	QUEBEC	CORMORANT ROCKS	50-07.30	60-03.70	15007.0	40613.5	00
ST LAWRENCE RIVER	QUEBEC	WYE ROCK BUOY H121	46-60.00	70-38.00	14578.03	32494.90	00
ST LAWRENCE RIVER	QUEBEC	HOSPITAL ROCK RANGE	47-08.00	70-28.00	14659.85	32484.16	00
ST LAWRENCE RIVER	QUEBEC	DEMERS ROCK BUOY H58	47-51.40	69-39.00	14998.57	32339.45	00

ROCKS

BODY OF WATER	PROV/STATE	NAME	LAT	LON	TD#1	TD#2	DEPTH
ST LAWRENCE RIVER	QUEBEC	WEST ROCKS	50-07.30	66-26.00	15262.7	42943.2	00
ST LAWRENCE RIVER	QUEBEC	MARINA DE GASPE ENTR	48-49.70	64-28.50	15146.75	30534.75	00
ST LAWRENCE RIVER	QUEBEC	MARINA DE GASPE BRKWTR	48-49.70	64-28.50	15146.75	30534.75	00

CHAPTER 10

LOVELY LEDGES

When at anchor, we have found it is not easy to keep the stern of the boat right above a ledge, what with the tides, winds, or current all trying to keep us away from the fish. We have found that a marker placed on the ledge will at least let us know how far we have drifted away from our ideal fishing location.

When we are going to troll a ledge, we place markers about every hundred yards or so apart. Then we troll a zigzagging course, trying not to catch our markers. Unfortunately, this technique doesn't work worth a hoot when there's lots of traffic!

We have also found that other fishermen will pull up to our markers and anchor there, just *knowing* that there must be fish by a marker. To alleviate this situation, we start trolling at about 3:30 in the evening and finish well after dark; this improves our chance to creel fish without interference.

Fishing at night is great fun, especially when we catch a real lunker that doesn't want to go home with us. We can't see what we are about to catch until just before we boat it. We heartily recommend that you give night-fishing a try.

Coordinates in this chapter are listed by body of water or province, depth, description, latitude, longitude, time delay one, and time delay two. When diving near ledges, as elsewhere, use the depth-finding equipment on your boat or charter boat to determine actual water depth. Also, use the time delay (TD) numbers in lieu of the latitude/longitude listings near ledges (see the introduction to Chapter 7).

WIT & WISDOM

If free-board is the amount of boat above the water line, then expensive-board is when the free-board finds itself below the water line.

HELPFUL HINT

We found the auto pilot to be a very useful tool, once we learned we could relax and enjoy the moment; then we found ourselves aground when we were relaxing.

DAFFYNITION

LORAN: Acronym for LOng RAnge Navigation. The coastal waters of the United States are covered with several Group Repetition Intervals (GRIs): GRI 7960 (Gulf of Alaska Chain), GRI 5990 (Canadian West Coast Chain), GRI 9940 (US West Coast Chain), GRI 9960 (Northeast US Chain), GRI 8970 (Great Lakes Chain), and GRI 7980 (Southeast US Chain). While the credentials of the loran are impressive, the machine cannot think for itself and should not be used as a substitute for good common sense.

LEDGES

BODY OF WATER	PROV/STATE	NAME	LAT	LON	TD#1	TD#2	DEPTH
GEORGIAN BAY	ONTARIO	SHOAL ISLAND	46-18.80	84-04.55	30934.06	47954.58	00
GEORGIAN BAY	ONTARIO	CREAK ISLAND SHOAL	45-56.58	81-41.73	30172.73	48390.25	00
GEORGIAN BAY	ONTARIO	BEARS RUMP SHOAL NO T3	45-18.24	81-34.70	30167.54	48677.82	00
GEORGIAN BAY	ONTARIO	SANDY COVE LEDGE	45-57.05	81-32.15	30116.37	48400.24	00
GEORGIAN BAY	ONTARIO	SURPRISE SHOAL NO T5	45-03.47	81-01.67	29966.01	48816.39	00
GEORGIAN BAY	ONTARIO	SQUAW POINT SHOAL NO T9	44-37.08	80-54.98	29942.19	49007.61	00
GEORGIAN BAY	ONTARIO	VAIL POINT SHOAL NO T7	44-44.75	80-47.30	29882.25	48958.82	00
GEORGIAN BAY	ONTARIO	HALL ROCK SHOAL NO P16	45-20.47	80-19.56	29689.28	48734.52	00
GEORGIAN BAY	ONTARIO	HOOPER ISLAND SHOAL P24	45-19.78	80-18.30	29681.33	48740.22	00
GEORGIAN BAY	ONTARIO	SPRUCE ISLAND SHOAL P27	45-19.83	80-15.50	29663.85	48742.18	00
GEORGIAN BAY	ONTARIO	BUSTY SHOAL LIGHT P35	45-20.82	80-03.75	29591.20	48744.97	00
GEORGIAN BAY	ONTARIO	MIDLAND BAY SHOAL NO M20	44-45.95	79-52.73	29508.56	48982.29	00
GEORGIAN BAY	ONTARIO	CANDLEMAS SHOAL NO M13	44-49.25	79-52.48	29507.87	48960.77	00
LAKE ERIE		MAMAJUDA SHOAL BUOY	42-10.90	83-08.20	43851.00	56913.77	00
LAKE ERIE		GR LAKES STL SHOAL NO 1	42-15.70	83-06.90	43884.37	56945.51	00
LAKE ERIE		MIDDLE HARBOR SHOAL NO 1	41-34.20	82-47.70	43649.90	56929.94	00
LAKE ERIE		SOUTHEAST SHOAL "EE"	41-48.70	82-27.85	16493.17	57163.35	00
LAKE ERIE		SOUTHEAST SHOAL LIGHT	41-49.60	82-27.80	43805.48	57167.52	00
LAKE ERIE		SOUTHEAST SHOAL NO "EE"	41-48.70	82-27.80	43799.15	57163.78	00
LAKE ERIE		SOUTHEAST SHOAL	41-49.58	82-27.78	16491.75	57167.61	00
LAKE ERIE		NANTICOKE SHOAL NO EA8	42-43.70	80-03.63	16453.78	58611.06	00
LAKE ERIE		WAVERLY SHOAL "EU"	42-51.70	78-56.20	44917.01	59217.70	00
LAKE HURON		WEST SISTER SHOAL J2	45-22.08	81-47.87	30246.88	48634.48	00
LAKE HURON		SOUTHWEST BANK NO TA1	45-14.03	81-45.44	30241.67	48696.85	00
ST LAWRENCE GULF	NEW BRUNSWICK	SAPIN LEDGE BUOY	46-58.40	64-44.70	14858.96	43738.46	00
	NEW BRUNSWICK	POMPEY LEDGE	44-58.80	66-56.70	14016.43	44757.28	00
	NEW BRUNSWICK	LETITE HARBOUR LEDGE	45-02.90	66-54.10	14063.57	44750.27	00
	NEW BRUNSWICK	MATTHEWS LEDGE	45-03.10	66-53.80	14065.98	44749.13	00
	NEW BRUNSWICK	MORGAN LEDGE	45-02.20	66-53.60	14056.22	44747.25	00
	NEW BRUNSWICK	NET ROCKS LEDGES "XV6"	44-45.30	66-44.50	13879.38	44688.91	00
	NEW BRUNSWICK	FARMER LEDGE	44-43.40	66-43.60	13859.73	44683.03	00
	NEW BRUNSWICK	OLD PROPRIETOR LEDGE BELL	44-33.00	66-39.70	13752.22	44655.71	00
	NOVA SCOTIA	SW LEDGE WHISTLE "M2"	44-10.30	66-27.20	13529.97	44581.09	00
	NOVA SCOTIA	NW LEDGE WHISTLE BUOY	44-18.30	66-26.00	13614.16	44582.60	00
	NOVA SCOTIA	COW LEDGE SHOAL BELL	44-17.10	66-20.30	13609.06	44556.45	00
	NOVA SCOTIA	TRINITY LEDGE WHISTLE	43-58.80	66-18.50	13426.10	44534.52	00
	NOVA SCOTIA	RAN ISLAND LEDGE	43-42.10	66-02.05	13289.17	44454.27	00
	NOVA SCOTIA	VIGNEAU LEDGE	43-32.20	65-46.20	13225.99	44378.31	00
	NOVA SCOTIA	WESTERN WAY LEDGE	43-31.70	65-45.10	13223.45	44373.28	00
	NOVA SCOTIA	WOODS HARBOUR/BIG LEDGE	43-31.20	65-44.80	13219.44	44371.73	00
	NOVA SCOTIA	THE FALLS LEDGE	43-32.10	65-44.70	13227.84	44371.73	00
	NOVA SCOTIA	WHITE KNOLL LEDGE BELL	43-25.20	65-34.40	13184.93	44323.68	00
	NOVA SCOTIA	QUACO LEDGE BELL K16	45-14.70	65-22.20	14189.16	44262.43	00
	NOVA SCOTIA	HORSESHOE LEDGE WHISTLE	44-28.30	63-58.40	13812.70	43819.84	00

LEDGES

BODY OF WATER	PROV/STATE	NAME	LAT	LON	TD#1	TD#2	DEPTH
	NOVA SCOTIA	BOWEN LEDGE BELL	44-52.00	62-10.60	13983.86	43146.61	00
	NOVA SCOTIA	WHITE PT LEDGES WHISTLE	45-13.50	60-58.60	14090.55	42655.88	00
ST LAWRENCE RIVER	QUEBEC	BARRETT LEDGE BUOY H56	47-53.00	69-37.20	15007.73	32330.85	00

CHAPTER 11

REEFS

The thought of vessels split open by reefs and sent down to Davy Jones' Locker makes our skin crawl with excitement and conjures up visions of hauling in countless treasures. While this sort of treasure-hunting is certainly a possibility, the real treasure of a reef lies in its beauty and in the beauty of the living creatures that call it home.

But don't be lulled into carelessness by the beauty of a reef. Right under the surface lurk rocks that can cause great harm and loss without a whimper of a warning. The anticipation and excitement that comes with the desire for discovery is very strong, but if it isn't tempered with caution, this emotion may give birth to a trip fraught with hazards that might threaten equipment, if not lives.

If you plan to venture to open-water diving and fishing spots, we urge you to consult with those who have made the trip and take heed of any warnings. Most places are safe and can be great fun to visit, but there are those that require special precautions.

We strongly endorse having up-to-date charts of the area aboard, along with tide tables where applicable. Both should be consulted to determine the proper course of action prior to venturing into unfamiliar waters. Listings are as usual (please refer to the first two paragraphs of Chapter 7), and again we urge divers to determine water depth prior to venturing beneath the surface.

Diving most of these structures is easy, but some of the dives are deep and should be attempted only by the experienced. Those who are not as experienced as others need not feel bad about missing out, as they can gain the necessary experience over time. In the meantime, there are lots of pretties listed in this publication that can be found in dives less than 30 feet deep. And that's where we find all of the color anyway!

Reef diving and fishing require special skills. If you're new to this type of diving and fishing, it would be wise to seek out local knowledge before attempting something that could become dangerous very quickly.

Then good luck and happy hunting!

DAFFYNITION

VHF RADIO: Communications equipment sometimes referred to as a "ship-to-shore," "marine telephone," and/or "two-way radio." Its purpose is to provide communications between vessels and to provide position information in the event it is required to do so. The "universal distress and call channel" is Channel 16. Radio checks and unnecessary communications should be avoided at all costs on Channel 16. Use channels designated for ship-to-ship for personal uses.

HELPFUL HINT

Fish for savory things near ledges, wrecks, reefs, rocks, and most structures. It is best to drift about a ledge, bounce over rocks, and set a hook at reefs and wrecks.

REEFS

BODY OF WATER	PROV/STATE	NAME	LAT	LON	TD#1	TD#2	DEPTH
GEORGIAN BAY	ONTARIO	CAMBRIA BANK LIGHT K33	46-19.48	84-06.20	30941.06	47945.24	00
GEORGIAN BAY	ONTARIO	PLUMMER BANK K8	46-17.80	83-54.63	30884.07	47985.54	00
GEORGIAN BAY	ONTARIO	BURNT ISLAND REEF KE7	46-06.83	83-49.97	30884.91	48083.62	00
GEORGIAN BAY	ONTARIO	O'DONNELL BANK LIGHT KE4	46-07.97	83-46.30	30862.25	48082.46	00
GEORGIAN BAY	ONTARIO	MIDDLE BANK LIGHT JD14	45-59.70	82-19.05	30386.38	48310.82	00
GEORGIAN BAY	ONTARIO	LOGAN REEF LIGHT J71	46-02.00	82-11.17	30337.91	48306.39	00
GEORGIAN BAY	ONTARIO	CARON REEF LIGHT J19	45-57.87	81-50.27	30221.38	48368.61	00
GEORGIAN BAY	ONTARIO	CENTRE ISLAND BANK J16	45-55.13	81-39.37	30160.17	48404.03	00
GEORGIAN BAY	ONTARIO	BURNT ISLAND BANK J13	45-54.28	81-35.35	30137.28	48415.70	00
GEORGIAN BAY	ONTARIO	ANN LONG BANK E11	45-58.47	81-32.50	30117.36	48389.61	00
GEORGIAN BAY	ONTARIO	ROOSTER REEF NO D86	45-55.17	81-13.98	30011.37	48437.72	00
GEORGIAN BAY	ONTARIO	BURTON BANK S LIGHT H12	45-44.57	80-40.88	29819.36	48550.32	00
GEORGIAN BAY	ONTARIO	BURTON BANK LIGHT H13	45-44.65	80-40.73	29818.47	48549.93	00
GEORGIAN BAY	ONTARIO	SEGUIN BANK NO P1	45-18.70	80-31.50	29764.27	48736.41	00
GEORGIAN BAY	ONTARIO	NEW BANK LIGHT TN2	44-36.80	80-20.10	29697.02	49029.30	00
GEORGIAN BAY	ONTARIO	BORER BANK LIGHT P26	45-19.67	80-16.92	29672.69	48742.09	00
GEORGIAN BAY	ONTARIO	BENNET BANK NO M3	44-52.41	80-01.47	29568.55	48934.98	00
LAKE ERIE		BALLARDS REEF CHAN NO 71D	42-07.40	83-07.10	43831.21	56907.71	00
LAKE ERIE		LOCUST POINT REEF	41-39.30	83-04.49	43648.20	56806.90	00
LAKE ERIE		CONE REEF	41-40.54	83-03.30	43659.40	56822.60	00
LAKE ERIE		CRIB REEF	41-39.47	83-00.63	43657.80	56840.90	00
LAKE ERIE		CRIB REEF BUOY NO 7	41-38.80	82-60.00	43655.39	56843.25	00
LAKE ERIE		ROUND REEF	41-37.44	82-59.53	43646.00	56841.60	00
LAKE ERIE		COLCHESTER REEF LIGHT	41-56.00	82-54.00	43786.89	56969.26	00
LAKE ERIE		WEST REEF SOUTH HUMP	41-43.32	82-51.26	43705.50	56938.40	00
LAKE ERIE		NORTH HARBOR I REEF "E13"	41-51.00	82-51.00	43760.00	56973.46	00
LAKE ERIE		WEST REEF NORTH HUMP	41-43.54	82-50.81	43708.00	56943.20	00
LAKE ERIE		ENNIS REEF	41-45.78	82-50.09	43725.20	56959.00	00
LAKE ERIE		SUNKEN CHICK	41-47.11	82-49.14	43736.60	56972.90	00
LAKE ERIE		TRANSPORT	41-47.05	82-47.67	43739.60	56985.30	00
LAKE ERIE		GRUBB REEF BUOY "E8"	41-51.90	82-33.60	43807.43	57127.01	00
LAKE ERIE		LORAIN REEF BUOY "A"	41-28.10	82-12.90	43684.41	57207.98	00
LAKE ERIE		MOSS POINT REEF "B"	41-30.20	81-47.60	43761.88	57438.32	00
LAKE ERIE		MOSS POINT REEF "A"	41-30.20	81-47.10	43763.13	57442.70	00
LAKE ERIE		TECUMSEH REEF EA6	42-47.65	79-43.47	16453.58	58796.52	00
LAKE ERIE		MIDDLE REEFS "EU4"	42-52.73	78-55.27	16465.22	59227.68	00
LAKE HURON		BURT LAKE OBSTR BUOY	45-24.90	84-47.70	31325.37	48307.62	00
LAKE HURON		GROS CAP REEFS LIGHT	46-30.70	84-36.90	31069.70	47778.28	00
LAKE HURON		MARTIN REEF LIGHT	45-54.80	84-08.90	31019.02	48139.88	00
LAKE HURON		SPECTACLE REEF LIGHT	45-46.40	84-08.20	31038.25	48211.07	00
LAKE HURON		DE TOUR REEF LIGHT	45-56.90	83-54.20	30932.54	48154.73	00
LAKE HURON		PORT AUSTIN REEF LIGHT	44-04.90	82-58.90	30899.26	49161.77	00
LAKE HURON		KETTLE POINT REEF NO V4	43-14.38	72-03.07	28006.56	49413.33	00
LAKE MICHIGAN		RACINE REEF BUOY NO 1	42-43.50	87-46.00	33082.70	49491.92	00

REEFS

BODY OF WATER	PROV/STATE	NAME	LAT	LON	TD#1	TD#2	DEPTH
LAKE MICHIGAN		RACINE REEF LIGHT	42-43.60	87-44.20	33074.45	49496.28	00
LAKE MICHIGAN		PESHTIGO REEF LIGHT	44-57.40	87-34.80	32270.63	48095.85	00
LAKE MICHIGAN		BOULDER REEF NO 1	45-35.20	85-59.00	31661.61	48031.37	00
LAKE MICHIGAN		HOG ISLAND REEF "HI"	45-43.50	85-20.40	31435.83	48063.02	00
LAKE MICHIGAN		SIMMONS REEF NO 2	45-54.20	85-12.90	31360.65	47989.04	00
LAKE MICHIGAN		GRAYS REEF LIGHT	45-46.00	85-09.20	31369.09	48070.25	00
LAKE MICHIGAN		GRAYS REEF NO 3	45-45.80	85-08.40	31365.60	48074.06	00
LAKE SUPERIOR		CAPSTAN REEF LIGHT	48-38.10	93-03.00	32328.38	44548.36	00
LAKE SUPERIOR		OLD DUMPING GROUND SHOAL P2	48-23.13	89-10.69	31803.94	45886.36	00
LAKE SUPERIOR		WELCOME SHOAL LIGHT A6	48-20.57	89-08.55	31805.60	45913.77	00
LAKE SUPERIOR		HARE ISLAND REEF LIGHT A2	48-17.92	88-59.20	31785.63	45975.68	00
LAKE SUPERIOR		HOLDEN SHOAL LIGHT J8	48-56.65	88-08.42	31513.93	45955.57	00
LAKE SUPERIOR		PANCAKE SHOAL NO X2	46-54.50	84-50.30	31073.38	47551.84	00
ST LAWRENCE GULF	MAGDALEN ISLANDS	PEARL REEF BELL "Y16"	47-19.50	61-34.40	14681.47	42315.86	00
ST LAWRENCE GULF	NEW BRUNSWICK	TORMINTINE REEFS BELL "X5"	46-06.60	63-41.10	14484.20	43500.52	00
	NEW BRUNSWICK	CHANCE HARBOUR/REEF PT	45-07.10	66-20.90	14122.57	44592.25	00
	NOVA SCOTIA	SKINNER REEF BELL	45-44.80	62-37.20	14302.24	43154.61	00
	NOVA SCOTIA	BASSOON REEFS BELL	44-50.60	62-13.60	13975.69	43167.95	00
ST LAWRENCE GULF	PRINCE EDWARD I	NORTH POINT REEF WHISTLE	47-05.00	64-00.10	14813.96	43388.86	00
ST LAWRENCE GULF	PRINCE EDWARD I	PRIM REEFS WHISTLE	46-02.70	63-07.00	14427.05	43286.31	00
ST LAWRENCE GULF	PRINCE EDWARD I	BEAR REEF WHISTE "N4"	46-00.60	62-24.30	14378.55	43014.46	00
ST LAWRENCE RIVER	QUEBEC	BEAUMONT REEFS K-147	46-50.90	70-60.00	12408.8	60135.6	00
ST LAWRENCE RIVER	QUEBEC	MADAME ISLAND REEF	46-55.90	70-50.50	12318.7	60134.4	00
ST LAWRENCE RIVER	QUEBEC	LARK REEF S-7	48-07.20	69-40.50	11715.6	60071.7	00
ST LAWRENCE RIVER	QUEBEC	T AUX VACHES REEF S-8	48-07.50	69-40.30	11714.5	60071.4	00
ST LAWRENCE RIVER	QUEBEC	BAR REEF S-5	48-06.90	69-39.10	11707.5	60073.3	00
ST LAWRENCE RIVER	QUEBEC	LARK REEF K-58	48-04.60	69-38.60	11704.1	60077.3	00
ST LAWRENCE RIVER	QUEBEC	WHITE ISLAND REEF K59	47-59.10	69-38.00	15016.85	32305.60	00
ST LAWRENCE RIVER	QUEBEC	WHITE ISLAND REEF	47-54.60	69-37.80	11698.2	60093.6	00
ST LAWRENCE RIVER	QUEBEC	LARK REEF K-56	48-04.60	69-37.60	11698.3	60078.0	00
ST LAWRENCE RIVER	QUEBEC	BASQUE REEF BELL D-6	50-10.90	66-22.00	15262.6	42894.0	00

CHAPTER 12

WRECKS

Navigating in waters that have caused wrecks in the past can be very hazardous. Most of the wrecks in the Florida Keys and Bahamas, for example, are on the ocean floor because they ventured into shallow water and ran afoul of coral reefs so sharp and hard that they literally cut their way right into the heart of the boats. Just about any kind of boat can be ripped apart, and some of these reefs lie right in the middle of vast expanses of open water. Only a heart-stopping bump will alert you to their presence.

As always, check charts, tide tables (where applicable), and exercise caution. See the introduction to Chapter 7 for tips on using these coordinates.

WIT & WISDOM

There has never been anything said nearer the truth than the old adage, "It is not important to catch fish; it is important to go fishing."

It would take a lot of words to explain the thrill of getting a hard strike at night without knowing what's on the other end of the line. Or to find a lunker at the end of the fight staring up at you in defiance. Or to watch a 100-pound woman land a 150-pound tarpon. There is nothing quite so heartbreaking as losing a fish that pulled so hard you had to cut the line to save the pole, and there is no laughter so fulfilling as watching a loved one catch a fish smaller than the hook.

Then there's the love you feel when you watch your child catch his first "keeper" fish and then argue for its life by insisting it be put in a glass of water instead of being killed for the supper table. There is no sorrow quite like losing a pet rod and reel or having someone step on a brand-new pole and break the tip off. There is no sound quite like that of line whizzing off the reel, and there is no finer feeling of joy than knowing you have caught what might be a prize.

Fishing is fast, slow, frustrating, rewarding, pensive, and promising all at the same time, but most of all, it's just plain fun.

When Susie and I fish as a team, which is most of the time, we are constantly teasing each other about who might lose the bets on the first, smallest, and biggest fish. We bet things like who cooks dinner, who has to clean and fillet the fish, who does the dishes, and — by far the worst bet I have ever made and lost — who was going to be boss the next day. Susie had great fun with the "Honey, get me . . ." game.

We used to try to fill our freezers with fish during the winter so that we could have fish during the summer until we found out that during the summer, it is by far cheaper to catch fish at a local fish market than to run the boat out to water depths of 70 to 80 feet. Now, we have great fun fishing without having to catch anything. The bets are the same.

WRECKS

BODY OF WATER	PROV/STATE	NAME	LAT	LON	TD#1	TD#2	DEPTH
LAKE HURON		THUNDER BAY WRECK "WR2"	45-03.70	83-23.60	30892.20	48648.34	00
LAKE HURON		NORDMEER WRECK "WR1"	45-08.10	83-09.30	30790.47	48634.05	00
LAKE MICHIGAN		SYDNEY McLOUTH WRECK "WR2"	44-49.80	87-48.80	32366.33	48124.88	00
LAKE MICHIGAN		DREDGE 906 WRECK BUOY "WR"	42-58.20	87-47.00	32991.93	49325.83	00
LAKE MICHIGAN		WILMETTE WRECK BUOY "WR2"	42-05.70	87-39.00	33309.72	49935.88	00
LAKE MICHIGAN		OUTER SHOAL WRECK BUOY	41-46.00	87-23.70	33382.07	50198.68	00
LAKE MICHIGAN		NOVADOC WRECK BUOY "WR1"	43-41.90	86-31.10	32363.43	49060.02	00
ST LAWRENCE GULF	PRINCE EDWARD I	SHIPWRECK POINT	46-28.20	62-25.50	14519.38	42910.31	00

CHAPTER 13

FINE FISH'N

Coordinates for fishing are included to provide you with a listing of bottom structures that have proved to be productive fishing grounds. We've also listed areas that produce fish for reasons that seem unfathomable.

Before you head to the marina, be sure to investigate local regulations regarding the taking of some special species of fish. Such restrictions are not uncommon. A state or province may have one restriction and some counties may have additional restrictions. A quick phone call to the local wildlife people may save you from gaining some expensive experience.

Coordinates in this chapter are listed by province or body of water, latitude, longitude, time delay one, and time delay two. Use the time delay numbers in lieu of the Lat/Lon coordinates, as explained in Chapter 7.

DAFFYNITION

TRUST ME: This statement is almost always used when doubt has been raised about something that should have been done, might have needed to be done, was promised to be done, but that almost never has been done. Beware of this statement when used in conjunction with wine, song, and sunsets.

FISHING

BODY OF WATER	PROV/STATE	NAME	LAT	LON	TD#1	TD#2	DEPTH
GEORGIAN BAY	ONTARIO	CAMBRIA BANK LIGHT K33	46-19.48	84-06.20	30941.06	47945.24	00
GEORGIAN BAY	ONTARIO	SHOAL ISLAND	46-18.80	84-04.55	30934.06	47954.58	00
GEORGIAN BAY	ONTARIO	WEST SISTER ROCK	46-18.22	83-54.93	30884.67	47981.51	00
GEORGIAN BAY	ONTARIO	PLUMMER BANK K8	46-17.80	83-54.63	30884.07	47985.54	00
GEORGIAN BAY	ONTARIO	BURNT ISLAND REEF KE7	46-06.83	83-49.97	30884.91	48083.62	00
GEORGIAN BAY	ONTARIO	O'DONNELL BANK LIGHT KE4	46-07.97	83-46.30	30862.25	48082.46	00
GEORGIAN BAY	ONTARIO	MIDDLE BANK LIGHT JD14	45-59.70	82-19.05	30386.38	48310.82	00
GEORGIAN BAY	ONTARIO	MEREDITH ROCK	45-58.95	82-14.42	30360.58	48323.82	00
GEORGIAN BAY	ONTARIO	ROBERTSON ROCK LIGHT J72	46-03.45	82-13.47	30349.32	48291.98	00
GEORGIAN BAY	ONTARIO	LOGAN REEF LIGHT J71	46-02.00	82-11.17	30337.91	48306.39	00
GEORGIAN BAY	ONTARIO	CARON REEF LIGHT J19	45-57.87	81-50.27	30221.38	48368.61	00
GEORGIAN BAY	ONTARIO	DUNCAN CITY ROCK EE5	46-00.23	81-43.45	30179.53	48361.45	00
GEORGIAN BAY	ONTARIO	CAROLINE ROCKS EE6	46-00.15	81-43.23	30178.32	48362.35	00
GEORGIAN BAY	ONTARIO	CREAK ISLAND SHOAL	45-56.58	81-41.73	30172.73	48390.25	00
GEORGIAN BAY	ONTARIO	CENTRE ISLAND BANK J16	45-55.13	81-39.37	30160.17	48404.03	00
GEORGIAN BAY	ONTARIO	BURNT ISLAND BANK J13	45-54.28	81-35.35	30137.28	48415.70	00
GEORGIAN BAY	ONTARIO	BEARS RUMP SHOAL NO T3	45-18.24	81-34.70	30167.54	48677.82	00
GEORGIAN BAY	ONTARIO	CAMPBELL ROCK J12	45-49.62	81-33.23	30128.53	48452.05	00
GEORGIAN BAY	ONTARIO	ANN LONG BANK E11	45-58.47	81-32.50	30117.36	48389.61	00
GEORGIAN BAY	ONTARIO	SANDY COVE LEDGE	45-57.05	81-32.15	30116.37	48400.24	00
GEORGIAN BAY	ONTARIO	JACKMAN ROCK NO E1	45-57.98	81-29.63	30101.01	48397.06	00
GEORGIAN BAY	ONTARIO	FLAT ROCK	45-58.98	81-25.58	30076.78	48395.47	00
GEORGIAN BAY	ONTARIO	ROOSTER REEF NO D86	45-55.17	81-13.98	30011.37	48437.72	00
GEORGIAN BAY	ONTARIO	SURPRISE SHOAL NO T5	45-03.47	81-01.67	29966.01	48816.39	00
GEORGIAN BAY	ONTARIO	SQUAW POINT SHOAL NO T9	44-37.08	80-54.98	29942.19	49007.61	00
GEORGIAN BAY	ONTARIO	VAIL POINT SHOAL NO T7	44-44.75	80-47.30	29882.25	48958.82	00
GEORGIAN BAY	ONTARIO	BURTON BANK S LIGHT H12	45-44.57	80-40.88	29819.36	48550.32	00
GEORGIAN BAY	ONTARIO	BURTON BANK LIGHT H13	45-44.65	80-40.73	29818.47	48549.93	00
GEORGIAN BAY	ONTARIO	KEYSTONE ROCK LIGHT H21	45-45.23	80-39.00	29808.18	48547.82	00
GEORGIAN BAY	ONTARIO	TIZARD ROCK LIGHT AL	45-34.08	80-33.30	29774.41	48629.77	00
GEORGIAN BAY	ONTARIO	SEGUIN BANK NO P1	45-18.70	80-31.50	29764.27	48736.41	00
GEORGIAN BAY	ONTARIO	RED ROCK	45-21.60	80-24.48	29720.08	48722.72	00
GEORGIAN BAY	ONTARIO	FARR ROCK LIGHT NO P7	45-21.42	80-22.77	29709.39	48725.40	00
GEORGIAN BAY	ONTARIO	ARIEL ROCK LIGHT NO P12	45-21.28	80-20.75	29696.78	48728.06	00
GEORGIAN BAY	ONTARIO	ARTHUR ORR ROCK NO P13	45-21.10	80-20.33	29694.15	48729.63	00
GEORGIAN BAY	ONTARIO	NEW BANK LIGHT TN2	44-36.80	80-20.10	29697.02	49029.30	00
GEORGIAN BAY	ONTARIO	HALL ROCK SHOAL NO P16	45-20.47	80-19.56	29689.28	48734.52	00
GEORGIAN BAY	ONTARIO	TELEGRAPH ROCK NO P22	45-20.10	80-18.88	29684.99	48737.58	00
GEORGIAN BAY	ONTARIO	HOOPER ISLAND SHOAL P24	45-19.78	80-18.30	29681.33	48740.22	00
GEORGIAN BAY	ONTARIO	BORER BANK LIGHT P26	45-19.67	80-16.92	29672.69	48742.09	00
GEORGIAN BAY	ONTARIO	SPRUCE ISLAND SHOAL P27	45-19.83	80-15.50	29663.85	48742.18	00
GEORGIAN BAY	ONTARIO	McCLELLAND ROCK P28	45-19.78	80-15.48	29663.72	48742.53	00
GEORGIAN BAY	ONTARIO	CARLING ROCK NO P30	45-20.08	80-14.17	29655.60	48741.58	00
GEORGIAN BAY	ONTARIO	LOCKERBIE ROCK NO TN11	44-32.23	80-13.81	29654.15	49063.11	00

FISHING

BODY OF WATER	PROV/STATE	NAME	LAT	LON	TD#1	TD#2	DEPTH
GEORGIAN BAY	ONTARIO	LOTTIE WOLF ROCK NO M2	44-55.75	80-10.41	29628.35	48907.37	00
GEORGIAN BAY	ONTARIO	BUSTY SHOAL LIGHT P35	45-20.82	80-03.75	29591.20	48744.97	00
GEORGIAN BAY	ONTARIO	McKERREL ROCK NO P37	45-20.59	80-03.17	29587.54	48746.95	00
GEORGIAN BAY	ONTARIO	BENNET BANK NO M3	44-52.41	80-01.47	29568.55	48934.98	00
GEORGIAN BAY	ONTARIO	RED ROCK GO HOME BAY	44-58.21	79-57.66	29544.84	48898.88	00
GEORGIAN BAY	ONTARIO	MIDLAND BAY SHOAL NO M20	44-45.95	79-52.73	29508.56	48982.29	00
GEORGIAN BAY	ONTARIO	CANDLEMAS SHOAL NO M13	44-49.25	79-52.48	29507.87	48960.77	00
GEORGIAN BAY	ONTARIO	TURNING ROCK HONEY HARBOUR	44-50.93	79-49.53	29488.84	48951.33	00
GEORGIAN BAY	ONTARIO	TURNING ROCK WAUBAUSHENE	44-46.33	79-44.40	29452.82	48983.93	00
GEORGIAN BAY	ONTARIO	MARY ROCKS	44-46.20	79-43.40	29446.08	48985.25	00
LABRADOR SEA	NEWFOUNDLAND	BAD NEIGHBOR ROCK BELL	47-34.50	58-54.20	Suggest	GPS	00
LABRADOR SEA	NEWFOUNDLAND	CHRISTMAS HEAD	47-40.50	58-23.50	Suggest	GPS	00
LABRADOR SEA	NEWFOUNDLAND	FRENCHMANS HEAD	49-03.40	58-09.50	Suggest	GPS	00
LABRADOR SEA	NEWFOUNDLAND	COW HEAD	49-55.10	57-48.90	Suggest	GPS	00
LABRADOR SEA	NEWFOUNDLAND	NORTHWEST HEADS	47-31.00	57-25.00	Suggest	GPS	00
LABRADOR SEA	NEWFOUNDLAND	MAQUELON ROCKS BUOY	47-04.00	56-13.00	Suggest	GPS	00
LABRADOR SEA	NEWFOUNDLAND	BAD ROCK	50-47.00	56-10.00	Suggest	GPS	00
LABRADOR SEA	NEWFOUNDLAND	TINKER ROCK	47-37.00	56-03.00	Suggest	GPS	00
LABRADOR SEA	NEWFOUNDLAND	COCK BANK WHISTLE	46-50.40	55-59.20	Suggest	GPS	00
LABRADOR SEA	NEWFOUNDLAND	FORTUNE BAY HEAD	47-04.00	55-52.00	Suggest	GPS	00
LABRADOR SEA	NEWFOUNDLAND	ROCKY POINT, BRETON	47-29.00	55-48.00	Suggest	GPS	00
LABRADOR SEA	NEWFOUNDLAND	ALANS ISLAND, BLUFF HD	46-51.00	55-48.00	Suggest	GPS	00
LABRADOR SEA	NEWFOUNDLAND	GULL ROCK	49-41.00	55-41.00	Suggest	GPS	00
LABRADOR SEA	NEWFOUNDLAND	BLACK HEAD	46-54.00	55-34.00	Suggest	GPS	00
LABRADOR SEA	NEWFOUNDLAND	HARBOUR ROCK	51-22.00	55-34.00	Suggest	GPS	00
LABRADOR SEA	NEWFOUNDLAND	FISHING POINT	51-21.00	55-33.00	Suggest	GPS	00
LABRADOR SEA	NEWFOUNDLAND	DRUNKARDS POINT BELL	46-54.00	55-31.00	Suggest	GPS	00
LABRADOR SEA	NEWFOUNDLAND	MIDDLE HEAD	46-54.00	55-21.00	Suggest	GPS	00
LABRADOR SEA	NEWFOUNDLAND	CORBIN HARBOUR LG PT	46-57.00	55-14.00	Suggest	GPS	00
LABRADOR SEA	NEWFOUNDLAND	STAG ROCK	47-02.00	55-11.00	Suggest	GPS	00
LABRADOR SEA	NEWFOUNDLAND	DODDING HEAD	47-00.00	55-09.00	Suggest	GPS	00
LABRADOR SEA	NEWFOUNDLAND	LONG HARBOUR POINT	47-35.00	55-08.00	Suggest	GPS	00
LABRADOR SEA	NEWFOUNDLAND	STURGEON COVE HEAD	49-31.00	55-07.00	Suggest	GPS	00
LABRADOR SEA	NEWFOUNDLAND	DUCK ROCK	47-09.00	55-05.00	Suggest	GPS	00
LABRADOR SEA	NEWFOUNDLAND	RED HARBOUR HEAD	47-17.00	54-59.00	Suggest	GPS	00
LABRADOR SEA	NEWFOUNDLAND	STANLEY ROCKS BELL	47-15.00	54-59.00	Suggest	GPS	00
LABRADOR SEA	NEWFOUNDLAND	STEERING ROCK	47-21.00	54-54.00	Suggest	GPS	00
LABRADOR SEA	NEWFOUNDLAND	ROCKY BAY	49-26.90	54-13.80	Suggest	GPS	00
LABRADOR SEA	NEWFOUNDLAND	TINKER ROCK	49-35.00	54-11.00	Suggest	GPS	00
LABRADOR SEA	NEWFOUNDLAND	JOE BATTS ARM ROCKS	49-44.00	54-10.00	Suggest	GPS	00
LABRADOR SEA	NEWFOUNDLAND	IRONSKULL ROCK	47-27.00	54-05.00	Suggest	GPS	00
LABRADOR SEA	NEWFOUNDLAND	SHAG ROCKS	47-25.00	53-55.00	Suggest	GPS	00
LABRADOR SEA	NEWFOUNDLAND	CANDLE COVE ROCKS	49-06.00	53-36.00	Suggest	GPS	00
LABRADOR SEA	NEWFOUNDLAND	BENBURRY ROCK BUOY "JV4"	49-07.00	53-36.00	Suggest	GPS	00

FISHING

BODY OF WATER	PROV/STATE	NAME	LAT	LON	TD#1	TD#2	DEPTH
LABRADOR SEA	NEWFOUNDLAND	SEINE ROCK	49-04.00	53-34.30	Suggest	GPS	00
LABRADOR SEA	NEWFOUNDLAND	POUND ROCKS	49-04.00	53-34.00	Suggest	GPS	00
LABRADOR SEA	NEWFOUNDLAND	KENNYS ROCKS	49-13.00	53-28.00	Suggest	GPS	00
LABRADOR SEA	NEWFOUNDLAND	POWELLS HEAD	46-41.40	53-24.20	Suggest	GPS	00
LABRADOR SEA	NEWFOUNDLAND	CHARGE ROCK WHISTLE "JX"	49-15.00	53-22.00	Suggest	GPS	00
LABRADOR SEA	NEWFOUNDLAND	BAIT ROCKS, COLEYS PT	47-35.00	53-15.00	Suggest	GPS	00
LABRADOR SEA	NEWFOUNDLAND	BLOW ME DOWN BLUFF	47-25.70	53-07.70	Suggest	GPS	00
LABRADOR SEA	NEWFOUNDLAND	CHAIN ROCKS	47-34.00	52-41.00	Suggest	GPS	00
LABRADOR SEA	NEWFOUNDLAND	NORTH HEAD	47-34.00	52-41.00	Suggest	GPS	00
LABRADOR SEA	NEWFOUNDLAND	VIRGIN ROCKS WHISTLE	46-29.00	50-46.00	Suggest	GPS	00
LAKE ERIE		MAUMEE RIVER BRKWTR "A"	41-37.60	83-32.70	43578.60	56557.18	00
LAKE ERIE		COOLEY CANAL E BRKWTR	41-40.60	83-17.00	43631.34	56704.98	00
LAKE ERIE		COOLEY CANAL W BRKWTR	41-40.60	83-17.00	43631.34	56704.98	00
LAKE ERIE		TOLEDO WW INTAKE CRIB	41-42.00	83-16.00	43643.01	56719.79	00
LAKE ERIE		ENRICO PERMI PWR INTAKES	41-58.60	83-14.70	43756.77	56804.89	00
LAKE ERIE		HURON VALLEY OUTFALL "E"	42-03.10	83-09.80	43797.20	56866.13	00
LAKE ERIE		HURON VALLEY OUTFALL "C"	42-03.10	83-09.80	43797.20	56866.13	00
LAKE ERIE		MAMAJUDA SHOAL BUOY	42-10.90	83-08.20	43851.00	56913.77	00
LAKE ERIE		BALLARDS REEF CHAN NO 71D	42-07.40	83-07.10	43831.21	56907.71	00
LAKE ERIE		WEST SISTER	41-44.72	83-07.04	43680.00	56808.80	00
LAKE ERIE		GR LAKES STL SHOAL NO 1	42-15.70	83-06.90	43884.37	56945.51	00
LAKE ERIE		WEST SISTER LIGHT	41-44.65	83-06.82	43680.00	56810.40	00
LAKE ERIE		LOCUST POINT REEF	41-39.30	83-04.49	43648.20	56806.90	00
LAKE ERIE		FLAT ROCK	41-40.45	83-04.11	43657.00	56815.20	00
LAKE ERIE		CONE REEF	41-40.54	83-03.30	43659.40	56822.60	00
LAKE ERIE		LITTLE PICKERAL	41-40.79	83-01.67	43664.70	56837.70	00
LAKE ERIE		TOUSSAINT SOUTH HUMP	41-38.38	83-01.65	43648.00	56827.40	00
LAKE ERIE		BIG PICKERAL	41-40.02	83-01.61	43659.50	56834.90	00
LAKE ERIE		TOUSSAINT MIDDLE HUMP	41-38.59	83-01.38	43650.00	56830.60	00
LAKE ERIE		TOUSSAINT NORTH HUMP	41-38.69	83-01.20	43651.10	56832.60	00
LAKE ERIE		CRIB HUMP	41-39.30	83-00.87	43656.10	56838.10	00
LAKE ERIE		CRIB REEF	41-39.47	83-00.63	43657.80	56840.90	00
LAKE ERIE		CRIB EAST HUMP	41-39.41	83-00.22	43658.30	56844.20	00
LAKE ERIE		CRIB REEF BUOY NO 7	41-38.80	82-60.00	43655.39	56843.25	00
LAKE ERIE		MIDDLE SISTER	41-51.41	82-59.94	43741.30	56898.80	00
LAKE ERIE		MIDDLE SISTER ISLAND HUMP	41-50.75	82-59.80	43737.20	56897.20	00
LAKE ERIE		ROUND REEF	41-37.44	82-59.53	43646.00	56841.60	00
LAKE ERIE		NIAGARA HUMP	41-40.52	82-58.91	43668.90	56860.30	00
LAKE ERIE		WATERWORKS INTAKE CRIB	42-21.10	82-58.00	43939.55	57042.75	00
LAKE ERIE		PORTAGE RIVER	41-31.68	82-56.52	43611.80	56842.70	00
LAKE ERIE		PORT CLINTON INTAKE CRIB	41-31.20	82-56.40	43609.47	56841.49	00
LAKE ERIE		COLCHESTER REEF LIGHT	41-56.00	82-54.00	43786.89	56969.26	00
LAKE ERIE		COLCHESTER	41-56.57	82-53.93	43789.90	56972.40	00
LAKE ERIE		EAST SISTER ISLAND	41-49.45	82-52.23	43745.60	56956.40	00

FISHING

BODY OF WATER	PROV/STATE	NAME	LAT	LON	TD#1	TD#2	DEPTH
LAKE ERIE		EAST SISTER SHOAL	41-49.45	82-52.23	43745.60	56956.40	00
LAKE ERIE		NORTH HARBOR SHOAL	41-50.44	82-52.21	43752.40	56960.80	00
LAKE ERIE		NORTH HARBOR ISLAND	41-50.18	82-52.14	43750.80	56960.30	00
LAKE ERIE		COLONY CLUB MARINA LIGHT	41-33.20	82-51.40	43634.60	56893.52	00
LAKE ERIE		WEST REEF SOUTH HUMP	41-43.32	82-51.26	43705.50	56938.40	00
LAKE ERIE		NORTH HARBOR I REEF "E13"	41-51.00	82-51.00	43760.00	56973.46	00
LAKE ERIE		EAST SISTER SHOAL HUMP	41-50.04	82-50.82	43752.90	56971.00	00
LAKE ERIE		WEST REEF NORTH HUMP	41-43.54	82-50.81	43708.00	56943.20	00
LAKE ERIE		ENNIS REEF	41-45.78	82-50.09	43725.20	56959.00	00
LAKE ERIE		ENNIS WEST HUMP	41-45.59	82-49.53	43725.20	56963.00	00
LAKE ERIE		BIG CHICK ISLAND	41-46.79	82-49.36	43733.90	56969.60	00
LAKE ERIE		SUNKEN CHICK	41-47.11	82-49.14	43736.60	56972.90	00
LAKE ERIE		NEW GEM BEACH	41-34.70	82-48.96	43649.80	56921.30	00
LAKE ERIE		NORTH BASS CAN	41-44.32	82-48.63	43718.40	56965.30	00
LAKE ERIE		ENNIS MIDDLE HUMP	41-45.66	82-48.52	43728.00	56972.00	00
LAKE ERIE		HEN ISLAND	41-47.89	82-48.43	43743.60	56982.30	00
LAKE ERIE		ENNIS EAST HUMP	41-44.81	82-48.38	43722.40	56969.60	00
LAKE ERIE		E HARBOR E BRKWTR LIGHT	41-33.70	82-48.20	43645.21	56923.46	00
LAKE ERIE		HEN ISLAND SHOAL	41-49.14	82-47.77	43753.80	56993.40	00
LAKE ERIE		MIDDLE HARBOR SHOAL NO 1	41-34.20	82-47.70	43649.90	56929.94	00
LAKE ERIE		TRANSPORT	41-47.05	82-47.67	43739.60	56985.30	00
LAKE ERIE		LITTLE CHICK	41-46.92	82-47.62	43738.80	56985.20	00
LAKE ERIE		HEN ISLAND SHOAL HUMP	41-49.12	82-47.45	43754.40	56996.00	00
LAKE ERIE		BALLAST ISLAND CAN	41-40.91	82-47.25	43697.70	56962.70	00
LAKE ERIE		SCHROCKS MARINA E BRKWTR	41-32.60	82-46.10	43641.95	56937.02	00
LAKE ERIE		WAGON WHEEL	41-47.22	82-44.39	43748.40	57014.30	00
LAKE ERIE		KELLEYS ISLAND POPEYE'S	41-36.14	82-43.10	43673.20	56978.30	00
LAKE ERIE		MARBLEHEAD LIGHT	41-33.02	82-42.85	43651.30	56967.20	00
LAKE ERIE		MOSELEY CHANNEL RANGE	41-29.20	82-42.20	43625.90	56956.50	00
LAKE ERIE		WEST DOCK	41-46.41	82-41.82	43748.70	57033.00	00
LAKE ERIE		GULL ISLAND SHOAL	41-39.87	82-41.69	43703.00	57006.40	00
LAKE ERIE		CEDAR POINT WATER INTAKE	41-29.00	82-41.60	43625.77	56960.89	00
LAKE ERIE		KING GEORGE	41-41.85	82-40.39	43720.00	57026.00	00
LAKE ERIE		KELLY SHOAL	41-38.97	82-39.76	43701.00	57019.30	00
LAKE ERIE		SOUTH DOCK	41-45.11	82-39.15	43745.90	57050.60	00
LAKE ERIE		WINTER POINT	41-49.01	82-37.41	43777.20	57082.00	00
LAKE ERIE		MILL POINT	41-45.20	82-36.81	43752.00	57071.20	00
LAKE ERIE		MIDDLE GROUNDS	41-51.84	82-35.27	43802.00	57112.40	00
LAKE ERIE		GRUBB REEF BUOY "E8"	41-51.90	82-33.60	43807.43	57127.01	00
LAKE ERIE		SOUTHEAST SHOAL "EE"	41-48.70	82-27.85	16493.17	57163.35	00
LAKE ERIE		SOUTHEAST SHOAL NO "EE"	41-48.70	82-27.80	43799.15	57163.78	00
LAKE ERIE		SOUTHEAST SHOAL LIGHT	41-49.60	82-27.80	43805.48	57167.52	00
LAKE ERIE		SOUTHEAST SHOAL	41-49.58	82-27.78	16491.75	57167.61	00
LAKE ERIE		LORAIN REEF BUOY "A"	41-28.10	82-12.90	43684.41	57207.98	00

FISHING

BODY OF WATER	PROV/STATE	NAME	LAT	LON	TD#1	TD#2	DEPTH
LAKE ERIE		CEDAR SPRINGS WATER INTAKE	42-14.70	82-05.75	16456.46	57458.80	00
LAKE ERIE		MOSS POINT REEF "B"	41-30.20	81-47.60	43761.88	57438.32	00
LAKE ERIE		MOSS POINT REEF "A"	41-30.20	81-47.10	43763.13	57442.70	00
LAKE ERIE		WILDWOOD PARK C BRKWTR	41-35.30	81-34.00	43836.32	57578.34	00
LAKE ERIE		WILDWOOD PARK E BRKWTR	41-35.40	81-34.00	43837.10	57578.75	00
LAKE ERIE		EASTLAKE INTAKE BRKWTR	41-40.50	81-26.50	43896.59	57665.10	00
LAKE ERIE		ASHTABULA INNER BRKWTR	41-54.70	80-47.70	44118.02	58061.20	00
LAKE ERIE		ASHTABULA E BRKWTR	41-54.80	80-46.50	44122.46	58072.11	00
LAKE ERIE		CONNEAUT HARB W BRKWTR	41-58.80	80-33.50	44193.86	58201.43	00
LAKE ERIE		NANTICOKE SHOAL NO EA8	42-43.70	80-03.63	16453.78	58611.06	00
LAKE ERIE		TECUMSEH REEF EA6	42-47.65	79-43.47	16453.58	58796.52	00
LAKE ERIE		DUNKIRK BRKWTR W NO 4	42-29.30	79-20.50	44677.50	58948.96	00
LAKE ERIE		BIG SIX MILE CREEK LIGHT	43-01.60	79-00.70	44951.68	59194.42	00
LAKE ERIE		NIAGARA MOHAWK PWR LIGHT	43-04.20	78-60.00	44967.39	59203.84	00
LAKE ERIE		BUCKHORN I INTAKE CRIB	43-04.00	78-60.00	44966.41	59203.59	00
LAKE ERIE		HOOKER ELEC OUTFALL CRIB	43-03.90	78-59.60	44967.52	59206.90	00
LAKE ERIE		WAVERLY SHOAL "EU"	42-51.70	78-56.20	44917.01	59217.70	00
LAKE ERIE		ASHLAND REFINERY LIGHT	42-60.00	78-55.80	44963.26	59234.50	00
LAKE ERIE		MIDDLE REEFS "EU4"	42-52.73	78-55.27	16465.22	59227.68	00
LAKE ERIE		BUFFALO INTAKE CRIB LIGHT	42-52.80	78-54.70	44929.32	59232.78	00
LAKE ERIE		UPPER RANGE LIGHT	42-57.20	78-54.60	44953.59	59240.84	00
LAKE ERIE		BUFFALO INTAKE CRIB LIGHT	42-54.50	78-54.30	44940.32	59239.17	00
LAKE ERIE		FISHERIES CONTROL SITE	42-51.20	78-54.00	44923.20	59236.03	00
LAKE HURON		GROS CAP REEFS LIGHT	46-30.70	84-36.90	31069.70	47778.28	00
LAKE HURON		BAYFIELD ROCK RANGE	46-29.30	84-17.00	30972.86	47840.48	00
LAKE HURON		ROCK CUT LOW LEADING LIGHT	46-15.10	84-10.60	30975.04	47970.08	00
LAKE HURON		MARTIN REEF LIGHT	45-54.80	84-08.90	31019.02	48139.88	00
LAKE HURON		SPECTACLE REEF LIGHT	45-46.40	84-08.20	31038.25	48211.07	00
LAKE HURON		DE TOUR REEF LIGHT	45-56.90	83-54.20	30932.54	48154.73	00
LAKE HURON		THUNDER BAY WRECK "WR2"	45-03.70	83-23.60	30892.20	48648.34	00
LAKE HURON		ROCKPORT HARBOR LIGHT	45-12.30	83-22.90	30864.64	48578.70	00
LAKE HURON		NORDMEER WRECK "WR1"	45-08.10	83-09.30	30790.47	48634.05	00
LAKE HURON		PORT AUSTIN REEF LIGHT	44-04.90	82-58.90	30899.26	49161.77	00
LAKE HURON		INKSTER ROCK LIGHT JS5	45-33.12	82-01.10	30315.17	48535.74	00
LAKE HURON		WEST SISTER SHOAL J2	45-22.08	81-47.87	30246.88	48634.48	00
LAKE HURON		SOUTHWEST BANK NO TA1	45-14.03	81-45.44	30241.67	48696.85	00
LAKE HURON		KETTLE POINT REEF NO V4	43-14.38	72-03.07	28006.56	49413.33	00
LAKE MICHIGAN		SYDNEY McLOUTH WRECK "WR2"	44-49.80	87-48.80	32366.33	48124.88	00
LAKE MICHIGAN		DREDGE 906 WRECK BUOY "WR"	42-58.20	87-47.00	32991.93	49325.83	00
LAKE MICHIGAN		RACINE REEF BUOY NO 1	42-43.50	87-46.00	33082.70	49491.92	00
LAKE MICHIGAN		RACINE REEF LIGHT	42-43.60	87-44.20	33074.45	49496.28	00
LAKE MICHIGAN		WILMETTE WRECK BUOY "WR2"	42-05.70	87-39.00	33309.72	49935.88	00
LAKE MICHIGAN		PESHTIGO REEF LIGHT	44-57.40	87-34.80	32270.63	48095.85	00
LAKE MICHIGAN		OUTER SHOAL WRECK BUOY	41-46.00	87-23.70	33382.07	50198.68	00

FISHING

BODY OF WATER	PROV/STATE	NAME	LAT	LON	TD#1	TD#2	DEPTH
LAKE MICHIGAN		ROCK ISLAND BUOY "RI"	45-26.10	86-44.50	31916.16	47978.93	00
LAKE MICHIGAN		NOVADOC WRECK BUOY "WR1"	43-41.90	86-31.10	32363.43	49060.02	00
LAKE MICHIGAN		BOULDER REEF NO 1	45-35.20	85-59.00	31661.61	48031.37	00
LAKE MICHIGAN		HOG ISLAND REEF "HI"	45-43.50	85-20.40	31435.83	48063.02	00
LAKE MICHIGAN		SIMMONS REEF NO 2	45-54.20	85-12.90	31360.65	47989.04	00
LAKE MICHIGAN		GRAYS REEF LIGHT	45-46.00	85-09.20	31369.09	48070.25	00
LAKE MICHIGAN		GRAYS REEF NO 3	45-45.80	85-08.40	31365.60	48074.06	00
LAKE SUPERIOR		GULL ROCK LIGHT	48-59.00	95-03.60	32476.71	44004.36	00
LAKE SUPERIOR		ROCKY POINT LIGHT	48-57.50	94-32.30	32429.98	44023.87	00
LAKE SUPERIOR		BALD ROCK LIGHT NO 8	48-37.40	93-10.90	32346.24	44505.23	00
LAKE SUPERIOR		CAPSTAN REEF LIGHT	48-38.10	93-03.00	32328.38	44548.36	00
LAKE SUPERIOR		GULL ROCKS LIGHT	48-33.80	92-46.60	32309.41	44669.60	00
LAKE SUPERIOR		JARVIS ROCK LIGHT	48-06.20	89-17.60	31879.16	45971.38	00
LAKE SUPERIOR		JARVIS ROCK	48-06.17	89-17.58	31879.20	45971.69	00
LAKE SUPERIOR		OLD DUMPING GROUND SHOAL P2	48-23.13	89-10.69	31803.94	45886.36	00
LAKE SUPERIOR		WELCOME SHOAL LIGHT A6	48-20.57	89-08.55	31805.60	45913.77	00
LAKE SUPERIOR		HARE ISLAND REEF LIGHT A2	48-17.92	88-59.20	31785.63	45975.68	00
LAKE SUPERIOR		ROCK OF AGES LIGHT	47-53.40	88-53.20	31846.51	46179.99	00
LAKE SUPERIOR		ROCK HARBOR W ENTR	48-05.70	88-34.40	31746.62	46175.29	00
LAKE SUPERIOR		HOLDEN SHOAL LIGHT J8	48-56.65	88-08.42	31513.93	45955.57	00
LAKE SUPERIOR		GULL ROCK LIGHT	47-25.00	87-39.80	31692.11	46720.39	00
LAKE SUPERIOR		BARWIS ROCK LIGHT JC	48-50.22	87-36.95	31429.70	46127.16	00
LAKE SUPERIOR		STANNARD ROCK LIGHT	47-11.00	87-13.50	31640.08	46938.38	00
LAKE SUPERIOR		PANCAKE SHOAL NO X2	46-54.50	84-50.30	31073.38	47551.84	00
ST LAWRENCE GULF	CAPE BRETON I	CERBERUS ROCK WHISTLE	45-27.60	61-06.30	14164.06	42651.27	00
ST LAWRENCE GULF	CAPE BRETON I	ORPHEUS ROCK BELL	45-28.70	60-51.20	14164.17	42557.20	00
ST LAWRENCE GULF	CAPE BRETON I	BLACK ROCK POINT	46-18.30	60-23.50	14376.60	42180.48	00
ST LAWRENCE GULF	CAPE BRETON I	MAD DOG ROCK BELL	45-60.00	59-49.40	14280.69	42063.24	00
ST LAWRENCE GULF	MAGDALEN ISLANDS	PEARL REEF BELL "Y16"	47-19.50	61-34.40	14681.47	42315.86	00
ST LAWRENCE GULF	MAGDALEN ISLANDS	BIRD ROCKS	47-50.30	61-08.70	14758.56	41967.29	00
ST LAWRENCE GULF	NEW BRUNSWICK	TORMINTINE REEFS BELL "X5"	46-06.60	63-41.10	14484.20	43500.52	00
	NEW BRUNSWICK	BULL ROCK WHISTLE "XA1"	44-30.20	66-56.60	13701.29	44723.88	00
	NEW BRUNSWICK	TWO HOUR ROCK	45-01.80	66-56.20	14049.96	44758.46	00
	NEW BRUNSWICK	GANNET ROCK/GRAND MANAN	44-30.60	66-46.90	13718.03	44684.20	00
	NEW BRUNSWICK	NET ROCKS LEDGES "XV6"	44-45.30	66-44.50	13879.38	44688.91	00
	NEW BRUNSWICK	HALF TIDE ROCK/CHENEY	44-39.30	66-43.70	13815.46	44679.38	00
	NEW BRUNSWICK	EDMUNDS ROCK	44-40.40	66-43.30	13827.71	44678.72	00
	NOVA SCOTIA	GULL ROCK BELL BUOY	44-12.00	66-23.20	13553.06	44565.22	00
	NEW BRUNSWICK	CHANCE HARBOUR/REEF PT	45-07.10	66-20.90	14122.57	44592.25	00
	NEW BRUNSWICK	SPLIT ROCK BELL BUOY	45-07.10	66-14.60	14123.67	44559.32	00
	NOVA SCOTIA	CAT ROCK BELL "Y3"	43-47.00	66-09.50	13324.21	44487.44	00
	NOVA SCOTIA	BLONDE ROCK WHISTLE "N4"	43-18.60	66-00.10	13073.12	44429.19	00
	NOVA SCOTIA	PIQUET ROCK	43-29.40	65-43.00	13206.41	44363.05	00
	NOVA SCOTIA	CROW NECK ISLAND/GATE ROCK	43-28.70	65-27.20	13229.05	44293.05	00

FISHING

BODY OF WATER	PROV/STATE	NAME	LAT	LON	TD#1	TD#2	DEPTH
	NOVA SCOTIA	WHALEBACK ROCK	43-29.60	65-27.00	13237.32	44292.44	00
	NOVA SCOTIA	BRAZIL ROCK WHISTLE	43-21.00	65-26.80	13162.51	44288.75	00
	NOVA SCOTIA	BULL ROCK BELL BUOY	43-37.50	65-08.30	13336.64	44208.09	00
	NOVA SCOTIA	GULL ROCK ENTRANCE	43-39.30	65-06.00	13355.48	44197.36	00
	NOVA SCOTIA	BLACK ROCK	45-10.20	64-45.80	14139.54	44048.10	00
	NOVA SCOTIA	WHITE POINT ROCK BELL	43-55.60	64-43.10	13521.83	44083.12	00
	NOVA SCOTIA	BELL ROCK BELL	44-29.00	63-31.10	13826.60	43663.76	00
	NOVA SCOTIA	RAT ROCK	44-37.60	63-16.20	13889.97	43563.91	00
	NOVA SCOTIA	JEDDORE ROCK	44-39.80	63-00.70	13906.69	43469.41	00
	NOVA SCOTIA	GULL ROCK BELL	45-46.50	62-40.50	14314.17	43170.09	00
	NOVA SCOTIA	SKINNER REEF BELL	45-44.80	62-37.20	14302.24	43154.61	00
	NOVA SCOTIA	BASSOON REEFS BELL	44-50.60	62-13.60	13975.69	43167.95	00
	NOVA SCOTIA	SMITH ROCK BELL	44-53.80	62-01.50	13993.78	43088.06	00
	NOVA SCOTIA	CAHIL ROCK RANGE	45-34.20	61-21.30	14203.40	42717.62	00
	NOVA SCOTIA	ROCK ISLAND	45-17.00	61-01.80	14109.11	42662.48	00
	NOVA SCOTIA	DOVER BAY/GULF ROCK	45-16.80	61-01.00	14107.88	42658.46	00
	NOVA SCOTIA	MAN OF WAR ROCK BELL	45-19.70	60-57.00	14121.42	42624.57	00
ST LAWRENCE GULF	PRINCE EDWARD I	NORTH POINT REEF WHISTLE	47-05.00	64-00.10	14813.96	43388.86	00
ST LAWRENCE GULF	PRINCE EDWARD I	PRIM REEFS WHISTLE	46-02.70	63-07.00	14427.05	43286.31	00
ST LAWRENCE GULF	PRINCE EDWARD I	FITZROY ROCK BELL	46-07.10	63-06.70	14451.46	43268.60	00
ST LAWRENCE GULF	PRINCE EDWARD I	INDIAN ROCKS WHISTLE	45-55.00	62-49.20	14368.05	43196.38	00
ST LAWRENCE GULF	PRINCE EDWARD I	SHIPWRECK POINT	46-28.20	62-25.50	14519.38	42910.31	00
ST LAWRENCE GULF	PRINCE EDWARD I	BEAR REEF WHISTE "N4"	46-00.60	62-24.30	14378.55	43014.46	00
ST LAWRENCE GULF	QUEBEC	CAIRNTORR ROCK "C64"	50-07.30	60-18.60	15019.2	40709.9	00
ST LAWRENCE GULF	QUEBEC	CORMORANT ROCKS	50-07.30	60-03.70	15007.0	40613.5	00
ST LAWRENCE RIVER	QUEBEC	WYE ROCK BUOY H121	46-60.00	70-38.00	14578.03	32494.90	00
ST LAWRENCE RIVER	QUEBEC	HOSPITAL ROCK RANGE	47-08.00	70-28.00	14659.85	32484.16	00
ST LAWRENCE RIVER	QUEBEC	LARK REEF S-7	48-07.20	69-40.50	11715.6	60071.7	00
ST LAWRENCE RIVER	QUEBEC	T AUX VACHES REEF S-8	48-07.50	69-40.30	11714.5	60071.4	00
ST LAWRENCE RIVER	QUEBEC	BAR REEF S-5	48-06.90	69-39.10	11707.5	60073.3	00
ST LAWRENCE RIVER	QUEBEC	DEMERS ROCK BUOY H58	47-51.40	69-39.00	14998.57	32339.45	00
ST LAWRENCE RIVER	QUEBEC	LARK REEF K-58	48-04.60	69-38.60	11704.1	60077.3	00
ST LAWRENCE RIVER	QUEBEC	WHITE ISLAND REEF K59	47-59.10	69-38.00	15016.85	32305.60	00
ST LAWRENCE RIVER	QUEBEC	WHITE ISLAND REEF	47-54.60	69-37.80	11698.2	60093.6	00
ST LAWRENCE RIVER	QUEBEC	LARK REEF K-56	48-04.60	69-37.60	11698.3	60078.0	00
ST LAWRENCE RIVER	QUEBEC	WEST ROCKS	50-07.30	66-26.00	15262.7	42943.2	00
ST LAWRENCE RIVER	QUEBEC	BASQUE REEF BELL D-6	50-10.90	66-22.00	15262.6	42894.0	00

CHAPTER 14

SEA BOUNTY

This chapter is very near and dear to my heart. I would rather eat fish that Susie cooks than some of the things that great chefs have built their reputations on. Susie always complains about my weight, yet at dinner time she'll make a meal fit for six King Henry the Eighths. She is inventive and willing to try just about anything (on me).

One nice thing about planning a cruise or a camping trip is that we are home when we're thinking about menus and how to prepare the meals. Heat and humidity are the major drawbacks to cooking inside the boat in Florida between April and December.

We have two solutions. During the summer months, we barbecue most of the foods on board. We purchased one of those neat stainless steel things that mounts of the stern of the boat and hangs over the side. We like using the easy-starting kind of charcoal the best, rather than starter fluids, because they are so highly flammable and hazardous.

Lighting the charcoal in a breeze can be a real challenge, however. A friend of ours showed us the following method of firing up the barbecue with no fuss or mess. We call this the Joe Potts Barbecue Chimney Method. We are sure that Joe didn't invent the method, but we can't prove he didn't and he ain't talkin', so we are going to be safe and name it after him.

First, always have a large can of V-8 juice on the boat for breakfast (any can about the same size will do). We pour the juice into a plastic container and keep it on ice for frequent sipping. Next, take a can opener and remove the top and bottom of the can, then take a beer can opener (of the church key variety) and make several triangular openings around the perimeter of one end. A small hole at the top will serve as a pick-up point or a wire can be hooked through the hole for the purpose of picking up the chimney when it is hot. What you end up with is a fine little chimney to stack self-starting charcoal in.

The size of the can is just about the right measure for the charcoal to fill the bottom of the grill. When the chimney is placed into the barbecue grill, the triangular openings must be on the bottom. It is through these holes that we light the briquettes, but more important, they are the air draft holes that fire the charcoal briquettes into rosy red cinders packed with pure cooking power in short order.

Once all the briquettes are aglow and a perky red, lift the chimney with a fork or knife, and, being careful not to touch it to any plastic parts of the boat, lower it into water. After a loud hiss and a couple of seconds, it is ready to be stowed away.

We space the hot briquettes evenly about the bottom of the barbecue grill and add only enough more regular briquettes on top of the hot ones to cook our dinner. Usually, in 10 to 20 minutes we can start our steaks, fish, or whatever else is in need of barbecuing.

HELPFUL HINT

We have learned that we can increase our visibility range while underway in the fog by having the First Mate or Captain stand on the bow. A rain coat, a life jacket, and a thermos full of hot coffee are also very helpful.

We almost always barbecue the first night out. This way we can cook several things in a row. We have learned that cooked food lasts longer in the cooler than raw food, especially meats of any kind. Once the food is cooked, we divert our talents to the generator and the microwave.

The combination of a generator and a microwave on a boat is hard to beat. Our baked potatoes, fresh veggies, baked apples for dessert — to say nothing about freshly caught poached fish — make Susie the envy of the fleet. We installed a regular icemaking unit under the seat, and while making ice, we can also keep food frozen. The ice maker becomes a freezer.

The second method of solving the cooking problem, of course, is to precook all of the food in the comfort of your air-conditioned home. As mentioned before, the additional benefit of using this method is that food lasts a lot longer once cooked and on ice than raw foods do.

Now, for the things you catch, find, spear, or grab while on a cruise: Preserving fish and seafood for any length of time is at least complicated and at best uncertain. So we have become what our friends term "opportunity eaters."

Creatures like lobster, crabs, and clams are very hearty animals and survive well for a day or so in the livewell, where they get a constant supply of fresh salt water. Crabs are very fond of the heads of freshly caught fish (leftovers from the filleting operation) and will survive for some time. The only problem with crabs is that you have to have lots of them to make a meal.

Clams, scallops, and oysters don't last long, as they are either eaten right away or put in the perpetual chowder pot. We have never been able to put too many of any of these into our pot, and the chowder makes for a terrific snack source during the day.

Scallops should never be eaten raw, because if you start eating the little fellers right away, there will never be any left over for the stew pot. Scallops, freshly caught, freshly cleaned, and eaten immediately are our favorite morsels from the sea. We also like to include them in our salads, soups, egg dishes, and chowders, or to cook them by themselves in garlic and drawn butter with just a touch of rice wine vinegar added for dash.

When we catch a fish that is to be our dinner, we immediately fillet it and put the meat on ice within a plastic zipper-type bag. We catch only what we can eat that day and release everything else.

The following recipes are some that Susie prepares exceptionally well. She has become deservedly famous for them among our boating friends, and once you try them, you'll become the envy of your friends, too. Though Susie developed these recipes using South Florida fish and shellfish, they will work as well with local substitutions. Experiment — take a chance — and even odds, you will love the result.

WIT & WISDOM

He who trusts his fuel gauge must also be a good swimmer.

RECIPES

POTATO-OYSTER STEW

This dish is our perpetual chowder. As the days go on, you can add more potatoes, onions, clams, crab meat, and leftover fish to the pot and in no time have a splendid dish. Do not salt the chowder each time you add ingredients, however, or it will soon begin to taste like the Gulf of Mexico! Serves four.

INGREDIENTS:

1	large handful of shucked raw oysters
3	cups of water
1	teaspoon of salt
1	large onion, diced
1	stalk of celery
1	bay leaf
2	dried tarragon leaves
2	potatoes, peeled and diced
2	cups of milk (or cream)
1	cup of whole small mushrooms

PREPARATION:

Place the potatoes, onion, water, and salt in a pot and simmer for 20 minutes or until the potatoes are tender. Stirring constantly, add everything else to the pot and simmer for three to five minutes, being careful not to burn the milk. Cover and turn the fire off. Let stand for 20 to 30 minutes. Heat again to bring stew to serving temperature, stirring constantly. Add pepper as needed.

When "perpetuating the pot," remember that any kind of fish that has been previously prepared in any way may be dumped into this pot, even if it has been breaded. Never add salt to the pot. As the various veggies are consumed, just add more with milk or cream, but don't burn the milk. The milk or cream will tone down the flavor of the chowder's previous incarnation and allow the new mess to develop its own character. If you like the dish thicker, add more cream, and don't be afraid to experiment with spices. There will come a time (at about the fourth generation) when you will want to start over!

CLAMS A LA SUSIE

The preparation of this dish is as simple as throwing everything into a pot! This soup is very rich and is great served with French garlic bread. We especially enjoy it during the winter months when the evenings are a bit cool and on winter days while fishing — this and hot coffee. Mmmmmmmm. This soup is best made ahead of time at home and carried to the boat. Serves four.

INGREDIENTS:

2	large handfuls of fresh clams
2	quarts of water
1	teaspoon of salt
1	medium onion, diced
2	stalks of celery
1	bay leaf
4-6	whole peppercorns
2	tablespoons of minced parsley
4	tablespoons of butter or margarine
4	tablespoons of all-purpose flour
2-3	tablespoons of lemon juice
1	10-ounce package of frozen carrots
1	10-ounce package of frozen peas
2	potatoes, peeled and diced
1	half quart of milk
1/4	cup of whipping cream

PREPARATION:

Place the clams in the bathtub (or in a large sink or bowl) and cover with fresh water for two to three hours. It helps to stir them a couple of times. This encourages the clams to spit out sand instead of saving it for the soup.

Put two quarts of water in the bottom of a double-boiler pot and bring to a boil (don't use the water the clams have been sitting in). Place all of the fresh clams, still in their shells, in the top of the double-boiler and steam the clams until they open.

Remove the meat, being careful to save the juices. Put all of the meat and juices into the boiling water in the bottom of the double-boiler. (You may have to add water to bring the level back to two quarts.) Add all the raw veggies and spices and return to a rolling boil.

After five minutes, reduce the heat to a slow simmer and cover the pot. Simmer for one to one and half hours, then add the butter to the pot. Add the flour to one cup of cold water and blend completely. Slowly add the flour-water mixture to the pot, stirring constantly. Cook, two or three minutes. Add lemon juice and the frozen carrots. Cover and simmer for about five to seven minutes.

Add the peas and simmer two to three minutes. Stir in the cream and then add the milk. Add salt and pepper to taste. Refrigerate the whole mess and take to the boat. Keep the soup on ice, then heat it up and serve it.

CORNY FISH CHOWDER

This dish is a neat way to serve fish to those who are not real fish-eating aficionados, and also makes use of fish fillets that got too small during the cleaning operation. Serve with hot buttered French bread and a glass of chilled light white wine of your choice. This is a dinner that can be enjoyed on the bridge while slowly putt-putting back to home port. Serves four.

INGREDIENTS:

1	pound of fresh fish fillets, cut into "fingers"
1	medium onion, diced
1/2	cup finely diced celery
2	tablespoons butter or margarine
1	tablespoon of all-purpose flour
2	chicken bouillon cubes
2	cups of water
1	bay leaf
2	dried tarragon leaves
2	cups of potatoes, peeled and diced
1	13-ounce can of evaporated milk
1	8.5-ounce can of cream-style corn
1	teaspoon dill weed
1/2	cup of chopped parsley

PREPARATION:

Saute dill weed, onion, and celery in butter until the onion is clear and tender. Stir in flour and add bouillon cubes, water, and potatoes. Bring to a boil. Cover and simmer for 15 to 20 minutes until potatoes are tender.

Add fish and corn, and stir in milk and the rest of the ingredients. Add salt and pepper to taste. Cover and simmer until the fish is tender, but not overcooked. Turn the fire off and let stand for 10 to 15 minutes before serving.

Just before serving, heat to serving temperature. When serving, be very careful not to get in the way of the mad rush to the table!

BAKED FISH WITH DILLY CHEESE SAUCE

Many varieties of fish are especially suitable for this dish. Try snapper, grouper, shark, halibut, cod, sea bass, barracuda, flounder, or just about anything that has gills and swims. We fold small fillets when we don't have fillets that are three quarters of an inch thick, as called for. If you are going to fold fillets, try stuffing them with a bit of pimento and anchovies. Another variation is to spread the inside of the fillet with a bit of Miracle Whip. Experimenting with this dish is fun. Serves four.

INGREDIENTS:

- 1.5 pounds of fish fillets (three quarters of an inch thick)
- 3 tablespoons of butter or margarine
- 3 tablespoons of all-purpose flour
- 1 tablespoon of salt
- 1/2 teaspoon of dry mustard
- 1/4 teaspoon of dried dill weed
- 1 dash of cayenne
- 1.5 cups half and half cream
- 1.5 cups shredded cheddar cheese
- 1 four-ounce can of mussels, drained
- 1 four-ounce can of diced clams, drained
- 1/4 pound of small shrimp, cooked and peeled

PREPARATION:

Preheat oven to 400 degrees. Cut fish fillets into serving pieces and place them into a greased two-quart baking dish. In a two-quart sauce pan, melt the butter. Stir in the flour and cook until it bubbles. Add salt, dry mustard, dill, and cayenne. Remove for heat and gradually stir in half and half cream.

Return sauce to heat and cook, stirring constantly until thickened. Mix in one cup of cheese, stirring until melted. Mix in the mussels, small shrimp, and clams. Pour cheese sauce evenly over the fish. Sprinkle with the remaining cheese.

Bake at 400 degrees for about 20 minutes or until top browns and fish flakes evenly when tested with a fork in the thickest part. This dish is best served with white wine or ice cold beer, green beans, and a baked potato.

SUSIE'S POTATO-FISH PIE

The fish that are especially suitable for this dish are snapper, grouper, shark, halibut, cod, sea bass, barracuda, flounder, and spotted sea trout. The leftovers are great when reheated in the oven or microwave and served with ice cold milk. Serves four.

INGREDIENTS:

- 1/2 pound of fish fillets
- 4 cups of potatoes, peeled and thinly sliced
- 3/4 teaspoon of salt
- 2 tablespoons of minced parsley
- 1 small onion, minced
- 1/8 teaspoon of black pepper
- 2 tablespoons of butter or margarine
- 1/2 teaspoon of dried dill weed
- 1/2 cup of whipping cream
- 1/2 cup fresh parsley for garnish
- 1 anchovy
- 1 pie crust

TO MAKE PIE CRUST:

Mix two cups of all-purpose flour and three quarters of a teaspoon of salt. Cut in half a cup of softened butter or margarine and a third of a cup of lard (shortening) until small particles are formed. Mix well with a fork while adding a couple of tablespoons of cold water a few drops at a time, stirring until particles hold together. Form this mess into a ball and divide into two equal parts. Roll half of the dough until it is an eighth of an inch thick and will fit over a nine-inch pie plate. Trim edges evenly around the plate. (The second half will cover the pie once the other ingredients have been added.)

PREPARATION:

Preheat oven to 375 degrees. Prepare a nine-inch pie shell as above. Toss together the potatoes, salt, parsley, onion, and black pepper, and spread half around the bottom of the pie crust. Place the fish fillets over the potato mess and sprinkle the dill weed over the fillets. Add remaining potatoes and dot with butter. Roll out remaining crust and cover the pie filling. Cut slits to allow the steam to escape. Trim the edges and crimp the crusts together with a fork.

Bake at 375 degrees for about one hour. Remove from the oven and carefully cut out a round hole in the middle of the pie and save. Then, *very* gradually pour the cream into the pie through the hole just cut, allowing the cream to settle before continuing. Replace the pastry cut-out and place the one anchovy over the plug. Return the pie to the oven and bake for 10 more minutes. Cut into wedges and serve warm. Garnish with the fresh parsley.

FISHY HOME FRIED POTATOES

This dish is great in the morning when there are leftover fried or oven-baked fish. Try this dish along with eggs or your favorite breakfast dish. It can be prepared in minutes and is very tasty. We guarantee the crew will love it. This is an outstanding recipe for shark, dolphin, large grouper, yellowfin tuna, king mackerel, and large jacks (all de-boned). Serves four.

INGREDIENTS:

- 1 pound fresh fish fillets, cut into "fingers"
- 3 cups of potatoes, peeled and diced
- 3 tablespoons of butter or margarine
- 2-4 green onions, chopped
- 1 cup sliced mushrooms, if available
- 1/2 teaspoon of salt
- 1 teaspoon of dill weed
- 1 dash of black pepper
- 1 dash of cayenne

PREPARATION:

Remove all skin and bones from the fish after baking for 20 minutes and then break fish meat into small pieces. Set aside. In a large frying pan, saute the potatoes in two tablespoons of the butter or margarine for about 15 minutes or until lightly browned and tender. Remove potatoes and keep warm.

In the same pan, melt the remaining butter or margarine and add the onions. Saute for 10 minutes or until the onions are just clear, then stir in black pepper, salt, dill, and cayenne. Roll in the potatoes and the fish without stirring too much. Heat through on very low flame or in the microwave. Transfer to the serving dish, and sprinkle with the fresh parsley.

For variety, try placing a couple of butter-basted eggs on the plate, lightly sprinkled with paprika, salt, and pepper.

SUSIE'S KOREAN SHARK STEAKS

We are very fond of shark and look for every opportunity to put small ones (less than four feet long) on our table. Once we have caught one, we clean our catch as soon as possible (immediately is best). We tie the shark's tail to a line attached to the aft cleat, then we clean the feller and let him "bleed" for a bit while he's in the water before we start carving out thick fillets. We remove the blood line from the fillets, and keep a supply of freezer-type plastic bags on board to store them (our ice maker doubles as a small freezer). This recipe serves four.

INGREDIENTS:

1.5	pounds of fresh shark steaks (one-inch thick)
2	tablespoons of soy sauce
2	tablespoons of rice wine vinegar
2	tablespoons of lemon juice
2	tablespoons of vegetable oil
1/2	tablespoon of chopped parsley
1	clove garlic, minced or pressed
1/2	teaspoon of freshly ground pepper
1/2	teaspoon of minced green onion

PREPARATION:

Place the steaks in a bowl. Combine the soy sauce, vinegar, lemon juice, oil, parsley, garlic, and black pepper to create a marinade. Pour the marinade over the steaks and allow them to soak for about 30 minutes. Turn often to expose all surfaces of the steaks to the marinade.

Remove the steaks from the marinade and barbecue them on the boat's grill (over charcoal). Cover the barbecue and grill for about four to five minutes per side. Brush on a little marinade after turning.

When the steaks are done, serve them on a dish and sprinkle the steaks lightly with the minced green onions and parsley. We like to serve them with baked sweet potatoes, garlic bread, and a large salad. Top the meal off with your favorite red or white wine (full bodied port is our favorite), chilled to a pucker.

For variety, Susie likes to ladle nacho-type melted cheese over the fish, topped with sliced jalapenos. When Susie does this we play Mexican music and dance a lot. It seems the more jalapenos we eat, the better we dance.

SUSIE'S HOT-DAMN SHRIMP CASSEROLE

This dish is for the romantics who have a flair for the unusual and for those who like the wonderful combination of spices from the Orient coupled with a dash of Americana. This dish teems with flavor, and it will drive you to say, "Hot damn, got any more?" If you are not too fond of spices, you may exclaim, "Hot damn pass the ice cream!"

This is one of Susie's best creations, and it's made from the fresh bait shrimp that are still alive and left over after fishing. Fresh scallops can be used instead of the shrimp, or you can try a fifty-fifty combination. Serves four.

INGREDIENTS:

2	cups (one and a quarter pounds) fresh peeled shrimp
3	tablespoons of butter or margarine
3/4	cup of chopped celery
1/2	cup coarsely chopped green peppers
4	onions, chopped
1/2	cup diced mushrooms
3	tablespoons of all-purpose flour
1	tablespoon of salt
1/4	teaspoon of curry powder
1/4	teaspoon of red pepper
2	teaspoons of Worcestershire sauce
1	tablespoon of soy sauce
1	13-ounce can of evaporated milk, warmed
1/4	cup of grated Parmesan cheese
1/4	teaspoon of paprika
4	Prayers

PREPARATION:

Preheat oven to 425 degrees. In a large skillet, melt the butter or margarine over medium heat. Add celery, green pepper, mushrooms, and onions. Saute for about 10 minutes or until the onions are clear, stirring constantly (stirring here is essential). Add flour, salt, all of the spices, Worcestershire and soy sauces, stirring until well blended. Saute for about three minutes or until everything is well cooked and heated.

Stir in the warmed condensed milk. Cook, stirring continuously, until sauce is smooth and thickened. Add shrimp and cook for three to six minutes. Taste and correct seasoning to suit. Pour this mess into a buttered six-inch by 10-inch casserole dish. Sprinkle top with Parmesan cheese and paprika and cover. Bake at 425 degrees for 20 minutes and serve hot.

Use the prayers freely to keep everyone's fingers out of the mess before baking in the casserole. For dessert, try French vanilla ice cream! Talk about good!

KOREAN CIOPPINO

Cioppino is a combination of various fish and shellfish, and here is Susie's variation on this classic dish. We often make this when we have been fishing and have caught a mixture of all kinds of fish. Obviously, we use up the bait shrimp that are still alive, fresh scallops from our freezer, clams (diced or minced, canned or fresh), and any available crab meat. All are chucked into the stew with no holds barred. Just about anything goes, because this dish is so forgiving. Garfeldasteinski (the Damned Cat) could make it. Serves four.

INGREDIENTS:

1-1/2	pounds fresh fish fillets, cut into "fingers"
1/2	pound of scallops
1	pound fresh shelled shrimp
2	tablespoons of vegetable oil
2	tablespoons of butter or margarine
1-1/2	cups sliced onions
2	cloves of garlic, pressed
1	can (one pound, 12 ounces) Italian plum tomatoes
1	can (10-3/4 ounces) chicken broth
1	cup dry white drinking wine
1	cup of water
2	tablespoons of chopped parsley
1-1/2	teaspoons dried basil leaves
1-1/2	teaspoons of salt
1/2	teaspoon of dried oregano leaves
1	eight-ounce can minced or diced clams; not drained
5 to 6	cups cooked white, brown, or wild rice
1-1/2	cups sliced mushrooms
2	large chicken breasts (boned and cooked)

PREPARATION:

Cut fish fillets into one-inch chunks and set aside. Heat oil, butter or margarine, onions, and garlic in a heavy skillet. Saute about two minutes or until onions are soft. Add tomatoes, wine, water, parsley, basil, salt, and oregano. Cover and simmer for about 20 minutes.

Add fish and chicken and simmer for about 10 minutes. Add the rest of the seafood (shrimp, clams, etc.) and simmer for about five minutes. Avoid stirring the stew at all after adding the fish. Using a large wooden spoon, "roll" the seafood into the sauce. (Overcooking and stirring will make the stew mushy.)

To serve, spoon hot rice into large, shallow soup dishes. Ladle the stew over the top of the rice and cap with a pat of butter. Place a sprig of parsley into the stew and call it a tree. Serve this dish with a light, dry white wine, tossed salad, French garlic bread, and a mound of your favorite veggies. A hug from the captain and crew is guaranteed.

CHAPTER 15

DAFFYNITIONS

The following "daffynitions" are being provided to clarify recreational boating terminology, not to confuse our dear readers. The Captains of small vessels use certain words for deep-seated psychological reasons, while other words just need defining. In all our wisdom (guessing), we will attempt to clear the air and to put doubt to rest forever.

ANCHOR: A heavy device usually found at the bow of the boat. Its intended use is to hold the boat firmly when you want to go home and to slip its grip at night when you're laying to.

BOAT: (1) Anything that floats, carries people, passengers, guests, animals, food, drinks, and costs lots of money. (2) Also, a vessel that consumes excess cash proportionately to the availability of same. (3) An object of senseless love. (4) A personal yacht.

BOW: Pointed end of the vessel or the end of the vessel that usually parts the water and leaves the port first, i.e., the front of the boat.

BUMPERS: Improper boating form of the word "fender."

CABIN: The area on the boat where cooking and all sorts of fun games take place.

CAPTAIN: Lord and Master.

CAPTAIN'S CHAIR: A place to park the Captain so that work can get done.

CAPTAIN'S PRIVILEGE: Those things the Captain's wife or First Mate says that the Captain can or cannot do.

CHART: A sailor's map.

COCKPIT: (1) A place that is usually surrounded by a gunnel. (2) A weather deck usually found near or at the stern of the boat. (3) A convenient place to observe sunsets and feed the First Mate a line.

COVE: (1) A quiet indentation within the landmass where sailors and powerboat drivers attempt to anchor their boats for the night so that they can use the phrase "trust me." (2) A place where boats gather to tell lies about their adventures. (3) A haven. (4) A wonderful place to camp on the boat while playing soft music, cooking dinner, relaxing, and making plans for the next day's journey while your neighbor shows off his bigger boat.

DECK: Floor.

DECK, WEATHER: A floor that gets rained on.

DEPTH INDICATOR: (1) Indicates depth and quits working in shallow water. (2) A "passifier."

DINGHY: (1) Very small boat, see TENDER, BOAT. (2) What the Captain usually is.

DOCK: (1) A place where one might want to put his boat. (2) To some, home base.

FENDER: (1) Inflated rubber "things" that hang over the side of the boat to protect it from rubbing and bumping. (2) Bumper.

FISH: Those things that become scarcer proportionate to the amount of money spent to catch them.

FISHFINDER: (1) A device that is believed to be able to alert fishermen regarding where to catch a fish. (2) Fancy name for a depth indicator. (3) A device that helps the Captain frustrate fishermen who can't catch fish.

FISHING: The art of attempting to catch fish while presenting live, frozen, dead, cut, wood, or plastic baits with sharp hooks so designed to catch grass, rocks, and coral while at the same time providing frustration and lessons in patience.

FLASHLIGHT: Sometimes called a search light, it always works during the day, it works only intermittently at night, and it never works in tight channels.

GALLEY: Kitchen.

HALYARD: (1) A line used to raise or lower a sail or flag. (2) Line. (3) Rope.

HEAD: (1) A place where a cap or hat is placed. (2) Toilet. (3) A place that is too small for the Captain and just right for people who don't know how to operate the equipment.

HELM: Driving or steering station.

HELMSMAN: The driver of the boat.

LINE: (1) "Thing" used to tie the boat to the dock, pier, or other boat with. (2) Proper boating term for the words rope, string, or cord. (3) The one "thing" that always has knots in it. (4) The "thing" the Captain tries to feed to the First Mate while apologizing for yelling, hoping for forgiveness and secretly anticipating good things to come.

NAVIGATION: (1) The art of knowing where one is going. (2) The ability to figure out where one is.

NAVIGATOR: A person able to find shore; which usually excludes the Captain, who can find the shore only when he's not trying to.

PFD: Personal Flotation Device, or life jacket.

PORT: (1) Opposite of starboard; the left side of the vessel when one is looking at the bow. (2) Place where all good Captains hope to get to often. (3) A spot where services such as repairs, food, marinas, restaurants, and supplies abound and where they always cost more.

RADAR: An electronic device that works all of the time when the sun is shining, seldom at night, and almost never in the fog.

ROPE: Line.

SEARCH LIGHT: See FLASHLIGHT.

STARBOARD: The right side of the vessel when one is looking at the bow.

STATEROOM: The place where the beds are kept.

STERN: The blunt end of the vessel or the end of the vessel that leaves port last.

SUNSETS: An invention designed to impress the First Mate into a sense of nostalgia and lesser resistance; filled with a special something that is never present during sunrises.

TENDER, BOAT: A very small boat that is always in the way.

THING: The word "thing" is used as a substitute word for any other word the Captain of the vessel cannot remember, or never knew.

"Get me that thing. Tie the boat to that thing. That thing over there. Bring me the thing to fix this thing." REAL MEANING: I don't know what I'm talking about, but I sure hope you do.

TOILET: See HEAD.

TROLLING: The act of washing artificial lures while pretending to fish.

WAKE: Waves left behind the boat that will most certainly cause someone to express profanities on the nicest days.

WAVES: (1) A natural saltwater phenomenon which, when encountered, causes violent motion; waves are guaranteed to be present when pouring hot drinks. (2) "Things" that Captains make to irritate the First Mate, as in "Don't make waves, honey!" (3) Female sailors.

WHITE LINE RECORDER: (1) Makes mysterious writings on small paper to tease the operator into believing that fish are waiting to pounce on anything presented in the form of bait. (2) Draws profiles of the sea bottom in sufficient detail to identify ledges, rocks, and other shapes, such as wrecks and reefs. (3) Substitute for an inoperative depth indicator.

WINDLASS: An electrical and/or mechanical device designed to haul in line, such as the anchor windlass, halyard windlass.

YACHT: A boat owned by a proud person.

CHAPTER 17

WAYPOINT LOG

Most all modern loran machines have some kind of waypoint memory for storing your waypoints. The following log will allow you to list your waypoints right in this book for easy reference. We suggest leaving the first 10 waypoints in your memory open for special entries.

We have entered the coordinates we use all of the time at the very end of our log. This way, we can flip directly to our pass coordinates without having to look them up.

This is your very own log book; please enjoy it.

MEMORY	DESTINATION	TD #1	TD #2
WPT 01			
WPT 02			
WPT 03			
WPT 04			
WPT 05			
WPT 06			
WPT 07			
WPT 08			
WPT 09			
WPT 10			
WPT 11			
WPT 12			
WPT 13			
WPT 14			

MEMORY	DESTINATION	TD #1	TD #2
WPT 15			
WPT 16			
WPT 17			
WPT 18			
WPT 19			
WPT 20			
WPT 21			
WPT 22			
WPT 23			
WPT 24			
WPT 25			
WPT 26			
WPT 27			
WPT 28			
WPT 29			
WPT 30			
WPT 31			
WPT 32			
WPT 33			
WPT 34			
WPT 35			
WPT 36			

MEMORY	DESTINATION	TD #1	TD #2
WPT 37			
WPT 38			
WPT 39			
WPT 40			
WPT 41			
WPT 42			
WPT 43			
WPT 44			
WPT 45			
WPT 46			
WPT 47			
WPT 48			
WPT 49			
WPT 50			
WPT 51			
WPT 52			
WPT 53			
WPT 54			
WPT 55			
WPT 56			
WPT 57			
WPT 58			

MEMORY	DESTINATION	TD #1	TD #2
WPT 59			
WPT 60			
WPT 61			
WPT 62			
WPT 63			
WPT 64			
WPT 65			
WPT 66			
WPT 67			
WPT 68			
WPT 69			
WPT 70			
WPT 71			
WPT 72			
WPT 73			
WPT 74			
WPT 75			
WPT 76			
WPT 77			
WPT 78			
WPT 79			
WPT 80			

MEMORY	DESTINATION	TD #1	TD #2
WPT 81			
WPT 82			
WPT 83			
WPT 84			
WPT 85			
WPT 86			
WPT 87			
WPT 88			
WPT 89			
WPT 90			
WPT 91			
WPT 92			
WPT 93			
WPT 94			
WPT 95			
WPT 96			
WPT 97			
WPT 98			
WPT 99			
WPT 100			
WPT 101			
WPT 102			

MEMORY	DESTINATION	TD #1	TD #2
WPT 103			
WPT 104			
WPT 105			
WPT 106			
WPT 107			
WPT 108			
WPT 109			
WPT 110			
WPT 111			
WPT 112			
WPT 113			
WPT 114			
WPT 115			
WPT 116			
WPT 117			
WPT 118			
WPT 119			
WPT 120			
WPT 121			
WPT 122			
WPT 123			
WPT 124			